MIDNIGHT MARQUEE ACTORS SERIES

LON CHANEY, JR.

MIDNIGHT MARQUEE ACTORS SERIES

LON CHANEY, JR.

Edited by Gary J. and Susan Svehla

MIDNIGHT MARQUEE PRESS, INC.
BALTIMORE, MARYLAND

ISBN 1-887664-15-7
Library of Congress Catalog Card Number 97-73133
Manufactured in the United States of America
Printed by Kirby Lithographic Company, Arlington, VA
First Printing by Midnight Marquee Press, Inc., July 1997

Acknowledgments: John Antosiewicz Photo Archives, Richard Bojarski, Ronald V. Borst/Hollywood Movie Posters, Michael Brunas, Eric Hoffman, Leonard J. Kohl, Greg Mank, Mark A. Miller, Ted Okuda, John E. Parnun, Photofest, Gary Don Rhodes, Bryan Senn, Larry Springer, Linda J. Walter

for Lon Chaney, Jr.

CHANEY

TABLE OF CONTENTS

INTRODUCTION

For the third installment in the *Midnight Marquee Actors Series*, we have decided to profile Lon Chaney, Jr., the least documented of all the horror film icons. Unlike Boris Karloff and Bela Lugosi, Lon Chaney, Jr. never worked for Universal Pictures during the classic horror heyday of the 1930s; he arrived on the Universal lot at the beginning of the 1940s as their new horror movie star debuting with both *Man Made Monster* and *The Wolf Man*. Almost immediately the studio's artistic decline led to the Monster Rallies and the *Inner Sanctum* series—the era of classic horror was over. Unfortunately for him, Chaney, Jr. arrived on the horror scene one decade too late!

After losing his Universal contract by the end of 1945, Chaney, Jr. was forced to freelance and played supporting character roles in mainstream A productions, starred in some interesting B productions, or drifted into low-budget dreck that tarnished his reputation. But one thing was certain, Chaney, Jr. wanted to continue working in movies. He appeared before the camera constantly until the bitter end when his declining health (alcoholism, cancer, and other ailments) silenced him forever in 1973 (his filmography, while it lacked the "quality" of Karloff and Lugosi, contained the "quantity" of a working professional, impressive by its numbers alone).

Lon Chaney, Jr. is the most controversial of all the horror icons, simply because two camps of opinion exist about his work: the first stating that Chaney, Jr. was a real trouper who performed some outstanding work in movies—Lennie in *Of Mice of Men*, Larry Talbot in *The Wolf Man*, etc.—and deserves to take his place among Hollywood's greatest screen personalities; the second saying that Chaney, Jr. was a one-note, very limited, and inexpressive Hollywood presence, generally lucky to have risen above mediocrity in a handful of roles, only to sink to the nadir of embarrassment by the last decades of his career.

While volumes exist on the lives and careers of Karloff and Lugosi, precious little has come to light on Lon Chaney, Jr. He is the performer who stunned audiences with his portrayal of The Wolf Man, but Chaney, Jr. is also the same man who groped through *Dracula vs. Frankenstein* toward the end of his career. This is the actor who returned to form at Universal-International for *Abbott and Costello Meet Frankenstein*, but the same man who, even before the film saw release, tried to commit suicide by intentionally overdosing on pills. Always being compared to his even more talented and famous father Lon Chaney, Chaney, Jr. faced demons throughout both his personal life and his professional career.

The *Midnight Marquee Actors Series* cannot provide answers to all these and other questions, but by delving into pivotal films made throughout his career (not just the mainstream Universal and horror classics, but his stunning performance in *Of Mice and Men*, his B Western career, his low-budget horror/exploitation movie career, his prestigious character performances in A productions, his television work, etc.), by having different authors offer distinct reflections and individual insights, and by including several first-hand interviews from people who worked with Chaney, Jr., we hope to offer the most complete and balanced portrait yet seen of Lon Chaney, Jr., working actor.

Gary J. Svehla
July 1997

LON CHA
©1939 HR-F28

OF MICE AND MEN (1939)

by Gary D. Rhodes

"(Creighton Chaney) has been heralded as a possible successor to Clark Gable. But he isn't like Clark. He isn't like quite any other actor. He isn't quite sure, himself, if he is an actor at all. But he swears to all and sundry that he is going to be!"
—*Movie Classic*, January 1933

"I'm so green at this Hollywood game, I don't even know many other actors. My pals at the studio are the fellows in the publicity department and others like that about the lot. When my father was here—well, he wasn't too keen about having me around the studios. I only visited his sets once or twice in all the years he was a movie star. I don't think my Dad wanted me to be an actor. But I guess that is natural. A lawyer seldom wants his son to be a lawyer, and doctors have all sorts of reasons why they don't want their boys to follow in their footsteps," actor Creighton Chaney told Nancy Pryor of *Movie Classic* magazine in 1933.

"I had a couple of film bids after Dad's death—from studios that wanted to bill me as 'Lon Chaney, Jr.' I refused them. Then one day a friend took me over to the RKO studios and introduced me to the casting director. He explained that I was willing to do anything at first—that I would accept extra work at seven-fifty a day. The casting director asked me the usual questions and seemed interested. I wasn't fooled about that interest though—I knew the fact that I was Lon Chaney's son had a lot to do with any impression I might have had.

"He told me to come back the next day. I thought there would probably be an 'extra' job. You can imagine my surprise when I was presented with a contract and asked again to change my name to Lon Chaney, Jr. I was just about floored with joy over the contract—but I flatly refused to change my name, even though that refusal might lose me the chance I so wanted. They begged me to reconsider. That night I told my mother all about it. Incidentally, my mother knows more about the workings and inner-workings of the movies than anybody I have ever met. She knew why they had offered me a contract. She knew why they wanted to change my name. Her advice was, 'Don't do it.'

"When I told them, the next day, that I couldn't accept the contract if it meant changing my name to my father's for exploitation purposes, I was all set to have that contract withdrawn. I thought it was pretty fine when they said it was all right—if I didn't want to agree to the changed name, the contract offer went, anyway.

"I'm honestly grateful to them for giving me a chance to make good under my own steam as Creighton Chaney. I figure they must think I have something to offer on my own. I'm putting my movie fate in their hands, and if one of my jobs is to jump out of a tree onto the back of a horse—well, I'm going to do it!

"'I don't exactly know my true screen place, yet,' he philosophized. 'I sometimes think I would like to do westerns. Maybe that is because I'm not quite sure of myself as an actor,' he smiled, one of those rare occasions, 'and not an awful lot of acting ability is required for westerns.'"

That was a Creighton Chaney quoted by the fan press while still a bit player in films. He prophesied his connection with genre films, mentioning Westerns in particular. Implicitly, he perhaps had an inkling of his ability as a character actor over the kind of mesmerizing persona radiated by Chaney Sr., Bela Lugosi, or Boris Karloff. A bit of understandable pride surfaced in his desire to keep the name Creighton. Four decades later, a November 1973 *Films in Review* quoted his bitter remarks regarding his name: "I am most proud of the name Lon Chaney. I am *not* proud of Lon Chaney, Jr., because they had to starve me to make me take this name." The boyish enthusiasm had evaporated.

"I'm still scared stiff in front of the camera.
In spite of my three pictures, I shake and shiver with nervousness
when the camera is trained on me.
A lot of people seem to have the idea
that I have had previous screen or stage experience.
They figure that because I come from a theatrical family,
I must have been trained in that sort of work. But it isn't true."
—Creighton Chaney, 1933

Three years after his father's death in 1930, Creighton Chaney seemed to believe a film career outside his father's shadow was possible, even if it meant starting at the most minimal of roles. After becoming "Lon Chaney, Jr." for the box office, then simply "Lon Chaney," that desire proved impossible.

"Creighton flushed," the journalist for *Movie Classic* wrote. "He poked about nervously at his Brown Derby salad and said: 'Do me a favor, will you? If you are going to write me up in a story, don't say anything comparing me with my father? There isn't any comparison between us. Dad was an artist—a real actor. I'm just a fellow trying to get along in the movies. I'd rather be compared to anybody else but my Dad, because I know I'm not worthy of that comparison. When the first publicity I earned was a story to the effect that I was glad because I figured that if I was being compared to Mr. Gable,

A studio portrait of Lon Chaney, Jr. as Lennie from *Of Mice and Men.*

it would sidetrack other comparisons to my Dad. I will say this, though—I know the sacrifices and great physical suffering my father went through for his screen roles. I know, perhaps better than anybody, except my little, excitable, Italian mother. I know that that suffering did not stop with the completion of a role, either. My father was afflicted with almost chronic headaches, his eyesight was strained, his body was weakened under the grueling make-ups he created for the camera.

"I would never be big enough, or enough of an artist to make the sacrifices my Dad did. In the first place, I haven't his great talent for makeup and characterization—so I couldn't if I wanted to. But I also know this: *I'm not going to ask for a double for just ordinary athletic stunts any fellow my size and build should be able to do—even if I break my neck attempting to do them!* My Dad would feel disgraced at the idea of a double for a Chaney in any role that requires only the physical ability any man should have!"

As he bristled under the possibility of similarities to his father, he unintentionally furthered the comparisons by speaking of stunt doubles. The year *Movie Classic* wrote their Creighton Chaney article, the shadow of his father still loomed prominently over the entire movie industry. The two prior years—1931 and 1932—found more articles written in the fan magazines on a deceased Chaney, Sr. than on both Bela Lugosi and Boris Karloff combined.

Despite Creighton's efforts, he became Lon Chaney, Jr., standing directly in that prominent Chaney shadow. Even still, success was not easily grasped. The actor had multiple personal problems throughout the thirties, and his screen career was no better in the late thirties than it had been with early films like *Girl Crazy* (1932). But as Creighton's problems mounted, so did those of an entire country. And understanding and analyzing those problems, those social ills, was author John Steinbeck, who pinpointed the difficulties of a nation while unknowingly paving the way for the arrival of Lon Chaney, Jr., star of the silver screen.

"Guys like us, that work on ranches,
are the loneliest guys in the world.
They got no family. They don't belong no place.
The come to a ranch an' work up a stake
and then they go into town and blow their stake,
and the first thing you know
they're poundin' their tail on some other ranch.
They ain't got nothing to look ahead to."
—George Milton to Lennie Small in Steinbeck's novel *Of Mice and Men*

One of novelist John Steinbeck's letters (dated February 1935) informed an agent, "I'm doing a play now. I don't know what will come of it. If I can do it well enough it will be a play. I mean the theme is swell." This reference is probably to *Of Mice and Men* in its earliest stages. A year later, in an April 1936 letter, Steinbeck wrote that he was working hard on the new project, but that he had "struck a snag." The next month, the snag proved particularly daunting. "Minor tragedy stalked," he penned. "My setter pup, left alone one night, made confetti of about half of my manuscript book. Two months work to do over again. It sets me back. There was no other draft. I was pretty mad, but the poor little fellow may have been acting critically. I didn't want to ruin a good dog for a manuscript I'm not so sure is good at all. He only got an ordinary spanking."

The finished novel, after regrouping from the confetti, was published in 1937. The now-familiar tale allowed Steinbeck to create and explore the character Lennie, "a huge man, shapeless of face, with large, pale eyes, and wide, sloping shoulders; and he walked heavily, the way a bear drags his paws." The story consistently likens Lennie to an animal, describing how he "dabbled his big paw in the water like a horse" and how "he drinks with long gulps, snorting into the water like a horse." Lennie is a misfit and outcast, less symbolic of the everyday man than an indication of a society that itself was sick.

French poster for *Of Mice and Men*.

Critical reviews were mixed, as Steinbeck encountered detractors to both his political framework and his highly realistic style of writing. Critic Maxwell Geismar's judgment, reprinted in John H. Timmerman's *John Steinbeck's Fiction: The Aesthetics of the Road Taken*, deemed the novel "thin" and "full of easy sensations." He continued by suggesting, "We see here the dominance of the creative fire over common sense, so that we are held by such apparitions as these characters who, when removed from the framework of the play, crumble under the weight of their own improbability." On other

Lon Chaney, Jr. won the coveted role of Lennie over twenty-five other actors.

fronts, many took offense at the novel's profanity, even though the language does not extend beyond the use of "hell" and "son of a bitch."

Most readers at the time, as well as in retrospect, understood the novel's power and insightful social commentary. While the author himself would mutter of the time-consuming and troublesome aspects of fame, his base of readers continued to grow. *Of Mice and Men* quickly sold 300,000 copies, while Steinbeck would brush off the novel's importance, referring to it almost dismissively as "the Mice book."

Years later, Steinbeck would also write that "M & M may seem to be unrelieved tragedy, but it is not. A careful reading will show that while the audience knows, against its hopes, that the dream [of Lennie's] will not come true, the protagonists must, during the play, become convinced that it will come true. Everyone in the world has a dream he knows can't come off but he spends his life hoping it may. This is at once sadness, the greatness and the triumph of our species. And this belief on stage must go from skepticism to possibility to probability before it is nipped off by whatever the modern word for fate is. And in hopelessness—George is able to rise to greatness—to kill his friend to save him. George is a hero and only heroes are worth writing about."

"Simply stated, *Of Mice and Men* was an attempt to write a novel that could be played from the lines, or a play that could be read."
—John Steinbeck in the January 1938 issue of *Stage*

Steinbeck never hid his intentions that *Of Mice and Men* was planned for the stage, writing the novel in such a way that a stage production would easily follow from it. For example, over eighty percent of the lines in the novel went directly into the play, which he himself scripted. Almost immediately after publication, *Of Mice and Men* was illuminated by stage lights.

The San Francisco Theatre Union produced a version of the play in 1937, drawing its performances from workers who had to rehearse in their spare time over several months. A variety of reviews resulted, though due more to the theme of the play than the performance itself. Perhaps the most lengthy critique, as well as the most difficult to reconcile in retrospect, is Margaret Shedd's in the October 1937 *Theater Arts Monthly*. Her overtly political reading of the play caused her to question the "whole socially-minded theatre," believing the author "does not know what dynamite he has in those characters. Nor does the so-called left-wing theatre know what it has. And exactly because, in the case of the left-wing theatre, it does not know what it wants." To Shedd, Steinbeck "destroys epic material... over and over in *Of Mice and Men*."

She also spends much time in an examination of Lennie: "The very core of the play, Lennie's obsession for stroking mice, is an example of the confusion and of the lack of motivation. It is widely known that many itinerants carry small animals with them on their travels—rats, dogs, rabbits; this has in it the raw element of human interest. It is also a matter of common knowledge that a great many bindlestiffs are feeble-minded; there is certainly the raw element of human tragedy in that. But for an author merely to throw together these two facts to make a curiosity is not enough. Steinbeck at no point establishes whether Lennie's destruction of the animals he strokes is a matter of abnormality or accident. He implies it is an accident, which, happening so often, is not convincing. The audience assumes it is sadism and gets a little excitement out of that. Actually there is no excuse for this confusion. If Lennie is to be any sort of universal symbol, anything more than an isolated monstrosity... then all questions of behavior psychology must be settled before they arise."

Steinbeck did receive more favorable critiques of his work, which was already slated for a Broadway opening. Appearing in a season that included such distinguished plays as *Our Town*, *Golden Boy*, *Susan and God*, and *On Borrowed Time*, Steinbeck's *Of Mice and Men* opened at the Music Box Theatre on November 23, 1937. The venerable George S. Kaufman directed the Broadway version, and Sam H. Harris produced.

Wallace Ford portrayed the migrant George, and Broderick Crawford appeared as his friend, the unfortunate Lennie. The cast also included Will Geer as Slim, Sam Byrd as Curley, and Claire Luce as Curley's wife. Though reviewers praised each for their performances, Broderick Crawford generally made the strongest impression. John Mason Brown of *The New York Evening Post* believed that "in every unsparing detail, he suggests the blind devotion, the feeble-mindedness, the depravity, and the brute strength of Mr. Steinbeck's amazing character." *Stage* (January 1938) realized Crawford "makes Lennie's stupidity tangible and convinces you that he could kill a man without half tryin, accidental like." *The New York Times* (November 22, 1937) called his Lennie the "perfect counterpart" to Wallace Ford's George, later interpreting the role "admirably vitalized in the patient and subdued acting of Broderick Crawford" (December 12, 1937). An impressed *Time* (December 6, 1937) magazine dubbed his performance "gooseflesy."

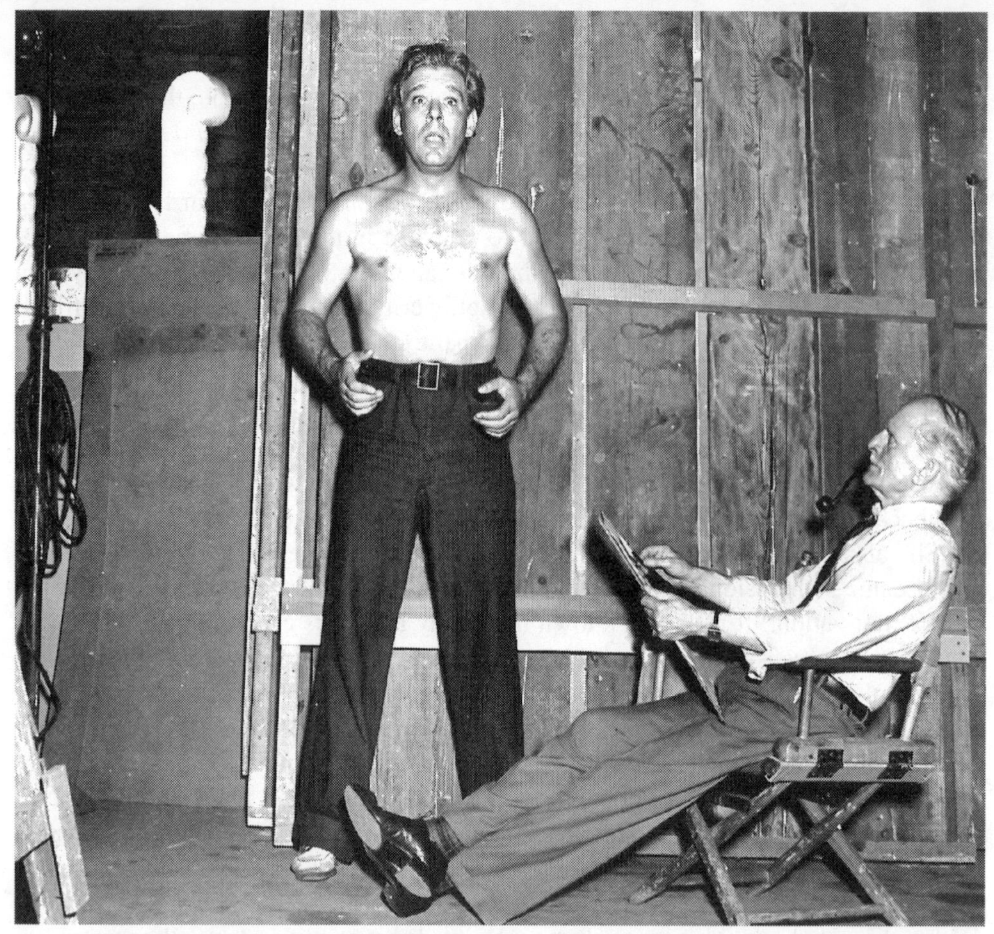

Artist Carl Bohnen making a sketch of Lon Chaney, Jr. as Lennie. [Photofest]

According to Donald Oenslager, who took strong reviews for his set design, Steinbeck himself attended a pre-rehearsal meeting with the creative minds behind the play. The author offered various suggestions for the actors' speech and movements, as well as settings, and mentioned he believed the play was in good hands. He left to purchase a Chevrolet, never seeing the play itself after it opened. Steinbeck was beginning the road to *The Grapes of Wrath*.

The play ran 207 performances. Brooks Atkinson of *The New York Times* called it a "masterpiece" of the New York stage. Burns Mantle dubbed it one of the "Best Plays of the Year," and it won the prestigious Drama Critics Circle Award for the 1937-38 season. On the whole, critics found *Of Mice and Men* a thought-provoking social drama that wisely avoided preaching to audiences. That the profanity of Steinbeck's novel remained caused some shocked reactions, but even then most believed the language indicative of the realism demanded by the story. Versions of the play then hit other cities, including a highly successful San Francisco run in May of 1939. Very probably, film director Lewis Milestone and screenwriter Eugene Solow heard of that particular version.

"They had a two-month option by the tail, no funds to back the movie, and, to top it all, they were afraid of the Hays office.

Nevertheless, you'll soon be seeing *Of Mice and Men*."
—*Collier's*, January 6, 1940

"Can it be that *Mice and Men* was from the beginning a Hollywood story?"
—*The Nation*, January 20, 1940

"They'd been writing a picture together, Lewis Milestone and Gene Solow, and it was finished now, so they thought they'd take a week off," Quentin Reynolds wrote in a January 6, 1940 *Collier's*. "When anyone who lives in Hollywood has a week off, he takes it in New York. So Solow and Milestone found themselves at the bar in 21 one afternoon, just talking of this and that. Then, Milestone said, 'What would you like to do next, Gene?' Solow said, 'Milly, I want to do *Of Mice and Men*. That would be a great picture.'

"Milestone said, 'Sure it would but George Kaufman and Sam Harris own the picture rights with Steinbeck and they'll want a lot of money for it. Then the Hays office would never pass it.' 'That's right,' Solow said gloomily, 'but I'd love to do that script. Just suppose we had a lot of money, Milly. We could buy it, do the script, and then you could direct it.'

"Milly looked thoughtful. 'I wonder,' Solow said casually, 'if Kaufman and Harris would gamble with us. We'd do the script and then get backing somewhere and cut up the profits.' 'No one in Hollywood ever heard of doing business that way,' Milestone said. 'Besides, who would back us?' 'If the script was good,' Solow said, 'and it passed the Hays office and people knew that you were going to direct it, we might get some company to put up the production costs for a cut of the profits.'

"'Well, it only costs a nickel to phone George Kaufman,' Milly said. Two minutes later Solow was talking to Kaufman. Kaufman listened in silence while Solow outlined his idea. 'We have no security to put up,' he said, 'except this. Milly and I are crazy about the play and we'll break our necks to do a good script. Then you know Milly is a great director.'

"Kaufman said, 'It all sounds good to me. I'll talk to Sam about it and to Alec Woollcott too. He owns ten percent of it.' The next day Sam Harris phoned Solow. 'I like your nerve,' he said. 'Kaufman and I are agreeable, so is Woollcott. We'll string along on a percentage basis, but you'll have to get Steinbeck's okay first. Matter of fact Steinbeck is in Chicago. I'll phone him.' Sam phoned him and Steinbeck chuckled. 'Sure, I'll go along. I'd like to see the script first, though.'"

The entire tale described by *Collier's* took place in less than 24 hours.

The Hays Office did initially prove to be the greatest obstacle to producing the film. While the profanity of the novel and play could be quickly eradicated, the story's conclusion was a problem. Out of mercy, the hapless bindlestiff George shoots Lennie at the end of the novel; technically, this violated the production code in that George gets away with murder. "But if you want to do a thing," Milestone said at the time, "you can find a way to do it." Without changing the impact of the novel's climax, Milestone has the film's George kill Lennie, then immediately hand over his gun to a sheriff. The problem was solved, and the duo moved ahead.

Solow and Milestone also wanted Steinbeck's approval on the script, and a meeting was arranged at Steinbeck's ranch. At the author's request, Solow read the script aloud

Images unfold offering both beauty and a wistful air of the nature that Lennie embraces.

while Steinbeck rested on a couch. An hour later, Steinbeck made his first comment, asking what part of the country Solow had grown up in. After answering "New England," Solow heard Steinbeck grumble, "One of those Harvard guys." The author pinpointed a Northeastern expression Solow used that the characters would not have known. Solow then continued to read aloud, finishing the script at 5 a.m., desperately wanting a drink. Steinbeck quickly praised the integrity of Solow's work, mentioning that the addition of one short scene would finish the script. The novelist spent thirty minutes on his typewriter, producing seven pages of what Solow would claim to be the most beautiful dialogue he had ever read. The finished script made its way back to Hollywood.

Milestone and Solow heard that Hal Roach might be interested in backing the project. Or, given other accounts, the duo heard Roach would offer to finance the film in lieu of a $90,000 out-of-court settlement made by the renowned producer of Laurel and Hardy shorts and Milestone, whom he had removed from helming *Road Show* in 1937. At any rate, at Roach's office the duo explained the co-operative nature of the financial structure, with producers, writers, and the director sharing in the profits. Then they announced that they could produce the entire film for $250,000. Roach was dubious about an A picture resulting from such little money, but he agreed to back the project. In fact, Roach was so enthused about a film adapted from the novel that he didn't even want to read the script before committing.

The project was quickly becoming a reality.

According to a December 1939 issue of *Esquire*, Milestone sent a location scout roving over all of California to find the ideal ranch for the film. After no discovery was made, Milestone rented a corner of the vast William Randolph Hearst ranch, where the needed barns, houses, and sheds were erected. *Esquire* noted the irony, and wondered to whom the joke of fate was directed; Steinbeck's novel actually makes a subtle reference to Hearst.

Nicholai Ramisoff designed models of the sets, which were approved by Steinbeck. Ramisoff had first come to America as art director for Chauve Souris, who did Max Reinhardt's much-talked about version of *Faust.* His models for *Of Mice and Men* were turned into life-size sets in the space of a week.

Of the rest of the cast and crew, *Esquire* claimed, "currently, the highest ambition of any film worker who believes in the dignity of the medium, is to be permitted to work in either *Of Mice and Men* or *Grapes of Wrath.* The Steinbeck worship has almost assumed cult proportions."

Even before getting the financial go-ahead from Roach, Milestone and Solow agreed to cast actors and actresses that were best-suited for the film as a whole, without regard to "star" status. A clause in the contract with Roach acknowledged this, adding that any disagreements between the writer and director on whom to cast would be settled by third party Leo McCarey. Allegedly, Jimmy Cagney was very interested in playing George; such actors as Spencer Tracy and John Garfield were also anxious to get involved. Studio commitments, however, prevented any of the three from being cast.

Milestone and Solow tested some twenty actors for the part of George before deciding on Burgess Meredith, whose name was known mainly to Broadway fans. His only well-known film had been *Winterset* (1936). From friends Sam and Bella Spewack, Solow also heard of Hollywood newcomer Betty Field. Her screen test solidified Milestone and Solow's excitement, and she went on to portray Mae. The writer and director team chose Charles Bickford as the old mule skinner Slim, Noah Beery, Jr. as Whit, and Western genre star Bob Steele as Curley. Roman Bohnen of the Group Theatre was selected as Candy, the old swamper.

And Lon Chaney, Jr., winning out over twenty-five other actors—including Broderick Crawford—became Lennie.

The various tests had taken approximately $50,000 of the budget, leaving some $200,000 for Milestone to work with. Norbert Brodine shot the film, working with Milestone for the first time in twenty years. The two had arrived in Hollywood at about the same time, both getting jobs bicycling cans of film for the studios to the railroad station. They hadn't worked together since those early days of Tinseltown.

The production phase lasted thirty-nine days, finishing one day earlier than Milestone's original schedule. *Of Mice and Men* came in on budget, and close friends like Jimmy Cagney and Leo McCarey—watching the film before its release—agreed that it was one of Hollywood's best. Audiences and critics first glimpsed the film in late 1939, with much attention given to the younger Chaney.

"Lon Chaney, Jr. is a name to which the mass audience should respond,
out of simple curiosity, if for no other reason.
The other reason is that Chaney, Jr. is a mighty fine actor."
—*Esquire*, December 1939

Variety (January 3, 1940) believed "Lon Chaney, Jr. dominates throughout with a fine portrayal of the childish giant," and *Newsweek* (January 15, 1940) spoke of the "compelling performances" of both Chaney and Meredith. He impressed critics writing in the movie trades and popular press, as well as the literati in the movie audiences that turned out to see the Steinbeck adaptation.

Kind reviews of Chaney did not ring out in chorus, however. *The New York Times* (February 19, 1940) felt "young Mr. Chaney does not quite erase the memory of Broderick Crawford's Lennie," and Franz Hoellering at *The Nation* (January 20, 1940) also found disappointment in the characterization. The latter believed "that one is never really captivated by the Lennie of Lon Chaney, Jr. is not the actor's fault, and it would be a gross injustice to call him the weakest of the lot. He is as good if not better than Burgess Meredith as George, but no enduring interest can be held by the repetitious, unchangeable stupidity of the character he has to play."

The film itself took strong reviews overall, with the February 19, 1940 *New Republic* announcing "you can put *Of Mice and Men* down on the list of the ten best of 1940." *Variety* concluded "Milestone has exercised skill in retaining the poignant and dramatic motivations of Steinbeck's work. His deft direction provides one of the best production achievements of the season...." A January 15, 1940 *Time* called it "more tender than the tough stage version, the impact of the picture is tough and raw." In the same manner as the New York stage production, however, the film gave a few critics a chance to again challenge the merits of the Steinbeck novel, as Franz Hoellering did more than once in *The Nation*.

Regardless of its occasional detractors, the film took an Academy Award nomination for Best Picture, losing to the sweep made by *Gone With the Wind* (1939). It was the first filmic adaptation of a Steinbeck novel, though John Ford's classic *The Grapes of Wrath* (1940) quickly followed it at the box-office. And, even though Ford's film may have taken greater accolades than *Of Mice and Men* at the time, in retrospect the Milestone film deserves the name "milestone" in more than one way. *Of Mice and Men* remains the most faithful and effective Steinbeck adaptation in cinema history.

Much of this is due to Milestone's own beliefs about filmmaking. "Throughout my career," he once said, "I've tried not so much to express a philosophy as to restate in filmic terms my agreement with whatever the author of a story I like is trying to say." He also claimed, "My approach, my style is governed by the story, not the story by my style." Milestone's reputation today is one of a highly competent studio director, the man behind such important films as *All Quiet on the Western Front* (1930), *The Front Page* (1931), *Rain* (1932), and *A Walk in the Sun* (1945).

Regrettably, even if *Of Mice and Men* made filmgoers aware of Lon Chaney, Jr., the film itself proved a failure at the box office. Though audiences immediately made the connection between the film and the famed Steinbeck novel, United Artists even tried to add a spice of sexuality in some movie posters. These featured Betty Field in alluring poses, with tag lines like, "Unwanted, she fought for the one thing which is every woman's birthright."

In retrospect, the film remains a classic, and—unlike the whole of Milestone's career—a film much unlike the usual studio product. *Of Mice and Men* makes this clear from its opening moments, which feature a dramatic prologue prior to its opening credits, a radical innovation for the time. More importantly, the device forces spectators to consider the drama unfolding to be one of a realistic nature.

Lon Chaney, Jr.'s portrayal of Lennie is a brilliant characterization, and it also provides a unique insight to the paradox of Chaney's entire career.

The film continues in its particularly realistic treatment of the story through its cinematic composition. Camera angles avoid any hint of the omniscient, with Milestone and Brodine opting instead for eye level compositions. Brodine's cinematography also repeatedly and beautifully constructs the important theme of nature in the film. A careful examination of specific shots also reveals the care with which some shots were devised. For example, George and Lennie walking along an old highway past a billboard is almost certainly rooted in Dorothea Lange's 1937 Farm Security Administration photograph of two tramps and a billboard. Other moments are reminiscent of such important Depression-era documentaries as Pare Lorentz's *The River* (1937). These images unfold with Aaron Copeland's music score offering both beauty and a wistful air of the nature that Lennie embraces.

Chaney's raw talent as a character actor had nabbed him the role of Lennie over such actors as Broderick Crawford, but, like Lugosi's Dracula, it proved in many ways a curse.

Lennie's accidental murder of Mae itself becomes a cinematically innovative and terrifying experience. In the same manner as films like Fritz Lang's *M* (1931), the murder is not seen except in the expression of Lennie's face, which is composed between the bars of the stall, metaphorically imprisoning him and subtly indicating the nature of his crime.

While the film's conclusion satisfied the Hays office, it becomes a quite realistic aspect of the film. George does offer his gun to the sheriff after firing it into Lennie's head, but the punishment is unspoken... the ending is unclear. Along with being a triumph in the face of the production code, it preserves the intentions of Steinbeck's novel and the film's bent toward reality. And, as Lennie falls dead into a pool of water, the film completes a circular pattern that began with him drinking water in the prologue, and it returns Lennie forever to the nature he so loved.

Lennie's accidental murder of Mae itself becomes a cinematically innovative and terrifying experience.

"...in the seeing of a play there are the author, the play, the players,
and the whole audience,
and each one of these contributes
a vital part to the whole effect."
—John Steinbeck in the January 1938 issue of *Stage*

Lon Chaney, Jr., Betty Field, and Burgess Meredith, the stars of *Of Mice and Men.*

Lon Chaney, Jr.'s portrayal of Lennie is a brilliant characterization, and it also provides a unique insight to the paradox of Chaney's entire career. Steinbeck's quotation regarding the confluence of elements that make the "whole effect" of a play also helps to explain the Chaney, Jr. film career. He instills much pathos into Lennie, and would later do so again in such roles as the Frankenstein Monster in *The Ghost of Frankenstein* (1942). Whatever emotions he conveyed, Chaney, Jr. was at his best as a character actor working as a part of a greater whole. This is certainly the case in *Of Mice and Men*. His early quotations from *Movie Classic* seemingly anticipated that reality, and on that basis the already reductive desire to compare him to his father becomes all the more irrelevant.

In films like *Of Mice and Men* and *The Wolf Man* (1941), Chaney would become a successful player on a team, a character actor surrounded by other talented performers and backed up by worthwhile production values and a skilled crew. Unlike his father or Boris Karloff or certainly Bela Lugosi, Chaney, Jr. was not a persona in and of himself. However crucial a character Lennie is in *Of Mice and Men*, the film is an integration of all its characters into a strong thematic line. When Universal Studios thrust him into star status in their cheaply made horror films of the forties, it becomes unsurprising that, however brilliant at times he was as a character actor, Chaney, Jr. was not a personality capable of carrying a film by himself. Moreover, he lacked the "man of a thousand faces" mystique of his father and the foreign intrigue of Lugosi and Karloff that roles like Count Alucard in *Son of Dracula* (1943) demanded.

As Lennie in *Of Mice and Men*, however, he stands among the greats in the tradition of cinematic character actors. In perhaps his strongest similarity to horror stars

Lugosi and Karloff, Chaney, Jr. became typed as Lennie, even as he moved into the horror genre. This extended to innumerable roles patterned after Lennie, as in *My Favorite Brunette* (1947) and *The Black Castle* (1952). And, if the shadow of his father prompted his name change, the shadow of Lennie also prompted many horror films to feature him as a "helper" or a less-than-intelligent assistant to another villain. It's true of course that horror films featuring more than one name actor often used this tactic as a plot device. Lugosi became Ygor in *Son of Frankenstein* (1939) as a result of this method, as well as the character Joseph in *The Body Snatcher* (1945). But in Chaney's case it was a more pronounced and more often repeated aspect of his roles, whether in *The Haunted Palace* (1963) or *Dracula vs. Frankenstein* (1971).

A November 1973 *Films in Review* quoted him on this issue: "It haunts me. I get a call to play a dumb guy and the director tells me not to be Lennie, but he's never happy until I play the part like Lennie. Then he doesn't know why he likes it."

Chaney's raw talent as a character actor had nabbed him the role of Lennie over such actors as Broderick Crawford, but, like Lugosi's Dracula, it proved in many ways a curse. Creighton Chaney was a character actor, forced to carry entire films as a "star" persona following the critical acclaim of *Of Mice and Men*. But a character actor was the true outlet for Chaney's acting; however, in the same fashion as he accidentally kills Mae, the ignorant brute Lennie murdered any real chance for Chaney to explore other kinds of character roles. At the same time, Lennie propelled Lon Chaney, Jr. to fame, saved him from perpetual financial ruin, and carved out a unique place for him in cinema history.

Film collector and archivist Forrest J Ackerman once recalled, "I observed a real magic moment with Chaney once when the Count Dracula Society had him as the guest of honor at their annual banquet. I was sitting opposite him and I saw he didn't eat a morsel of food at the banquet; he just sat there drinking. It worried me because I knew from experience that he was only good until afternoon and from then on he was blotto... When he name was announced at the banquet, I made the introductory speech about him. He then appeared on stage and he got a standing ovation and that really turned him on. He said, 'Would you like to see me do Lennie?' Everyone said yes and he did Lennie. And he really had it down pat. He stood up there and became that powerful figure from *Of Mice and Men* and it brought tears to everybody's eyes to see how great he could be when he tried."

CREDITS: Producer and Director: Lewis Milestone; Screenwriter: Eugene Solow; Cinematography: Norbert Brodine; Music: Aaron Copeland; Editor: Bert Jordan; Art Direction; Nicolai Remisoff; Special Effects: Roy Seawright; Based on the novel by John Steinbeck; United Artists, 1939

CAST: Burgess Meredith (George); Betty Field (Mae); Lon Chaney, Jr. (Lennie); Charles Bickford (Slim); Roman Bohnen (Candy); Bob Steele (Curley); Noah Beery, Jr. (Whit); Oscar O'Shea (Jackson); Granville Bates (Carlson); Leigh Whipper (Crooks); Leona Roberts (Aunt Clara); Helen Lynd (Susie); Barbara Pepper (Second Girl); Henriette Kay (Third Girl); Eddie Dunn (Bus Driver); Howard Mitchell (Sheriff); Whitney de Rhan (Ranch Hand); Baldy Cooke (Ranch Hand); Charles Watt (Ranch Hand); Jack Lawrence (Ranch Hand); Carl Pitti (Ranch Hand); John Beach (Ranch Hand)

MAN MADE MONSTER (1941)

by Bryan Senn

"After witnessing the torture my father endured in his various make-ups," commented Lon Chaney, Jr. in a Universal studio publicity piece, "I was more than ready to heed his advice about not doing that type of work. And yet, I suppose the fact that I'm here proves that some people just can't escape their destiny." Indeed he could not, as evidenced by his first foray into the horror field, *Man Made Monster*. "There on the identical spot where his father performed in his famed character guises," marveled the film's pressbook, "young Chaney, disguised in a gruesome facial covering and encased in a 70-pound rubber suit, played the role of a human electrical man." Studio publicity also claimed that Chaney, Jr. lost sixteen pounds while walking about in this "70-pound rubber suit." Destiny can sometimes be a severe taskmaster.

Chaney plays Dan McCormick, the sole survivor of a bus accident (a convincing and atmospheric bit of modelwork courtesy of John P. Fulton's special effects department) which left all the passengers but him dead of electrocution. Dan runs a "mostly phony" carnival act as "Dynamo Dan the Electrical Man" and this continual fooling around with electricity seems to have given him some kind of immunity.

Famous electro-biologist Dr. Lawrence (Samuel S. Hinds) invites Dan to come stay at his home/laboratory so that he and his colleague, Dr. Rigas (Lionel Atwill), can study this phenomenon. When the kindly Dr. Lawrence departs for a conference, Dr. Rigas begins conducting his own experiments on Dan, using the trusting unfortunate as a human guinea pig in his mad goal to create electricity-powered automatons ("a race of superior men... whose only wants are electricity"). To this end, he exposes Dan to larger and larger doses of electricity until the formerly vivacious Dan becomes "a walking shell waiting for the life-giving current" (as Rigas writes in his notebook).

When the returning Dr. Lawrence stumbles upon Rigas' final experiment with Dan, Rigas orders Dan ("whose every impulse is controlled by me") to stop the elderly man from calling the police. At this, the now super-powered Dan breaks his former benefactor's neck. When Dan is arrested for the crime, he can only intone "I killed him" over and over (as ordered by Dr. Rigas). Dan is convicted and sentenced to die—in the electric chair.

When three jolts in "the chair" only transform Dan into an electrically charged killing machine (electrocuting everyone he touches), Dan uses the warden as a hostage to break out of the prison and instinctively head back to the laboratory. At that moment, June (Anne Nagel), Dr. Lawrence's sympathetic niece, finds Rigas' notebook. Rigas, unfortunately, immediately finds *her*. "I've always found that the female of the species was more sensitive to electrical impulses than was the male," he states, smiling malevolently. Just then, Dan breaks into the lab and somehow overcomes Rigas' hypnotic hold to attack and kill the mad medico. Dan then dons an insulated suit to prevent his precious electrical life-force from running out through his touch and scoops up June.

As Junior looked on, five survivors of the original *Phantom of the Opera* crew unveiled a plaque reading: "Dedicated to the memory of Lon Chaney, for whose picture *The Phantom of the Opera* this stage was erected in 1924."

With the police in pursuit, Dan carries her off into the woods. Becoming entangled on a barbed wire fence, his suit rips and Dan's life-giving electricity runs out of his body into the wire until he finally collapses, drained and dead. Back at the lab, June and her reporter boyfriend, Mark (Frank Albertson), burn Rigas' notebook so that no one can ever again do what was done to Dan.

After Lon Chaney, Jr.'s breakthrough roles in *Of Mice and Men* (1939) and *One Million B.C.* (1940), Universal sought to sign the rising actor to their roster. The acid test they set for him was *Man Made Monster*. He passed with flying colors, and the studio was so pleased with the young Chaney that they awarded him an exclusive, long-term contract beginning at $500 a week (with frequent and significant raises to come). With this, Chaney, Jr. took up residence at the same studio that had helped make his father a huge success—and vice-versa. (In fact, between scenes on *Man Made Monster*—and reportedly while still in make-up—Chaney, Jr. attended a brief commemorative ceremony on the original Phantom soundstage honoring his father. As Junior looked on, five survivors of the original *Phantom of the Opera* crew unveiled a plaque reading: "Dedicated to the memory of Lon Chaney, for whose picture *The Phantom of the Opera* this stage was erected in 1924.")

It's likely that Lon Chaney, Jr. was fully aware that *Man Made Monster* was extremely important to his future career. As such, the previously struggling actor (who

was deathly afraid of poverty and later in life reportedly kept meatlockers full of food stashed at various locations so that he'd never have to go hungry) undoubtedly threw his heart and soul into the role. It shows. Also likely was that Chaney, in trying to win over Universal to his cause, was on his best behavior (i.e., no drinking). As a consequence, his focused performance as Dan McCormick ranks among his best. It's too bad that soon after his mammoth success with this picture's horror follow-up, *The Wolf Man*, the troubled actor seemingly either lost his focus or became too overconfident in his position and soon embarked upon the troubling behavior (drinking and brawling) that adversely affected his subsequent work and career. (Just compare Chaney's 1941 performances to his substandard work only a few years later in such films as *The Ghost of Frankenstein*, *Son of Dracula*, and the *Inner Sanctum* pictures—a series the actor took great stock in yet could not fully capitalize upon.)

In any case, *Man Made Monster* proved a propitious "coming out" venue well-suited to Chaney's specific persona and talents. From his introductory scene, Chaney's Dan McCormick comes across as a likable, easy-going, everyday Joe, and his friendly manner and straightforward demeanor immediately win over the viewer. Chaney's wide, bright smile and good-natured attitude as he sits up in a hospital bed with his open face tilted upwards, eager to shoot the breeze with the doctors, quickly establishes his character as a modest, out-going, warm-hearted guy.

With his subsequent scenes Chaney continues to effectively flesh out his character. When June comes across Dan in the garden, for instance, she asks him what happened to the circus girl he was once "sweet on." "Well," answers Chaney with a frown, "she ran away with the fire eater." But Chaney's frown instantaneously gives way to another big smile at her sympathetic laughter, and he immediately resumes playing with Corky the dog. Dan is not one to let past misfortunes get him down. (In this respect, Chaney's performance here is even more effective than in his signature film, *The Wolf Man*, for in that picture his initial character-building scenes—in which he accosts and flirts with the heroine—seem forced and insincere; Chaney reportedly never felt comfortable with love scenes.)

When Dr. Lawrence proposes Dan come to work for him as a test subject, the scientist adds, "You can live right here too." At this, Chaney's face lights up and he asks enthusiastically, "You mean I get to *eat* here too?" Obviously Dan is a man of basic wants and pleasures (borne out in the next tranquil scene which shows him happily frolicking with the dog in the garden). Then, when June comes across Dan outdoors and comments, "Lovely day isn't it," Chaney replies, "Oh, it sure is!" with such sincerity that you have to believe it—and believe that he's a man who fully enjoys life and its simple pleasures. This makes it doubly shocking (pardon the pun) when these things are so cruelly taken from him—first his capacity for joy (as he becomes a shell of his former self) and finally his very life.

Dan is no simplistic hedonist, however, for he later shows real concern when he sees that a rabbit is missing from its usual laboratory cage. Chaney's worried, "Hey doc, where's Pete?" shows both a warm consideration and a charming naiveté. (This scene also allows Lionel Atwill as the sinister Dr. Rigas a great throwaway line when he casually answers, "Oh, he worked yesterday," with just a hint of amusement at the innocence of his *present* subject over the welfare of his *former* subject.)

This scene also becomes an effective instance of foreshadowing—since Dan is destined to follow in Pete's unhappy footsteps. Chaney's acting adds to the moment's ominous feel; his worried countenance and continual glances over at the empty cage while Rigas straps him down to the forbidding apparatus both echo and intensify the uneasy concern felt by the viewer.

After becoming "the shell of a man, electrically alive," Chaney, though now robbed of dialogue (apparently the process has left him mute), uses his face and body language to depict both the physical change and his raging emotions. For instance, in sharp contrast to his formerly open and kind visage, as the "Man Made Monster" Chaney's face becomes strained, his smooth forehead now furrowed, and his smiling mouth a contorted grimace. When, after his prison break, the electrified Dan meets up with a group out for an evening hayride, Chaney holds up his hands to the people, squeezes them into fists out of frustration (perhaps knowing he can no longer touch his fellow human beings), and then opens them again in a gesture of supplication. His face also takes on a look of tortured pleading. Much like Karloff's more famous man made monster, however, all he gets for his troubles is a whip across his back. Even as a murderous dynamo of destruction, Chaney continues to elicit some small pity.

While not exactly (ahem) electrifying, *Man Made Monster*'s story can stand on its own two (rubber-soled) feet as an original and solid piece of construction. (The same can *not* be said for a number of Universal's other—and better known—horror entries of the 1940s.) This perhaps stems from the fact that the film originated as an intended Karloff/Lugosi vehicle called *The Man in the Cab* (based on a story titled *The Electric Man* by Harry J. Essex, Sid Schwartz, and Len Golos) during the genre's Golden Age (the 1930s) when originality was not such a rare concept. George Waggner dusted off the property, rewrote the script under his pseudonym Joseph West, and retitled it *The Human Robot* (which became *The Mysterious Dr. R* during shooting and finally meta-

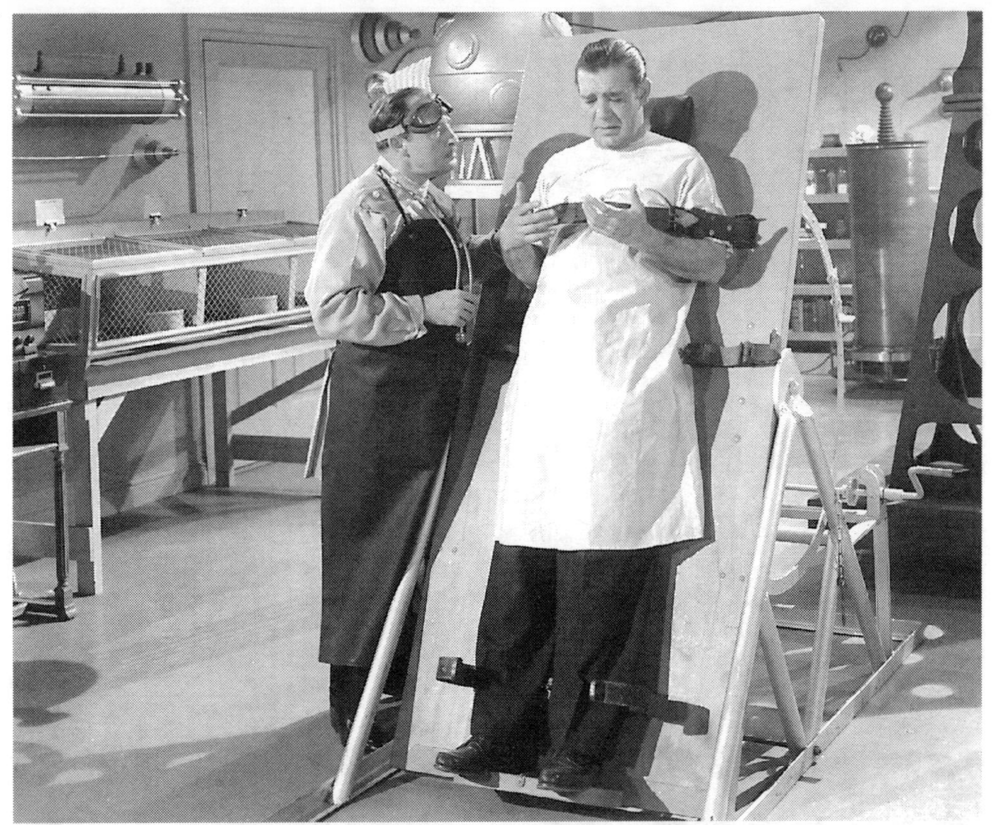

Lionel Atwill receives top billing in *Man Made Monster* and rightly so, for his bravura playing gives the story its spark (literally as well as figuratively).

morphosed into the snappier *Man Made Monster* in post-production). While it's easy to imagine Bela Lugosi in the Lionel Atwill part of the mad Dr. Rigas, it's difficult to picture Karloff in the effusive role of Dan McCormick. This only serves as further testament to Lon Chaney, Jr.'s effective performance, one that he made his own.

This being one of the cheapest Universal horrors of the 1940s (sporting a cut-rate budget of only $86,000), it's little wonder that much of the film's action takes place off-screen. For instance, the potentially sensational scene of McCormick's failed execution is only *talked* about rather than shown, albeit in a more immediate fashion than the standard newspaper headline method (with a reporter, guard, and prison electrician frantically phoning back and forth to find out—and reveal—what's happening). While this proves initially disappointing (since such a tableau is potentially rife with macabre excitement), keeping it hidden from view allows the audience to stretch their imagination a bit and at the same time helps preserve sympathy for the film's monster/protagonist (for seeing the electrified Dan commit two murders couldn't do his hero image any good—in fact, with the justifiable exception of Dr. Rigas, we only see Dan kill when he's attacked first).

Obviously, given his limited resources, Waggner had to pick and choose his moments, and those action sequences that do make it into the final print are well-realized. One of the best comes when the escaped Dan encounters the horse-drawn haywagon full of laughing riders. As the horses neigh and toss their heads in terror at the startling vision of the glowing Dan at the side of the track, the belligerent and frightened driver

It's likely that Lon Chaney, Jr. was fully aware that *Man Made Monster* was extremely important to his future career.

flicks his whip at Dan and is promptly electrocuted for his actions. Then the terrified horses bolt, sending the panicked passengers toppling from the rig. As the wagon passes, Dan reaches out as if to stop it, but his touch only causes a fearful spark that sets the hay alight. As the last of the passengers leaps from the burning wagon, the fear-maddened animals break free and the cart tips sideways to spill its fiery load down an embankment, the flaming material rolling and flowing like scorching lava. With shadowy lighting, rapid edits (terrified horses, fearful passengers, dying driver, the glowing Dan), and frantic music playing on the soundtrack, it becomes a moment both frightening and exciting (and, thanks to Chaney's effective pantomime, a little sad).

Lionel Atwill receives top billing in *Man Made Monster* and rightly so, for his bravura playing gives the story its spark (literally as well as figuratively). Though essaying a rather one-dimensional character, Atwill imbues the fanatical, unscrupulous Dr. Rigas with a boundless energy and an evil gleam, bringing his full powers to bear on the limiting role by employing subtle gestures and inflections to flesh out and enhance his character as well as project a broad grandness worthy of a monomaniacal mad scientist.

The way Atwill undertakes a simple task in his very first scene speaks volumes about his character's state at the moment. After employing a stethoscope to listen intently to something offscreen, he raises up slowly, then removes the listening prongs from his ears with a quick jerk and abrupt snap. His shoulders slump ever so slightly as he begins to disconnect the wires. Through Atwill's subtle body language, we feel first his character's disappointment, then a brief surge of anger, and finally a resignation at his failure—all without a single word spoken.

When the character finally does speak, Atwill exhibits his deft control of voice as well as body. When Dr. Lawrence suggests he give up his experiment, Rigas' first words are "It *will* work, I *know* it." Innocuous enough, but as Atwill delivers them (his voice low, the words seemingly forced out through a constricted throat), they become a verbal badge of desperate and dangerous determination.

When Lawrence further admonishes, "Sometimes I think you're mad," Atwill lifts the safety goggles from his eyes and answers almost happily, "I am! So was Archimedes, Galileo, Newton, Pasteur, Lister, and all the others who dared to dream!" Atwill's eyes have gone a bit too wide and a subtle half-smile plays across his face; it seems as if he revels in the idea of being thought mad. He spouts his litany with such pride and enthusiasm that one can't help but admire his verve.

With a plethora of sinister roles in films such as *Doctor X* (1932), *Mystery of the Wax Museum* (1933*), The Vampire Bat* (1933), *Secret of the Blue Room* (1933), *Murders in the Zoo* (1933), and *The Man Who Reclaimed His Head* (1935), Lionel Atwill had become one of Hollywood's foremost screen villains. In 1933 (a year in which he appeared in *eight* films), *Motion Picture* magazine dubbed the actor "The MENTAL Lon Chaney" (that's *Senior*, not Junior), going on to say, "Here is a *handsome* man who makes women's hearts beat faster—*until he stops them.* Here is a charming and very polished gentleman who makes women's blood run warmer—*until he chills it.* This man murders with a smile, violates with a chilling laugh.... Here is a man with the most sardonic mouth I have ever seen, the coldest and most merciless eyes ever set in a man's skull."

Atwill, a complex man both in front of and behind the camera, enjoyed playing villainous roles. While still a matinee idol on the Broadway stage, he began acting in early silents. In a 1919 interview for *Motion Picture Classic*, Atwill commented on the future of moving pictures and his views on screen villainy: "I honestly think pictures have possibilities, but not until some of these old-fashioned ideas are combed out of them. For instance, to the picture director, a character is either a hero, who is all good, or a villain, who is all bad.... No one is wholly good or evil.... I, for one, will never play in pictures again until I am assured that the director is broad-minded enough to present a villain who has lovable qualities, or a hero who has a few weaknesses." Though his

Dr. Rigas sports very few "lovable qualities," Atwill manages to imbue in him a few *human* traits at least.

Later, in 1933, after becoming an established screen star, Atwill further expounded upon his convictions as to the duality of man (and himself) in *Motion Picture* magazine: "See, one side of my face is gentle and kind, incapable of anything but love of my fellow man. The other side, the other profile, is cruel and predatory and evil, incapable of anything but the lusts and dark passions. It all depends on which side of my face is turned toward you—or the camera. It all depends on which side faces the moon at the ebb of the tide." For his Dr. Rigas, Atwill's face seemed fixed more intently upon the *dark* side of the moon.

Even though given little to work with in *Man Made Monster*, Atwill still manages to add a few subtle touches that transform his (as written) one-dimensional villain into a more human and three-dimensional antagonist. For instance, though Rigas orders Dan to "Stop him!" when Dr. Lawrence begins to phone the police, the real shock displayed on Atwill's face when he kneels over his colleague's body and says wonderingly, "You killed him," (as if he intended nothing so drastic) shows that he's not above human feeling (at least toward a fellow scientist).

During the filming of one of his four horror pictures made in 1933 (*The Vampire Bat*), the former Broadway star told reporters that he was happier doing horror films than stage plays. "So long as I've got something definite and picturesque to get my teeth into I feel I can have a field day and enjoy myself, whether the role is equal to Hamlet or not." Whether he still felt this way after nearly a decade of largely villainous roles is questionable, but with *Man Made Monster* he stayed true to his word as he sunk his teeth into the part and indeed appears to be enjoying himself. He returns the favor as well, for his bravura turn as the obsessed Dr. Rigas remains one of the most enjoyable aspects presented to the viewers of *Man Made Monster*.

Samuel S. Hinds provides solid support as the well-meaning Dr. Lawrence, his calm and kindly scientist serving as marked contrast to Atwill's amoral fanatic. Hinds' reasonable demeanor (when he gently chides Rigas' dismissal of common humanity as "nonentities" and then smoothes it over with a friendly insistence to join him for a beer and a snack in the kitchen) temporarily diffuses Atwill's mania, allowing that actor to relax his intensity for a moment and reveal a bit more of his character's humanity as he finally gives in and even smiles at his colleague's kindness.

After 35 years as a practicing lawyer (and amateur thespian; he was co-founder of the Pasadena Community Playhouse), the loss of Samuel Hinds' considerable fortune during the stock market crash served as catalyst for a career change. Hinds made his professional acting debut in 1932 at age 58, going on to appear in over 150 films over the next sixteen years (he died in 1948), including such varied genre entries as *The Raven* (1935), *She* (1935), *Son of Dracula* (1943), and *Jungle Woman* (1944).

As the imperiled heroine, Anne Nagel makes for a plucky protagonist, both compassionate and competent. When she tells her beau that she fears something strange is going on and states determinedly, "I'm worried and I'm scared," before pressing to go back and investigate, one believes that she'll indeed try and *do* something about it. Thanks to Ms. Nagel's no-nonsense playing, June becomes much more than just the standard window-dressing screamer (in fact, she refreshingly doesn't scream once).

Born Anne Dolan in 1912, Anne Nagel appeared in nightclubs as a professional dancer before making her film debut in 1933's *I Loved You Yesterday*. Over the next

While not exactly electrifying, *Man Made Monster*'s story can stand on its own two feet as an original and solid piece of construction. Pictured: Chaney, Jr. and Anne Nagel.

fifteen years she appeared in more than 75 features and serials. Her horror/fantasy credits include *Black Friday* (1940), *The Invisible Woman* (1940), *The Mad Doctor of Market Street* (1942; again with Lionel Atwill), and *The Mad Monster* (1942). Absent from films since 1949, she succumbed to cancer in 1966 at the age of 54.

Not only was Universal well pleased with their new star, Lon Chaney, Jr., but with writer/director George Waggner as well, who took the disparate elements and fashioned them into a well-crafted whole. Waggner takes full advantage of his stars' talents—*and* those of his technicians, particularly playing up cinematographer Elwood Bredell's moody lighting. Bredell's atmospheric illumination perfectly complements the fog-shrouded woodland sets, turning the trees into sinister, twisted figures and the over-hanging branches into spindly fingers and spiderwebs. Even on a mundane set such as the hospital foyer, backlighting casts long, ominous shadows before an approaching figure, and corners of the room are steeped in pools of darkness. Upon completion of

Man Made Monster and *Horror Island* (its companion feature also directed by Waggner), the studio offered Waggner a seven-year contract.

Born George Waggoner in 1894, Waggner graduated from the Philadelphia College of Pharmacy, then served as an Army officer from 1916 to 1920. Relocating to Hollywood after his discharge, he entered the film industry as an actor, appearing in such silent features as *The Sheik* (1921), *Desert Driven* (1923), and *The Iron Horse* (1924; playing Buffalo Bill). With the advent of sound, Waggner turned both songwriter (composing over 100 songs, some of which were recorded by Bing Crosby) and screenwriter (penning or collaborating on nearly two dozen features in only five years!). Graduating to director in 1938, he helmed his first six films in less than a year—all Westerns. While the *Man Made Monster/Horror Island* tandem was his first foray into the horror genre, it was thankfully not his last. Waggner directed (*and* produced) *The Wolf Man* (1941) and *The Climax* (1944), and produced *The Ghost of Frankenstein* (1942), *Frankenstein Meets the Wolf Man* (1943), and *Phantom of the Opera* (1943). In the 1950s, Waggner turned to television, where he wrote and directed over 50 episodes of *77 Sunset Strip* and worked on more than 20 other series, including *Bonanza*, *The Untouchables*, *The Man from U.N.C.L.E.*, *Maverick*, *Batman*, and *The Green Hornet*. He died at the Motion Picture Home in 1984 at the age of 90.

Man Made Monster scored a moderate success at the box office but did less well with the critics. One of its few good reviews came from *Variety*, which called the film a "strong programmer tailored for dualers" and a "shocker that's in the groove for the horror fans. It makes no pretense of being anything but a freakish chiller, going directly to the point and proving mighty successful." Of the fledgling horror star, the reviewer noted, "This picture has the added box-office draw of Lon Chaney, Jr., in monster role, which is calculated to whet curiosity as to the son's ability to follow in the footsteps of his father with this type of characterization. Young Chaney looks like he is on his way."

Though the *Motion Picture Exhibitor* dismissed *Man Made Monster* as "a more-or-less routine thriller," the reviewer conceded that "the cast does well with its opportunities, and the direction is reasonably smooth." Like *Variety*, this trade publication also urged exhibitors to play up the son-following-in-famous-father's-footsteps angle: "Sell the fact that Lon Chaney, Jr., is playing the same kind of roles his father did."

Harrison's Reports called *Man Made Monster* "just a program horror melodrama" and the *New York Journal-American* felt the film was "pretty much on the silly side." Across town at *The New York Times,* cranky critic Bosley Crowther dismissed it as "low-grade shocker fare," but *The New York World-Telegram* proved even harsher: "The film is pretty static and bankrupt of suspense and excitement."

Unlike many a Universal horror, *Man Made Monster* hasn't gotten much in-depth retrospective attention, despite the fact that (as noted by Michael Brunas, John Brunas, and Tom Weaver in *Universal Horrors*) "Lon Chaney's Dan McCormick ranks with [*The Wolf Man*'s] Larry Talbot as his best horror performance." Surprisingly, even in the (slim) volume *Lon Chaney, Jr.: Horror Film Star*, author Don G. Smith simply calls *Man Made Monster* "as quintessential a horror film as one is likely to find" without further elaboration. Denis Gifford's equally vague assessment in *A Pictorial History of Horror Movies* labeled the movie "good, typical stuff." Phil Hardy, in *The Encyclopedia of Horror Movies*, opined that "Chaney, a dull actor... can make little of the role." Of the film itself, Hardy complained about the script "generating little suspense" and noted that "[Elwood] Bredell's excellent camerawork lends the film more distinction than it deserves." In *Classic Movie Monsters*, however, Donald F. Glut felt that "not only was Chaney a viable commodity, because of his father's name and reputation, he also had a youthful appeal and considerable acting talent. Chaney's performances often brought out tragedy and aroused the sympathy of his audience."

For his *Classics of the Horror Film*, William K. Everson provided one of the few substantial analyses the film has received. Everson called *Man Made Monster* "an expert little made-to-measure horror vehicle, delivering everything that the fans expected, including clichés that were still new enough to be welcome friends." Though feeling that "it was Atwill's show all the way," Everson noted that "Chaney... played his fairly well-written role for pathos and tragedy as much as menace, and came as close as he ever would to Karloff's genius for making an audience feel sorry for him even while they feared him."

Man Made Monster made it to England (minus the death-house sequence, which was excised in the interest of "good taste") as *The Electric Man*, a title change that no doubt allowed the anti-horror British censors to breathe a little easier. The film acquired yet another moniker about a decade later when it was reissued under the absurd appellation *The Atomic Monster* (presumably in an effort to cash in on the post-WWII "Atomic" craze).

By whatever name, *Man Made Monster* remains a taut, well-acted, entertaining thriller, not least because it proved to be one of the few happy occasions in which Universal used the specific talents of Lon Chaney, Jr. to best advantage. For Chaney fans, it is not to be missed.

CREDITS: Alternate Titles: *The Electric Man* (British), *The Atomic Monster* (reissue); Director: George Waggner; Associate Producer: Jack Bernhard; Screenplay: Joseph West (George Waggner); Based on the Story *The Electric Man* by H. J. Essex, Sid Schwartz, and Len Golos; Director of Photography: Elwood Bredell; Art Director: Jack Otterson; Associate Art Director: Harold H. MacArthur; Film Editor: Arthur Hilton; Musical Director: Hans J. Salter; Sound Supervisor: Bernard B. Brown; Technician: Charles Carroll; Gowns: Vera West; Set Decorator: R. A. Gausman; Special Photography: John P. Fulton; Make-up: Jack P. Pierce; Released March 1941 by Universal; 59 minutes

CAST: Lionel Atwill (Dr. Rigas); Lon Chaney, Jr. (Dan McCormick); Anne Nagel (June Lawrence); Frank Albertson (Mark Adams); Samuel S. Hinds (Dr. Lawrence); William Davidson (District Attorney); Ben Taggart (Detective Sergeant); Connie Bergen (Nurse); Ivan Miller (Doctor); Chester Gan (Chinese Boy); George Meader (Dr. Bruno); Frank O'Connor (Detective); Jon Dilson (Medical Examiner); Byron Foulger (Second Alienist); Russell Hicks (Warden)

[Courtesy Ronald V. Borst/Hollywood Movie Posters]

THE WOLF MAN (1941)

by John Stell

The only creation produced during the 1940s that can stand proudly beside the 1930s' Dracula, Frankenstein Monster, Mummy, and Invisible Man, *The Wolf Man* is also the lone classic monster that was played, throughout its Universal run, by only one actor: Lon Chaney, Jr. After yielding impressive results in *Man Made Monster* in the spring of 1941, young Lon was cast in his immortal role, which served as Universal's second attempt at the werewolf legend after the uneven *Werewolf of London* (1935). The film itself, constructed as a gothic-tragedy by writer Curt Siodmak, is perhaps the last of Universal's adult horror films, as its sequel, *Frankenstein Meets the Wolf Man*, was the beginning of the juvenile monster rallies that ultimately had the Wolf Man playing second fiddle to Abbott and Costello in 1948. And *The Wolf Man* is truly an adult tale: one of lust, betrayal, scandal, and, of course, good versus evil.

Young Larry Talbot (Lon Chaney, Jr.) is returning home after being away 18 years. His older brother, John, is dead, killed in a hunting accident, and now Larry must take his place as the family heir. After a few uncomfortable moments with his father, Sir John (Claude Rains), Larry is more than willing to embrace his new life.

Larry is also ready to embrace his new neighbor, Gwen Conliffe (Evelyn Ankers), the beauty he spots while working on Dad's telescope. Even though she is engaged to Frank Andrews (Patric Knowles), Gwen agrees to accompany Larry to a gypsy fair, bringing along her friend Jenny Williams (Fay Helm). When Jenny is attacked by a wolf, Larry comes to her aid, only to be bitten by the wolf in the ensuing struggle. He insists that he killed the wolf with his silver tipped walking cane. But the body found near Jenny's is that of a fortune-telling gypsy, Bela (Bela Lugosi).

When returning to the gypsy camp Larry is confronted by Maleva (Maria Ouspenskaya), Bela's mother. She warns him he will turn into a wolf, because whoever is bitten by a werewolf and lives, becomes a werewolf himself. After the brutal murder of a gravedigger, and some unexplained nightly prowls, Larry suspects the truth.

While the authorities refuse to believe in werewolves, Larry tells his father and Gwen he is leaving. Hoping to convince his son he is wrong, Sir John straps Larry in a chair and then joins the others who are hunting the wolf. Larry escapes, transforms, and discovers Gwen, who is in the forest looking for the man she now loves. The Wolf Man attacks Gwen, but Sir John hears the screams and attacks the beast with the very same cane that killed Bela—the same cane that Larry insisted his father take with him. Sir John looks in horror as the wolf transforms back into his beloved son.

Of all the classic horror tales, *The Wolf Man* is the most tragic. At the end of the film, a likable fellow is dead, a father has killed the last of his offspring, and a woman has lost the man she loves. It is hardly a happy ending, and the death of the werewolf hardly brings cheers.

Although the film makes it obvious that the man-into-wolf story represents the struggle between good and evil that exists in everyone, *The Wolf Man* also personifies the warning that mothers give their daughters: all men are wolves. This sexual identity is driven home by the fact that all of the Talbot men are traditionally "manly." Sir John's idea of showing affection to his son is to shake his hand. Larry's brother died in a hunting accident. Larry himself is great with tools, and when he spots Gwen, he unabashedly tells her they will go out that very night, acting like the metaphorical wolf. Later Larry shows himself to be quite a shot. And he is "heroic" when he comes to the aid of Jenny Williams, or unselfishly breaks off his romance with Gwen. There was even a bear wrestling scene that was cut from the final print.

But it is perhaps the relationship with Gwen that is the "reason" for Larry's suffering. Considering the time the film takes place, Larry's spending time with the engaged Gwen could be viewed as "adultery." While such a thing wouldn't raise an eyebrow today, such a tryst is positively scandalous in *The Wolf Man*. At one point Larry is forced out of church when the entire congregation stares him down. In the horror films of the 1980s some critics believed that the way to survive an ax-wielding maniac was to remain a virgin because the teens getting murdered were being "punished" for having premarital sex. Perhaps Larry Talbot was being punished for tearing asunder what God had almost joined.

Like James Whale's *The Bride of Frankenstein* (1935), *The Wolf Man* features many religious allusions. Larry is "the prodigal son" who has returned to claim wealth; the way to bring temporary comfort to the accursed is by prayer; Larry covets what he sees through the telescope; and the protective pentagram medallion Maleva gives Larry is similar to a cross. Whether or not these references were deliberate (Whale's certainly were) is of course debatable. But they fit comfortably with the good versus evil theme.

Adding to the adult nature of the film are the complex relationships that develop: Larry-Sir John, Larry-Gwen, Larry-Maleva, Gwen-Frank, Maleva-Bela, and Gwen-Jenny. In other words, few characters stand alone. They have friends and family. And most of these relationships meet with tragic ends. The later Universals of the 1940s would end with monster vs. monster, or human villain vs. good guy vs. monster. *The Wolf Man* hits an emotional chord that Universal was never able to strike again because Larry Talbot is as much a victim as anyone else.

Although his finest performance can be found in the 1939 production of *Of Mice and Men*, Lon Chaney's Larry Talbot is the best performance Chaney ever gave in a horror film. When we first see Larry, riding back to greet his father, he is all smiles. A jovial presence, Larry is eager to make amends with Sir John and start afresh. Although he's as subtle as a train wreck when meeting Gwen, his flirtations are more sweet than offensive. (At this point we don't know Gwen's engaged nor does she share this information with Larry until later.) Larry's good-natured manner is prevalent throughout the film's beginning. But when Chaney is in Jack Pierce's classic make-up, there is no doubting the savagery of the Wolf Man: standing tall, snarling uncontrollably, and ultimately lunging at his intended prey.

Larry Talbot is an easy character to like. He means well. He isn't deliberately trying to make trouble. He does try to save Jenny. And the cold treatment he gets from the town for doing so only makes us sympathize with him more. When he first meets his "competition" for Gwen—Frank Andrews—he offers Frank his hand in friendship, only to be ignored. Nobody ever gave poor Larry a chance.

Playing the pivotal part of the wise Maleva, Maria Ouspenskaya is intense and stern as the only one who truly knows the ways of the werewolf.

One moment truly stands out in terms of Chaney's performance. Maleva discovers the Wolf Man caught in a bear trap. She prays over Larry, bringing him back to his normal self. As Larry realizes what has happened and hears the barking dogs approaching, he desperately tries to free himself, his face a mask of panic, shock, and fear, i.e., the face of a hunted animal. This is such a different "face" than the one we saw as the film opened that the impact is startling.

Only once does Chaney overdo it a bit. Sir John tells Larry that they are searching for a wolf. With his back to his father he "innocently" asks, "Where do you suppose a wolf came from?" Unfortunately the audience can see the guilt written all over Larry's human face—a face so guilty it approaches parody. But this is a small misstep in an otherwise first-rate performance.

Offering outstanding support as Sir John is top-billed Claude Rains. Rains had not made a horror film since his motion picture debut in Universal's *The Invisible Man* in 1933. Although Rains did appear in several mystery-thrillers such as *Crime Without Passion* (1934), *The Clairvoyant* (1934), *The Man Who Reclaimed His Head* (1935) (which was remade as *Strange Confession* in 1945 as a vehicle for Lon Chaney, Jr.'s *Inner Sanctum* series), and *The Mystery of Edwin Drood* (1935), *The Wolf Man* marks his triumphant return to the genre that started his film career.

Rains' agonized expression, after realizing he has killed his son, is one of the most memorable and sad moments from 1940s' horror films.

Rains is excellent as Sir John. When Sir John and Larry reunite as the film begins, one can sense the awkwardness of the situation thanks to the great chemistry between Rains and Chaney. Sir John is a bit shy, a bit unsure. Still grieving over the loss of his oldest son, Sir John nonetheless is happy at Larry's return. This bittersweet scene sets the tone for *The Wolf Man*, as Sir John will have no sons by film's end.

Rains' agonized expression, after realizing he has killed his son, is one of the most memorable and sad moments from 1940s' horror films. Clutching the tree beside him, and then staggering away, Sir John pays the ultimate price for not believing his son. As always, Rains brings conviction and dignity to his role. Rains would go on to play the title role in Universal's 1943 color remake of *The Phantom of the Opera*, as well as making his mark in classics like *Casablanca* (1942).

Although seventh billed, Evelyn Ankers is the other key player in *The Wolf Man*. One of the earliest "scream queens," Ankers had just appeared with Abbott and Costello in *Hold That Ghost* (1941). With *The Wolf Man*, she became identified with the horror genre, even though fewer than ten of her more than fifty films are truly genre pictures: *The Ghost of Frankenstein* (1942), *Captive Wild Woman* (1943), *The Mad Ghoul* (1943), *Son of Dracula* (1943), *Weird Woman* (1944), *The Invisible Man's Revenge* (1944), and *Jungle Woman* (1944).

Despite the reports that Ankers and Chaney did not get along on the set when the cameras weren't rolling, the two crackle as the doomed lovers of *The Wolf Man*. Their first scene in the antique shop, with Chaney turning on the charm full blast, is cute and

Despite the reports that Evelyn Ankers and Chaney did not get along on the set when the cameras weren't rolling, the two crackle as the doomed lovers of *The Wolf Man.*

playful. Chaney is clearly coming on to her, while perfunctorily shopping for a walking stick. She notices a cane topped with a canine and says, "How 'bout a little dog. That would suit you." She plays yet another harmless trick on him when she invites her friend Jenny to accompany them to the gypsy camp on their "date."

Perhaps it's Larry Talbot's confidence that attracts her to him, but there is little doubt something passes between them that first evening. After being unfairly blamed for "allowing" Jenny to be killed, Gwen is ready to go with Larry when he tells her he's leaving. It's a touching scene, and, more importantly, a believable one. When Larry, in wolf form, tries to kill her just moments later, *The Wolf Man* reaches its truly horrific climax.

Playing the pivotal part of the wise Maleva, Maria Ouspenskaya is intense and stern as the only one who truly knows the ways of the werewolf. Born in 1876, the Russian actress made her American debut in *Dodsworth* (1936) for which she received an Oscar nomination. She reprised the role of Maleva in *Frankenstein Meets the Wolf Man* in 1943, this time helping Larry Talbot find Dr. Frankenstein. She died in 1949 when a fire broke out in her Los Angeles apartment.

Maleva is yet another of *The Wolf Man*'s suffering characters. Like Sir John, she has lost her son. But instead of holding Larry Talbot responsible for her son's death, she attempts to help him, giving Larry the pendant that might protect him from the curse. She stays behind after the other gypsies have fled, and offers peace at every opportunity to her new "son." She is in fact more of a mother to Larry than Sir John is a father.

Maleva (Maria Ouspenskaya) is a truly classic and noble character.

One of the best scenes in *The Wolf Man* takes place between the biological father and spiritual mother of Larry Talbot. Although Sir John claims not to believe the werewolf myth, he breaks off from his hunting party to check on the son he left strapped in a chair. Sir John meets Maleva on the road, and the two engage in a verbal showdown, with Maleva clearly being the winner:

Sir John: Who are you?
Maleva: Hasn't your son told you?

Sir John: You're the gypsy that's been filling his mind with this werewolf nonsense.
Maleva: Nonsense, Sir John?
Sir John: Yes. You've been praying on his gullibility with your witch's tales.
Maleva: But you fixed him, didn't you Sir John? You don't believe the witch's tales, do you?
Sir John: Not for a minute.
Maleva: Then where were you going, Sir John? Why aren't you back there, at the shooting stand?
Sir John: I was.
Maleva: Were you hurrying back to the castle? Did you have a moment's doubt? Were you hurrying to make sure he's all right?
Sir John: I wanted to be with my son. I was going back...
Shots are heard
Maleva: Yes Sir John? You were going...
More shots. Sir John starts to run
Maleva: Hurry, Sir John, hurry.

Maleva is slightly contemptuous of the "knowledgeable" Sir John. But one can still sense the sympathy she has for him, knowing that he will soon know her own pain. Maleva is a truly classic and noble character. She is a very important element in *The Wolf Man*'s success.

The rest of the cast is okay, but they pale in comparison to the work of Chaney, Rains, Ankers, and Ouspenskaya. Patric Knowles is fine as Ankers' fiancé, but he isn't given much screen time. Warren Williams as Dr. Lloyd thinks that the best medicine is simply "rest." Ralph Bellamy as Captain Paul Montford doesn't do anything to distinguish himself from other police officers in other horror films. Fay Helm is good as Jenny Williams, Gwen's friend who is in on Gwen's little joke. And Bela Lugosi is actually quite memorable as the other troubled werewolf of the film. His pleas for Jenny to leave the camp have an authentically urgent feel to them. Given that the character's name is Bela, it's likely the part was tailor made for Lugosi.

The original screenplay for *The Wolf Man* was written by Curt Siodmak, and it's one of his best. Siodmak had co-written the screenplays for *Black Friday* and *The Invisible Man Returns* in 1940 for Universal, as well as *The Ape*, Monogram's only Boris Karloff vehicle. His 1943 novel *Donovan's Brain* has been adapted no less than three times: in 1944 as *The Lady and the Monster*, in 1953 as *Donovan's Brain*, and in 1963 as *The Brain.* He turned director in 1951 with *Bride of the Gorilla.* But his screenplay for *The Wolf Man*, along with his work on *I Walked With A Zombie,* represents his best screen work.

Siodmak's script is a finely constructed story that features many parallel scenes. The film opens with son reuniting with father while it ends with father killing son. The playful scene in the antique shop with Larry wooing Gwen is later contrasted with another moment in the antique shop when Larry tells Gwen to stay away. There's much tragic irony in the fact that Larry buys the weapon that is ultimately used to kill him. Larry's brother was killed in a hunting accident, and so too is Larry. Siodmak has fun with the fable *Little Red Riding Hood*, having Larry tell Gwen what big eyes she has.

Other times, however, the "knowing" irony goes a bit too far. The earrings that Larry notices are moon shaped. The silver handle on the cane is that of a wolf. At the

Universal's titans of terror: Chaney, Jr. and Bela Lugosi (as Bela the Gypsy).

shooting gallery Larry cannot bring himself to pull the trigger when the wolf figure appears. The constant references to what is to come seem a bit heavy handed at times. When Frank Andrews meets Larry for the first time he tells Gwen, "There's something very tragic about that man. And I'm sure that nothing but harm will come to you through him." It's a curious scene because suddenly Frank is a fortune teller, and it suggests an ability to judge character that comes out of nowhere and doesn't appear again.

There's also a moment that just doesn't belong in the film. Jenny's mother (Doris Lloyd) and some of her friends come directly from Jenny's wake and start making ridiculous accusations against Gwen. Why didn't she stay with Jenny? Why didn't she protect her? What was she doing with that Larry Talbot? Later Mrs. Williams all but accuses Larry of the murders. This sort of character feels more at home in the superstitious villages of *Dracula* or *Frankenstein,* not in the more modern era of *The Wolf Man*. Unlike the gothic villagers of the 1930s' horror films, the key players of *The Wolf Man* don't believe in monsters. Thus the Mrs. Williams character seems a forced way to lend yet more sympathy to the already tragic relationship between Larry and Gwen. (Imagine if Mrs. Williams had been played by Una O'Connor!)

Siodmak, on the other hand, is to be commended for not taking an obvious route in terms of victims. In a lesser film, the victims would have been the same townsfolk who

Of all the classic horror tales, *The Wolf Man* is the most tragic.

taunted the "hero," thereby giving the audience an "out" when the attacks take place. But in *The Wolf Man* the victims are truly innocent people who have done nothing to "deserve" their deaths. It may be a small point, but it attests to the film's integrity.

While many of Siodmak's genre contributions were more science-fiction themed, *The Wolf Man* is a pure horror tale. The film's first shot is a camera panning several large volumes, as a hand removes one hefty tome and opens it to the section on lycanthropy, or, werewolfism. But the affliction is deemed to be "a state of mind." Thus the set-up of ancient legend in modern time is instantly in place. Later, while Larry picks out his cane, Gwen tells him the legend of the werewolf, and delivers Siodmak's most memorable lines: "Even a man who is pure in heart, and says his prayers by night, may become a wolf when the wolfbane blooms, and the autumn moon is bright." This same poem is later repeated by Sir John and Jenny Williams. Gwen also tells him about the pentagram that appears on the next victim's palm. And Maleva relays how the only way to kill a werewolf is with a silver bullet or something made of silver—much like the wooden stake is to a vampire's heart. These elements, combined with Jack Otterson's fog-enshrouded forest sets, give *The Wolf Man* a truly Gothic feel, even though it is a more "modern" horror film than its 1930s' predecessors.

George Waggner's direction of *The Wolf Man* is efficient but uninspired. Having directed Chaney in *Man Made Monster* the same year, as well as *Horror Island*, producer turned director Waggner was on his way to becoming one of Universal's horror

Lon Chaney, Jr. will always be remembered for the role of Larry Talbot, a role he made his own.

"specialists," producing *The Ghost of Frankenstein* in 1942, and *Frankenstein Meets the Wolf Man* and *Phantom of the Opera* in 1943. But with his 1944 failure *The Climax*, Waggner fell from Universal's graces.

Most of *The Wolf Man* is performance/relationship driven, and so the moments leading up to the first genuine attack by Lon Chaney, Jr. rely on the talents of the cast, who do not disappoint. The first scene where Chaney attacks the grave digger is done well enough. But the next Wolf Man appearance is a letdown. The Wolf Man just suddenly shows up, with no build-up from Waggner, and then gets caught in the bear trap. Certainly some more suspense could have been milked out of the scene. Also, a montage sequence where Chaney "sees" distorted images of wolves, Gwen, Bela, and Maleva feels out of place. As directed it doesn't seem to belong in this movie.

There are also a few inconsistencies that could be anybody's fault. When Bela is found, he is fully clothed, save for his bare feet. But that means that the wolf must have been wearing clothes when it attacked Jenny and Larry, a fact not supported when viewing the film (it would have been pretty silly looking). Furthermore, the werewolves of legend walk on all fours, as does Bela's wolf. But Chaney's wolf walks on two legs. Why is he different from every description of the werewolf that has been given to the audience up to that point? It is never explained, although the reason is probably the most obvious one: it would have been impossible in 1941 to achieve the make-up effects necessary to pull off a werewolf that could walk on all fours in a convincing close-up.

Jack Pierce's yak hair wolf make-up is yet another of his classic creations. The two transformation scenes, which show Larry turning into a wolf and then back into a man, respectively, make for some great early horror memories. Pierce would recreate this effect for future wolf man outings, each time with greater results.

Putting a crowning touch on *The Wolf Man* are Hans J. Salter and Frank Skinner, whose score for the film is one of the finest of any horror film. The music was so impressive that it became the standard score for the twelve Universal-produced *Sherlock Holmes* adventures as well as appearing in some way, shape, or form in many other 1940s' Universals. The intense, sometimes thundering music matches perfectly with Larry's mounting tension and desperate situation.

With Chaney's excellent performance in a very successful film, Universal made him their new horror star, casting him as the Frankenstein Monster in 1942, the Mummy and Dracula in 1943, and of course, as the Wolf Man in the sequels to the 1941 classic. But none of these monsters had the dimensions that Chaney brought to Larry Talbot. They were just killing machines. Even *The Wolf Man*'s sequels fail to capture the complexities of the original. The sequels were "fun" in their own way, but a far cry (or howl) from the original.

Lon Chaney, Jr. will always be remembered for the role of Larry Talbot, a role he made his own. No matter what reaction one has to his subsequent films, one cannot deny the strength and power of his performance in *The Wolf Man*, the last true classic of Universal's monster films. But the film is memorable because Chaney's Talbot is more than just a monster. He is a tragic figure with whom anyone can identify. And that is the real horror of *The Wolf Man*.

CREDITS: Producer: George Waggner; Director: George Waggner; Screenplay: Curt Siodmak; Director of Photography: Joseph Valentine; Art Director: Jack Otterson; Film Editor: Ted Kent; Music: Hans J. Salter and Frank Skinner; Make-up: Jack P. Pierce; Special Effects: John P. Fulton; Released December 12, 1941 by Universal Studios; 70 minutes

CAST: Claude Rains (Sir John Talbot); Warren William (Dr. Lloyd); Ralph Bellamy (Captain Paul Montford); Patric Knowles (Frank Andrews); Bela Lugosi (Bela); Maria Ouspenskaya (Maleva); Evelyn Ankers (Gwen Conliffe); Lon Chaney (Larry Talbot); Fay Helm (Jenny Williams); Leyland Hodgson (Kendall); Forrester Harvey (Victor Twiddle); J. M. Kerrigan (Charles Conliffe); Doris Lloyd (Mrs. Williams)

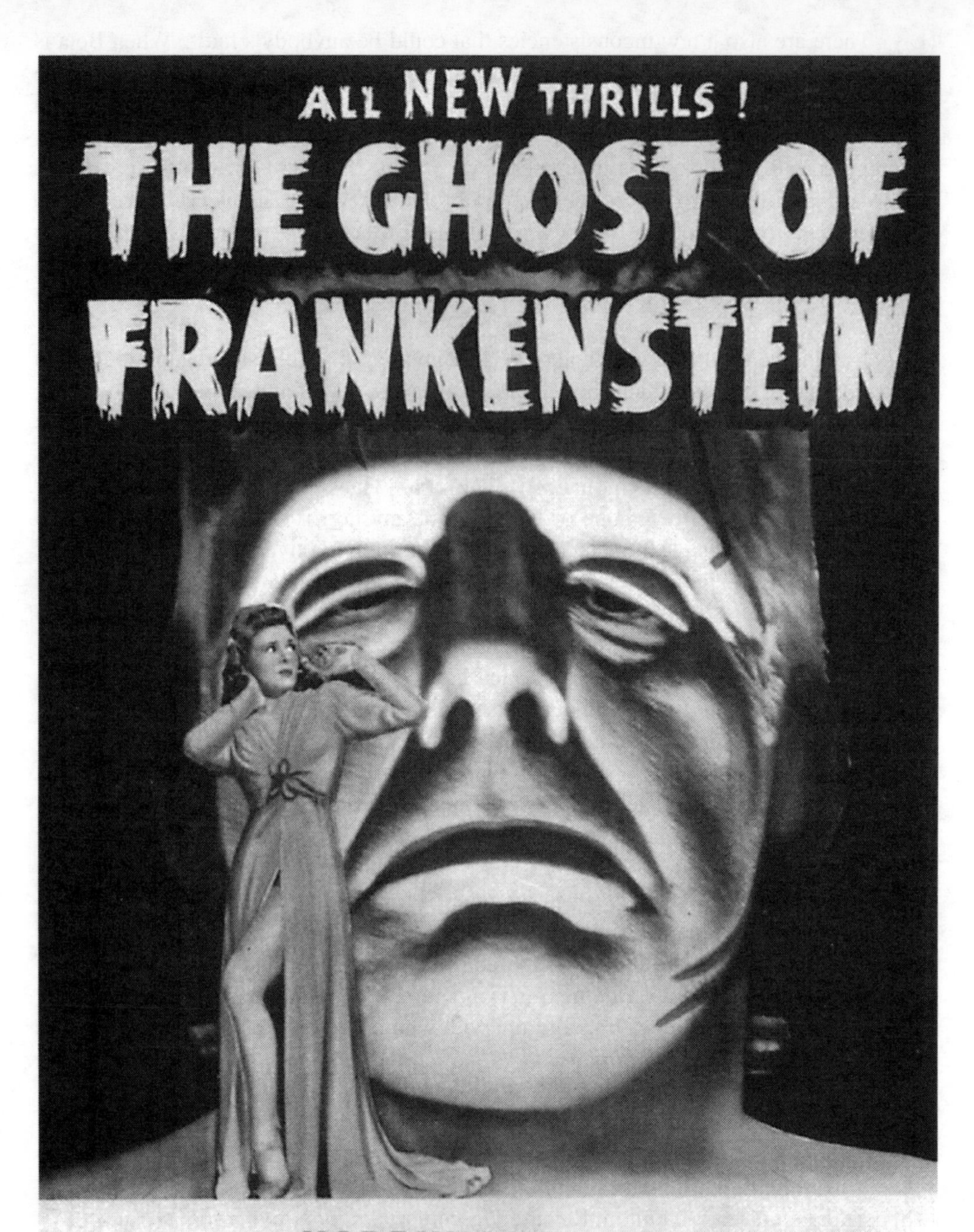
ALL NEW THRILLS !
THE GHOST OF
FRANKENSTEIN
with Sir Cedric HARDWICKE Ralph BELLAMY
Lionel ATWILL Bela LUGOSI Evelyn ANKERS
and LON CHANEY

THE GHOST OF FRANKENSTEIN (1942)
by Leonard J. Kohl

> "He [Lon Chaney, Jr.] got off to a 'good' and a 'bad' start. He deserved an award for *Of Mice and Men*, I think. You know, it was really an excellent job, but he made a reputation by that blank face that didn't seem to understand really what was going on? (laughs) I think that sort of stuck on him."—Ford I. Beebe[1]

After ten years as a struggling actor in Hollywood, Lon Chaney, Jr. was finally a "movie star." The younger Chaney got his big break in *Of Mice and Men* (1939) where he portrayed the slow-witted Lennie Small, a powerful but tragic figure from John Steinbeck's famous novel. Like Bela Lugosi's Count Dracula, and Boris Karloff's Frankenstein Monster, Lennie and Lon Chaney, Jr. became one and the same in the eyes of many movie casting people. However, by 1942, Chaney, Jr. had eclipsed Lennie with the doomed Larry Talbot, the tragic hero in *The Wolf Man* (1941). It was a new monster, but one who could equally stand his ground with Karloff's Monster and Lugosi's Transylvanian vampire, or even the Phantom or Hunchback as characterized by his dad. Chaney, Jr. was so good in *The Wolf Man* that the Universal executives decided that young Lon would be their new horror star since Boris Karloff was on Broadway in *Arsenic and Old Lace*, and Bela Lugosi was foolishly starring in low-budget thrillers like *Invisible Ghost* and *Spooks Run Wild* (both 1941) at Monogram. Lon Chaney, Jr., from *The Ghost of Frankenstein* on, was declared Universal's "new Lon Chaney" and he wasn't happy about it. Years later, the late director, Reginald LeBorg, had some interesting things to say about the troubled actor:

> Lon Chaney, Sr. was called "The Man of a Thousand Faces." I believe Lon Chaney, Jr. could be called "the Man of a Thousand Contradictions." He was gentle and violent, sentimental and hard-boiled, liberal and conservative, a family man and a loner, an introvert and a show off. He was capable of great love, yet one impassioned with hate. He was ambitious yet resigned—to the fact that he would never have the opportunity to prove himself as great an actor as his father, and to the realization that whatever stardom he attained was due in part to his trading on his father's celebrated name. His was a career and, I believe, a personality that resulted directly from trying to

embrace and, at the same time, disown the career and image of his own father.—Reginald LeBorg[2]

In doing research for an upcoming book on the serials of Boris Karloff, Bela Lugosi, and Lon Chaney, Jr., I contacted Ford Beebe, Jr., son of the famous serial director Ford Beebe. The younger Beebe certainly could sympathize in a way with Chaney, Jr., for he was also the son of a famous father. However, Chaney, Sr. wasn't just famous, he had been a world famous movie star. The young Ford Beebe visited the set of *Son of Dracula* (1943)—which was produced by his father—and met young Lon Chaney, albeit briefly, but he had a few interesting observations which he shared:

> Well, he [Lon Chaney, Jr.] was a little self-contained; I don't mean at all egotistical. Certainly not a "back slapper," but he was very nice, a very friendly guy. I do think that he used to do maybe a little personal drinking [off the set], but he never was a "carouser" type, and I never heard it personally from my Dad, or anyone else, that he was any trouble in production, or anything like that. I think—like a lot of second generation picture people—that he had a little trouble getting away from his father's image. It was tough to do, it still is! You hear the younger generation today, you know, and they have a hard time trying to make it—even when they really care for their parents—it's just something that they're stuck with, and they don't know how to handle it. It's a psychological thing, they don't want to get a reputation for being like their parents, they want to be their own actor, or whatever their field is, and it presents a problem.
>
> Truthfully, he [Chaney, Jr.] off the screen was a lot like he was on camera. He was not too expressive, unless, in a picture, he would have usually some kind of psychological part. He never was the "leading man," or anything like that. I mean in the sense of the "romantic lead," and his facial features, and everything, tended to be unexpressive. He was very much like that—to look at, off the screen, but, if you talked to him, or anything, he'd brighten up—if it called for it—and, as I say, he was quite friendly. I think he probably could have appreciated a couple more friends himself. He struck you as a person who didn't know how to go about being appreciated.—Ford I. Beebe, Jr.[3]

Lon Chaney, Jr. wanted to be a leading man but he very seldom ever got the chance. It is ironic that shortly before *The Ghost of Frankenstein* was released, Chaney, Jr. played a leading man—which he clearly enjoyed—in his last serial *Overland Mail* (1942) directed by the elder Ford Beebe and John Rawlins. The studio movers and shakers saw

***The Ghost of Frankenstein* (1942) was the first film in which Lon Chaney, Jr. tackled one of the classic monsters, inheriting the part of Karloff's Frankenstein Monster.**

him as someone who could play monsters (new and old) and villains as his father had often done. *The Ghost of Frankenstein* (1942) was the first film in which he tackled one of the classic monsters, inheriting the part of Karloff's Frankenstein Monster. *The Ghost of Frankenstein* was a direct sequel to *Son of Frankenstein* (1939), and earlier it had been planned that Basil Rathbone would reprise his role of Wolf von Frankenstein. However, when Rathbone wasn't available (he may have been working in a Sherlock Holmes picture on the same lot), it was decided to let Wolf have an older brother,

Little Cloestine (Janet Ann Gallow) confronts the Monster (Chaney, Jr.).

Ludwig Frankenstein, played by Sir Cedric Hardwicke. In some ways *The Ghost of Frankenstein* was not only a sequel of *Son* but also a remake as well.

The few years after the unwelcome Wolf von Frankenstein, the youngest son of Dr. Frankenstein, had arrived and quickly departed from his ancestral birthplace, the village of Frankenstein (earlier known as Goldstadt) has remained a desolate community. True, the Monster has finally been destroyed, but the villagers believe that old Ygor is still alive, and many assume that a curse still hangs over the town. The Mayor is pressured by the angry townspeople into blowing up the Frankenstein estate. Ironically, the destruction of the castle actually frees the Monster who has been laying dormant in the now dried out sulfur pit. An overjoyed but sickly Ygor decides that he and the Monster should waste no time in visiting the home of Ludwig Frankenstein, the older brother of Wolf, who lives in another village, Vasaria.

Vasaria, apparently, is far enough away from the village of Frankenstein that the ugly rumors of the Monster's misdeeds haven't turned Vasaria's villagers against this Dr. Frankenstein. The doctor's housekeeper, Martha, is the only one who initially knows that Ludwig is brother to Wolf von Frankenstein, who had revived the Monster, created by their father, Henry Frankenstein, some 40 years before. Unfortunately, Ygor and the Monster's arrival in town threaten the happiness that Ludwig and his daughter Elsa share. The Monster befriends a little girl, Cloestine, but then brutally attacks a threatening villager. Ygor blackmails Ludwig into helping him restore the Monster's health, otherwise he will tell everyone of the doctor's notorious family and the stories that surround them. Ygor craftily surmises that this brother is the more conservative of the two, and that being in the community's good graces means more to the respectable Ludwig than it would to the highly strung Wolf.

While Ludwig reluctantly agrees to hide the Monster, the creature kills Dr. Kettering, the beloved assistant of Ludwig. His other assistant, the bitter Dr. Theodor Bohmer, on the other hand has resented Ludwig's success, and waits for a chance to grab the power and prestige that he believes rightly belong to him. Ludwig sees the ghost of his late father when he decides to dissect the Monster, which, apparently, is the only way the Monster can be destroyed. His father states that perhaps the Monster could be a source for good, if he had a normal brain instead of the decaying, criminal brain that presently inhabits the Monster's skull. Inspired, Ludwig decides to make the best out of a bad situation and install Kettering's brain into the Monster's skull, thereby bringing Kettering back to life (in a way), and creating a reasoning, intelligent being, thus vindicating his father. (Many of the themes from *Son of Frankenstein* were apparently reworked into the script by W. Scott Darling.) Initially, Ygor is not pleased when he learns of Ludwig's plans. Ygor pleads, "He is all that I have! Nothing else! You're going to make him your friend, and I will be alone!" When his pleading doesn't work, Ygor gets an evil brain storm. Why not put his brain into the Monster, noting that his body is all crippled and distorted—laying on a little guilt here—"lame and sick from the bullets your brother fired into me... You can make us one! We'll be together always." Ludwig admires Ygor's cunning, stating: "Hah! That would be a Monster, indeed!" When Ygor protests again, Ludwig states that he will have his way or the Monster will be destroyed. Ygor triumphantly laughs this off until Ludwig reminds him that the Monster can be dissected. Ygor seems to admit defeat, and goes along with this plan.

When the Monster comprehends that he will have a new brain, he wants the brain of the innocent little Cloestine in his skull! Ygor tries to explain that this would hurt the little girl, but suggests—after some clever persuasion by Dr. Bohmer—they use his brain instead! The Monster angrily imagines the evil in this action, and nearly crushes his friend to death. The dying Ygor and Bohmer are able to carry out their plan causing the Ygor/Monster to threaten the town, if not the whole country. The operation turns out to be a failure: the Monster goes blind, killing Bohmer, and eventually Ludwig. Ludwig's daughter and her boyfriend, along with the villagers, escape the horrendous fire in the laboratory, now totally consuming Ludwig's entire estate. Vasaria is a peaceful village once more—but not for long!

For his first Universal film, Lon Chaney, Jr. was given the Karloff role in the earlier proposed Karloff-Lugosi project, *The Electric Man*, which would become *Man Made Monster* (1941). Lon played the sympathetic Dan McCormick who is turned into an electrically charged monster by the insane Dr. Rigas (played by Lionel Atwill, who else?), and the film did well enough for him to star in the classic *The Wolf Man* (1941), which had been—as an earlier script treatment in the 1930s—thought of as a possible Karloff and/or Lugosi film. On the strength of this film, Universal executives cast Chaney, Jr. into roles that had been played earlier by Boris Karloff (the Frankenstein Monster, the Mummy) and Bela Lugosi (Dracula). The studio built Chaney, Jr. up as "The Master Character Creator" that supposedly made one think of his father, "The Man of A Thousand Faces." Creighton Chaney had resisted movie studio executives' pleas to change his name to "Lon Chaney, Jr." He finally gave in though realizing the move would forever make people compare him with his dad. Then, starting with *The Ghost of Frankenstein*, Universal dropped the "Junior" from his last name. In this film Lon Chaney,

"I remember during *The Ghost of Frankenstein* they had me pose on the old Phantom stage and put a picture of Dad floating in the sky behind me. It used to aggravate me to constantly be compared to him," stated Chaney, Jr.

Jr. was not only haunted by the "ghost" of "Frankenstein" (Karloff's performances of the Monster), but of the "ghost" of his father as well:

> I remember during *The Ghost of Frankenstein* they had me pose on the old Phantom stage and put a picture of Dad floating in the sky behind me. It used to aggravate me to constantly be compared to him. His style of acting was different than mine. He was from a different era. But by that time I had changed my name and Universal was calling me the Master of Character or something like that. Sometimes you just gotta flow along with life instead of fighting it.
>
> It was tough enough with the "ghost" of Dad floating around Universal, but when I had to take over the part of the Frankenstein Monster from Boris Karloff, the pressure was on.—Lon Chaney, Jr.[4]

In spite of these obstacles, Chaney, Jr. gives a fairly good performance in *The Ghost of Frankenstein*, probably the most underrated of the Universal Frankenstein films.

When the Monster comprehends that he will have a new brain, he wants the brain of the innocent little Cloestine in his skull! Ygor (Bela Lugosi) is about to be crushed.

Beginning with this film, just as Lon feared, he was constantly and perhaps unfairly compared to Chaney, Sr., Karloff, and Lugosi. Because of this, some horror film critics have been a little harsher on Chaney, Jr. than they needed to be. Carlos Clarens, for one, was critical of the monster film sequels and mysteries Universal was churning out in the 1940s, and of the star of many of them, Lon Chaney Jr.:

> In all of these, Chaney revealed himself as a monotonous actor of rather narrow range, possessing neither the voice or skill of Karloff, nor the demonic persuasion of Lugosi, and his rash of films were themselves mechanical, unimaginative, and hopelessly serialized in flavor.—Carlos Clarens, *An Illustrated History of the Horror Film.*

In a way, Clarens was right, because very few of the Universal horror sequels or the *Inner Sanctum* mystery films are as entertaining or well crafted as those of the earlier 1930s. Of the Universal horror and mystery films of the 1940s, the ones that still hold major interest are the Frankenstein and Wolf Man series, and of course, the Basil Rathbone/Nigel Bruce Sherlock Holmes series. Out of the Mummy series, most fans prefer the enjoyable *The Mummy's Hand* (1940) with Tom Tyler as the Mummy, which was the first and best of the 1940s Mummy films. Lon Chaney, Jr. played the mummified monster in the following three sequels, a role almost any actor could have played. The *Inner Sanctum* series were supernatural mysteries based on the radio show and mystery novels. Most of them are watchable, but they are nothing spectacular. As for *Son of Dracula* (1943), in which Lon plays Dracula, a.k.a. Count Alucard, there are those critics that consider the film to be something of a classic and under-appreciated by horror film fans, much like *The Ghost of Frankenstein*.

The film has certainly had its share of mixed reviews, and for knowledgeable horror film historians, *The Ghost of Frankenstein* fits into three groups. It is either enjoyed, tolerated, or disliked.

"*The Ghost of Frankenstein* resurrects both Lugosi as Ygor and the Monster, played this time in stodgy fashion by Lon Chaney, Jr...."—Martin Tropp, *Mary Shelley's Monster: The Story of Frankenstein*

"Another step on the downward path."—Ivan Butler, *Horror In the Cinema*

"*The Ghost of Frankenstein* is economically set, flatly lit and dully shot, and it lacks actors who care. Hardwicke walks through his role with something like contempt, Chaney might as well be a block of wood, and even Lugosi is less impressive than before. But the old malarkey struck a responsive chord at the box office, and Universal wanted to make more Frankenstein stories. Alas, they only made them badly."—Leslie Halliwell, *The Dead That Walk*

Some critics have grudgingly tolerated the film:

"Not having Karloff's lean, expressive face his monster was the inferior of the two, although Chaney obviously tried hard and managed to invest the role with a few of his 'Lennie' characteristics (actually Lennie and the monster have much in common—both are child-like creatures possessed of a great, and often uncontrollable strength)."—John Brosnan, *The Horror People*

"Karloff's monster remained unchanged, except by Chaney. Jack Pierce tried to mold him into a Karloff, but the taller, thicker, jowlier man remained a hulking Lennie, a flat-topped, jut-browed brute of a mute. His performance has robotic power, but lacks soul, even a man-made one."— Denis Gifford, *A Pictorial History of Horror Movies*

"Just as he would later demonstrate in his Mummy roles, Lon Chaney believed that all there was to playing a monster was to endure Jack Pierce's make-up sessions. Karloff's interpretation of the Monster had little influence on his performance and he inherited precious little of his father's legendary gift for mime."—Michael Brunas, John Brunas, and Tom Weaver, *Universal Horrors: The Studio's Classic Films, 1931-1946*

Finally, some critics have thoroughly enjoyed the film:

"...*Ghost of Frankenstein* was surprisingly good for a fourth-generation sequel... Though he attempted to make the Monster even more unsympathetic than ever, Chaney's fresh approach created a highly interesting characterization."—Calvin Thomas Beck, *Heroes of the Horrors*

"Though the film was not as frightening as its predecessors, it had impressive moments... Chaney was probably the best of the post-Karloff monsters. His brutish portrayal, like Ygor, winning audience sympathy."—Richard Bojarkski, *The Films of Bela Lugosi*

"*The Ghost of Frankenstein* is in many ways the last of the vintage horror films. Val Lewton, *The Uninvited* and *Dead of Night* were about to bring a new sophistication and literacy to the genre. If *The Ghost* is already an assembly line job, it's a good, thor-

In a posed studio publicity shot, Evelyn Ankers and Chaney, Jr. discuss "global" issues.

oughly professional, and highly entertaining one, an honorable close to a solid decade of first rate chillers."—William K. Everson, *Classics of the Horror Film*

In Don G. Smith's insightful biography of Lon Chaney, Jr., *Lon Chaney, Jr.: Horror Film Star (1906-1973),* he makes some interesting observations about the screenplay for *The Ghost of Frankenstein.* In scene after scene, the directions often given to Chaney state that the Monster should be played as "dull," or "lifeless." The idea was, of course, to be consistent with Boris Karloff's portrayal of the Monster as an almost mindless, sick being from *Son of Frankenstein* (1939). If a critic can make a rash assumption that Chaney didn't study Karloff's interpretation—which I seriously doubt—it's clear that the film's second scriptwriter did. Writer W. Scott Darling had vastly improved Eric

Chaney tried hard not to imitate the Karloffian grunts and growls of the Monster, and tried to create his own interpretation.

Taylor's earlier weird, and somewhat downbeat story treatment, and he also had paid fairly close attention to the characters and situations from *Son of Frankenstein*. Darling falters though, in that he missed giving Chaney's Monster the subtle touches of humanity that occur in the *Son of Frankenstein*'s revised shooting script. Darling may have modeled his Monster on Lon Chaney, Jr.'s performance in *Man Made Monster* (1941), where by the end of the film, the more electricity Dan McCormick receives, the stronger, and less human he becomes. Chaney walks around in much the same lifeless way he would later play the Monster. Of course, that's under the assumption that Lon Chaney, Jr. would be playing the Monster when the first script for *The Ghost* was being written! While historians have noted that Boris Karloff decided not to play the Monster again in this sequel, it's never been clear just at what stage of the production Karloff said "no thanks!" During the film's production, he was conquering Broadway in *Arsenic and Old Lace*. Karloff must have also been aware that the pivotal character in the film was not the Monster, but Ygor, played by his "rival," Bela Lugosi. As in *Son of Frankenstein* (1939), the main focus of the story is centered around Ygor's character. The Monster, once again, is a secondary character. With Karloff's body and facial movements, and the oddly expressive grunts and groans he gave to the Monster previously, he could have kept something of the Monster's dignity and humanity. That quality doesn't quite come across in Chaney's conception, but again, we can blame that more on the direction and the script than on the actor.

As some critics have noted, W. Scott Darling had written two-reel comedies in his earlier career, and was responsible for practically killing the careers of Laurel and Hardy at 20th Century-Fox with scripts for films like *The Dancing Masters* (1943) and *The Big Noise* (1944). As much as I'd like to take a good punch or two—if I could—at Darling for his Laurel and Hardy scripts, he did collaborate on some of the better Charlie Chan films at Fox in the later 1930s, and, some of the dialogue written for the characters in *The Ghost of Frankenstein*, as I have briefly stated, is absolutely first rate. In *The Ghost of Frankenstein*, Darling has been careful to depict the Monster as a sick, lumbering creature, but he didn't give the character more of the human touch he needed. The other characters in the film, however, are well crafted. So, despite the impression you might get from reading *Universal Horrors*, Universal's choice on having W. Scott Darling do the script rewrite was actually—in many ways—a good one. Unlike *Son of Frankenstein* which some critics dislike because it takes a while before the action gets underway, Darling sets things moving from the very first scene. One interesting thing about Darling's script is the introduction of Ludwig Frankenstein's character. When Ygor and the Monster leave the Frankenstein village, Ygor tells the Monster that they will go to see Ludwig, who will give the Monster back his strength, and perhaps some of his former intelligence. We are not shown how the Monster and Ygor get to Vasaria. My guess is that they hopped a freight train at night, or hid in a farmer's huge hay wagon for a good part of the trip, for Ygor looks pretty disheveled—and who wouldn't be with a few bullet holes in him?—and the Monster, caked in dried sulfur, looks like the stuff from which nightmares are made. (Ygor, however, has managed to get the Monster cleaned up and gotten him a new suit by the time the weird looking pair enter Vasaria!)

When Ygor approaches a young girl tending a flock of geese, he stops her for directions to the doctor's home. (The terrified geese get out of the way of the Monster, which is a nice comic touch!) When the girl asks Ygor if he knows the doctor, he replies in his sardonic way: "Very well! I knew his father, and his brother, too." Darling assumes the audience is somewhat familiar with the previous Frankenstein films. When we meet the second son of Dr. Frankenstein, he has just completed a successful brain operation, with the help of his colleagues, the optimistic Dr. Kettering, and the brooding, bitter Dr. Bohmer. This Dr. Frankenstein appears to be in command of the situation. When he is summoned to see the Monster, the creature smiles in recognition. It would make sense, don't you think, that Wolf would ask his older brother to come up to the old Frankenstein estate and see their other "brother"? However, Ludwig rather coolly lies to the state's prosecutor that he's never seen the Monster before, and "knows nothing about him." This enrages the Monster, but before he escapes the court room, he stares murderously into the eyes of Ludwig, who coolly stares the monster down. It is only with Ygor's arrival and threats of blackmail that Ludwig's smugness vanishes. Sir Cedric Hardwicke plays Ludwig Frankenstein wonderfully as a respected man with a past he wants to keep buried. Bela Lugosi, who once again does a splendid job repeating his role as Ygor, replies, "You wouldn't like to spoil that, Doctor? Would you? You wouldn't want me to tell them that you're the son of the Frankenstein that created him, that your brother made the thing live after it had been dead for years? Do you want me to tell them, Frankenstein?" Ygor threatens the doctor with exposure, unless he helps to hide and later helps to restore the heath of the Monster. Ludwig tries to regain his smug composure, and says, "Yes, I could do that." Ygor reminds him just who is in control, however, when he says, "And you will do it, Frankenstein!" Ludwig loses his composure, and orders him out, but Ygor's demands are met. Like *Son of Frankenstein*, the story revolves around Ygor and the Monster, who has become mentally ill. Ygor states: "He is more dangerous today than he ever was before." Ygor can no longer totally keep him under his control.

A specific example of one of the most glaring faults in *The Ghost of Frankenstein* script: the Monster should have shown more emotion in the scenes with the little girl, Cloestine, who befriends him. My guess is that Chaney tried hard not to imitate the Karloffian grunts and growls of the Monster, and tried to create his own interpretation. However, even if this is so, Chaney's performance, whether due to little direction by Kenton, Darling's script, or his own conception, sometimes headed toward unintentional comedy. In an almost ludicrous scene, Ygor raves to the Monster that he will have a new brain. When Ludwig Frankenstein asks Ygor if the Monster understands, Ygor chides him: "Can't you see? He is the first time happy in his life!" However, the Monster's face registers no emotion at all! Now, had a director like Rowland V. Lee or James Whale been at the helm, I believe that a minor problem like this in the script would be changed on the set. Erle C. Kenton, on the other hand, seemed to let the actors rely on their own judgments. Unlike a John Ford who would often sadistically bully everyone from a small character actor to a superstar like John Wayne to get the exact performance he wanted, Kenton seemed to do little more than "direct traffic" with actors or actresses he respected. Kenton has often been criticized for this, but his *Island of Lost Souls* (1933), for example, is still the best version of H. G. Wells' *The Island of Dr. Moreau*, and the rarely seen *You're Telling Me* (1934) belongs in the category of W. C. Fields classics like *It's A Gift* (1934), *The Old Fashioned Way* (1934), and *The Bank Dick* (1940).

While I have noted some of the weak points of Darling's script, I have to admit that he has written some thoughtful dialogue for his main characters. Ludwig Frankenstein's character is that of a cool, efficient scientist who, nevertheless, has some burning passion to prove to the scientific world that his father was a genius. When he decides to put the brain of the murdered Dr. Kettering into the Monster's body, he reflects on the irony of putting the murdered man's brain into the murderer's body and wonders if Kettering will thank him for a new lease on life, or despair at living in a Monster's body, a "human junk heap." Speaking of this "human junk heap," the existence of one of *The Ghost of Frankenstein*'s scripts shows that the faults in the Monster's portrayal aren't Chaney's fault, as some critics have surmised. Chaney, Jr.'s biographer, Don G. Smith, correctly surmises "that when the script calls for increased expression, Chaney provides it, but no more and no less." Smith also states that had Chaney been more imaginative or more secure in his role, perhaps he might argued with Kenton to give the Monster more

Chaney, Jr., always fond of children, poses with little Janet.

personality, but that is purely speculation. Certainly, as Don Smith notes, when the Monster is revived with Ygor's brain, Chaney's Monster is very effectively animated and mouths Lugosi's dubbed dialogue extremely well. Chaney seems, in fact, to be doing a comic take-off of Lugosi's facial expressions as Ygor/Frankenstein Monster, which for a fan of the film, can be seen as frightening and yet funny at the same time: "I am Ygor! I have the strength of a hundred men! I cannot die! I cannot be destroyed! I, Ygor, will live forever!"

Unfortunately for Bela Lugosi, *The Ghost of Frankenstein* would be the last film he would make at Universal until *Abbott and Costello Meet Frankenstein* (1948), a role worthy of his talents.

Apparently, Sir Cedric Hardwicke had little to say about the film when asked about it in his later years, but he gives a believable performance, and his scenes with Bela

Lugosi and Lionel Atwill are extremely good. If Sir Cedric Hardwicke disliked this film, as critic Leslie Halliwell suggested, then, he proved himself a fine actor, for there are several times in the film where he acts, I think, as an intelligent and even-tempered son of Dr. Frankenstein would act. Lionel Atwill, for me, plays one of his best roles here as the bitter and brooding Dr. Bohmer, and of course, Bela Lugosi has a field day once again as Ygor. After Lugosi and Hardwicke, the third outstanding performance in the film is that of Lionel Atwill. While a lot of critics (Bryan Senn, Tom Weaver, etc.) usually find fault with Atwill's performances, Weaver and the Brunas brothers actually give Atwill a back-handed compliment by noting how subtle and subdued his performance—until the climax—is in this film. As for young Lon Chaney as the Monster, who could have done a better job than Boris Karloff? Should Chaney have played the role imitating Karloff's conception? If Boris Karloff played the Monster he might have given the Monster more of a human touch. Again, we can only speculate here.

The other actors and actresses—like Ralph Bellamy and beautiful Evelyn Ankers as the romantic leads—are fine. As has been noted before, the camera work, the sets, the lighting, and particularly Hans J. Salter's powerful score—one of his very best—all make *The Ghost of Frankenstein* look and sound like anything but an "assembly line" production. (Baby boomers may notice that the laboratory props look a great deal like the Aurora "Mad Lab" model kits that you could order through *Famous Monsters of Filmland*!) Tony Thomas, who produced a few albums of Hans Salter's scores on record, remarked that Salter's score was an essential reason for much of the success of *The Ghost of Frankenstein*. While many of Salter's scores give the films an added dimension of quality (Salter's score for *Frankenstein Meets the Wolf Man* [1943] is a prime example!), here is one case where the film *would* really suffer without a musical score!

It is the climax—in which the blinded Monster (with Ygor's brain) goes berserk—that bothers most critics of the film. It's looking at the film in retrospect that we can see the whole idea of the brain switching would become plain silly by *House of Frankenstein* (1945), so, after a slightly better *House of Dracula* (1946), it was time to wrap things up, in the affectionate parody *Abbott and Costello Meet Frankenstein* (1948). Far from being a "quickie," or a "programmer," as some critics have asserted, *The Ghost of Frankenstein* was well put together and, like *Son of Frankenstein,* had a superb cast. One version of W. Scott Darling's script, reproduced in MagicImage Filmbooks' *The Ghost of Frankenstein,* shows that some rewriting would be done on the final script—something that would not have occurred were the film a run of the mill "quickie," or "another step in the downward path." This implies that *Son of Frankenstein* (1939) started the descent. Generally, *Son of Frankenstein* is a wonderful film, although maybe there is a little too much talking going on. *The Ghost of Frankenstein* however, is the shortest in the series, a half hour shorter than *Son.* Visually, and aurally, however, I believe it is just as dazzling. Interestingly, Karloff never spoke publicly on Chaney's or Lugosi's performance as the Monster, other than the fact that some fans confusingly thought that he was still behind the make up. *The Ghost of Frankenstein* may not be as good as the pervious Karloff Trilogy, but it is worthy enough to stand beside them.

CREDITS: Director: Erle C. Kenton: Producer: George Waggner; Screenplay: W. Scott Darling (based on a story by Eric Taylor); Photography: Milton Krasner, Woody Bredell; Art Direction: Jack Otterson, Herald H. MacArthur; Editor: Ted Kent; Sound: Bernard B. Brown; Music: Hans J. Salter; Gowns: Vera West; Set Decoration: Russell A. Grausman; Assistant Director: Charles B. Gould; Make-up: Jack P. Pierce; Universal Pictures, 1942; 67 minutes

CAST: Sir Cedric Hardwicke (Dr. Ludwig Frankenstein); Ralph Bellamy (Erik Ernst); Lionel Atwill (Dr. Theodor Bohmer); Bela Lugosi (Ygor); Evelyn Ankers (Elsa Frankenstein); Janet Ann Gallow (Cloestine Hussman); Lon Chaney (The Monster); Barton Yarborough (Dr. Kettering); Olaf Hytten (Hussman); Doris Lloyd (Martha); Leyland Hodgson (Chief Constable); Holmes Herbert (Magistrate of Vasaria); Lawrence Grant (Burgomaster of Frankenstein); Brandon Hurst (Hans); Julius Tannen (Sektal); Harry Cording (Frone); Lionel Belmore (First Councilor); Michael Mark (Second Councilor); Otto Hoffman (Villager No. 1); Dwight Frye (Villager No. 2); Ernie Stanton, George Eldredge (Constables); Eddie Parker (double for Lon Chaney)

Special thanks to Ford I. Beebe, Jr. and Mickey Gold for their help with this article.

1. Telephone interview with Ford I. Beebe, Jr., February 19, 1997. Beebe is the son of Ford Beebe, the man best known for directing (usually with a co-director) serials such as *Flash Gordon's Trip to Mars* (1938) and four serials Lon Chaney, Jr. made at Universal.
2. Reginald LeBorg, "Lon Chaney, Jr." A Man Living in a Shadow," *Close-Ups: The Movie Star Book*, edited by Danny Peary (New York, Workman Publishing, 1978), p. 336.
3. Telephone interview with Ford Beebe, Jr.
4. Philip J. Riley, editor *The Ghost of Frankenstein, Universal Filmscripts Series: Classic Horror Films: Volume 4* (Atlantic City, N.J.—Hollywood, CA, MagicImage Filmbooks, 1990), pp. 8 and 9.

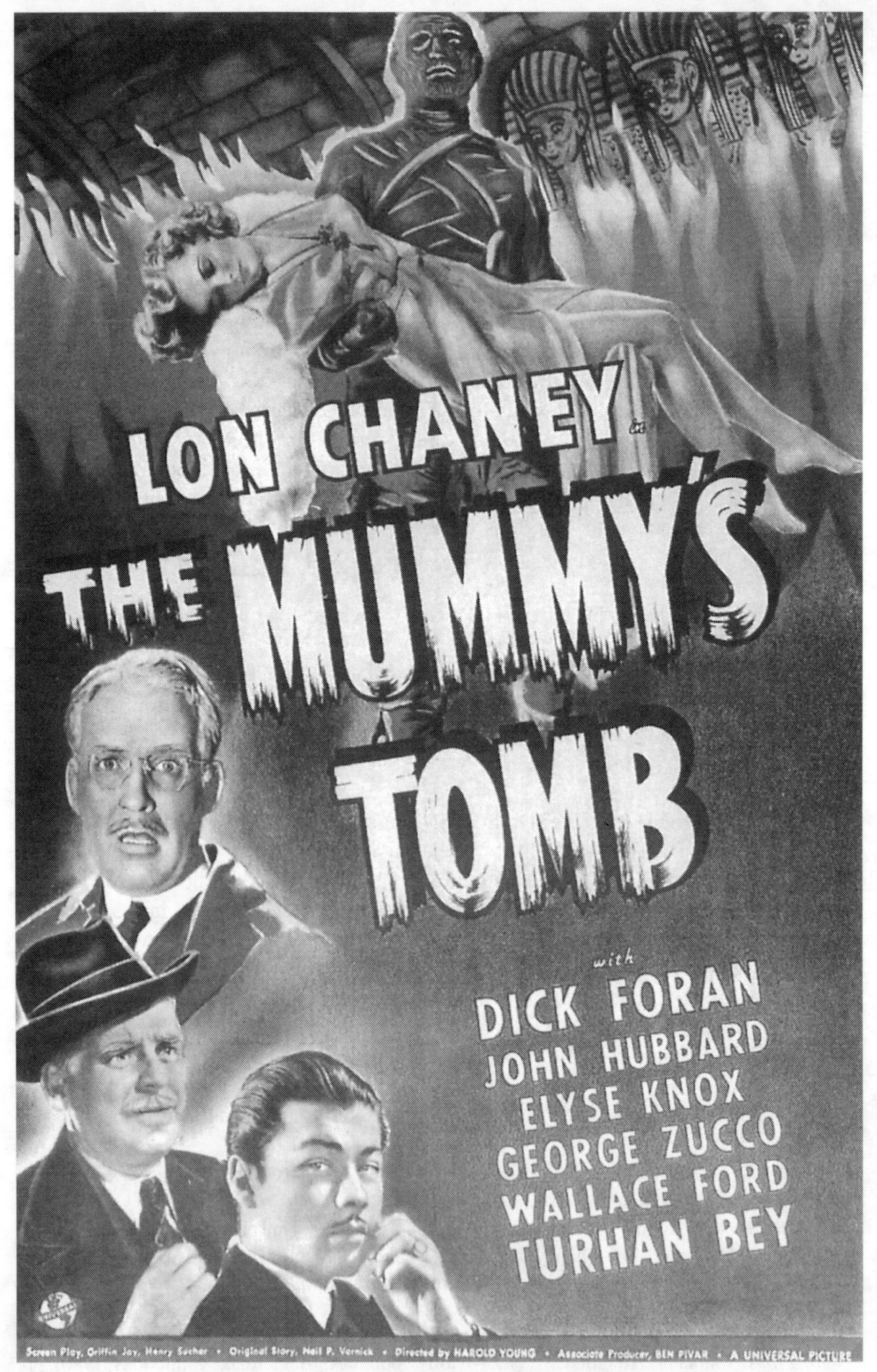

[Courtesy Ronald V. Borst/Hollywood Movie Posters]

THE MUMMY'S TOMB (1942) *THE MUMMY'S GHOST* (1944) *THE MUMMY'S CURSE* (1944)

by John Soister

If truth be told, the "Screen's Master Character Creator" spent more time rummaging through the rack of vintage horrors than he did creating them of whole cloth. While the Wolf Man rose and finally fell bearing no one's stamp save Lon Chaney's, Dracula, Frankenstein's Monster, and the Mummy had first been incarnated—sumptuously—by the Messrs. Lugosi and Karloff. There may have been no shame attached to picking up where the Masters had left off—by the forties, neither was quite the genre icon he had been during the earlier decade—but their signature roles were timeless, and anyone who dared to follow in their footsteps was doomed to languish in their shadows. (One can only presume that Chaney was bypassed for the Invisible Man sequels because—John Fulton's array of optical miracles having become rather familiar—success in the part lay largely upon its interpreter's commanding voice; vocal versatility would never top the list of Lon's professional strengths.)

Of the three retreads foisted upon the hapless Chaney, the Mummy was the least rewarding. After all, Alucard/Dracula was in essence the same master of the night who had throttled Renfield and who had come within inches of having the flinty Van Helsing succumb to his will. Even with his grimacing brute only a patch on the ingenuous yet deadly creature who first backed in through the watchtower door, Chaney's Frankenstein Monster was clearly linked to Karloff's, if only through such transparent devices as Ygor, the interplay with a little girl, and the mysterious reappearance of that damned black suit. The Mummy, however, was another kettle of fish altogether.

The Mummy's Hand—essentially a bowdlerized and simplified version of Karl Freund's moody melodrama from 1932—had been released before George Waggner had successfully pounded into submission the treatment for Chaney's "genre screen test" at Universal: *Man Made Monster.* The role of Kharis was thus created by action/cowboy star, Tom Tyler, whose angular good looks matched long shots of Karloff during flashback scenes, and whose strength and stamina allowed him to schlep an unconscious Peggy Moran through the hills of Southern California without complaint. Hence, for *The Mummy's Tomb,* Lon inherited a character which was *already* one step removed from the classic original. Forget the intricacies of the dual roles of Imhotep and Ardath Bey: Chaney's challenge lay in matching the mute menace of a one-note grotesque whose chief characteristic—his implacable, shuffling gait—may itself have been due primarily to Tom Tyler's chronic arthritis.

Chaney would don the bandages and rubber appliances of the Mummy for three features; each is a minor masterpiece of illogic, and when taken together, the trio is irrefutable proof of the studio's ultimate disregard for the importance of continuity in series' schlock. Still, even with the wisdom of hindsight, one somehow doesn't feel compelled to argue much over the policy, and the loopy disparities which exist among the pictures do help make them as enjoyable as they are nowadays.

The Mummy's Tomb picks up *thirty years* after the climax of *The Mummy's Hand.* We know that three decades have passed because Andoheb (George Zucco), now ensconced in Eduardo Ciannelli's chair (and wearing his robe and hair, too), has said as much to Mehemet Bey (Turhan Bey), whom we recognize as the latest in the venerable line of high priests of Karnak, if only because he's wearing *Zucco's* old clothes. Bullets may have shattered the old professor's arm, but there's nothing wrong with his mouth: "Kharis still lives... lives for the moment he will carry death and destruction to all those who dared violate the tomb of Ananka! That moment has now arrived!" In our hearts, we know why it's taken 30 years to arrive; Amon-Ra's anger can shatter the world, but he's still got to save up for those steamship tickets. Before setting up shop as cemetery caretaker in Mapleton, Massachusetts, Mehemet must be exposed to the tana leaf litany: "Three leaves will keep him alive; nine leaves will give him motivation." Andoheb doubtless means ''motion"; *Ananka* gives Kharis motivation.

Meanwhile, an older but still roguish Steve Banning (Dick Foran) is regaling his sister Jane (Mary Gordon), his son John (John Hubbard), and John's sweetheart Isobel (Elyse Knox) with ten minutes' worth of first rate flashbacks from *The Mummy's Hand.* While John—a physician and one smug son of a bitch—clucks haughtily, Mehemet has unpacked in the little cemetery's huge, atmospheric mortuary, and as a nearby wolf howls in jackal-like fashion, Kharis (Lon) sits erect in his sarcophagus. The scene is heavy with George Robinson's canny shadowplay; choreographed against an aural backdrop of Hans J. Salter's exotic melodies and Turhan Bey's ritual summons, it is one of the most effective sequences in the film.

Within a heartbeat (Robinson's camera demurs from recording the graceless Chaney's climb *out* of the sarcophagus), the Mummy is on his way. Albeit plopped in the middle of a country which had not existed when he first walked the earth; although targeting a foe whom he had confronted for mere moments, *30 years earlier,* Kharis somehow homes in on and strangles Banning in the old duffer's second-floor bedroom. *Whew!* Even Kharis' *shadow* is potent; its passing disturbs a sleeping woman and prompts a young couple to move elsewhere to neck.

The sheriff's all for palming the murder off on a "fiend" (why not on a burglar, caught in the act?), but this is nowhere near as disconcerting as the revelation that Mehemet Bey has the mystical power of *always being in the right place at the right time.* He catches Doctor John in Isobel's arms, and this sets off the genetic weakness for curvy heroines to which high priests of Karnak are particularly susceptible.

The 11:00 p.m. train unloads Babe Hanson, who used to be Babe Jenson, but who's hard to make out under all the old-age make-up (and *pince-nez!*) anyhow. Babe knows damn well that Kharis is on the loose, but even when the Banning groundskeeper is frightened into paralytic shock (he later succumbs), and old Scots-cadenced Aunt Jane is likewise throttled, nothing will deter smarmy Doctor John (or the sheriff) from that

Mehemet Bey (Turhan Bey) and Andoheb (George Zucco) examine Kharis (Chaney, Jr.) in *The Mummy's Tomb.*

"fiend" theory. Fed up with the young schmuck, Babe heads down to the local watering-hole, where he regales hordes of visiting reporters with his pet theory.

Mehemet *naturally* is having his tea at the same spot; he overhears Babe and runs back to push Kharis out into the streets. Despite the fact that he's only got one good eye and that he *never* saw Banning's sidekick face to face, Kharis spots Babe and dispatches him in a nearby blind alley. (Chaney does a great job in transcending his immobile rubber mask here; just by glaring daggers with his exposed eye and tightening further his slit of a mouth, the actor conveys the rage that consumes the Prince of the Royal House when he catches sight of Babe.) Newspaper blather about "The Fiend" continues, as John Banning consults Professor Norman (Frank Reicher) about a strip of bandage he's found. The mold taken from every victim's neck "has the odor of myrrh," states Norman; "that mold and this strip of linen come from the body of a mummy!" More to the point, "That inky hieroglyphic there is the same that's found on the body of the Princess Ananka!"

And with that dogmatic revelation, we've just shot past the sublime into the ridiculous. The idea that Kharis' *bandages* have somehow been imprinted with pictographs concerning his beloved princess leaves one with the unfortunate image of a flocked roll of toilet paper; this is neither screenwriter Griffin Jay's nor Henry Sucher's finest moment. "Whether you are ready to accept it or not," continues Norman, "we are

Kharis roams the streets of Mapleton looking for his victims, in *The Mummy's Tomb.*

dealing with the presence of the living dead." Ordinarily, this might make an impression on John, but he's just been called up to active duty, and he's much too busy adjusting to that idea to give the matter of the wholesale slaughter of his family much thought. Back in the garden, John sort of pops the question to Isobel, but the conversation *is overheard by Mehemet Bey,* who just happens to be stomping through the adjoining shrubbery.

Acting fast, Bey acquaints the bewildered Mummy with the facts of life and bids him snatch Isobel. (Unwisely, director Harold Young felt it necessary that Kharis react to the news of his boss's taking a wife; Chaney indulges in a series of doubletakes and visual sulks which would have shamed his father on the worst of his earliest days.) Again, without benefit of map or compass, the disenchanted prince knows exactly where to pounce.

The villagers gather in front of the Banning estate, where an old timer enjoying a moment of lucidity puts everyone onto the caretaker at the cemetery. The mob stirs dangerously at the late-breaking news that John's fiancée has been abducted by the Mummy, and the traditional doling out of the torches takes place; the crowd splits into two factions and off go Banning and his men to the town graveyard. Footage from *Frankenstein* obviates some second unit shots, as the hunt for Isobel covers land and water.

Already fastened to a casket in the mortuary, Isobel and Mehemet parry and thrust as glibly as two spouses having a spat over coffee. Bey is all for spoon-feeding the tana-leaf fluid to the young woman, thus making her immortal. (Along with a driving lust for the heroine, her ingestion of tana fluid is always uppermost in the minds of horny high priests; started by the bug-eyed Andoheb in *The Mummy's Hand,* this situation will prove to be almost as inevitable as the mangling of the tana leaf ritual for the balance of the series.) The clamor of the approaching mob, however, forces Mehemet to change plans midstream. "Kharis," he commands, "take her and hide her until I get rid of these fools." Off like a shot, Kharis hefts Isobel back to the Banning mansion; John and the other fools follow as soon as the sheriff has plugged the gabby caretaker.

Kharis carries the unconscious heroine over a log across a fast-running stream in one of George Robinson's most beautifully composed shots. Finding himself cut off at all turns, the Mummy climbs the trellis to the second story bedroom where Steve Banning had met his destiny. (Chaney, with the assistance of his "mummy strap"—a device designed to spread the weight of the lady of the moment over the actor's back and shoulders—lugs Elyse Knox across the second floor verandah with one arm. Way to go, Lon!) John Banning rushes up to confront Kharis, twice tries to brain him with his torch, and twice has to pick himself up from a supine position.

Only the intervention of a couple of the cops allows the young doctor and Isobel to make good their escape. Torches are hurled onto the portico by those members of the crowd who have chosen to remain out of harm's way (and that seems to include just about everyone), and following a spate of spastic armwaving, Kharis falls victim to the fire. The big news the next day is the Banning wedding; some people have short memories.

Forgetting those two sacerdotal underlings Kharis strangled before the release print went out to theaters, *The Mummy's Hand* is responsible for mold marks on only two throats: that of Ali, the Egyptian overseer, and Professor Petrie's. *The Mummy's Tomb* doubles that figure, with Babe, Steve and Jane Banning throttled, and Jim the groundskeeper frightened to death. Particularly distasteful this time around is the fact that, intentionally or not, the three strangulation victims are all unarmed seniors. Jim, the one person to act aggressively toward Kharis, is the only victim to be spared the sensation of those bandaged fingers at his neck; his most unpleasant contact is having the 3,700-year-old bully kick sand in his face.

Although *Tomb* was only the second outing for Kharis and Ananka, the cloth from which the details were cut was already showing its seams. The whole *raison d'être* for Kharis and the ministrations of the priests of Karnak—to bring death to those who seek to defile Ananka's tomb—has already dissipated in the face of more exciting chase and grab. Sure, there's plenty of death, but Ananka takes such a back seat here that Mehemet Bey, while waxing rhapsodically about the bride *he's* about to acquire, completely leaves the musty princess out of the game plan! "Together," he assures Kharis, while referring to Isobel, "we three until the world crumbles and there is no longer a stone or a rock or a tree or a blade of grass." Fortunately for the high priest, his having only one good eye prevents the Mummy from seeing that visions such as this have placed his own honey right in the crapper.

We are treated to portents of dreary routines to come: despite his seeming invisibility—only his shadow is noted by the townspeople early in the film—and his virtually noiseless shuffle, Kharis is never quite able to sneak up unseen on any of his targets. Each of his intended victims catches him shuffling toward them from a healthy distance away. For all that, the characters marked for death just stand there—like

Kharis spots Babe (Dick Foran) and dispatches him in a nearby blind alley, in *The Mummy's Tomb.*

condemned buildings awaiting demolition—or else they scramble into blind alleys or stumble over their own feet. As Bill Cosby once averred, "Anyone who couldn't outrun the Mummy deserved to die!"

It has also become apparent that most of these high priests are more interested in using their exalted office and mystic perks to pick up girls, rather than to get the job done. As none of these guys ever actually gets past first base, the continual source of high priests of Karnak (later Arkham) is uncertain. What's *not* uncertain is that, sooner or later, the project will be disrupted as the hereto celibate minister (or his flunky) lets a curvy brunette in a silken robe separate his good judgment from his sense of duty. What was novel and acceptable in *The Mummy's Hand,* though, had already begun to grow overly familiar.

A whale of an opportunity to indulge in a little gratuitous creativity was missed in the mad rush to kill off anyone who'd stand still long enough. Never explained is Kharis' ability to home in on his intended victims; some attempt at establishing a psychic tie between predator and prey might have at least enlivened the occult end of things, which had already dwindled to the occasional mention of Amon-Ra and tana leaves. The Mummy's omniscience concerning the whereabouts of the desecrators and their kin, taken along with Bey's knack for being Mehemet-on-the-spot whenever anything of portent is uttered, could have been woven into a mystical tapestry, threading elements

Bey acquaints the bewildered Mummy with the facts of life and bids him snatch Isobel (Elyse Knox) in *The Mummy's Tomb.*

of extrasensory perception, destiny, and that dreaded curse of the king of the gods. Opting to ignore such questions, or trusting that the presumption of coincidence would defuse the cynics, leaves the picture—and the saga—so much the worse for wear.

The pity is that Kharis didn't start his reign of terror with Steve's son, John. The part was written to illustrate the scientific inflexibility of some men, but as played by John Hubbard, Banning *fils* comes across like a stubborn mule. His one nod to the scientific process—having the mold found on his father's throat analyzed—leads nowhere. Unwilling to examine the physical evidence provided by the growing number of cadavers and refusing to pay the slightest attention to the frustrated and terrified Babe, he remains adamant in supporting the sheriff's facile claim that a "fiend" is responsible for the mayhem in Mapleton. Later, he only begrudgingly accedes to Professor Norman's conclusions; "Babe was right," he admits with a wry smirk. This concession made, he then devotes all his energies into arranging his wedding to Isobel before he's called up to serve in the Medical Corps. Kharis' passions—as black and white and one-dimensional as they may be—are still more authentically human than John Banning's.

Turhan Bey spends the whole of the movie glancing sideways, glazing over his eyes when in prayer, and leering at Elyse Knox. Well groomed and immaculately tailored, his Mehemet Bey is the only heavy in horror pictures to be better looking than both the hero *and* the heroine; had he used a come-on fresher than "What I can do for you, I can do for myself"—lifted almost verbatim from *The Mummy's Hand*—Isobel might very well have chosen everlasting life with him. Once again, a shot at intrigue was missed; perhaps Bey's exotic charms could have piqued Isobel's curiosity about him in spite of herself. A will she?/won't she? tana fluid scene at the mortuary—balanced by Kharis' winnowing the locals on the other side of town—would have made for some suspenseful interplay.

It's a treat to see Dick Foran and Wallace Ford again, even if the actors never share a scene together. Having been with him during the discovery of Ananka's tomb, we feel a certain kinship with Steve Banning, and it is numbing to watch Kharis snuff out his life. Babe's sartorial splendor and aggressive attitude denote his having prospered over the last few decades; he would never have been caught dead in a Homburg and a three-piece suit in his "Poopsie" days. The close interdependence that the two men had shared in their youth is never so apparent as in their death; Babe, denied his friend's courage and support, is picked off by the marauding Kharis. Alone—virtually ignored by the authority figures in Mapleton and without his buddy by his side—neither man can survive that vengeful curse of Amon-Ra.

Just as serial chapters would cheat while recapping the previous week's cliffhanger, the climactic conflagration which had consumed Tom Tyler resulted in scarcely more than a couple of smudges (and some conspicuously missing digits) on Lon Chaney. (This light cosmetic treatment was, in part, necessitated by the switch in casting. Kharis' reappearance as a profoundly charred and twisted wreck would have stood in peculiar contrast to his having apparently *gained* some 30 pounds in the interim.) Chaney didn't have to endure a primary application directly on his face (for close-ups) as did Tyler, so his rubber mask cut down on the number of hours he needed to spend in Jack Pierce's chair. More than just a nod to continuity, the blackening of the Kharis mask went a long way to hide the obvious eye-hole which allowed the visually challenged actor to keep from falling over the furniture at inopportune times; the later entries—wherein Kharis had somehow been restored to an almost pristine whiteness—made the contrast between musty facial rubber and bloodshot Chaney orb almost comical.

Kharis was among Lon Chaney's least favorite portrayals; the rigors of the get-up seemed to have elicited more grousing from him than did preparations for any other part. Despite this, the Mummy placed second only to the Wolf Man as Lon's most frequently enacted horror. As with the werewolf, Lon's performance levels as Kharis peaked early—his work in *The Mummy's Tomb* is the least affected of his outings in bandages (faint praise, that)—and then petered out as the remaining series' entries drove the actor to new dimensions of impatience and boredom. Unlike the Wolf Man, Kharis was not a dual role into which one could sink one's thespic teeth; no tortured Lawrence Talbot clone came with the territory.

Between *The Mummy's Tomb* and follow-up, *The Mummy's Ghost,* Chaney had gabbed his way through *Frankenstein Meets the Wolf Man, Son of Dracula,* and a brace of *Inner Sanctum* features. The law of healthy returns on limited investments dictated that that most frustrated of Egyptians would shuffle forth once again, this time under the direction of horror novice, Reginald LeBorg.

When we last saw Kharis, he had succumbed to the flames which were enveloping the second-floor portico of the Banning mansion in Mapleton, Massachusetts. Well, whereas that little bonfire at the end of *The Mummy's Hand* had resulted in the seared

A posed studio publicity shot of Chaney, Jr. from *The Mummy's Ghost.*

and blackened goblin of *Tomb*, the major-league conflagration during the closing moments of that film apparently had quite the opposite effect. Our first glimpse of Kharis in *The Mummy's Ghost*—second of the Lon Chaney sequels and next up on the Hit Parade—finds him positively squeaky clean, chalk white, and full of piss and vinegar. Go figure.

The fact that the picture at hand picks up with us still in Mapleton (albeit two years later) is gratifying. Stuffy John Banning and his beautiful Isobel have headed off to greener pastures, but the familiar faces of old Professor Norman (Frank Reicher) and older Professor Andoheb (George Zucco) tie us in nicely with the earlier film. (It's

Kharis appears from behind a sarcophagus to confront the night watchman at the museum, in *The Mummy's Ghost.*

reassuring to see that Emmett Vogan's nameless Coroner is also still around, checking for mold; between those called to the front [because of the war] and those called to their reward [because of Kharis], the people we used to know in Mapleton have become very scarce.)

Still hanging out in that Mayan-esque Temple on the banks of the Nile and still masterminding schemes to get Ananka and her beau back to the dilapidated comfort of their tombs, Andoheb has obviously loosened a few screws while quivering with age. In his standard introductory remarks to Youssef Bey (John Carradine), the wizened high priest actually demotes Kharis (hereto referred to as a "Prince of the Royal House") to the distinctly less exalted status of "a young man." (With the turn of such a phrase, our ancient anti-hero's biggest fault now seems not to have been sacrilege so much as trying to marry above his station.)

More alarmingly, the temple itself seems to have undergone a change in management: Karnak is out, Arkham (or something) is in. Just as several of the historical pharaohs had razed monuments and obliterated hieroglyphs lauding their predecessors, someone (Amon-Ra? Griffin Jay?) has unseated the Karnak organization, heedless of its long history of faithful—if somewhat inept—service to the cause. And: it seems that Ananka was not just another daughter of King Amenophis, but was also "a priestess-initiate of Arkham." As such, her carrying on with Kharis (or any other young wastrel) was doomed from the start; "Such a love was forbidden," clucks Andoheb to his disciple, never once indicating just what kind of love the gods would have okayed.

The museum's watchman (Oscar O'Shea) confronts the Mummy in *The Mummy's Ghost.*

Before the high priest can puncture any more dreams, we cut to Professor Norman, who lets on to his class how he was given some tana leaves by Steven Banning "for scientific research," and how Ananka's mummy is now "one of the choice possessions of the Scripps museum." Listening semi-intently is Tom Hervey (Robert Lowery), an aged student who has obviously chosen school over the draft. After class, Tom hustles over to shoot the breeze with his girlfriend, Amina Mansouri (Ramsey Ames), an Egyptian girl who can't manage to even *think* of her homeland without freezing up. When her *touching* a book on "The Tombs of Ancient Egypt" puts her within spitting distance of a good swoon, even Tom has had enough. Promising to meet her later that evening, he's out the door.

Back in Egypt, Andoheb is still droning on to Youssef Bey: The world believes it has destroyed Kharis, but through the sacred message brought to us by the most holy spirit of Amon-Ra, we know that he still lives... Lives only for the purpose for which he was created: to guard Ananka's tomb until the end of time.

As Kharis doesn't seem to have been terribly successful up to this point, Bey is instructed to return the two ancients to Egypt. But first, the tana leaf story. "Once each night, during the cycle of the full moon, you will brew nine tana leaves. Kharis will know and will come for the fluid which preserves him. He will find it, wherever it is." Now, anyone with a better memory than old Andoheb will recall that nameless high priest Eduardo Cianelli had very pointedly informed young Andoheb that *three* leaves was the standard dosage when the moon was full, and that it took nine to get the Mummy up on his pins whenever "unbelievers seek to desecrate the tomb of Ananka." What's more, considering the leaves are touted as being "totally extinct" time and again, Andoheb's profligacy—he brews up a handful for the hell of it while programming Youssef Bey—is *very* difficult to understand.

Back in Mapleton, there's that same full moon, and Professor Norman is screwing around with *his* cache of tana leaves. Heating up nine leaves lets off a hell of a lot of smoke (just how does one obtain *fluid* by heating up desiccated leaves?), so it's not surprising that Kharis, sniffing the air as Chaney's dog, Moose, must have done in the presence of barbecue, catches the scent and makes a beeline for the brew. (Another enigma: how has Kharis managed to conceal himself in the nearby shrubbery for two years without recourse to so much as a dollop of the stuff?) A block or so behind the Mummy is Amina, who had been awakened mystically from her sleep by the presence of something Egyptian. The lovely but entranced young woman remains under the old oak tree until Kharis—having dispatched both professor and fluid—shuffles out into the night; she then collapses.

Well. The next morning, the professor's body has been discovered, the coroner gets to identify the mold, and Amina is sprawled charmingly on the Normans' front lawn; the townspeople commence to grumble about mummies. And who do you think is in their midst, formally attired and Max Factored to the nines? None other than Youssef Bey, who had departed the outskirts of Cairo in the middle of the night and had planted himself in the Mapleton, Massachusetts, town square by the following morning! If Arkham can deliver the goods like this *all* the time, it's no wonder that Karnak got dumped. That night, Bey and his sacred brazier do their thing in the middle of a clearing: "Protect me in this strange and foreign land. Help me to dispatch with speed and glory the mission I have undertaken in your name. Bring Kharis to me, wherever he is!"

As it is now a given that tana fluid is not just the dinner, but the dinner bell as well, Kharis gets a whiff of those smoking leaves and makes for the woods. In order to get there, however, he must pass the jalopy containing Tom and Amina, and this is a pity. The young coed, rather fetching with a white streak in her hair, has just started chuckling up a storm with a much-relieved Tom when Kharis' shadow crosses them both. This causes Tom's dog to bark, an ominous organ tremolo to grow louder, and the decision to call it a night to be made. Tom snarls at a passing hunter, and who can blame him? Kharis keeps on lumbering toward that brazier, and if only because a straight line is the shortest distance between two points, he lumbers right into some poor bastard's barn. Pausing only to swat ineffectively at a dog and strangle its master, Kharis walks right *through* the barn wall to get to the fluid.

A cut, and *Voila!*—two and a half pictures after its first mention, finally—the Scripps Museum! Blending in with a band of tourists, Bey remains behind at Ananka's sarcophagus; he hides out until after closing, and then proceeds to appoint the area around the princess with a truckload of lamps and braziers. (We bow from the waist to Arkham's travel agents, who have moved the gawky high priest *and Kharis* from Mapleton to New York City without their being spotted.) Meanwhile, the night watchman settles in for an installment of *The Hour of Death* on his radio. (The old man [Oscar O'Shea] doesn't last long, but his penchant for mysteries allows scenarists Griffin Jay, Henry Sucher, Brenda Weisberg *et al.* a great inside joke, targeted at fans of Universal horror movies [among others]: "A killer is at large tonight, my friends," drones the narrator. "He enters the darkened study of *Doctor X, the Mad Doctor of Market Street!")*

When Ananka's swathed carcass crumbles at Kharis' touch, the sleeping Amina awakens in her bed in Mapleton with a scream. ("I don't know what happened," she confesses. "I thought there was someone here in the room. I could feel his hands, touching me.") Kharis is not happy, either, a fact which does not go unnoticed by Youssef Bey; the lanky priest does some fast calculating: "Amon-Ra, almighty god! Thy wrath is far-reaching! By thy will, her soul has entered another form!" Not entirely placated by this explanation, the mummy goes berserk and wrecks tens of dollars worth of the studio's props before choking the poor old watchman in a fit of pique. (Stills of this scene can be found showing the Mummy bleeding from the chin like a stuck pig; as related in *Universal Horrors*, Chaney had shattered a real plateglass door in a display of testosterone, and—per Blackie Seymour—Jack Pierce was forced to modify the actor's facial appliance to prevent his getting infected. The movie being shot out of sequence [naturally], scenes of Chaney in actual make-up alternate with scenes of him in the rubber mask from *Tomb*.)

While Kharis, Bey, and the night train are puffing back to New England, *two* investigations also pick up steam: in Mapleton, Sheriff Elwood (Harry Shannon) tells pushy old Tom to forget about taking Amina away from all this; she had been found unconscious by the scene of Professor Norman's murder, and that must mean something. In NYC, Inspector Walgreen (Barton MacLane) has the museum's curator, Doctor Ayad (Lester Sharpe), translate the hieroglyphs which have graced the inside of the princess's sarcophagus for millennia and have sat unheeded in the Big Apple for two years: "herein rests and must forever rest the body of Ananka, third daughter of Amenophis. In the hills of Arkhon shall Ananka lie, in the tomb appointed for her and in none other, because, freed from its resting place, her soul may find reincarnation in another form, again to seek out its salvation on earth." We're now left with a very awkward situation. Presumably, Ananka is not the only priestess-initiate of Arkham who has died within the last forty centuries. Is she, however, the only one to be saddled with the "curse" outlined above, or was this standard operating procedure for the cult? If the former, why aren't any of the high priests aware of this wrinkle? (Youssef Bey is nearly floored by it, and he and his forerunners have devoted *eons* of service to this particular princess.) If the latter, why haven't any of those high priests been concerned for the last 30 years?

(This reincarnation theme was, of course, lifted from the Karloff/Freund original and was very much an afterthought. Kharis' catching up with Ananka's mummy at the museum would have spelled "Dead End" for the series' narrative and profitability, so an out had to be arranged. The patently absurd pronouncement that moving the body would lead ineffably to the movement of the soul reeks of desperate improvisation on the part of Griffin Jay, Henry Sucher, and Brenda Weisberg, who had found the light at the end of their scripted tunnel to be New Jersey.)

Anyhow, Walgreen grumps a bit ("First it's a mummy, and now it's a reincarnated woman"), but he and Ayad jump on the train for Mapleton. Taking charge of *both* investigations, the New York cop orders a huge pit dug right in front of Professor Norman's French doors; this will prove to be of no value whatsoever, but it keeps the extras busy and pads the running time. Meanwhile, testy Tom and Amina have decided to make a run for it, planning to leave for New York the very next day. That night, though, Youssef Bey's prayers for a sign of Ananka's presence are answered, and Kharis is sent out to snatch the sleeping Egyptian student. (Rather than chance lurking in the bushes indefinitely, Bey and the Mummy have holed up in a shanty which must have

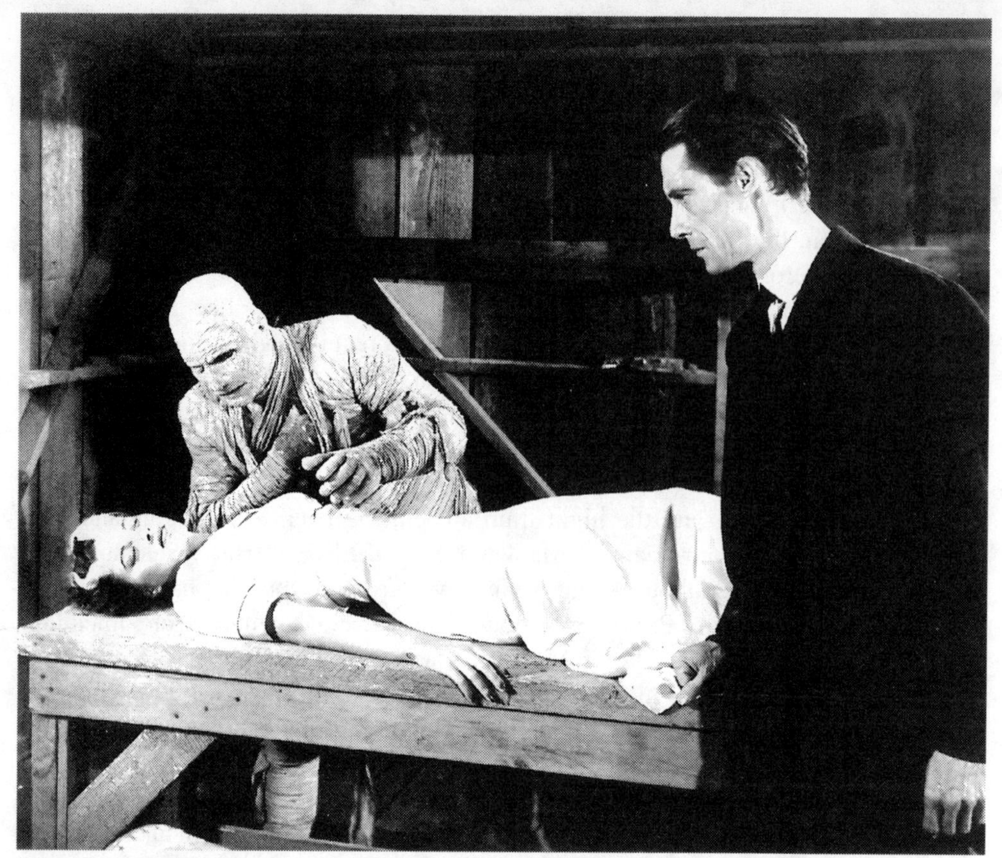

Kharis carries Amina (Ramsay Ames)—her hair growing progressively whiter—back to the shack. Youssef Bey (John Carradine) looks on, in *The Mummy's Ghost.*

been singularly useless to whatever mining concern had erected it: the secret lair is little more than a shack on stilts, which one may enter either through a vertical ladder leading to a window[!] or via a track-laden ramp. The structure contains but one wooden table, conveniently Amina-size; the two heavies presumably have to stretch out on the floor when sleep comes upon them.)

Kharis carries Amina—her hair growing progressively whiter—back to the shack, but he's let down once again by the raging hormones of the priests of Arkham (or Karnak. Or wherever.) As Youssef Bey has another extended dialogue with his conscience, he makes the fatal mistake of summing up aloud: "Here in this cup is my gift of life to you. I'm going to make you immortal and I, too, shall drink and be immortal! We will not return to Egypt! Our world shall be wide, our time shall be without end!" Kharis may not be able to move very well, but his shell-like ears work just fine; he gives Bey such a shot and tosses him out the window. More trouble. The hideout has been discovered by Tom, who has followed his yapping little doggie right to the ramp. The scrappy student, who has just been spoiling for a fight the whole film, is knocked down the ramp and onto his ass by Kharis; before he can finish the job, though, sounds of the approaching townspeople force the Mummy to grab Amina and take off.

Attending to the bloodied Tom, the crowd fails to notice Kharis and his lady (now gone completely white) hie *down the ladder* and head for the hills. Unfortunately, they never make it to the hills, as the swamps stand in their way. Pursued relentlessly by Tom, the mob, and Peanuts (the dog), Kharis and a withered Amina sink beneath the quicksand, bringing this chapter in the tale of the doomed lovers to a gritty and suffocating end.

There seems to be no valid reason why Arkham (however it may be spelled) was substituted for Karnak at this late date. Karnak was (and is) a real locale of great archaeological and historical significance in Egypt, and while I doubt there was any "cult" about to make trouble for Universal (as has been suggested), there has never been any shortage of lawyers willing to chase an ambulance (or a sarcophagus). A close look at John Carradine's *mouth* while Youssef Bey is fencing with his conscience toward the end of the picture will reveal a discrepancy: to paraphrase the old song, his lips tell you Karnak, but there's Arkham on the track. Obviously a looped moment, the vignette indicates that the switch from one august body to the other was made after shooting had already commenced.

That ramshackle mining shack had been prominently featured in *The Invisible Man Returns,* when it lent its wooden support to that film's baloney about the Radcliffe family's mining concerns. One of the studio's less impressive standing sets, the rickety structure was also seen (to better advantage) in *The Magnificent Brute* (1936; for which it had been constructed), *Black Diamonds* (1940; a Richard Arlen–Andy Devine adventure), and *Pittsburgh* (1942; with John Wayne *and* Randolph Scott). Insofar as there is a swamp only a few hundred yards from the shack, it's to be presumed that whatever excavation had once taken place in the area had to be abandoned when the tunnels began filling up with swamp grass, quicksand, and alligators (or other indigenous denizens of the Massachusetts underbrush).

Such blatant tampering and cheesy production values may not of themselves spell doom for the series, but they do indicate the catch-as-catch-can air that had befallen the Kharis pictures. Having cranked out a winner with *The Mummy's Hand,* the studio chiefs came to realize that the eponymous character would run out of gas much sooner than anticipated if left to his own devices. Scarcely much of a threat save to the elderly or the cornered, Kharis needed a catalyst. The assignment of lighting a fire under the old guy and providing ongoing exposition was allocated to the high priests, but even with the constant turnover in personnel, the repetitive droning still got old fast. Sadly, the priests themselves—a pathetic bunch, given to fezzes and fractured rhetoric—came to need a catalyst; unfortunately for them, the movers and shakers would be the sundry heroes' honeys (among whom was also *Kharis'* girlfriend, a wrinkle which would prove to be awkward and contrived, if not downright dangerous). By the time *Ghost* was in circulation, the bloom wasn't just off the rose, the petals had fallen from the stem. There was very little dramatic mileage left in the concept.

Once Frank Reicher has been squeezed into an early exit, John Carradine is without serious competition, and *The Mummy's Ghost* slips comfortably into his back pocket. It's doubtful whether anyone other than Carradine could have handled the trite and embarrassing dialogue exchanges with his "inner voice" and still have emerged with anything resembling dignity. Although released after *The Invisible Man's Revenge, Ghost* had been shot in late summer of 1943; it was thus Long John's second Universal fright flick (after *Captive Wild Woman)* since his bit days of *The Black Cat (*1934) and *The Bride of Frankenstein.* The intervening years had seen the flamboyant actor essay a wide variety of character parts in essentially A productions (or in B's for the more

The crowd fails to notice Kharis and his lady (now gone completely white) hie *down the ladder* and head for the hills, in *The Mummy's Ghost.*

major studios), and his forties' Universal bogeys shared in that panache. Carradine dismissed the lion's share of his movie work as merely a means to an end (to raise the funds for his itinerant Shakespearean company), but his stints for the more respected studios were almost always of a higher caliber (read: less outrageous) than were similar assignments for lesser firms, for which his name and patented ham-slicing were frequently all that was needed. Like Bela Lugosi, though, Carradine always gave his all, no matter how demeaning the part or ludicrous the film.

Robert Lowery and Ramsay Ames are the least interesting, most colorless romantic leads in this or any other horror film I've ever experienced (always excepting *Life Returns).* Miss Ames' Amina Mansouri is so lifeless, so completely devoid of expression, that the character seems almost an homage to Acquanetta, the only actress who could have actually done worse in the role. I'd cut Ames a minor break for the static nature of the role—Amina spends most of her time either nearly swooning or in mid-swoon—if only she could handle the elementary feelings outlined in her limited dialogue. She is much better (and this is a backhanded compliment) in *Calling Dr. Death,* where she's not forced to deal with such heady matters as extrasensory commands or reincarnation.

The word "reincarnation" seems very apropos when discussing Robert Lowery's Tom Hervey. The nominal hero is so overbearing, petulant, and contrary that he seems to have been possessed by the worst qualities of David Manners' Jonathan Harker without having inherited the earlier character's more redeeming features. As it had for Manners in *Dracula,* the screenplay here has given Lowery scant heroic potential, with respect to either action *or* attitude. A distinction must be made, however, between handling poor dialogue adroitly and surrendering to it entirely. Lowery appears to have followed the latter course; I can't sense any attempt on his part at making Tom other than the callow jerk delineated in the scenario. He gives the same testy reading to his other Universal genre "good guy"—Steve Morrow in *House of Horrors* (1946)—and isn't much fun to be around as Bruce Wayne in the 1949 Columbia serial, *Batman and Robin,* either.

Chaney is certainly more animated in *Ghost* than he had been in *Tomb,* but whether this was part of his unofficial campaign to bond with director Reginald LeBorg, or a reaction to the rococo acting style of John Carradine is anybody's guess. It wouldn't be too improbable to envision the actor perking up slightly when advised that reincarnation would rear its kinky head in *Ghost,* only to be disappointed (yet again) to discover that virtually none of the shtick had anything to do with his character. If the ghost of the title referred to the spirit of Ananka (and who can say for sure?), then the last of the sequels might well have been pegged *The Mummy Gives Up the Ghost.* In *Curse,* Chaney once again shuffles spiritlessly through those same old motions.

In fact, by the time *The Mummy's Curse* was being readied for production, no one appeared to give a damn about that old devil, continuity. Sure, Kharis was still there, and Ananka was still there, and the swamp was still there, but "there" wasn't where *it* used to be. "There" *had* been Mapleton, Massachusetts, home to the Banning family and site of that most frustrating of industries, marshland mining; all that, however, had changed. In the five or so months since *The Mummy's Ghost,* while our boys were overseas, someone had moved that swampland to Louisiana, doubtless hoping it would blend in, unnoticed, with the bayous.

With the swamp have come Kharis and Ananka, and they can't be any less confused than the rest of us. Twenty-five years have passed since they disappeared into that renowned New England quicksand, only to be resuscitated a couple of hundred yards from "Tante Berthe's Cafe," where *La Marseillaise* is an accordion favorite, French-ish accents come and go, and half the population have names more proper to Ancient Greece. The government (that's the U.S. government) has just started draining those swamps—no talk of eco-systems in 1944—but there's already a legend afoot. Cajun Joe (Kurt Katch) paints an exciting, if slightly premature, picture: "In the night, when the moon is so high in the heavens, the Mummy and his princess, they walk... This place, she's a-haunted!" Then, too, Antoine is missing.

Pat Walsh (Addison Richards), head of the drainage project, is the picture of aggravation. Not only have Dr. James Halsey (Dennis Moore) and Dr. Ilzor Zandaab

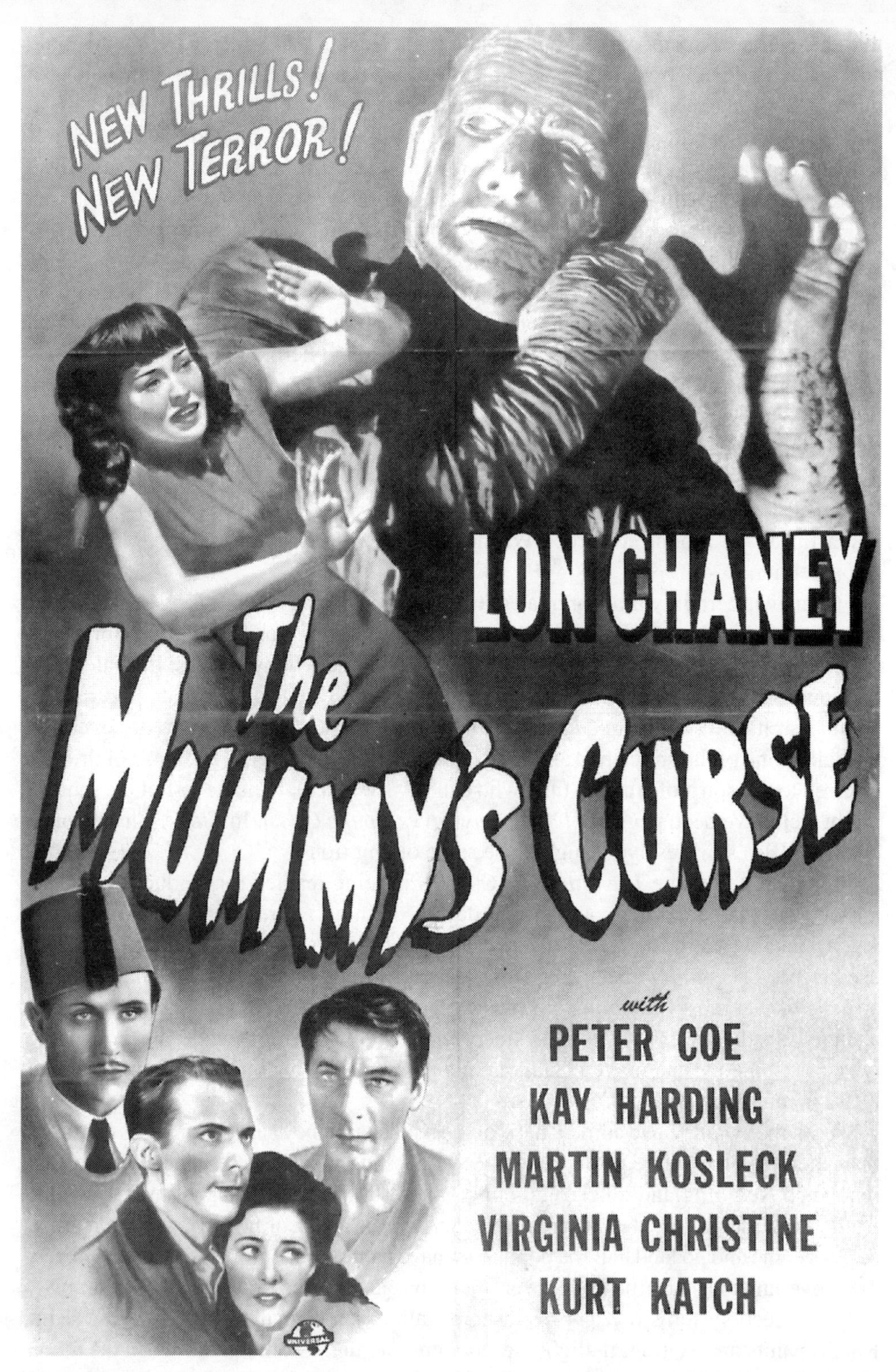

(Peter Coe) of the Scripps Museum got a note allowing them to poke around the job site, but Walsh's pretty niece, Betty (Kay Harding), is not at all subtle in her regard for Halsey. On top of this headache, everyone is upset that Antoine's been *found*—with a knife in his back and a piece of gauze clutched in his fist. As the poor bugger is sprawled next to a very large man-sized hole in the ground, Dr. Zandaab theorizes that "Whoever found the Mummy must have murdered Antoine." Skulking among the ragtag work force is Zandaab's man, Ragheb (Martin Kosleck); with the help of Antoine and several others, he had schlepped Kharis, a couple of sarcophagi, and a roomful of torches, urns, and flaming braziers to the ruins of an abandoned monastery not far from where they now stand. The colorful and highly ethnic Goobie (Napoleon Simpson) puts everything into perspective: "The devil's on the loose, and he's dancing with the Mummy!"

The two Egyptians pile into a small boat, and after a jaunt through the bayou pond locale exploited in *Son of Dracula,* arrive at the foot of the glass painting of an old monastery. This metamorphoses into some leftover *Tower of London* sets, and Ilzor strolls between two mummy cases (from a rather recent dynasty; the lid to Kharis' sarcophagus is on hinges.) The high priest now plunges into the tana leaf saga—basically unchanged since *The Mummy's Ghost*—and has Ragheb swear by the ancient gods of Egypt not to betray his trust; this, of course, guarantees that the shifty-eyed henchman will screw things up before the house lights are raised again.

Those neat Karloff-Tyler flashbacks kill a few moments while Ilzor provides the narration, and then the fluid of three tana leaves is ladled into Kharis' maw, and he begins to stir. (And you thought it took *nine* leaves to give him "motivation!") Down the stairs comes old Michael, the "self-ordained caretaker of this monastery" (William Farnum, decades after sharing [with his brother, Dustin] top honors for most popular player in motion pictures). Michael is nothing, if not polite: "This house of worship, although silent for many years, is not to be desecrated by such pagan customs. I'm afraid I shall have to ask you to take these sacrilegious things away. In a room beneath the chapel, I found the bodies of freshly murdered men." Also a master of understatement, he adds, "Never has this happened before." The caretaker is so well-mannered, he stands his ground while Kharis gets a good grip on his windpipe; less eloquent in death than he was in life, Michael lets out with what sounds suspiciously like "Nuts!" as the shadow-play on the wall reflects his demise.

Moving from the darkness of the tomb to the broad daylight in the bayou, quitting time the next day sees a figure rise painfully from the swamp mud. It is Ananka (Virginia Christine), and the actress's talent complements director Leslie Goodwins' crackerjack set-up; the resurrection of Kharis' own princess is easily the best bit in the picture. Stumbling slowly through the swamp, Ananka pauses to wash herself in a pond; by the time Cajun Joe catches up with her, the woman is bone dry, and her hair has been immaculately coiffured. As Joe leads her to Tante Berthe's, Ragheb—who shares old Mehemet Bey's gift for being in the right place at the right time—overhears her mention the "K" word.

Tante Berthe sends Joe to fetch a doctor, and Ilzor sends Kharis to fetch Ananka. "You shall go to take her," the high priest urges the Mummy; "you know the destination!" It never occurs to anyone that Kharis may *not* know the destination; the last time his good eye was open, he was in Massachusetts! Nonetheless, he makes his usual beeline—stopping momentarily to check a sign that's in English—and arrives at Tante Berthe's in two shakes. (How he's able to negotiate the little boat which connects the old monastery with the mainland is best ignored.) It's curtains for Berthe, as she gets between the Mummy and his beloved, but the noble Cajun woman buys time for Ananka. Clad only in a slinky, floor-length nightgown, the princess scoots out through the door; running at full speed, she pauses every ten feet or so to look behind her, and then, discovering a

Kharis claims another victim in *The Mummy's Curse.*

clearing which has good lighting and appears to be free of snakes and sharp sticks, collapses into a fetching heap.

In a scene right out of *The Villain Still Pursued Her,* Dr. Halsey and Betty stop to transfer the fallen Ananka into their convertible, leaving only a fraction of a second before Kharis, who should never have stopped for a double-take, can reach the car. Unlike earlier installments in the series, wherein the Mummy's *shadow* was enough to start dogs howling and organ pipes screeching, Kharis does everything here apart from getting down on one knee and breaking into song, and still no one can notice him for the trees. Back at the cafe, Cajun Joe sums it up: "Poor Tante Berthe; she's a-dead. And the girl, she's a-gone."

At Dr. Halsey's camp, the girl, she's a-wake up. Halsey and Dr. Cooper (Holmes Herbert) decide to keep her "mentally alert" by having her pitch in around the laboratory, and the very next day, she proves her worth. Tearing herself away from sun-bathing ("I can never get too much sun," she purrs, referring to John Fulton's optically enhanced orb), Ananka elaborates on the gauze she has under her microscope: "...they are mummy wrappings. The fabric was woven during the dynasty of King Amenophis, and worn by Kharis, Prince of the Royal House." (This impresses the hell out of Halsey, and rightly so. Could Britain's Princess Margaret divine the vintage and ownership of a swatch of English tweed under like circumstances?) Ananka has no idea how she knows this stuff, but slipping into a trance, she wanders smack into Ilzor. Recognizing immediately with whom he's dealing, the high priest makes for the monastery. That night, the Prince of the Royal House is prepped once again. "Hasten, then, while the moon is still high,"

Ilzor advises, so off goes Kharis, hastening as best as he can. Ananka awakens, trots on over to Dr. Cooper's tent, and fires off a load of exposition; she senses that Kharis is coming, but is hard-pressed to explain who he is, or just how she knows: "It's as though I were two different people. Sometimes it seems as if I belong to a different world. I find myself in strange surroundings, with strange people. I cannot ever seem to find rest. And now, Kharis..." Cooper rather predictably says he'll get her a little something to quiet her nerves, but is appalled to see Kharis coming at him—the usually stealthy Mummy has been making a racket audible in the next state—from the foliage. The brave physician's death is conveyed via some more shadow-play, and Ananka takes to her heels again.

Cooper's death and Ananka's disappearance have made Mr. Walsh testier than ever, and his men band together to search the swamps for "the girl." From the vantage point of his small boat, Cajun Joe spots her, but in a sequence which is as frightening as it is well choreographed, he runs headlong into Kharis. (Since he has already missed his princess by inches *twice,* you might think Kharis would pass on a little extraneous strangling in order to catch up with her here. Like Cajun Joe, old habits die hard.) Ananka makes for Betty's tent, where she hopes for a chance to catch her breath; as we're 55 minutes into a 62-minute picture, she's plumb out of luck. Ignoring the aghast Betty, the Mummy carries off Ananka, collapsing the tent in the process. Who should then turn up but Ragheb, who maneuvers the heroine out from under the canvas and promises to lead her to Dr. Halsey.

Hah! Dr. Halsey returns to camp in her absence and has to have it explained to him (by Goobie, of all people) that "Miss Betty sure am disappeared!" Finding *another* piece of wrapping on a branch (at this rate, Kharis will be fully unraveled by the Labor Day weekend), Halsey sends the annoying Goobie to alert Walsh and the men, and follows the tracks as best as he can.

Slowly making his way up the monastery steps (borrowed from the Mayan temple in *The Mummy's Hand),* Kharis finally delivers Ananka into the hands of the only high priest who has made it to the last reel without succumbing to rampaging lust. While Ilzor spoons tana fluid into the princess's mouth, Ragheb, who *does* have the hots—for Betty—craftily leads her to the monastery cellar. Before the treacherous toady can make his pitch, though, Ilzor strides in, assesses the situation at a glance, and waxes wroth: "The curse of Amon-Ra upon you, Ragheb... Your tongue shall be torn from your mouth for the vows you have sworn to. You have betrayed your trust. The secret of Kharis and his bride, Princess Ananka, cannot be preserved unless the girl dies!" Forgetting a) that everyone in this film and the previous two sequels has read, exhaustively, of the "secret" of Kharis and Ananka in their local newspapers, and b) that Ragheb, the sneaky little bastard, is carrying a knife, Ilzor attempts a dramatic exit. He gets none too far. With Zandaab down for good, Halsey shows up; this time, Ragheb is caught with his shiv showing, and a full-fledged struggle breaks out.

The noise attracts Kharis, who snatches the torch from Ragheb's hand before the murderous Egyptian can use it to brain Halsey. Locking himself in one of the monastery's cells(!?), Ragheb scrambles frantically to evade the Mummy's outstretched arm. Betty manages to help Halsey to his feet, just as Kharis gives a mighty heave, which tears the cell door from its frame and brings tons of masonry down on both him and Ragheb. Walsh and the men storm in, and everyone casts a look at the chalkwhite body of the young woman. Dr. Halsey elucidates: "Now I understand why she knew so much about

Kharis and the ancient Egyptians. This mummy is the girl we brought to the camp. She's the Princess Ananka!" Even Goobie is speechless.

The Mummy's Curse was Kharis' swan-song, and it would take another major-league leap in space and time—to 1959 England—before the epic tale of forbidden love would again reach the screen.

Virginia Christine has long been heralded as the most appealing of the female leads in the Chaney Mummy series, and that's the God's-honest truth, but the beautiful actress really had no competition. Elyse Knox, the only contender who had anything like a career after her shot (as Isobel Evans in *Tomb*), was barely allowed to open her mouth. Apart from that ludicrous debate with Turhan Bey—which she conducted while affixed to the lid of a casket—Miss Knox may have had a half-dozen lines, and most of those were played off her supercilious fiancé, John Hubbard. Miss Christine's immediate predecessor in the role was Ramsay Ames; suffice it to say, even had Miss Ames' part been better written, her performance most likely would not have been any more memorable. Be that as it may, the fact remains that Miss Christine has impressed *generations* of audiences with her portrayal. Little touches—like Ananka's assuming a frieze-like pose when first meeting Ilzor—were more probably improvised bits by the actress than carefully plotted details, masterminded by the likes of Leslie Goodwins.

Betty Walsh must have been little more than a walk-through for Kay Harding. Ostensibly the heroine—she *does* accompany the hero, stand up for him before her uncle, and allow herself to be led hither and yon by just about anybody in trousers—Betty's every gesture and sentiment are right out of the prompt book. It's tough to determine where to assign culpability here: there isn't a huge body of extant Kay Harding work with which to compare Betty. As with Ms. Harding, this was Dennis Moore's shot at the big-time (Universal-wise, at any rate). Much more comfortable (and appreciated) over at Gower Gulch, Moore (aka Denny Meadows) earned a living as the second (or third, or...) lead in an almost endless series of Monogram horse operas. The occasional action picture did intervene, naturally, and the actor's other genre appearances included *Boys of the City* (1940) and the East Side Kids horror, *Spooks Run Wild,* wherein Mr. Moore edged out Bela Lugosi as the titular creep. Dr. Halsey goes through all the usual heroic motions and is not unpleasant to look at; otherwise, he's as colorless as Goobie is embarrassing.

More familiar faces include Peter Coe and Martin Kosleck, both of whom would grace other of Universal's slick programmers before the merge with International saw them to the door. Coe has none of Zucco's or Carradine's wide-eyed lunacy, nor does he convey Turhan Bey's effortless charm. His Zandaab strikes one less as a fanatical high priest than a working stiff; he may be faced with more singular responsibilities than the average Joe, but only when his cushy and undemanding job (a spoonful here, a spoonful there) is threatened, does he exhibit any of the fire of his forerunners. Coming from his mouth, the company line is less than inspiring, and despite his steadfast celibacy, he is the last—and least—of that ancient line of horny servitors. None of the others would have been so stupid (there *is* no other word) to threaten a psycho like Ragheb, and then expose his back.

Martin Kosleck does his thing, and that means making Ragheb an unstable, duplicitous little shit. (The actor frequently was called upon to portray Nazis, assassins, and other, more true-to-life vermin; this usually resulted in their being drawn as unstable, duplicitous, and *sadistic* little shits.) Due more to Kosleck's ferret-like demeanor than

It's curtains for Berthe (Ann Codee), as she gets between the Mummy and his beloved, but the Cajun woman buys time for Ananka (Virginia Christine), in *The Mummy's Curse.*

to his rather natty attire, Ragheb never becomes just another face in the background. Saddled with the testosterone problems that the high priest (for once) is spared, the vile little henchman makes his one play for honor—defending Betty's life—for all the wrong reasons. His reminding Ilzor that he, too, can handle the tana leaf ritual is *another* stab in the back, as it pretty much exposes the sacred trust of Arkham for the rocket science that it is.

Cinematographer Virgil Miller—not a big genre name, by any means—hits the mark as often as he misses, and that's not so terribly bad. The shadow-work mentioned above is effective, if a trifle overdone, and Miller's camera is all over Ananka as she claws her way back to light and life. By varying the angles and the depths-of-field of the numerous set-ups, Miller (and Leslie Goodwins) reinforce the effort and the pain with which Miss Christine imbues the princess's revivification process. Denied even a single dose of that exhilarating tana fluid in *The Mummy's Ghost,* Ananka is forced to draw only upon the power of the sun and her own peculiar circumstances to overcome the atrophy of limbs which have been motionless for a quarter-century. Richly cinematic—and intelligent—the resurrection scene remains the film's visual highlight due to the talents of Miss Christine and the Messrs. Miller and Goodwins.

When Leslie Goodwins' name is raised 'round the genre campfire, it's usually in conjunction with *The Mummy's Curse,* but the director was also responsible for *Murder in the Blue Room* (1944), which I like better, and RKO's *Genius at Work* (1946), which I wish I could like more. The British-born Goodwins dabbled in film types, and moved constantly—happy as a clam—among low-budget musicals, Westerns, whodunits, comedies, and soap operas. Remembered chiefly for the enormously popular *Mexican Spitfire* series (with Lupe Velez and Leon Errol), the director struck industry types more as an amiable journeyman-technician than a source of tremendous leadership or insight.

Lon Chaney must have been tickled to death when it became known that *Curse* would be the last of the Kharis nightmares. With the exception of his baby, the Wolf Man, his monsters were all behind him, and those remaining installments in the *Inner Sanctum* series conformed very much more to the image Chaney was trying to foster. When, however, in 1946 Universal-International gave him and his image an hour to get off the lot, the resultant move to freelance work would reunite the actor with his moldy wrappings twice more: the screwy Mexican spooker, *La Casa del Terror* (1959), and his guest appearance(s) in the famed "Lizard's Leg and Owlet's Wing" episode of TV's *Route 66.*

Like so many other fans, I enjoy the body of Chaney's work without regarding him as an actor of great substance or high style. I don't mean to reduce his efforts to a one-line formula, but it always appeared to me that Chaney sought to simplify his "complex" roles, while looking to flesh out the one-dimensional jobs. Interviews with co-workers—held in *Universal Horrors* and elsewhere—make frequent mention of Lon's fear of wordy and involved dialogue. Given his well-known insecurities, the actor couldn't have felt totally adequate impersonating the spate of artistic and scientific geniuses around which the *Inner Sanctum* series revolved, either.

Striving to give a listless zombie-like Kharis some kind of personality would probably have been more to Chaney's liking had it not been for those stifling applications of rubber, gauze, and Fuller's earth. Yet, although drawing clothes on a stick figure is not as demanding as adding fine detail to a portrait done in oils, the dangers of excess are no less real. Unable to use his voice, Chaney overcompensated by having Kharis gesture and react with the same broad strokes that Eric Campbell and other comic heavies from the silent days had regarded as their own stock-in-trade. Chaney's turn in *The Mummy's Ghost* usually garners him some decent notices, but only in comparison with the other two entries in the series. His hand may well tremble near Ananka's cheek, but it's trembling for the back row; every one of Kharis' takes and reactions in *Ghost* is far more operatic than in either of the flanking films, and more doesn't necessarily mean better.

In order to evoke fully his personal horror, the role of Kharis demanded an actor adept at subtle pantomime; ironically, the three Mummy sequels might have attained near-classical status had Chaney *Senior* animated the bandages. As it was, it remained for Christopher Lee—at the top of his form, well removed from either Chaney—to covey via bodily movements the nobility and tragedy of the Prince of the Royal House. In all honesty, though, there's not a hell of a lot that *anyone* could have done with the character of Kharis as delineated in these three pictures. A pawn in the chess game of afterlife, he is constantly moved into the attack position, so as to take any pieces standing between himself and his queen. And without the guiding force of the high priest, the game is quickly lost; witness how, within moments of doing in those lustful Beys, Kharis rings down the end credits on his own head.

Lon Chaney must have been tickled to death when it became known that *Curse* would be the last of the Kharis nightmares.

This is not to say that the character remains static from film to film. In *Tomb,* Chaney's Prince is little more than a murderous zombie, and the ever-physical Lon is well suited for this limited role. The film allows us a glimpse of an *amenable* Chaney, suffering for his art, but willing to accept such chaff with the promise of wheat; resignation has not yet settled on his rubber-masked face. Nonetheless, following *The Mummy's Hand, Tomb* is like the second hill on a roller coaster: it may be fast and furious in its own right, but it's never a match for that first one.

In some ways, *Ghost* is the most creative of the Chaney Mummy series (in more ways, it's the most disingenuous); it boasts Carradine's tormented Youssef Bey and

Lon's most lively turn as Kharis. The vigor which both men bring to their roles, though, is almost (but not completely) negated by the grumpy, pedestrian portrayals by Robert Lowery and Ramsay Ames. It's only when the Kharis saga is saddled with flimsy, extra baggage—like the second rate reincarnation business here—that Chaney's recourse to body language falls short; essentially enacting a *silent movie ogre* during the height of the frantic, noisy forties, nothing in his personal or professional background could help him out.

Curse—a semi-hallucinatory shift in everything we've come to expect—is a meld of its two predecessors, uniting the impressive body count of *Tomb* with the reincarnation remnants of *Ghost.* It demands little of its nominal star and nothing of its audience; for all that, Lon's choicest moments remain those spent at the throats of the supporting cast.

The three Kharis epics—four, if we choose to include the Tyler original—obviously can't stand up to the kind of scrutiny which videotape technology and nit-picking pop critics (like *moi)* have made commonplace; *very* few films can. They do represent a casually linked series of the misadventures of unlikely lovers who are really nothing more than toys to the gods or the Scripps Museum. The charms of the Mummy films are palpable, if uneven, and their thrills juvenile and few. Still, I find myself going back to them, time and again, to enjoy the gasps as well as the gaffes, and to admire how each of these cheap and cheesy little pictures gave wartime audiences an hour's worth of peace of mind.

The Mummy's Tomb—released 23 October, 1942; 60 minutes
CREDITS: Associate Producer: Ben Pivar; Director: Harold Young; Screenplay: Griffin Jay and Henry Sucher; Original Story: Neil P. Varnick; Director of Photography: George Robinson, ASC; Art Director: Jack Otterson; Assoc. Art Director: Ralph M. DeLacy; Film Editor: Milton Carruth; Musical Director: Hans J. Salter; Sound Director: Bernard B. Brown; Technician: William Schwartz; Set Decorator: Russell A. Gausman; Assoc. Set Decorator: Andrew J. Gilmore; Assistant Director: Charles S. Gould; Make-up: Jack P. Pierce; Gowns: Vera West

CAST: Lon Chaney (Kharis); Dick Foran (Steve Banning); Wallace Ford (Babe Hanson); Elyse Knox (Isobel Evans); John Hubbard (John Banning); Mary Gordon (Jane Banning); Turhan Bey (Mehemet Bey); Cliff Clark (Sheriff); George Zucco (Andoheb); Paul E. Burns (Jim); Virginia Brissac (Mrs. Evans); Frank Reicher (Professor Norman); Eddy C. Waller (Chemist); Frank Darien (Old Man); Harry Cording (Vic); Myra McKinney (Mrs. Vic); John Rogers (Steward); Otto Hoffman (Cemetery Caretaker); Emmett Vogan (Coroner); Fern Emmett (Laura); Janet Shaw (Teenage Girl); Dick Hogan (Teenage Boy); Bill Ruhl (Nick); Guy Usher (Doctor); Pat McVey (Jake); Jack Arnold (Reporter); Glenn Strange (Farmer); Rex Lease (Al); Grace Cunard (Farmer's Wife); Lew Kelly (Bartender); Charles Marsh (Man); Walter Byron (Searcher); Edwin Parker (Stand-In for Lon Chaney)

The Mummy's Ghost—released 7 July, 1944; 60 minutes
CREDITS: Associate Producer: Ben Pivar; Executive Producer: Joseph Gershenson; Director: Reginald LeBorg; Screenplay: Griffin Jay, Henry Sucher, Brenda Weisberg; Original Story: Griffin Jay, Henry Sucher; Director of Photography: William Sickner,

ASC; Art Director: John B. Goodman, Abraham Grossman; Film Editor: Saul A. Goodkind; Musical Director: Hans J. Salter; Sound Director: Bernard B. Brown; Technician: Jess Moulin; Set Decorators: Russell A. Gausman, L.R. Smith; Make-up: Jack P. Pierce; Assistant Director: Melville Shyer; Gowns: Vera West

CAST: Lon Chaney (Kharis); John Carradine (Youssef Bey); Ramsay Ames (Amina Mansouri); Robert Lowery (Tom Hervey); Frank Reicher (Professor Norman); Barton MacLane (Inspector Walgreen); George Zucco (Andoheb, the High Priest); Lester Sharpe (Dr. Ayad); Harry Shannon (Sheriff Elwood); Emmett Vogan (Coroner); Claire Whitney (Ella Norman); Oscar O'Shea (Night Watchman); Jack C. Smith, Jack Rockwell (Deputies); Stephen Barclay (Harrison); Carl Vernell, Martha MacVicar (Students); Dorothy Vaughan (Ada Blade); Anthony Warde (Detective); Mira McKinney (Martha Evans); Bess Flowers, Caroline Cooke, Fay Holderness (Women); Eddy Waller (Ben Evans); Ivan Triesault (Museum Guide); Peter Sosso (Priest); David Bruce (voice only) (Radio Announcer)

The Mummy's Curse—released 22 December, 1944; 62 minutes
CREDITS: Associate Producer: Oliver Drake; Executive Producer: Ben Pivar; Director: Leslie Goodwins; Original Story/Adaptation: Leon Abrams, Dwight V. Babcock, Bernard L. Schubert, and T.H. Richmond; Screenplay: Bernard L. Schubert; Film Editor: Fred R. Feitshans, Jr.; Director of Photography: Virgil Miller, ASC; Camera Operator: William Dodds; Special Photographic Effects: John P. Fulton; Assistant Director: Mack Wright; Art Directors: John B. Goodman, Martin Obzina; Musical Director: Paul Sawtell; Song, "Hey, You!": Music: Oliver Drake, Lyrics: Frank Orth; Set Decorators: Russell A. Gausman, Victor A. Gangelin; Sound Director: Bernard B. Brown; Technician: Robert Pritchard; Make- up: Jack P. Pierce; Properties: Ernie Smith, Eddie Case; Gowns: Vera West

CAST: Lon Chaney (Kharis); Peter Coe (Ilzor Zandaab); Kay Harding (Betty Walsh); Martin Kosleck (Ragheb); Virginia Christine (Ananka); Dennis Moore (Dr. James Halsey); Addison Richards (Pat Walsh); Holmes Herbert (Dr. Cooper); Napoleon Simpson (Goobie); Kurt Katch (Cajun Joe); Charles Stevens (Achilles); William Farnum (Michael); Ann Codee (Tante Berthe); Holmes Heywood (Hill); Nina Bara (Cajun Girl); Eddie Abdo (Pierre); Tony Santoro (Ulysses); Eddie Parker (Double for Lon Chaney); With: Heenan Elliott; Al Ferguson, Budd Buster, Carey Loftin, Teddy Mangean

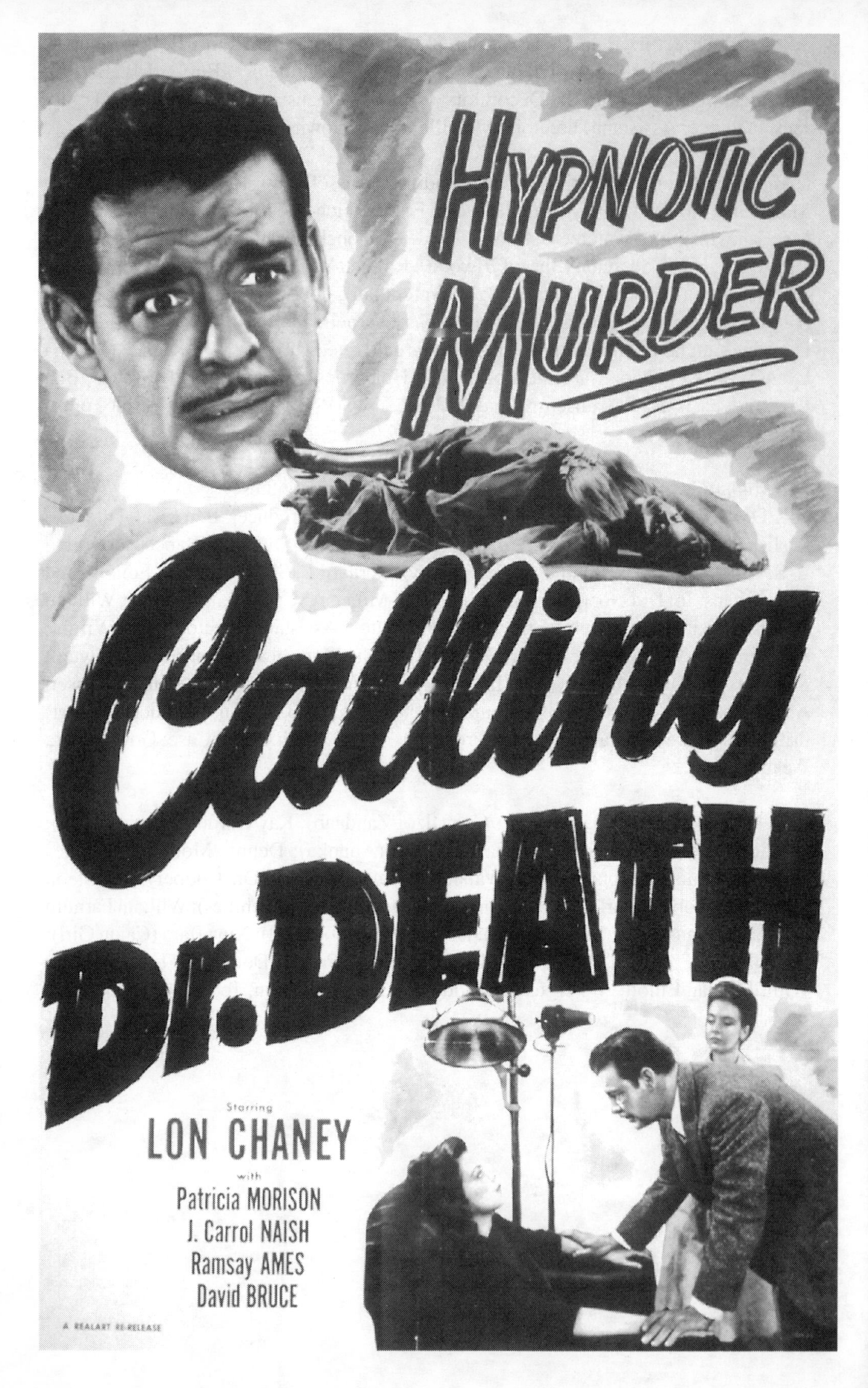
HYPNOTIC
MURDER
Calling
Dr. DEATH
Starring
LON CHANEY
with
Patricia MORISON
J. Carrol NAISH
Ramsay AMES
David BRUCE
A REALART RE-RELEASE

CALLING DR. DEATH (1943)

by Alan Warren

In his capable new study *Lon Chaney, Jr.*, author Don G. Smith notes that the six efforts that comprise the *Inner Sanctum* series "are probably the most critically maligned of any films Chaney did for Universal." Today, more than fifty years after their release, the films continue to take more than their share of potshots. Professed Universal fans find the films risible if not downright campy. Even John and Michael Brunas and Tom Weaver, the redoubtable authors of *Universal Horrors*, dismiss them as "...a half dozen feebly conceived melodramas with little to recommend beyond their camp qualities and the morose spectacle of seeing the badly miscast Chaney struggle his way through roles that were beyond his depth."

In truth, the *Inner Sanctum* films are quite variable in quality. They range from a high of *Strange Confession* (1945) to a low of *The Frozen Ghost* (also 1945). Chaney's acting is similarly variable. He is excellent in the former film, and quite bad in *Pillow of Death* (1945), in which he apparently was in the throes of an alcoholic haze. Brunas, Brunas, and Weaver describe his work in the *Inner Sanctum* films as "dreary," wondering what became of Chaney's talents in a few short years. The answer, of course, is alcohol. Martin Kosleck, his co-star in *The Frozen Ghost*, remembered Chaney as "roaring drunk," and several other performers (Elyse Knox, Peter Coe, Gloria Talbott) have similar recollections.

For many years Chaney was criticized for being, in Gregory Mank's description, "a sadly inferior second stringer," following in the footsteps of Karloff and Lugosi. In his biography of Lugosi, *The Count*, Arthur Lennig castigates Chaney as "an unexciting actor," complaining that he "created characters that were more to be pitied than respected, more cringing than aggressive, more plebeian than aristocratic." This kind of critical overkill disregards the fact that, for example, when Chaney played the Monster in *The Ghost of Frankenstein*, he had to follow Karloff's masterful portrayal. Inevitably, Chaney's Monster was inferior, due in part to the screenplay which specified a weakened and somnolent creature. Yet Lugosi and Glenn Strange, the actors who followed him, were less impressive in the role than Chaney. By the same token, fans who categorize Chaney as a limited actor, capable only of playing dimwitted thugs or variations on Lennie Small, refuse to accord Chaney's performance as Dracula the respect it deserves.

In recent years the critical pendulum has begun swinging back in Chaney's favor. Though the most frequent description of Chaney these days is "underrated," James B. Twitchell, the author of *Dreadful Pleasures*, describes him as "unexpectedly magnetic." His characterization of the Wolf Man holds an honored place in the pantheon of classic monsters. His nonhorror performances in such films as *Of Mice and Men*, *High Noon*,

The *Inner Sanctum* series presents Chaney as the ultimate social *insider*.

Not As a Stranger, and *The Defiant Ones* have earned him the kind of critical respect few horror stars received at any time during their careers.

The *Inner Sanctum* films may be in need of similar critical reconsideration. Quickly shot on low budgets, their B-movie status is immediately evident from the presence of associate producer Ben Pivar, surely the name most synonymous with "lowbrow" in the Universal lexicon. Pivar gave the world such lesser Universal horrors as *The Mad Ghoul* (1943), *She-Wolf of London* (1946), the Paula Dupree/Ape Woman series, and the Creeper films starring Rondo Hatton. According to director Reginald LeBorg in

Universal Horrors, "Pivar was the epitome of the artless, noncreative studio executive: he holed himself up in his office, was often crude, and displayed occasional flashes of illiteracy." In the same source, LeBorg offered an anecdote of the time that he wanted to rewrite a scene, and Pivar sent word that he was too busy even to discuss it. LeBorg sent an assistant director to see what was occupying Pivar's time. The assistant's reply to LeBorg was that "he's playing gin rummy!"

Given this pedigree, it is not surprising that the *Inner Sanctums* were intended to make a quick profit and be quickly forgotten. They were never intended to stand the test of time. Yet, surprisingly, the best ones do. Since horror films and mysteries have become increasingly violent and simple-minded with little interest in plot or character and wholly dependent on pyrotechnic visual special effects, the lesser horror films of the thirties and forties take on an added interest. The Monogram films of Bela Lugosi, for example, have been the subject of increased critical attention in recent years. Yet the *Inner Sanctums* are still routinely dismissed. A typical example is Greg Mank's description of them as "putrid" despite the fact that the *Inner Sanctums* are better scripted, directed, acted, and (most certainly) photographed than their Monogram counterparts.

In keeping with Chaney's status as Universal's leading horror star, several entries had semi-horrific overtones, but Universal hedged its bets by providing rational explanations that undercut the seemingly supernatural goings-on. With the exception of the atypical *Strange Confession*, all of the *Inner Sanctums* climaxed with the exposure of the mystery killer in standard whodunit tradition. Whether or not this provided the sought-after variety, these films were standard mysteries at heart and the juxtaposition of horror and mystery elements throughout the series was an interesting example of "crisscrossing" genres.

Even more interestingly, the series inverts the usual Universal formula of presenting Chaney as the social outsider who is turned into a monster, a literalization of his outsider status. This is particularly evident in *Man Made Monster* and *The Wolf Man*. In *Son of Dracula*, this allegory is clearly spelled out in the dialogue. Chaney's Count Alucard, having incurred the enmity of the socially genteel Southern aristocracy, warns Dr. Brewster (Frank Craven): "When I came to Dark Oaks, I was not graciously welcomed. Now the position is changed. *I* am master."

The *Inner Sanctum* series neatly reverses this formula by presenting Chaney as the ultimate social *insider*. As the series progresses he is depicted as a neurologist, author/teacher, artist, mesmerist, chemist, and attorney. These characters are genteel, usually wealthy, and married or engaged to someone of high social standing. As the melodramas unfold, Chaney is suspected of committing the ultimate social gaffe, murder. Invariably, his societal position is threatened. The films depict this ever-present threat with remarkable consistency, reminding us that one can lose control at any moment and forfeit all our material and societal gains. "Yes, even you, without knowing, can commit murder!" the bulbous head that introduces each entry warns us in advance. The murders usually occur when the protagonist (Chaney) has drunk himself into a stupor, inducing an alcoholic blackout during which he cannot account for his actions. He might, the films imply, be the murderer, even if he himself cannot remember committing the act. All it takes is one careless action, one unguarded moment.

On a more pragmatic level, it should be noted that the *Inner Sanctum* mysteries were extremely profitable for Universal. As noted in *Universal Horrors*, "Unbelievable as it may seem, the *Inner Sanctum* pictures were real moneymakers in their time.

Lon Chaney seems at home in the role of Mark Steele, making the physician's anguish believable throughout.

Dirt-cheap budgets, the popularity of the Simon and Schuster novels, and the renowned radio show had a positive effect on the profit margin." The first film, *Calling Dr. Death*, was released late in 1943, clearly Chaney's peak year as a box-office attraction. He had already played Universal's four classic monsters (the Wolf Man, the Frankenstein Monster, the Mummy, and Dracula) and was now having a series built around him. Originally he was to co-star with Gale Sondergaard, but the actress was axed a few days before shooting began. Her role was revamped and played by Patricia Morison. The film was completed in just twenty days, and was directed by veteran Reginald LeBorg, who clearly showed talent in such Universal films as *The Mummy's Ghost* (1944), though he could not rise above the script restrictions in what is arguably the lowest ebb of Universal horror, *Jungle Woman* (1944).

Calling Dr. Death begins well, with neurologist Dr. Mark Steele (Chaney) hypnotizing a young girl via the rhythmic ticking of a metronome. Through a series of whispered voice-overs we soon learn that Steele's own personal life is a failure. These voice-overs have been repeatedly criticized over the years, but Don G. Smith makes a convincing argument that they embody the concept of the mind as the true inner sanctum, allowing Chaney to provide exposition without resorting to lengthy drawn-out sequences.

When Steele goes home, he finds that his wife Maria (Ramsay Ames) has gone out with another man. Ramsay Ames' inadequate performance in this role is surely the worst in this film. Nor is Chaney's performance helped by the insipid dialogue as they

***Calling Dr. Death* was released late in 1943, clearly Chaney's peak year as a box-office attraction.**

argue: "You must listen to reason," Steele tells his wife, adding, "We can't go on like this." An effective scene follows, with the doctor advancing on his sleeping wife, apparently intent on strangling her until he is interrupted by the screech of a cockatoo (echoes of *Citizen Kane* and *Mad Love*). The inevitable does happen: Maria is found murdered. Steele is informed of this by two detectives, one of whom is played by Rex Lease, the star of *The Monster Walks* (1932), now reduced to doing bit parts. When Steele arrives at the lodge to view his wife's body, we see the scene unfold through his eyes via an effective use of first person camera technique, a device soon to be overused by Robert Montgomery in *The Lady in the Lake* (1946). This technique was not quite so innovative as Reginald LeBorg has claimed: Edgar G. Ulmer had used it in *The Black Cat* back in 1934. Still, it is undeniably effective in this sequence.

Maria has had her skull crushed by a blunt instrument, her face disfigured by acid. Steele is naturally suspected of the crime by the ubiquitous Inspector Gregg (J. Carrol Naish). Just as Steele comes to believe that he is responsible, the police arrest Robert Duval (David Bruce), Maria's lover. There is an interesting, almost Hitchcockian "transference of guilt" between Steele and Duval, with the doctor determined to help the imprisoned man. Steele is visited by Mrs. Duval (Fay Helm). A familiar actress from *The Wolf Man* and *Night Monster*, Fay Helm gives her customary effective performance. From here on the film reverts to a fairly standard, plot-driven melodrama. Duval is convicted of the murder and sentenced to death. Insp. Gregg continues to taunt Steele and urges him to confess to the crime. Then the doctor's office is mysteriously set ablaze. The finger of suspicion begins to point toward the apparently selfless Stella (Patricia Morison), Steele's devoted nurse, through the sheer paucity of other logical suspects.

On the night of Duval's execution Steele hypnotizes Stella, forcing her to relive the events of the night of the murder. Through a series of flashbacks, Stella sees herself nearly crushed by the walls of buildings that bend suddenly forward. We then see her crush Maria's head with a poker, and in a shockingly brutal scene for the forties, disfigure her face with acid. This sequence is discreetly photographed in shadow, but the implication is disturbingly realistic. Gregg turns up in time to save Duval, having overheard Stella's confession.

Calling Dr. Death is usually rated as the best of the *Inner Sanctums*, not surprising considering that *Strange Confession*, the other logical contender for that honor, was a lost film for forty years. Although packaged as part of the *Shock* television series in the late fifties, *Calling Dr. Death* makes no attempt to pass itself off as a horror film. It is, instead, a reasonably well plotted and competently acted mystery. It is clearly the best entry of the three directed by Reginald LeBorg. LeBorg was also at the helm of *Weird Woman* and *Dead Man's Eyes*, both made in 1944. The minor stylistic highlights he provides put the film a cut above most other *Inner Sanctums*.

Lon Chaney seems at home in the role of Mark Steele, making the physician's anguish believable throughout. Part of the problem with the later *Inner Sanctums* was that Chaney was required to play essentially the same character over and over, with inevitably diminishing returns. He is also spared the ignominy of playing a self-flagellating character, as he does in *Dead Man's Eyes*. Such a character becomes tiresome without being tragic. Here, Steele is sufficiently self-reliant to sustain audience identification throughout.

Patricia Morison, too, contributes a solid characterization as Stella Madden. Her obsessive devotion to Steele is continually hinted at, though her identity as the "mystery" killer would have been more effectively camouflaged with a few more suspects in evidence. There is an effective shock sequence in the flashback. Duval is shown walking the last mile, his outstretched arms held up by prison guards. He stumbles, falling out of the camera frame. When the guards raise the prisoner back into the frame, it is now Stella whom the guards are holding.

Morison had fond memories of the film, and of her co-star. As she recalled on A&E's *Biography* of Chaney, "It was a lovely experience... I remember when the film was over and we had a wrap, he came over and—it astonished me—he put his arm around me and said, 'Thank you so much, you know it was lovely working with you.' I was touched."

J. Carrol Naish has a congenial role as the ever-present Inspector Gregg. It is not a particularly showy part. If anything, it is that stock figure of mystery fiction, the persistent snoop who is forever rattling the nerves of the chief suspect. Television added a raincoat and a few endearing foibles and immortalized him as Columbo. The versatile Naish underplays it perfectly. There is a satisfying cat and mouse sequence following the destruction of Steele's office. Gregg attempts to prove Steele was in Spring Lake, where he placed a phone call to his office, upsetting a vial of acid, setting off the fire. When his ruse fails Gregg prepares to leave, then asks Steele for a light. Steele

Part of the problem with the later *Inner Sanctums* was that Chaney was required to play essentially the same character over and over, with inevitably diminishing returns.

produces a matchbook with the legend SPRING LAKE PHARMACY inscribed on the folder. "Mind if I keep these, doctor?" Gregg asks. To be sure, it is nothing revolutionary either in screenwriting or direction, but it is quietly effective, and Naish delivers the line with malevolent understatement.

Naish could be hammy or even saccharine on occasion. Henry Fonda remembered him as "one of those actors who loves to cry." He was usually excellent in his numerous horror parts. Fans remember him from *House of Frankenstein* (1944) with Chaney, but he was also good in *Dr. Renault's Secret* (1942) and *The Monster Maker* (1944). Oddly enough, he is exaggeratedly oily and overbearing in his other *Inner Sanctum*

On the night of Duval's execution Steele (Chaney, Jr.) hypnotizes Stella (Patricia Morison), forcing her to relive the events of the night of the murder.

appearance, *Strange Confession*, where he plays the villain. Naish sandwiched *Calling Dr. Death* between his Academy Award–nominated supporting roles in *Sahara* (1943) and *A Medal for Benny* (1944). He never won the Oscar, but he is better remembered than many of the stars he supported. Sadly, he wound up his career at the very bottom of the barrel, emoting (if it can be called that) with a dissipated Chaney in the execrable *Dracula vs. Frankenstein* (1971), notable for the immortal Zandor Vorkov's inimitable rendition of Dracula.

The other cast members, with the exception of Ramsay Ames, are adequate. David Bruce, fondly remembered as the star of *The Mad Ghoul*, is properly sympathetic as the wrongly accused Robert Duval, and Fay Helm is equally effective as his wife, despite her limited screen time. The only unfortunate casting flaw is Ramsay Ames, in her brief role as Maria Steele. Beautiful but sadly inadequate to the demands of the role, Ames was equally at sea in the otherwise above-average *The Mummy's Ghost* (1944), in which she appeared as the reincarnation of the Princess Ananka. Not surprisingly, Ames' acting career petered out after the forties, though she was seen in supporting roles in such later films as *Alexander the Great* (1956) and *The Running Man* (1963).

Over the years, *Calling Dr. Death* has accrued generally favorable reviews. *Castle of Frankenstein* tersely considered it "competently played and neatly plotted." Don G. Smith noted that "those who blindly see Chaney's Dr. Steele as a miscast Lennie fail to appreciate the actor's fine performance. Again, director LeBorg gets Chaney's best acting, which is enough to lift *Calling Dr. Death* at least to the upper levels of average, if not a little higher." The most interesting commentary comes from the normally hypercritical Donald C. Willis in his *Horror and Science Fiction Films II*: "The first entry in Universal's *Inner Sanctum* series plays like a cross between a typical Universal 'B' shocker and an experimental film: there are elaborate 'subjective' tracking shots, odd camera angles, and whole sequences featuring a 'subjective' soundtrack. And the climax is a (would-be) tour-de-force 'flashback' via hypnosis, including one segment in which the hypnotizer is hypnotized—a trance within a trance (it does get involved). But the story, dialogue (interior and exterior) and acting are poor, and even J. Carrol Naish's Inspector Columbo–like relationship with the suspect Lon Chaney, Jr. lacks something (like Peter Falk's sense of humor)."

All the foregoing is not meant to imply that *Calling Dr. Death* is an unsung classic, or the best mystery that Universal was capable of producing. It pales in comparison with the better Universal films made that year: *Frankenstein Meets the Wolf Man*, *Flesh and Fantasy*, and *Son of Dracula*. But it is one of the better *Inner Sanctum*s, undeserving of the critical scorn usually heaped upon it, and entitled to more respect than many horror aficionados and even "Universalists" accord it.

CREDITS: Director: Reginald LeBorg; Associate Producer: Ben Pivar; Original Screenplay: Edward Dein; Director of Photography: Virgil Miller; Special Photography: John P. Fulton; Editor: Norman A. Cerf; Art Directors: John B. Goodman and Ralph M. DeLacy; Set Decorators: Russell A. Gausman and Andrew J. Gilmore; Musical Director: Paul Sawtell; Sound Director: Bernard B. Brown; Gowns: Vera West

CAST: Lon Chaney (Dr. Mark Steele); Patricia Morison (Stella Madden); J. Carrol Naish (Inspector Gregg); Ramsay Ames (Maria Steele); David Bruce (Robert Duval); Fay Helm (Mrs. Duval); Holmes Herbert (Bryant); Alec Craig (Bill); Mary Hale (Marion); Fred Gierman (Father); Lisa Golm (Mother); George Elderedge (District Attorney); Charles Wagenheimer (Coroner); John Elliot (Priest); David Hoffman (Inner Sanctum); Norman Rainey (Governor); Rex Lease and Paul Philips (Detectives); Frank Marlowe (Newspaper Reporter)

FRANKENSTEIN
meets
THE WOLF MAN
starring
ILONA MASSEY
PATRIC KNOWLES
with
BELA LUGOSI
LIONEL ATWILL
MARIA OUSPENSKAYA
and
LON CHANEY
A UNIVERSAL PICTURE
Directed by ROY WILLIAM NEILL
Produced by GEORGE WAGGNER

FRANKENSTEIN MEETS THE WOLF MAN (1943)

by David H. Smith

"That darksome cave they enter, where they find
That cursed man, low sitting on the ground,
Musing full sadly in his sullen mind."
—Edmund Spenser, *The Faerie Queen*, xxxv

If ever Dickens' immortal opening lines to *A Tale of Two Cities* were embodied by a horror film actor, it would be Lon Chaney, Jr. in 1942. In retrospect, "It was the best of times, it was the worst of times," probably summed up Chaney's opinion of his personal life and professional career. In between his commercial and critical triumphs as the lead in *Man Made Monster* (1940) and *The Wolf Man* (1941), Chaney found himself bound by his Universal contract to appear in supporting parts in musical comedies (*Too Many Blondes*) and B Westerns (*Badlands of Dakota*) in between. With his star turns in the studio's stream of horror films, it probably dispirited him to bide his time playing character roles betwixt leads.

Success was undeniably sweet in his private life, though. With his new success came wealth, and Chaney was able to afford an enormous ranch of over 1,000 acres in California's El Dorado County. Only a few years after having their car and furniture repossessed, he and second wife Patsy (as well as sons Ron and Lon) were comfortably set. The years of hand-to-mouth living were behind them.

Not so for Universal screen-writer Curt Siodmak (b. 1902). After coming to America in 1937 from his native Germany, Siodmak produced a series of imaginative movie scripts that, while putting food on his and wife Henrietta's table, did little to place him in the upper echelons of the industry. With their heady mix of Gothic horror and science fiction, most of the subtlety of Siodmak's scripts was undone by studios' penny-pinching or by technicians' inadequacies. A screen-writer and already the author of 18 novels in Germany before emigrating, Siodmak would gain his greatest fame in literary circles for *Donovan's Brain*, published in 1943, and in the realm of cinema for his invention of Chaney's greatest role, the Wolf Man.

Sitting with Universal contract stars Yvonne De Carlo and Mary MacDonald one day at the studio commissary, Siodmak facetiously suggested to passerby producer George Waggner (1894-1984) a Wolf Man sequel wherein the werewolf met up with Frankenstein's Monster. To the writer's surprise, Waggner gave him the assignment some time later. Siodmak was forced to remove his Teutonic tongue from his cheek and seriously set about a union of Universal's two most famous screen monsters, the first such meeting in the studio's catena of horror films.

It is lamentable that, since the film's release in the spring of 1943, so much harsh criticism has been conferred on *Frankenstein Meets The Wolf Man.* True, the film suffers in its continuity, not only for what was excised from the final cut but, after such truncation, what remained of the performance of the actor who started the whole ball rolling in the thirties.

Bela Lugosi (1882-1956) was quite literally starved into the role of Frankenstein's derelict creation now, having dismissed it the decade before as beneath him. His star then on the rise with the success of *Dracula* (1931), the Hungarian-born actor gladly stepped out of the cement mason's boots and aside for an unknown named Boris Karloff (1887-1969), who was only too ready to submit to the tortures of make-up artist Jack P. Pierce (1889-1968) and four- to six-hour regimens of mortician's wax and collodion-soaked cotton.

In the years since, Lugosi's temperament and improficiency with the English language had inevitably caused that Universal rising star to collapse in on itself to become a Monogram black hole. Arguably, Lugosi had turned in the finest performances of his career as the broken-necked nursemaid Ygor in the two preceding films in the Frankenstein series. The second appearance of the character, *The Ghost of Frankenstein* (1942), had concluded with his brain (and apparently his larynx) transplanted into the Monster's skull, effectively killing off Karloff's misunderstood "child" in favor of a scarred megalomaniac. With a *deus ex machina* blood typing mismatch blinding this refurbished monstrosity, it was thematically (though not physically) logical for Lugosi to assume the role at this point. And it was a financial necessity at this point in his life as well; with a heavy heart, the vainglorious one-time headliner saw himself almost inconspicuous in screen billing, his character and name billed beneath even the village Burgermeister's.

But *Frankenstein Meets The Wolf Man*, for all of Siodmak's inventiveness, emerges as more a sequel to his earlier triumph *The Wolf Man* than *The Ghost of Frankenstein.* While werewolf Larry Talbot's seeking the scientific notes of the monster-maker in his quest for "real" death makes for a clever continuation of his saga, the interpolation of the Frankenstein Monster into the proceedings—when already half the motion picture has run its course—is clumsily done. In fact, except for the memorable skirmish at the end (even with its stunt man substitutions, the Monster's exposed underclothes, and machinery sent flying via obvious guywires), the story might have worked better had the Wolf Man stood on his own two lupine paws for a second film before Universal's matchmaking began pairing him off like some wallflower with others in its coterie of monsters.

Whatever its defects and deficiencies, however, *Frankenstein Meets The Wolf Man* represents Chaney's finest hour with Universal. In no other film for the studio would he fare as well, and be given such opportunities to display his range. As the tragic werewolf, the burly actor became the standard for all succeeding screen lycanthropes; other filmmakers seemed intent on copying that success by casting similarly built actors (i.e., Oliver Reed, Paul Naschy, and Earl Owensby) in similarly hirsute parts in the years and decades to come.

But Chaney yearned for the leading man status enjoyed by fellow Universal contractees Dick Foran, Donald O'Connor, Johnny Mack Brown, Allan Jones, and Robert Paige. No matter they could be suave, sing and dance, ride bucking broncos, or were even better looking. With the studio dropping the "Junior" from all his films' billing,

Lon Chaney, Jr. and Illona Massey take a break on the set.

Chaney wanted to be sure his parts cast no unfavorable shadows on his revered father's name. But, with nearly a decade behind him starving for his principles in bits and in crowd scenes, what little ego Chaney seemed to have was kept in check.

The part of the Wolf Man gave Chaney a chance to really shine as an actor, at least in this and in the werewolf's eponymous debut. As Lawrence Stewart Talbot, he got to romance the leading ladies, stand his own against the "villains," throw a punch or two, and—despite the grueling five hours of frightful make-up—still come across as the character most beloved by the audience. In *Frankenstein Meets The Wolf Man*, it all came together for the 36-year-old actor, and no amount of post-production pruning could undo the laurels on his crowning achievement.

Even the most cursory synopsis of *Frankenstein Meets The Wolf Man* gives ample substantiation of Chaney's talent. From his first conscious scene in the hospital in Cardiff, Chaney is on top of his game. Dr. Mannering (Patric Knowles) and Inspector Owen (Dennis Hoey) question Talbot, recovering at a phenomenal rate from the skull fracture given to him at the conclusion of *The Wolf Man*. Talbot innocently gives the two men his real name, ignorant of his four years of interment miles away in his native Llanwelly.

But even here Chaney invests the character with something more than a simple reading of lines. He is somewhat amnesiac, and plainly worried about what could have happened to him to leave him in such a state. Chaney's wordless entreaty to the doctor as the medico leaves his bedside speaks volumes.

Chaney, Jr., Patric Knowles, and Illona Massey seek a cure for Talbot's disease.

Later, confronted with the facts of Larry Talbot's accidental death and accused of being an impostor, Chaney, with only a grimace and furrowed brow, embodies his character's confusion and helplessness. When the full moon shines through the ward window (conveniently allowed by cafe curtains), Talbot at once comes to the realization of why he is there, what he becomes, and what is about to happen. Here, it is first detailed it takes a full moon to affect the change, whereas in the prequel an autumn moon would suffice.

After metamorphosing from man to beast—another screen first, *The Wolf Man* showed only the reverse—Talbot apparently dresses himself and murders a strolling bobby, returning to his hospital bed in the morning. He changes back into his pajamas and collapses tangled in the sheets. Though his memory of it is dim, Talbot confesses his crime to Mannering and Owen, displays the pentagonal Mark of the Beast, all the while maintaining he is the man proclaimed dead years before. When orderlies are summoned to calm him, Chaney really throws himself into the scene, engaging in a free-for-all with the attendants. Evidence of Chaney's enthusiasm for the rough and tumble stuff comes as his pajamas part briefly to reveal his belly in the struggle to straitjacket him, with everyone concerned really going at it. Similar expressions of exertion showed up in *The Ghost of Frankenstein* when Chaney's Frankenstein Monster grappled with courtroom bailiffs.

Mannering curtly dismisses Talbot as just "a man who imagines himself to be a wolf." The normatively gruff Owen pities Talbot now, so the two journey to Llanwelly to ferret out some clues to the patient's identity. They find the corpse of one of the graverobbers who first exhumed Talbot, then, as they confabulate back at the Welsh

It is a bedraggled and disheveled Talbot who awakens in the morning and sets about freeing the Frankenstein Monster from his frozen tomb.

police station, Mannering is notified his patient back in Cardiff has escaped his restraints by chewing through them.

Talbot reunites with Maleva (Maria Ouspenskaya), the reluctant gypsy woman who counseled him through his first episodes. She decides it would be best for them to seek out "a great doctor whom could help others no one else could cure" she has heard about in her travels with the gypsy caravan.

The hapless Talbot and Maleva wagon across Europe, arriving in Vasaria only to be met with disappointment and suspicious stares. This is the only scene in *Frankenstein Meets The Wolf Man* Chaney plays poorly, reining in the horse with a bilious "Whoa" and lumbering into the local inn like some bumpkin just off the turnip truck—or, more likely, like Lennie traipsing after George. Particularly galling is Chaney's wide-eyed regard for the village girl (Martha MacVicar) lighting the chandelier—at any second you expect him to burble something along the lines of "Gawrsh, whut a purty gal!" to Maleva.

Told the man they seek is dead and to leave with good riddance, Maleva and Talbot depart the inn. Soon after, the full moon rises and he transforms again, scampering off to murder (offscreen) the girl from the inn. The enraged villagers rally behind the rabble-rousing Vazec (Rex Evans) and track the Wolf Man. At the ruins of the Frankenstein estate, the metamorphosed Talbot falls through the wreckage into a glacial cellar. He scrambles about in the ice and snow, frustrated at his entrapment, then collapses.

With so much attention paid to Lugosi's inadequacies as the Monster (through no fault of his own), Chaney's performance usually gets short shrift.

It is a bedraggled and disheveled Talbot who awakens in the morning and, glimpsing the scarred features behind the hoarfrost of the nearby glacier, sets about freeing the Frankenstein Monster from his frozen tomb. Talbot reasons that if the doctor's research lead to creating life from the dead, then reversing the process should be a cinch. When the blind Monster is unable to help him find Frankenstein's records in the charred remains of the lab, Talbot schemes to contact the late doctor's beautiful daughter Elsa for help.

After tricking the young baroness (Ilona Massey) into returning to Vasaria under the pretense of wanting to buy her father's estate, another side of Chaney comes to the fore. He arrives at the mayor's (Lionel Atwill) office clean and groomed (the script says he is wearing one of Dr. Frankenstein's suits). He is somewhat taken aback by the woman's beauty, and asks to be left alone with her to hash out the details.

No doubt this is the sort of scene Chaney prayed for, and he was up to the task. With some judicious soft-focus photography smoothing his features, he is alternately charming and shy, and when he blurts out his ruse it is quite understandable why Elsa doesn't stalk out in a huff. Talbot's American sincerity and boyish enthusiasm overwhelm the morbidity of his ambition; Elsa, while sympathetic, believes her father's and grandfather's journals were irretrievably lost in the conflagration.

That evening at an outdoor festival, Talbot joins the baroness at her invitation, but cannot bring himself to share his date's enthusiasm. When a strolling minstrel (Russian musical comedy star Adia Kuznetzoff) serenades them, wishing them eternal life, Talbot explodes in rage. (As revealed in *The Psychotronic Encyclopedia of Film*, this was author Michael Weldon's favorite part.) He is at the end of his rope. Unable to exorcise the curse, the guilt of his actions weighing him down,, denied even the peace of the grave, Talbot starts to vent his anger on the naive singer.

Talbot quickly regains his composure with the sudden entrance of Dr. Mannering at the *fete champetre*. Tracking him across Europe, Mannering believes his former patient to be "insane at times," certainly not some supernatural were-creature. "I only want to die," Talbot insists. Before the discussion can continue, the Monster lumbers down from the ruins and breaks up the party, and he and Talbot beat a hasty retreat back to the Frankenstein estate.

Mannering allies himself with Elsa and Maleva and goes to the hiding place the next day. Unintimidated by the Monster's baleful roar, he examines the lab equipment strewn about and decides it can be restored. Coupled with Frankenstein's research on draining energy from living matter (appropriated by author Jeremy Kay for an entry in *The Secret Laboratory Journals of Dr. Victor Frankenstein*), Mannering hopes he can bring to an end both Talbot's suffering and the Monster's threat.

However, as horror movie scientists are wont to do, Mannering reneges on his promise to drain the Monster's life-force, eager to instead see Frankenstein's creation at full strength. Exchanging a couple of electrical leads with Talbot and revving up the generators, Mannering reenergizes the Monster, who breaks free from his operating table straps and scoops up the swooning Elsa and starts to carry her off (his legs swinging awkwardly to avoid being tangled in her bathrobe).

The full moon rises—somewhat fortuitously as it happens—and the Wolf Man tears loose from his restraints. He pounces upon the Monster (dumping poor Elsa to the flagstones) and the ensuing melee continues until Mannering leads Elsa to safety before the nearby dam is dynamited and both creatures are swept away in the deluge. And of poor Maleva, well, better not to wonder about those pesky loose ends too much.

With so much attention paid to Lugosi's inadequacies as the Monster (through no fault of his own), Chaney's performance usually gets short shrift. His efforts have received their due in several publications, however, and a selection of those recognize their worth. Bruce Dettmann and Michael Bedford, in *The Horror Factory*, noted Chaney stood out in *Frankenstein Meets The Wolf Man*, and, although he would play Talbot again and again, "never again would his portrayal reflect the desperation, mental imbalance, and anguished suffering as effectively as in this film."

Sam Gafford remarked in the second issue of *Chiller Theatre* that "this would be the last time that Talbot was given a good story." Similar sentiments about *Frankenstein Meets The Wolf Man* were shared by Richard Davis in *The Encyclopedia of Horror*, wherein "Chaney did well" but further sequels "became increasingly shoddy, though he still managed to make his Talbot a pitiable figure."

"Walt.," in a February 1943 issue of *Variety*, saw only "routine performances, with little opportunity to give out in picture of this type." The concurrent *Showmen's Trade Review*, however, made mention of "the cast turning in swell performances" with Chaney "especially good."

Gregory William Mank paid tribute to Chaney's contribution in *It's Alive!: The Classic Cinema Saga of Frankenstein*, writing it was he who carried *Frankenstein Meets The Wolf Man*. Further, "[Chaney's] performance is the best of his Universal sojourns,

Much as Chaney described the Wolf Man as a character, *Frankenstein Meets The Wolf Man* is the one motion picture whose success he pointed to as his "baby."

and he creates and sustains a level of pathos that conveys the tragedy, and not just the melodrama, of the lycanthropic Talbot."

Suspiciously like-minded *Vintage Monster Movies* author Robert Marrero reiterated that "Chaney carries the film from start to finish, delivering a performance of pathos that conveys the tragedy and melodrama of the character."

In *Heroes of the Horrors*, Calvin Thomas Beck stated Chaney "gives one of his best performances; his natural feeling for pathos was very impressive and the film's highlight." The uncredited review in *The Dark Side* #56 allowed "Chaney is pretty good," while Michael Brunas, John Brunas, and Tom Weaver agreed with one another that Chaney's portrayal "contributed in large part to the success and popularity of *Frankenstein Meets The Wolf Man*" in *Universal Horrors: The Studio's Classic Films, 1931-1946*. They continued, "Chaney gives a pent-up performance that is as good or (arguably) better than the one he gave in *The Wolf Man*.... [he] now seems more seasoned, more at ease with the character." The authors concluded "Chaney dominates the film, forlorn but no longer whiny, desperate but no longer panic-stricken, [bringing] new dimensions to the melancholy [part] and evokes yet-greater sympathy."

After such high praise, the old business adage "The higher you climb, the farther you fall" works for other reviews of Chaney's performance in *Frankenstein Meets The Wolf Man*. Ken Hanke didn't care for the actor's efforts so much as the characterization: "Chaney isn't bad in the role, but the role itself borders on the impossible," he wrote in *A Critical Guide To Horror Film Series*. "If ever a more self-pitying, moronic, and morose character graced the screen, it would be hard to imagine."

Great Horror Movies' Favius Friedman had little regard for the actor in *Frankenstein Meets The Wolf Man*, sniveling "poor Lon Chaney, Jr. could do very little werewolfing under the heavy load of make-up he wore," whatever that means. Jesse Obstbaum, in the fourth issue of *Chiller Theatre*, hated the movie in toto ("a major stinker!"), branding Chaney "an annoying nervous wreck."

Similarly opinionated, *Horrors!* author Drake Douglas said, "Little acting was needed for this role, which was chiefly a matter of looking with agonized eyes at the full moon." Thomas G. Aylesworth was in agreement in his *Monsters From The Movies*, saying with distressing sameness, "With all that make-up on, about the only acting that he was permitted to do was stare agonizingly up at the full moon."

Michael Mallory, touting what remained of Lugosi's earnest performance in the eighth issue of *Scarlet Street*, turned the tables and disparaged Chaney's "somewhat stilted way of speaking," wrestling as he had to with Siodmak's "purple dialogue" with his "normally thick and dull" voice. Contrary to Mallory's critique, the most lugubrious line from Siodmak's typewriter was bestowed on villager Rudi, played by Dwight Frye (1899-1943), who managed "Much as I'd like to kill the Monster I'd hate to crawl around through those dark catacombs of Frankenstein's castle in the black of the night" in one gulp of air. Chaney suffered from writers' pretension in the next year's *House of Frankenstein* (perhaps in a holdover from Siodmak's original story), when Larry Talbot, a regular American Joe, had to recite, "Who are you? Why have you freed me from the ice that imprisoned the beast that lived within me?"

Siodmak's script, even in its original form, fails some of the other characters as well. When confronted by the living, breathing Monster of her grandfather's invention—her own father's murderer—Elsa barely gives him a sideways glance as she frets over Mannering's scientific intentions. By an interesting and probably unintentional coincidence, the beauty mark on the cheek of top-billed Ilona Massey (1912-1974) (once dubbed by MGM as "The Singing Garbo," her Hungarian accent was forgiven, despite her assumption of a role originated by Afrikaner Evelyn Ankers) matched perfectly the one Jack Pierce gave the inheritors of Karloff's prototypical make-up to compare with his sunken cheek. Never before had the family resemblance between genetic and lab-created bearers of the Frankenstein family name been so pronounced.

Besides Massey, Chaney received capable support by everyone in the cast. Patric Knowles (1911-1995), that most handsome of the Universal loony medical corps., scarcely has time to realize he has not one but two wonders of science on his hands: the genuine Frankenstein's Monster and a verifiable shape-changing werewolf. The gleam in his eyes as he galvanizes the Monster (and Talbot too?) is not so much the glint of madness but the fires of awe.

Dennis Hoey (1893-1960), nowadays best remembered as the affable but dull-witted Inspector Lestrade in six of the Sherlock Holmes mysteries filmed on sound stages next door, naturally does well as a similarly skeptical police inspector. Though not sharing any scenes, Maria Ouspenskaya (1876-1949) wrapped herself in the babushka of Maleva for the second and last time, at first visibly terrified by Talbot's unexpected reappearance but grimly resigned to helping the man find the lasting peace denied him. Scrutinizers of *Frankenstein Meets The Wolf Man* wondered what becomes of the "old

Frankenstein Meets The Wolf Man **stands as a testimonial to Chaney's likability as a person and his capability as an actor.**

gypsy woman" at the finale, postulating theories and freeze framing their videos for a glimpse of her as the floodwaters inundate the castle, all to no avail. Maleva was simply lost in the hubbub. James Abery, reflecting on the movie in *Shivers* #40, made note of the chemistry between Ouspenskaya and Chaney, saying she "encourages a delicacy in his delivery that the actor seems otherwise afraid of."

Lionel Atwill (1885-1946), his appetite for scenery no doubt satisfied by his elegant chewing of it as the handicapped police inspector in *Son of Frankenstein* (1939) and as Ygor's devious surgical collaborator in *The Ghost of Frankenstein*, played here the voice of reason as the town mayor. In fact, there seem to be no lawmen in Vasaria at all. Apparently, Elsa's short-lived (and apparently unconsummated) exile with the district attorney from the previous Frankenstein film seems to have been all that was needed for the dissolution of the police force and an "every man for himself" kind of anarchy to hold sway.

The mayor's (and hence Talbot's, the Monster's, Mannering's, Elsa's, and especially poor old Maleva's) chief nemesis is portly innkeeper Vazec. In the part, actor Rex Evans (1903-1969) is an imposing, braggadocian figure, his eyes darting like some silent-film villain as he eavesdrops on secret conversations, his blustering cries for vigilante justice stoking the fires of bravado in the townspeople. A star in London vaudeville and on Broadway, Evans otherwise made a Hollywood career earning good notices in character parts, particularly in *Camille* (1936), *A Star Is Born* (1937), and, most famously, as the stately butler in *The Philadelphia Story* (1940). He retired from acting to run an art gallery on Hollywood's famous La Cienega Boulevard.

Director Roy William Neill (1886-1946), born Roland de Gostrie on a ship off Ireland, spent his career making serious and sometimes somber B movies. Reportedly a humorless man, he never made a color film in his lifetime, instead confining his talents to fast-moving movies with good effects and atmospheric set designs. He would ultimately direct nine of the entries in the series of Sherlock Holmes films mentioned earlier, only dipping his toes in full-blown Gothic horror with this, *The Black Room* (1935), and *Dr. Syn* (1937). He was slated to direct *The Lady Vanishes* before Alfred Hitchcock took over the project.

But, inevitably, one must come to the major failing of *Frankenstein Meets The Wolf Man*—Bela Lugosi, and all his spastic gestures and jerky movements. Directed to do so, looking down his patrician nose, lagging behind whoever was plowing through the lab wreckage or spilling stacks of books, the dollops of make-up putty separating his own skin with the forehead appliance glaringly obvious, the poor man looks ridiculous.

Had the powers-that-were at Universal chosen to overdub the Monster's dialogue rather than eliminate the thick Slavic accent they so detested by erasing it entirely, there would be far fewer critics of the film then and today. Even in its original form, Siodmak's script subtracted the necessary Ygor factor from the equation, as though whosever gray matter was inserted into the squared skull lost its individuality and became, simply, "The Monster." This would prove to be a problem later on in *House of Frankenstein*, as Siodmak's story would further the confusion of transplanted brains and personalities with bodies, as the evil scientist played a game of "hot potato" with the cerebellums of his betrayers.

Much as Chaney described the Wolf Man as a character, *Frankenstein Meets The Wolf Man* is the one motion picture whose success he pointed to as his "baby." Afterward, Chaney would grow a pencil-thin mustache and fulfill his professional ambition: go on to star in the *Inner Sanctum* films, roles calling for him to enact the urbane scholar rather than the rough-and-tumble Everyman. He was sadly unsuited for the parts, however.

Frankenstein Meets The Wolf Man is a triumphant culmination of production, writing, acting, and directing skill; it stands as a testimonial to Chaney's likability as a person and, in spite of the critics damning him with faint praise, his capability as an actor.

CREDITS: Producer: George Waggner; Director: Roy William Neill; Original Screenplay: Curt Siodmak; Director of Photography: George Robinson; Art Director: John B. Goodman; Associate Art Director: Martin Obzina; Director of Sound: Bernard B. Brown; Technician: William Fox; Set Decorator: Russell A. Gausman; Associate: Edward R. Robinson; Film Editor: Edward Curtiss; Gowns: Vera West; Musical Director: Hans J. Salter; Make-up Artist: Jack P. Pierce; Assistant Director: Melville Shyer; Special Photographic Effects: John P. Fulton; copyright 1942 by Universal Pictures Company, Inc.; released March 5, 1943 with a running time of 72 minutes

CAST: Lon Chaney (Lawrence Talbot/The Wolf Man); Ilona Massey (Baroness Elsa Frankenstein); Patric Knowles (Dr. Frank Mannering); Lionel Atwill (Mayor); Bela Lugosi (The Frankenstein Monster); Maria Ouspenskaya (Maleva); Dennis Hoey (Police Inspector Owen); Don Barclay (Franzec); Rex Evans (Vazec); Dwight Frye (Rudi); Harry Stubbs (Guno); Beatrice Roberts (Varja); Adia Kuznetzoff (Singer); Torben Meyer (Erno); Doris Lloyd (Nurse); Jeff Corey (Gravedigger); David Clyde (Police Sergeant); Tom Stevenson (Grave Robber); Cyril Delevanti (Second Grave Robber); Martha MacVicar (Margareta); Charles Irwin (Constable); Eddie Parker and Gil Perkins (stunts)

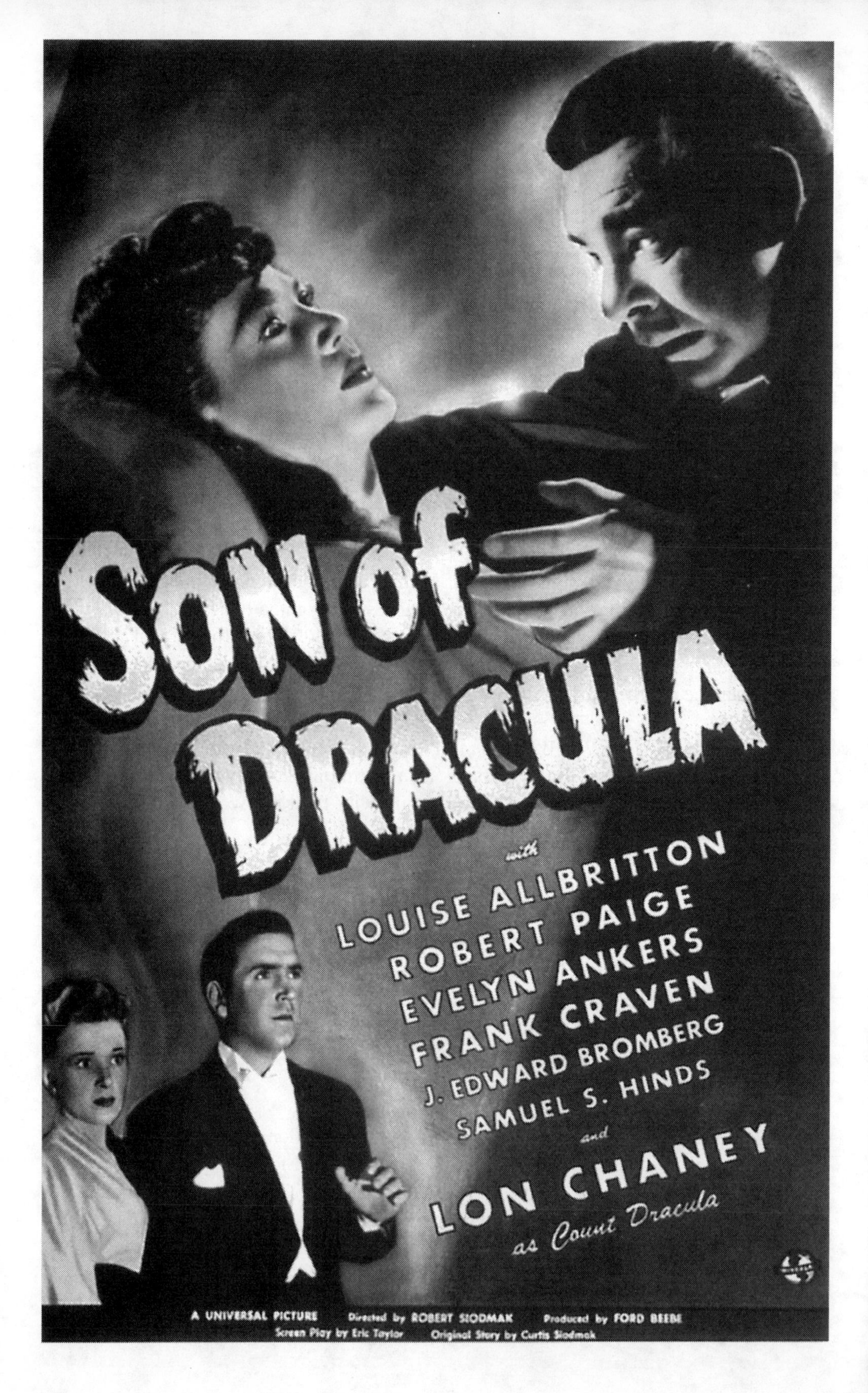
SON of DRACULA
with
LOUISE ALLBRITTON
ROBERT PAIGE
EVELYN ANKERS
FRANK CRAVEN
J. EDWARD BROMBERG
SAMUEL S. HINDS
and
LON CHANEY
as Count Dracula
A UNIVERSAL PICTURE
Directed by ROBERT SIODMAK
Produced by FORD BEEBE
Screen Play by Eric Taylor
Original Story by Curtis Siodmak

SON OF DRACULA (1943)

by Bruce Dettman

Of late, thanks primarily to the excessive (and seemingly ongoing) mythological revisionism of Anne Rice and her legion of sycophantic followers, vampires have not only earned a certain unfounded respectability, but in some curious quarters are now considered the ultimate personification of romanticism. While this image is not a totally new one (John Polidori's 1819 tale *The Vampire*, ostensibly based on the physician's bullying mentor Lord Byron, got the ball rolling by placing his creation, Lord Ruthven, in a highly proper setting and giving him the manners and trappings of a gentleman, an image which may or may not have influenced Bram Stoker when he created Count Dracula some years later), things have currently gone noticeably overboard. The latest crop of vampires, portrayed on the screen by a homogeneous gaggle of pretty boy Hollywood types, seems to approach their need for the red stuff more as yuppies in search of an acceptable merlot than as spawn of the devil out to satisfy an insatiable thirst. Vampires, folks, have become too damn civilized! Sure, to be fair, Stoker's Dracula did practice certain niceties of civilization (apparently including the household chores of bed making and cooking), but he also had hair in the palms of his hands, breath that would melt an iceberg, and the humanity of a rabid pit bull.

A kind of nostalgic yearning on the part of hardcore vampire purists for the more classic bloodsuckers of yesterday has perhaps been responsible, although not entirely, for a serious reappraisal of Lon Chaney, Jr.'s interpretation of Dracula (or his descendent—Eric Taylor's script is a bit unclear on this point and has caused much debate over the years) in Universal Pictures' 1943 production *Son of Dracula.* Miscasting at the Universal horror factory has always been a serious issue with fans, and on the list of cinematic flubs Chaney, Jr.'s tour of duty as the Count has invariably been lumped in with the likes of Henry Hull (*The Werewolf of London*), Gloria Holden (*Dracula's Daughter*), and Bela Lugosi (*Frankenstein Meets The Wolf Man*) as a candidate for most unfortunate and ill-advised performances. The prevailing attitude toward Chaney (one admittedly shared by this author in his younger days) was that with Karloff and Lugosi more or less removed from the Universal scene, the studio, wishing to exploit the moniker they had foisted on him and most pleased by his success as Lawrence Talbot in *The Wolf Man* (1941), simply tossed the younger Chaney into as many horror ventures as possible. Placed in the unenviable role of following up Boris Karloff as the Monster in *The Ghost of Frankenstein* (1942), he was mute, bestial, single-directed, and only marginally acceptable. As Kharis the Mummy (reportedly his least favorite role) he was so invisible that over the years there have been numerous claims, all unfounded, that he was rarely even beneath the bandages (anyone familiar with certain of Chaney's exaggerated gestures and expressions can nonetheless often spot them in the movements of the snail-like Egyptian). The harshest criticism, however, came from his one-shot performance as Transylvania's favorite son. His critics were quick to point out that not only was he too well fed and stocky for the part of a five-hundred-year-old vampire (is there some rule that says a vampire must be skinny?), but that he failed to bring so much as a hint of old world mystery to the part, that he was stiff and awkward and not at all convincing. There were grudging concessions that he tried his best but little else. Then slowly over the years something began to happen. Fans started to take a second and third look at the film and to appreciate much of what they were seeing. Although a good deal of early complaints were undeniably valid—his lack of continental bearing, his visible uncomfortableness projecting that remote and mysterious aristocratic style so important to the character—Chaney nonetheless manages to provide a perfect transitional Count Dracula between the suave and baroque pretensions of Lugosi and the bestial fanged satyrism of Christopher Lee, lending a strength of will and uncompromising physical power to the role heretofore unseen. John Carradine, who would follow Chaney with his two performances of the vampire in Universal's *House of Frankenstein* (1944) and *House of Dracula* (1945), was, as has been stated over and over again, physically closer to Stoker's literary conception of the character, but the actor comes off about as menacing as a tipsy drawing room Lothario. If nothing else, Chaney was a Dracula definitely worthy of reckoning with.

A certain Count Alucard is expected to arrive at Dark Oaks, a Southern plantation, as a guest of Kay Caldwell (Louise Allbritton), a woman long entrenched in the supernatural, whom he met recently in Europe. Meeting him at the train station is Frank Stanley (Robert Paige), Kay's fiancé, and a family friend Dr. Brewster (Frank Craven). Alucard is seemingly not aboard the scheduled train although his baggage, consisting of a few trunks, has arrived. Saying nothing about it, Dr. Brewster notes that Alucard is Dracula spelled backwards, a fact he later reveals by phone to Professor Lazlo (J. Edward Bromberg), an authority on occult matters.

That evening at a party given at Dark Oaks in honor of the still absent nobleman, Kay's father is killed by Alucard although the death is attributed to heart failure. Alucard later shows up and his relationship with Kay, who has inherited Dark Oaks, is immediately the target of suspicion by Claire Caldwell (Evelyn Ankers), Brewster, and (particularly) a jealous Frank, despite Kay's insistence that there is no reason to worry.

Kay and Alucard secretly marry and pledge they will live together in a special union throughout eternity. Arriving on the scene, an enraged Frank threatens Alucard, but the Count knocks him down, and Frank retaliates by shooting at his rival. The bullets, however, pass harmlessly through Alucard and kill Kay who has been standing behind him. Out of his mind with what he has witnessed, Frank gives himself up to the police who are at first skeptical of his claims, particularly as Dr. Brewster testifies to having seen Kay after the supposed shooting incident, but change their minds and detain Frank once Kay's body is discovered in a crypt.

Professor Lazlo arrives in town and convinces Brewster of Alucard's vampiric credentials. Alucard materializes out of mist during their conversation and attacks the men, but Lazlo deflects his advances with a crucifix. The two men subsequently agree that Kay, because of her long interest in the supernatural and excessive fear of death, probably entered into the pact with Alucard of her own accord. They decide they must have her body cremated and then find and destroy the Count.

Transforming into a bat, Kay visits Frank in his cell and explains her plan, most importantly that she is not in love with Alucard but has only used him to gain immortality for herself which she then plans to share with Frank. To complete the scheme,

Chaney (with Louise Allbritton) manages to provide a perfect transitional Dracula, lending a strength of will and uncompromising physical power to the role heretofore unseen.

however, Frank must agree to destroy Alucard and possibly even Dr. Brewster and Claire as well.

Frank breaks jail and makes his way to Dark Oaks where he discovers Alucard's hidden coffin, which he burns. Caught in the act by the Count, Frank is overpowered and nearly strangled but the sun rises and turns the vampire into a skeleton. Frank makes his way to Dark Oaks only minutes before the authorities and cremates Kay.

As with its creation of the Mummy, Universal would take its sweet time coming up with a sequel to further showcase the Count. For many reasons this might seem a peculiar chain of events given the popular success of *Dracula* with Bela Lugosi back in

Alucard materializes out of mist and attacks, but Lazlo (J. Edward Bromberg) deflects his advances with a crucifix.

1931. Not only did that film enormously aid Universal's floundering box office receipts and usher in the first great era of sound horror films, but it gave a firm nod to the concept of legitimate supernaturalism in motion pictures since most such depictions during the silent period were revealed in the last reel to be either dreams or the product of hoaxes. Had *Dracula* been produced a few years later, after those seminal European directors, writers, and producers who put their decidedly quirky stamp on the first wave of Universal horror products were replaced by the quick buck factory output of the 1940s, the sequels would have come fast and furious. However, *Dracula* was a surprise hit, new and uncertain and many in the business were unclear about what exactly to do with this untested product, how to target it. Certainly the success of *Frankenstei*n later in the year as well as horror productions such as *Dr. Jekyll And Mr. Hyde*, *Mystery of The Wax Museum*, and *Island of Lost Souls* at other studios definitely cemented the genre, but by this time Lugosi, whose fortunes had so suddenly risen, was no longer the only kid on the horror block. Most importantly, Karloff had arrived. Still, *Dracula* would have a sequel, one first rumored to star the Hungarian but which in 1936 became *Dracula's Daughter* sans Bela (his image would be replaced by a brief shot of a waxen effigy almost immediately incinerated by his offspring in a funeral pyre). It would not be until the 1940s (with a new regime at Universal and a time-tested horror formula) that the era of the sequels truly got underway.

Chaney, Jr. was the ultimate, perhaps the only choice for the part, at least at this juncture of the Universal story and particularly when he had already made such an impression as Lawrence Talbot in *The Wolf Man* and replaced Karloff as the Monster in *The Ghost of Frankenstein.* Both films had made money and that was all that mattered. Aside from an occasional reunion film with the studio, both Karloff and Lugosi had left Universal behind and Chaney, Jr. would have to do.

With Dracula the next monster on the assembly line it was up to the studio to create a story and select a director. Writer Curt Siodmak, responsible for *The Wolf Man,* was hired to pen the script but ended up with only an original story credit, the screenplay assignment being turned over to Eric Taylor (*The Ghost of Frankenstein*, *The Black Cat, Phantom of the Opera*). The director, on his first Universal assignment, was Curt's older brother Robert, who wasted little time on the project before pink slipping his younger sibling. The famed rivalry between the two reportedly went on their entire lives, although they had worked together as early as 1929 on the ground-breaking German documentary *Menschen am Sonntag,* along with future Hollywood statesmen Billy Wilder, Edgar Ulmer, and Fred Zinnemann. Following an impressive stint working at UFA Studios where he made several memorable films, Robert, noting the darkening political situation in Germany, migrated first to Paris, where he directed the musical *La Crise Est Finie* (1934), and then to America. An uninspiring career at Paramount, Fox, and even Republic followed, but at Universal he finally was allowed some measure of artistic control. Such films as *Phantom Lady*, *Christmas Holiday,* and *Uncle Harry* would follow.

If for no other reason, the downbeat nature of *Son Of Dracula* makes it unique in Universal horror film annals. A leaden sort of gloominess presides throughout the proceedings and, given the content and character development, there is really no room for a happy ending as was usually the case in such films. This is refreshing.

The idea of setting the story in the isolated deep south, itself a harbinger of certain mythology and rural legends, was good thinking on the part of the writers, acting as an acceptable transition from the old to new worlds. Even if the central characters seemed more like New England aristocrats than cornbread gentry, the swamp locations with their dripping Spanish Moss, deep pockets of uncertain darkness, and vocal night life brought an evocative and most effective backdrop against which Dracula's machinations were set. The plantation Dark Oaks, although only glimpsed in part, also made for a gloomy, shadow infested and highly suspect locale, both sites benefiting from photographer George Robinson's smooth and shadow anointed camera work. As usual in Universal horror films, the exact time frame of the story is unclear (someone once sat down and computed that if one were to go by the script references, the events in the final Mummy film *The Mummy's Curse* wouldn't occur until after the year 2,000), although contemporary automobiles are glimpsed.

One of the most interesting aspects of the script is Kay's willingness to enter into a blood-swapping alliance with Dracula, not to share immortality with him as Dracula believes, but to actually perpetuate for eternity her relationship with Frank Stanley (although I can't say why). Unlike most other vampire films, not to mention traditional mythology, where the nosferatu's kiss robs the soul as well as the arteries (remember the effect on such ladies as Helen Chandler, Anne Gwynne, and Lenore Aubert in other Universal horror films featuring Dracula), in *Son Of Dracula,* becoming one of the undead seemingly has little effect upon Kay's very human motivations and earthly goals.

Chaney, Jr. was the ultimate, perhaps the only choice for the part.

Now I don't happen to buy this premise, but it certainly makes for a more complex and non-conventional storyline.

Certainly the film is not without its share of faults. Siodmak's slow and deliberate buildup and methodical pacing is somewhat compromised by scenes in the jailhouse with the rube sheriff and his underlings, all of whom would not be out of place in a Republic Western. These moments are jarring to say the least. The stereotypical depiction of the black workers is also a detriment but unfortunately pretty typical of the times. Minor quibblings would include Alucard/Dracula feeling the silly need to carry

Kay over the threshold after their nuptials and Dr. Brewster painting an iodine cross on a young victim's neck.

Although early writeups on the film stressed that the movie possessed several good moments, save when the lead is on the screen, Chaney actually enjoys numerous impressive scenes as Dracula (for the record I'm simply going to ignore this "Son" business just as I have my doubts that the furry albino wimp in *Son of Kong* was related to the great Kong), many opposite Frank Craven, and it is certainly to his credit that he fares so well against that fine and always steady character actor. Particularly memorable is the scene in Dark Oaks, just after Brewster has learned from Kay that she has married Alucard. Before he leaves, the Count steps into the darkened corridor with the doctor and warns him that visitors will no longer be tolerated at the estate without his permission. Chaney is controlled and polite but it is the very nature of this control, the icy unequivocalness which runs molten hot beneath it, which makes the conversation so disconcerting and hedged with a malevolent menace which is anything but hidden. My personal favorite moment, however, comes after a rather lengthy conversation between Brewster and Professor Lazlo on the subject of vampires (not only is Bromberg physically made up to look like Edward Van Sloan from the original *Dracula,* but like the old Dutchman, certainly enjoys hearing the sound of his own voice as well—must all vampire hunters pontificate?) when Dracula in a heavy mist suddenly oozes beneath the locked door and assumes corporal form. Upon hearing the conclusion of Lazlo's long-winded dissertation (actually acceptable, as screenwriter Taylor must have figured contemporary audiences, not steeped in vampire lore, as is the case today, needed a rehashing of the old legends), he mockingly compliments the academician: "You are very brilliant, aren't you, Doctor?" If a snake, watching a lizard vulnerably sunning itself on a hot rock, could talk, I think it would sound very much like Chaney in this scene.

Robert Paige (who unfortunately bears a certain disconcerting resemblance to Jim Nabors of *Gomer Pyle* fame) as Frank Stanley (he was a last minute replacement for actor Alan Curtis) couldn't possibly be any different than your run of the mill obligatory male lead in nearly all other horror pictures of the period. Once he has glimpsed Dracula's power he goes totally over the edge of reality and never returns. A somewhat unimaginative and hot-headed guy to begin with (during their first physical confrontation, once Dracula has easily brushed him aside with a quick choke and push, Frank wastes no time in blazing away at the unarmed nobleman with his pistol, even though at this point he hasn't a clue his adversary is a supernatural creature), he simply cannot believe the truth of what he has seen. For the remainder of the film he is a broken, inarticulate shell of his former self, a nice change of pace from the conventional dunderheaded and usually lukewarm heroics of such Universal leading men as David Manners, Lester Matthews, and Robert Lowery. Paige, who began his film career in short subjects under the name David Carlyle and later moved from Columbia to Paramount before settling at Universal, was most often cast in light-hearted comedy and musical engagements such as *Hellzapoppin* and *Can't Help Singing*. He would eventually retire from the screen and tackle various careers, among which was a stint as a TV quiz show host. Arguably *Son of Dracula* is his best and most memorable work.

Universal contract player and Pasadena Playhouse graduate, Louise Allbritton, usually a fixture in lighter studio fare such as *Not A Ladies' Man* and *San Diego, I Love You*, is rumored to have disliked the part of Kay tremendously and was most resentful

The downbeat nature of *Son Of Dracula* makes it unique in Universal horror film annals.

of the studio's decision to place her in a horror film. Certainly the majority of critics, both contemporary and those who would write later in monster magazines and film books, make an almost mean-spirited point of trashing her performance nearly as vehemently as Chaney's. Personally I find most of these unfavorable reviews excessive and largely unfounded. Allbritton, decked out in a jet black wig, with her classically chiseled good looks, gives a distant, almost catatonic reading of the lines which I believe to be totally in keeping with the veiled slyness and aloofness of this cold and calculating character. In what may be her finest moment (and to many the most memorable scene in the film), she stands alone and mute on the shore of the swamp appearing at a distance like a white flame as Alucard's coffin rises from beneath the murky waters with Alucard standing atop it as the coffin is propelled towards her.

The rest of the cast is professional and competent, although J. Edward Bromberg is a bit ripe as the vampire hunter Lazlo. Evelyn Ankers, who always added a steadiness and almost regal balance to her roles, has little more than a cameo, but it's always good to see her. Such stalwarts as Samuel S. Hinds, George Irving, and Walter Sande fill out the supporting cast.

All in all, *Son of Dracula* is a smoothly engineered and carefully crafted film, hardly flawless but certainly one of Universal's best horror offerings of the 1940s. Frosting on the cake is supplied by Hans Salter's fine score, most of it lifted from the earlier *The Invisible Man Returns* (1940), and John P. Fulton's always reliable special effects which richly enhance but never overwhelm the action. The vampire-into-bat transformations, the first witnessed in a Universal film, are particularly well-handled. Although animated, they are accomplished in a smoother, more rapid and believable style than those later attempted with the top-hatted John Carradine in either *House of Frankenstein* (1943) or *House of Dracula* (1945) or the later *Abbott and Costello Meet Frankenstein* (1948).

In the end Lon Chaney, Jr. would be remembered for a handful of horror roles by a legion of young fans and largely ignored by film critics who mostly recalled him as a mediocre talent at best, a mere shadow of his famous father, an actor who almost by accident acquired a certain amount of fame as the Wolf Man. The exceptions, and there were many of them, would almost be passed off as curious flukes. He belongs to the "They weren't very good except in..." school of performers. In Chaney's case he wasn't very good *except* in *High Noon* and *The Defiant Ones* and *Of Mice And Men* and *Not As A Stranger* and many more. And for this writer that list would and should now include *Son Of Dracula.*

CREDITS: Director: Robert Siodmak; Producer: Ford Beebe; Screenplay: Eric Taylor; Original Story: Curt Siodmak; Director of Photography: George Robinson; Editor: Saul A. Goodkind; Art Director: John Goodman and Martin Obzina; Music: Hans Salter; Special Effects: John P. Fulton; Make-up: Jack Pierce; Running Time: 78 minutes; Released November 5, 1943

CAST: Lon Chaney (Count Alucard/Count Dracula); Louise Allbritton (Katherine Caldwell); Robert Paige (Frank Stanley); Evelyn Ankers (Claire Caldwell); Frank Craven (Dr. Harry Brewster); J. Edward Bromberg (Professor Lazlo); Samuel S. Hinds (Judge Simmons); Adeline De Walt Reynolds (Queen Zimba); George Irving (Col. Caldwell); Patrick Moriarity (Sheriff Dawes); Walter Sande (Matt)

ALL NEW... ALL TOGETHER!
DRACULA
FRANKENSTEIN'S
MONSTER
WOLF MAN
MAD DOCTOR
HUNCHBACK
HOUSE OF DRACULA
with
LON CHANEY
MARTHA O'DRISCOLL
JOHN CARRADINE
LIONEL ATWILL
ONSLOW STEVENS
GLENN STRANGE
JANE ADAMS
LUDWIG STOSSEL
A
UNIVERSAL

HOUSE OF FRANKENSTEIN (1944) *HOUSE OF DRACULA* (1945)

by John E. Parnum

"With each full moon I turn into a werewolf. I kill. I want to die! Only death can bring me release...."
—Larry Talbot to Dr. Niemann in *House of Frankenstein*

"There's something tragic about him, Doctor."
—Nurse Miliza to Dr. Edelmann in *House of Dracula*

There's a scene in the 1945 Universal Pictures monster rally, *House of Dracula*, in which Lawrence Stewart Talbot impulsively decides to seek that final release from the curse first placed on him three films prior when he was bitten by a werewolf gypsy named Bela. Unwilling to endure another agonizing transformation, and frustrated by the kindly Dr. Edelmann's inability to effect an immediate cure, he dashes to the edge of a precipice and throws himself into the turbulent sea. Silly man. He should have known by then that such a feeble attempt would be ineffectual. After all, he had already had his brains bashed in from a silver cane wielded by his father (*The Wolf Man*, 1941), been swept away when an irate villager blew up a dam, sending him and the Frankenstein Monster to an icy grave (*Frankenstein Meets the Wolf Man*, 1943), and, most efficiently, been shot "by a silver bullet, fired by the hand of someone who loves him enough to understand"—a tried and true method of werewolf disposal (*House of Frankenstein,* 1944). So while Talbot's leap into the surf is but another botched death release, it serendipitously results in discovering conditions that do indeed bring about the Wolf Man's cure (at least, in *House of Dracula*).

Talbot, as portrayed by Lon Chaney, Jr., was not always inclined to suicide, just as the actor himself had been free of depression before the ravages of alcohol took their toll on him. To all appearances, the young Creighton Tull Chaney (his birthright name) was a happy, gregarious family man, married 37 years to the same woman and devoted to his two sons, but who subconsciously lived in the shadow of his famous father, Lon Chaney, Sr., to whom he would always be compared This chapter will examine Chaney, Jr.'s, psyche and how it was mirrored as Larry Talbot in his Wolf Man films especially in *House of Frankenstein* and *House of Dracula*.

In *The Wolf Man*, Talbot returns to his ancestral home in England after many years of studying in America. And while he and his father, Sir John (Claude Rains), have had their differences, Talbot is amenable to helping the senior Talbot. These differences are not identified in the film, but Chaney himself certainly experienced traumatizing ones with Lon, Sr., who had put him in boarding schools and foster homes and finally sent him to live with his deaf mute grandparents. Most damning of all, however, was when Lon, Jr. discovered that his mother, Cleva, was *not* dead as his father had told him, thereby causing an estrangement between father and son. In *The Wolf Man*, Talbot is a big, burly, happy fellow, given to mischievousness, especially when he tries to come on to the pretty Gwen Conliffe (Evelyn Ankers). But his transformations into the Wolf Man after he has been bitten leave him confused and anxious, even with some doubt at first of his participation in the resulting killing sprees. When he finally accepts that he is the creature that has been terrorizing the countryside, he is frightened and concerned for Gwen. After an unsuccessful attack on Gwen as the Wolf Man, Larry is "killed" by Sir John.

Resurrected in *Frankenstein Meets the Wolf Man*, Talbot seeks out the gypsy woman, Maleva (Maria Ouspenskaya), to watch over him the way she protected her son Bela (Bela Lugosi) who had bitten him. When Maleva informs him that a Dr. Frankenstein might help him, Talbot's spirits are raised, then dashed upon learning that Frankenstein is dead. Hopes are lifted again when they are told that a daughter Elsa (Ilona Massey) might have access to her father's records. When Elsa accuses Talbot of being insane, Maleva speaks up: "Insane? He's not insane. He simply wants to die." And "die" again he does when the dam blows up.

This brings us to Chaney's third outing as the Wolf Man, this time in the first of two monsterthons, *House of Frankenstein*. Boasting an all-star cast that features Boris Karloff as the mad Dr. Niemann, John Carradine as Dracula, J. Carrol Naish as the murderous hunchback, Daniel, and Glenn Strange as the Frankenstein Monster, Chaney's Lawrence Talbot was relegated to the second half of this episodic Universal shocker, based on a story by Curt Siodmak who had penned the two previous Wolf Man scripts. In this tale, however, Edward T. Lowe's screenplay portrays Talbot (whose manic-depression is relieved only by occasional outbursts of anger) as a victim obsessed with wanting to die—his only release from the curse of lycanthropy.

Dr. Niemann and Daniel discover Talbot in the form of the Wolf Man, along with Frankenstein's Monster, frozen in ice beneath the castle laboratory where they had been swept when the waters from the burst dam interrupted their climactic battle. This is a lucky break for Niemann since he hopes the two monsters will help him locate Frankenstein's records, which will aid him in pursuing his own insane experiments. He, along with Daniel, has escaped from Neustadt prison where he had served 15 years for giving a dog the mind of a human being. Two events have transpired between the time of their escape and their discovery of the Wolf Man and the Monster and these events take up the first half of *House of Frankenstein*.

The first is the dastardly duo's takeover of Professor Lampini's traveling Chamber of Horrors, with Niemann assuming the circus owner's identity. Daniel has murdered Lampini (George Zucco) and his driver at Niemann's bidding, hoping that his obedience will seal Niemann's promise to give him a handsome body like other men. Among the displays in the horror show is the actual skeleton of Count Dracula, sealed in his soil-lined coffin with a wooden stake through his heart. Once in the village of Riegelberg,

Dr. Niemann (Boris Karloff) agrees to help the tortured Larry Talbot (Chaney, Jr.) in *House of Frankenstein.*

Niemann removes the stake, returning the skeleton to human form, and the vengeful doctor persuades Dracula to kill Burgomaster Ludwig Hussman who had incarcerated him years before. Dracula seduces Hussman's granddaughter-in-law Rita (Anne Gwynne), but, with the intervention of her husband, Carl (Peter Coe), and Inspector Arnz (Lionel Atwill), the young bride is saved as the rising sun reduces Dracula to bones again.

The second event is Niemann and Daniel's arrival at a gypsy camp, with the hunchback being attracted to the dancer, Ilonka (Elena Verdugo). When the lass is brutally beaten by her partner for not turning over her money to him, Daniel thrashes the man mercilessly. Daniel pleads with Niemann to let him take the hurt Ilonka with them and nurse her back to health, and Niemann reluctantly agrees. Ilonka regains consciousness under the driver's seat. At first she teases Daniel coyly but, upon discovering his deformity, is repulsed by his ugliness. By the time they arrive at the Frankenstein ruins, Ilonka has accepted the hunchback because of his kindness to her.

It should be pointed out that while screenwriters for this series usually provided continuity within these films, they sometimes slipped up. Frankenstein's castle (or sanitarium as writer W. Scott Darling called it in *The Ghost of Frankenstein)* was actu-

Talbot babysits the Frankenstein Monster (Glenn Strange) as Niemann looks on in *House of Frankenstein.*

ally the home of Frankenstein's second son, Ludwig, and was located in the town of Vasaria. Curt Siodmak's screenplay for *Frankenstein Meets the Wolf Man* accurately follows through with the location, but when Edward T. Lowe wrote his script based on Siodmak's story idea he sloppily changed the name of the village to Frankenstein, with Niemann's final destination being his own home in V*i*saria (now spelled with an "i").

When Niemann and Daniel discover the Wolf Man and the Monster frozen in ice, they immediately thaw them out: "They may know where the records are kept, friend Daniel; we'll set them free and they will help us," a ludicrous assumption by Niemann. The Wolf Man is the first to thaw and he transforms back into Lawrence Talbot, whose first words are not a "Howdy" or a "Thank you," but a gloomy and stilted "Who are you? Why have you freed me from the ice that imprisoned the beast within me?" Talbot's mood elevates when Niemann informs him that he, like Frankenstein, is a scientist and could build Talbot a new brain to lift the curse from him forever.

Niemann relegates Talbot to driver since he needs Daniel to help him apply hot compresses to the Monster, whose tissues have been severely damaged by the ice. Ilonka, playfully tickling Talbot's legs, is pleasantly startled to discover the deformed hunchback has been replaced. Bubbling over with enthusiasm, this coy gypsy girl is puzzled, however, by Talbot's depressed mood and to his reply as to his identity. "Just the driver," he intones sadly. When he answers that his name is Lawrence, Ilonka asks if they call him Larry, to which he reflects, "They used to."

At a rest stop, Ilonka brings Talbot flowers and finally coaxes him to smile for her. Daniel suffers in silence as he sees a romance developing between Talbot and Ilonka and pleads with Niemann to let him drive part of the time. But the doctor is adamant, claiming that Talbot bothers him with his "everlasting impatience." Upon their arrival at Niemann's estate, Daniel cruelly displays the Monster to a horrified Ilonka who runs to Talbot's arms for protection. Glenn Strange's garb for the Monster consisted of the same clothes that Chaney had worn in *The Ghost of Frankenstein* since the two actors had approximately the same build.

With the approach of the full moon, Talbot becomes more impatient, telling Niemann he can't go through that torture again. Daniel begs Niemann to give him Talbot's body. But the mad doctor's ultimate plans are far from humanitarian. He tells Daniel that "Talbot's body is the perfect home for the Monster's brain which I will add to and subtract." Primarily, Niemann seeks vengeance on the two who testified against him, Ullman and Strauss. He tells Ullman that he'll place his brain in the skull of the Frankenstein Monster and give Strauss the brain of the Wolf Man, "so all your waking hours will be spent in untold agony." If this sounds confusing and cartoonish, it should be noted that an earlier version of the script explained that all this body and brain switching would give Niemann the knowledge and experience to create the perfect man.

In an effort to protect Ilonka and turn her against Talbot, Daniel spills the beans about Larry being a werewolf. It achieves only the opposite effect, with Ilonka, hysterical in her anger, calling the hunchback mean and ugly and telling him she hates him. Daniel then takes out his frustrations on the Monster, conscious but weakened, strapped to an operating table. In the meantime, Talbot transforms into a werewolf in a cost- and time-saving effect: first he sits on the edge of the bed and removes his shoes; then he runs from the room, peers up at the rising full moon, and covers his face with his hands as the camera travels down to his feet. As Talbot runs off, it follows his footprints along the ground as they become wolf prints, finally ending in a long shot of the Wolf Man bounding into the woods.

The next day Ilonka finds a very dejected and repentant Larry seated in the garden. She tells him that she is aware of his "condition" and that he didn't know what he was doing. Talbot argues that he did; that he wanted to kill; and that when the moon rises, he'll kill again. He warns her that he might even kill her. It is a tender scene, with Chaney giving his most moving speech. In an odd prediction he says, "Only death can bring *us* peace of mind"—not "*me*." He then explains that the only way a werewolf can be killed is by a silver bullet, fired by the hand of someone who loves him enough to understand. And so, sadly, Ilonka goes to work on fashioning bullets from her silver charm bracelet.

Niemann and Daniel switch on Kenneth Strickfaden's electrical generators, although the equipment is not as elaborate as it has appeared in previous Frankenstein films. In the midst of impregnating the Monster with energy, Talbot charges into the lab, seizes Niemann by the throat, and angrily demands he stop what he's doing and operate on him. Niemann reminds Talbot that if he kills him, he'll destroy his only hope of release. In the nearby woods, having discovered a villager with his throat torn out, an angry torch-wielding mob searches for the killer and observes lights in Niemann's old abandoned estate. It is distracting to hear several members of the search party pronouncing "Niemann" differently in the same scene.

Once resurrected, the Monster snarls furiously at the hunchback who had whipped him earlier. Several reviewers have suggested that the Monster is cruelly laughing at Daniel's deformity, but it seems more natural that the Monster's initial reaction to the hunchback would be one of anger and not mirth. Niemann prepares for his next patient:

"Tell Talbot I'm ready for him," he instructs Daniel. An earlier script had Niemann always referring to Talbot as the Wolf Man, but to say "Tell the Wolf Man I'm ready" seems comical and mood-breaking. At the moment, however, Talbot is transforming, as Ilonka stands by the door, gun in hand, watching him. Unable to pull the trigger, Ilonka sees her lover fully transformed into a snarling beast and come crashing through the glass door. (Strangely, Jack Pierce's astonishing make-up precluded transforming Talbot's hands—an oversight? Or cost-cutting measure?) As Ilonka pursues him down the walk, the werewolf leaps from behind a hedge, grabs her by the throat, and bites her neck, as they both tumble behind some bushes. A scream and a shot are heard and the Wolf Man reappears clutching his stomach. Ilonka, also mortally wounded, crawls to her attacker, now transformed back to a lifeless Larry, a smile of peace on his face at last. It is a dramatic final embrace, one that may have indeed inspired David O. Selznick to repeat it in the climactic shoot-out between Gregory Peck and Jennifer Jones in the 1946 *Duel in the Sun*. Once again, economy rears its head as Chaney's final transformation involves only the feet.

House of Frankenstein then moves to a rapid finish. Daniel, finding the two dead lovers, carries Ilonka to Niemann's lab where he strangles the mad scientist. The Monster breaks free of his restraining straps and hurls Daniel through a skylight to his death. The mob arrives and drives the Monster, who is carrying the dying Niemann, into the swamps where the two are swallowed up by the quicksand.

According to Greg Mank in his Production Notes for *House of Frankenstein: Universal Filmscripts Series, Classic Horror Films-Volume 6* (MagicImage Filmbooks, Atlantic City/Hollywood, 1991, page 20), Lon Chaney was feeling animosity toward Universal during the shooting of the film: "...the studio had promised him his father's role in the remake of *Phantom of the Opera*, and then signed Claude Rains for the part." Since Chaney was always trying to compete with his famous father, perhaps Universal's decision was a wise one. He may also have had mixed feelings about sharing the spotlight with other Universal monsters, especially being relegated to the second half of the film, even though his part was the most dramatic. Still, Chaney must have been pleased to play the Wolf Man for a third time; as he has said so often, the character was his "baby" and it is the role for which he is best remembered.

Much credit, of course, must be given to Jack Pierce for creating the effective Wolf Man make-up, even though Chaney's acting breathed life into the character. Chaney's acting as the Wolf Man far exceeds his stint as Talbot, with his werewolf character exhibiting bestial fury, athletic prowess, and excruciating agony when mortally wounded. Nineteen-year-old Elena Verdugo reported in an interview in Mank's *House of Frankenstein MagicImage FilmScript* (page 14): "For the horror films at Universal, they used to have professional screamers on the sets. For the scene in which the Wolf Man attacked me, they called one of those 'screamers' to our stage... I hadn't seen Lon in his make-up. Well, when the Wolf Man jumped out at me, I was so scared and screamed so wildly that they canceled the professional screamer!"

The entire troupe of actors perform professionally. While Chaney turns in a fine performance, J. Carrol Naish and Elena Verdugo are outstanding, with young Verdugo's range of emotions equaling those of a more seasoned actress. Her only "goof" occurs when Daniel lifts Ilonka's corpse into his arms and Verdugo instinctively slips her arm under her dress to prevent the camera from peering up her skirt, a totally unnecessary action since she had already displayed even more thigh during her earlier gypsy dance.

At a rest stop, Ilonka (Elena Verdugo) brings Talbot flowers and finally coaxes him to smile for her, in *House of Frankenstein.*

All in all, production values are excellent for this type of picture, with the possible exception of the glass mattes used in the ice cave. John P. Fulton's special effects (Dracula changing into a bat and Chaney's time-exposure werewolf transformation) are magically superb for their time. And George Robinson's eerie photography is particularly effective, especially when showing some of the more graphic murders in shadow. In *Universal Horrors* by Michael and John Brunas and Tom Weaver (McFarland & Company, Inc., Jefferson, North Carolina, and London, 1990, page 472), the authors praise the film: "High-keyed, aggressive and shrewdly calculated, *House of Frankenstein* is horror filmmaking at its slick, superficial best. The abundance of thrills are logged in with clockwork precision. Cherished clichés are dusted off and polished to a shine. That the whole picture tastes of yesterday's leftovers is beside the point and in this instance almost forgivable." About Chaney's performance, they state (page 473), "Although Lon Chaney's gloom-and-despair schtick was quickly reaching the point of parody by now, the actor does infuse the qualities of sincerity and dignity in his performance. Providing Talbot with a gypsy love interest, however brief, is a bittersweet touch, particularly in light of the fact it was a gypsy who passed the curse of the lycanthrope onto him."

As Ilonka purses Talbot, the werewolf leaps from behind a hedge, grabs her by the throat, and bites her neck, as they both tumble behind some bushes, in *House of Frankenstein*.

Producer Paul Malvern was delighted by the stupendous box office receipts for *House of Frankenstein* and thought that a sequel was only natural. He dusted off an unrealized script—*Wolf Man vs. Dracula*—which had been written during the filming of *Frankenstein Meets the Wolf Man* and had been shelved because of contractual difficulties and censorship problems. By the time Edward T. Lowe had rewritten the many versions and changed the title to *House of Dracula*, *Wolf Man vs. Dracula* looked nothing like its original draft. *House of Dracula* is really just a sanitized *House of Frankenstein.* Gone is the stinking slimy dungeon from which Niemann and Daniel escaped. Gone is the bizarre traveling Chamber of Horrors which displayed the actual skeleton of Count Dracula. Gone are the crumbling ruins of Frankenstein's castle and Niemann's grotesque laboratory which are replaced by Dr. Edelmann's spiffy-clean sanitarium (surrounded by a well-tended garden and seaside vista) furnished with modern machinery. An old torture chamber is even turned into a botanical hothouse. J. Carrol Naish's grotesque hunchback is replaced by pleasant and self-giving lab assistant Nina (Jane Adams) whose modified hump does not detract from the actress's pretty face. Gone also are the supernatural elements that are now replaced by scientific explanations of why Dracula must survive on human blood and why Larry Talbot turns into a werewolf when the moon is full. Gothic horror has become science fiction.

What is missing most are the explanations of how Dracula and the Wolf Man are resurrected from *House of Frankenstein,* with scripter Edward T. Lowe being the first writer not to afford any explanation of how the destroyed monsters from a previous film survived to appear in his screenplay. A repentant Dracula (John Carradine again), posing as Baron Latos as he did in *House of Frankenstein*, just shows up one evening at the medical facility of Dr. Franz Edelmann (Onslow Stevens) apologetically seeking a cure for his vampirism. The next evening when Latos arrives for a consultation (he actually resides in a coffin in Edelmann's basement), he bumps into the doctor's other nurse, Miliza Morelle (Martha O'Driscoll), with whom he had been briefly acquainted in Bistritz. Coincidentally, while the doctor is busy explaining to Dracula that a parasite resides in his blood which might be destroyed by an antitoxin, Lawrence Talbot also appears on the scene to ask for Edelmann's help. Impatient as ever, he dashes into the night, leaving Miliza puzzled, but sympathetic.

Shortly afterward, Edelman receives a phone call from Inspector Holtz (Lionel Atwill) who has honored Talbot's request to be locked up in the town jail. When Edelmann and Miliza arrive at the cell, Talbot recounts his problem just as the full moon rises and he is transformed into the Wolf Man. Chaney is particularly effective as he clambers about the cell and rolls on the floor like a trapped animal, a scene reminiscent of his floundering in the trap in *The Wolf Man* and his thrashings about the ice cave in *Frankenstein Meets the Wolf Man*. This is the only time in *House of Dracula* that we see Talbot change *into* the Wolf Man and, unfortunately, the metamorphosis is marred. The blunder is related in the Brunas brothers and Weaver's *Universal Horrors* (page 523): "...Chaney is allowed to open and close his mouth in bestial fashion during his Wolf Man transformations; consequently, John P. Fulton's double exposures give the actor twin sets of upper and lower teeth." Perhaps the sloppiness can be excused when one realizes that these transformation scenes required Chaney to remain immobile during 16 hours of filming.

The next day at Edelmann's estate, the doctor explains to Talbot that his condition is caused by pressure on the brain, due to improper enlargement of the cavity. This, coupled with self hypnosis that he can change into a wolf, releases hormones from certain glands that bring about the physical transformation. A cure is possible by using a mold from a hybrid mimosa plant that can soften hard structures composed of calcium. Thus, with a sufficient amount of this mold, Edelmann could not only reshape Nina's deformed body, but could relieve the pressure on Talbot's brain. Unfortunately, there's not enough mold since the plants take time to mature. Talbot reminds Edelmann that the moon will be full in another hour and that he can't go through another transformation. He dashes from the house, rushes toward the cliffs, then throws himself into the churning sea. Edelmann comforts Miliza by saying that there is some hope that he may have been washed into an underground cave and that they will look for him at dawn. Edelmann's rescue must be timed so that he finds Talbot just as the werewolf seizure is passing but before Talbot in human form can try to kill himself again.

Searching the darkness of the underwater cave, Edelmann is attacked by the Wolf Man who tries to strangle the doctor. The moon sets just in time, however, and the werewolf changes back to Talbot. This, too, is an interesting transformation. Chaney's Talbot, for the first time, was sporting a mustache, something the actor had been wearing since the 1943 *Son of Dracula*, hoping the appearance would make him more distinguished and give him a leading man look for those dreadful *Inner Sanctum* mysteries. It is a bit comical to see the Wolf Man's hirsute face come clean and then develop hair again on his upper lip.

While Talbot bemoans the fact that he has been brought back to a life of despair, Edelmann discovers that the humidity of the caves is ideal for speeding up the growth of the mold-producing plants, so they should have sufficient quantity by the next full moon. Then, from a fissure in the wall from which quicksand has seeped, they discover Frankenstein's undying Monster and the skeleton of Dr. Niemann, Edward T. Lowe's one concession to continuity in the film. Once again playing the Monster, Glenn Strange relates in Donald F. Glut's *The Frankenstein Legend* (The Scarecrow Press, Inc., Metuchen, N.J., 1973, page 176) how Chaney saved him with a bottle of booze. "...I was in there [the quicksand] all day long and that stuff was cold.... And Chaney came down with a fifth and I think I got most of it. He poured it down me and it warmed me up some. They finished shooting and I went up to the dressing room.... They took the make-up off and by the time I got about half undressed I was so looped I could hardly get up. I got warm. And then I got tight. But I think he just about saved my life that day." Chaney was always willing to have company during his drinking adventures, rationalizing his excessive boozing early on as benign if he could get his buddies to keep up with him..

Then follows a group discussion about the ethics of restoring the Monster, with Nina convincing Edelmann "...that Man's first responsibility is to man...to bring him back would unleash worse than murder on humanity." Edelmann promises those assembled that Frankenstein's creation "...will never wreak havoc again." But Dracula, apparently, has changed his mind about being cured and tries to persuade Miliza to join him in his world of "people who are dead—and who are yet alive." Edelmann and Nina interrupt Dracula's tryst with Miliza and perform another transfusion on him. But the crafty vampire sends Nina into a trance and reverses the transfusion process, tainting Edelmann's blood with that of his own. When Edelmann sees a giant bat enter Miliza's bedroom, he grabs a crucifix and rushes to save her while Nina recruits Talbot. Once more in human form, Dracula's final seduction of Miliza is interrupted by Edelmann, Nina, and Talbot (who catches the fainting Miliza in his arms). Edelmann pursues Dracula to the basement coffin, dragging the casket into the rising sun, which reduces the vampire to bones. Director Erle C. Kenton, however, was oblivious to the fact that opening the lid of the coffin inadvertently blocked the rays of the sun from the vampire's body. End of Dracula segment, which unlike *House of Frankenstein* was integrated with other plots.

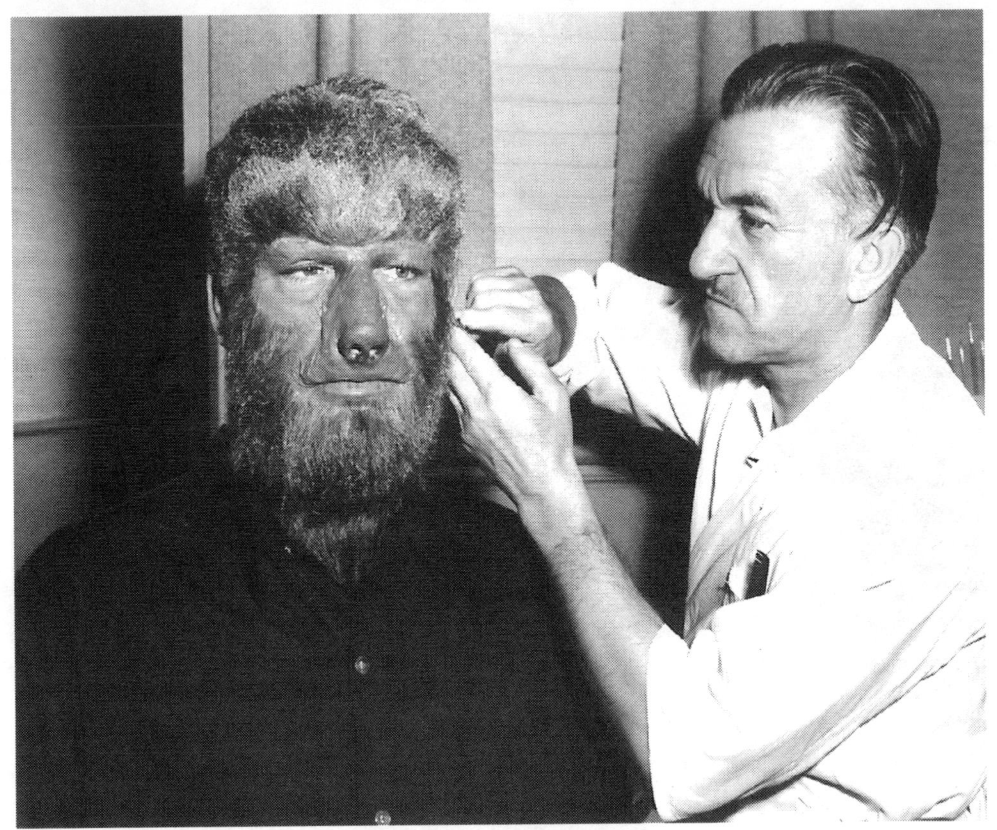

Yak hair was used by Jack Pierce to make up Chaney in all four of his werewolf films and the last shipment from Central Asia had arrived before the start of World War II.

Edelmann now has become a monster in his own right. In a montage of Freudian symbolism, probably inspired by the 1941 *Dr. Jekyll and Mr. Hyde*, Edelmann dreams of domination and sexual obsession. Breaking his promise, he sets to work on restoring the Monster, but is interrupted by Nina who fears for his sanity. When he admits he is sick, he tells Nina that he will operate on her next. Nina selflessly encourages him to cure Talbot first. After the operation, Miliza comforts Larry, who is not convinced that Edelmann has been successful: "Time after time, I've clung to the hope that someone might be able to help me—and time after time those who tried, have failed." Miliza encourages him to think of the night as beautiful. "Until the moon turns it into a thing of ugliness and horror," he argues. She persists that soon he'll "see it as everyone sees it—restful, tranquil, and serene." "Until that time comes," Talbot reflects, "I'll live a thousand hopes and die a thousand deaths."

Edelmann in his "Mr. Hyde" form then commits a particularly sadistic murder, which is witnessed by the villagers. They alert the police who pursue the unrecognized killer to Edelman's estate. The police think Talbot committed the murder, but are assured by the now kindly Edelmann that his condition precludes any exertion. Talbot, however, has seen Edelmann from his window and confronts the doctor. When Edelmann asks why he didn't inform Inspector Holtz, Talbot acknowledges his debt to the doctor. Edelmann promises Talbot, "You wish to help me, there's one way in which you can; say nothing to Inspector Holtz of what you know. Not to protect me! Only to give me time—time to do for Nina what I've done for you. After that, this evil thing shall be

Miliza (Martha O'Driscoll), Nina (Jane Adams), and Dr. Edelmann (Onslow Stevens) console Larry Talbot in *House of Dracula.*

destroyed. You have my word it will be, my boy—but if things become too bad, and I fail, then you must do it for me."

The village undertaker finds a gold watch with Dr. Edelmann's name on it clutched in the victim's hand. The police set out once again for the doctor's estate as a mob of townsfolk gather to take justice into their own hands. Back at Edelmann's, all is tranquil as Talbot waits stoically for the moon to rise. Reminiscent of his famous father's pantomimes, Chaney silently portrays a once-despondent man's victory over the curse that has haunted him in four films for so many years. He walks to the terrace, but neglects to take off his shoes—a tradition that he and all lycanthropes adhere to before they become werewolves. The moon shines full on his face. He averts his eyes to the ground. Then looks up hesitantly. He feels his face and is encouraged. Finally, he stands erect. Though he does not smile, he throws his shoulders back and looks proud. The music swells to a crescendo. He has lived his thousandth hope and "died" his final time. Miliza rushes to him and they embrace.

Nina turns to Edelmann to congratulate him, but he is gone. The now evil doctor is putting the final touches on restoring the Monster. When Nina interrupts, Edelmann strangles and tosses her body through a trap door. Talbot and Miliza enter with the police. The Monster pulverizes one policeman with a crushing blow as Edelmann hurls Inspector Holtz into machinery, electrocuting him. Talbot picks up the policeman's gun as Edelmann approaches him and Miliza menacingly. Talbot remembers Edelmann's words, "you must do it for me," and fires. Edelmann smiles serenely and sinks to the floor, leaving Larry to deal with the fury-ridden Monster. He topples a row of shelves filled with chemicals onto the creature, causing an explosion. In an abrupt ending, Talbot, Miliza, and the mob flee the fire-engulfed mansion into the safety of a moonlit night as the Monster is buried under burning timbers. *Deja vu*, anyone?

While *House of Dracula* may have been a more sanitized version of *House of Frankenstein*, it was certainly not as polished. Cost-cutting is evident in every department, from the musical score (which for the most part was picked up by Edgar Fairchild from Hans J. Salter's magnificent themes in other horror movies) to clips used from other Frankenstein films to supplement the action. The latter is especially disconcerting since *House of Dracula* actually has scenes with four different actors playing the part of the Monster: Glenn Strange got the credit; Boris Karloff's Monster from *The Bride of Frankenstein* running amuck in the village and toppling cemetery tombstones occupy this film's dream montage sequence; Lon Chaney's Monster, along with stuntman Eddie Parker's from *The Ghost of Frankenstein,* is snipped in for the entire conflagration finale of *House of Dracula*. Russell Schoengarth's sloppy editing accounted for three policemen entering Edelmann estate, but showing only two once they were inside. Also, it was unfortunate he couldn't eliminate Lionel Atwill's offscreen coughing, a prelude to the bronchial cancer that killed him a year later. The set from the 1939 *Tower of London* was cleaned up and painted for Edelmann's estate, just as it had been used for Neustadt prison in *House of Frankenstein*.

Yak hair was used to make up Chaney in all four of his films and the last shipment from Central Asia had arrived before the start of World War II. This may account for the Wolf Man's bare hands after his transformation in *House of Frankenstein* and for his limited screen time in *House of Dracula*, which according to *Universal Horrors* (page 523), was "...probably to satisfy censors who didn't want the Wolf Man killing anyone in a film where Talbot survives to the end." It should be pointed out, however, that in *House of Dracula*, Talbot in *human* form does kill someone (Edelmann) for the first time in the series—an act of both mercy and self defense. Chaney's Talbot had now become the hero, winning the heroine. Greg Mank points out in *It's Alive* (A.S. Barnes & Company, Inc., San Diego/New York, 1981, page 146), "Chaney had surrendered hopes of a studio build-up as a romantic lead, and was content to just remain on contract, the loss of which he desperately feared."

But this stint as leading man in *House of Dracula*, with his name at the top of the credits, was short lived. Changes were taking place at Universal. There were whispers of new management. Just as it had in 1936, the studio was eliminating horror films from its roster. As summed up in *Universal Horrors* (page 524): "...*House of Dracula* represents one of the last Universal credits for most of the people involved. It was the final horror film for burly Lon Chaney, Universal's Master Character Creator. Chaney, whose hard drinking and boisterous hijinks won him few friends on the lot, was dropped from the studio payroll shortly after *House of Dracula* wrapped, and was forced to work as a freelancer." Interestingly, Chaney in his last role as a Universal contract player gives his most subdued portrayal both as Talbot and the Wolf Man, possibly due to the fact he could see the handwriting on the wall.

Chaney felt that the Wolf Man character was one for which he would always be remembered, just as his father was remembered as the Hunchback of Notre Dame and the Phantom of the Opera. Perpetually in competition with his father's successes, Lon hoped that achieving his own stardom might make up for the elder Chaney's seeming lack of affection for his son. As Don G. Smith notes in his book *Lon Chaney, Jr.* (McFarland & Company, Inc., Jefferson, North Carolina and London, 1996, page 188), Lon attempted "...not only to emulate him but to surpass him. Although he later denied it, he fought hard to play some of the roles made famous by his father. Born Creighton Chaney, he was at first too proud to accept the moniker of Lon Chaney, Jr., even when it was obvious that such a move would advance his career. Instead he wanted to achieve fame on his own. He finally did agree to change his name to Lon Chaney, Jr. But when Universal dropped "Jr." from his billing, he fought to retain it, probably because—even during his peak at Universal—he never felt himself his father's equal."

Most striking of all, however, is the similarity between the temperaments of Chaney, the man, and Chaney's Wolf Man/Talbot characters. Lawrence Talbot, before he was bitten, was carefree, happy-go-lucky, and burly (he even wrestles a circus bear, a scene cut from the script of *The Wolf Man*). As the Wolf Man, his entire personality changed to one of cruelty and viciousness. Whether leaping over tree stumps to strangle a fleeing damsel or thrashing about on the floor of a cramped prison cell, the Wolf Man was an uncontrollable beast with only mayhem on his mind. Chaney, under the influence of alcohol, underwent drastic changes in personality—also for the worse.

Stories about Chaney's drinking are legendary. Once he'd imbibed enough booze, his entire personality changed. Peter Coe became good friends with Chaney while working with him in *The Mummy's Curse* and *House of Frankenstein* and related incidents of Chaney's drinking and shenanigans in the Introduction to the *Universal Filmscript Series House of Frankenstein* (page 10): "They even had a club called 'The Shin-Kicking Club.' All the guys at Universal, and some of them were big and rugged like Chaney and Brod Crawford, would meet at a bar called 'Fosters' near the studio. The whole idea was when a member greeted you with a less than 'big and rugged' greeting like 'Hi, Luv' or 'Hi Baby' it was swiftly followed by a hard kick in the shins. If you showed any pain or let out any choice words, you had to buy a round of drinks for everybody. Believe me, when a man the size of Chaney kicks you in the shins, you end up buying a lot of drinks."

Paul Malvern, who had produced both *House* pictures, states in the Foreword to the *Universal Filmscripts House of Dracula* book (pages 13 and 14), "I was a very close friend of Lon, Jr. There never was a nicer guy. He got along with everybody. He and Broderick Crawford and Andy Devine were all pals and they used to get together and do a lot of drinking. When we went on location [for *North of the Klondike*] to Big Bear [California] the three of them didn't have to worry about keeping warm. If they weren't beating the hell out of each other, they drank enough to generate enough heat to keep us all warm." It has been well documented that Chaney would begin drinking early in the day and would instruct his directors to get the most out of his acting by noon.

Malvern's comment about Chaney being liked by everyone is not quite true. Lon had his detractors, such as Curt Siodmak, who accused Chaney of being "sexually confused." But perhaps no one disliked Lon more than his co-star of five horror films, Evelyn Ankers, who relates in the introduction to Doug McClelland's *The Golden Age of "B" Movies* (Charter House Inc., Nashville, 1978, page 9) several incidents of Lon's mischievousness (sneaking up from behind and grabbing her) and hot temper on the sets. The most famous incident occurred during a promotional dinner when Lon chided Ankers' husband, Richard Denning, about being in the Navy but not having been sent overseas. When Denning retaliated with, "'It's a lot better than not being in the service

Chaney in his last role as a Universal contract player gives his most subdued portrayal both as Talbot and the Wolf Man, in *House of Dracula.*

at all during wartime,'—which was Lon's situation," Chaney took his revenge by wiping ice cream on Denning's uniform. "That did it. Dick took his ice cream—which was pistachio green...—and pushed it in Lon's face.... Lon was about to heave his coffee at Dick, thus starting one of the brawls he so dearly loved, when I intervened and quieted things down."

But for all of his detractors, there were many more who dearly liked the man. Elena Verdugo in *It's Alive* (page 136) says "Lon Chaney was a lovely, friendly man. I remember often sitting and chatting with him." Also in Mank's book (page 117), Ilona Massey states, "I think Lon Chaney is one of the nicest, sweetest people in the world. It was a great deal of fun.... I never had any difficulty with my co-stars, but Chaney was something special" (James Miller in "Interview with Ilona Massey," *Varulven* magazine No. 4). Other praises appear in *Universal Horrors* (pages 524-526): producer Howard W. Koch "reminisces, 'He was a sweet, compassionate, wonderful man. He was great with me, and I was really crazy about him.' Anthony Eisley, who worked with Chaney toward the end of the actor's life in 1971's *Dracula vs. Frankenstein*, recalls, 'He was very, very ill then—he would have to lie down after every take—but to talk with him and to hear his stories was just incredible. He was a wonderful, lovely, unbelievably interesting man.'... But it was probably Gloria Talbott, star of *The Cyclops* (1957), who summed it up: 'He was a darling, darling man—but drunk as a skunk!'"

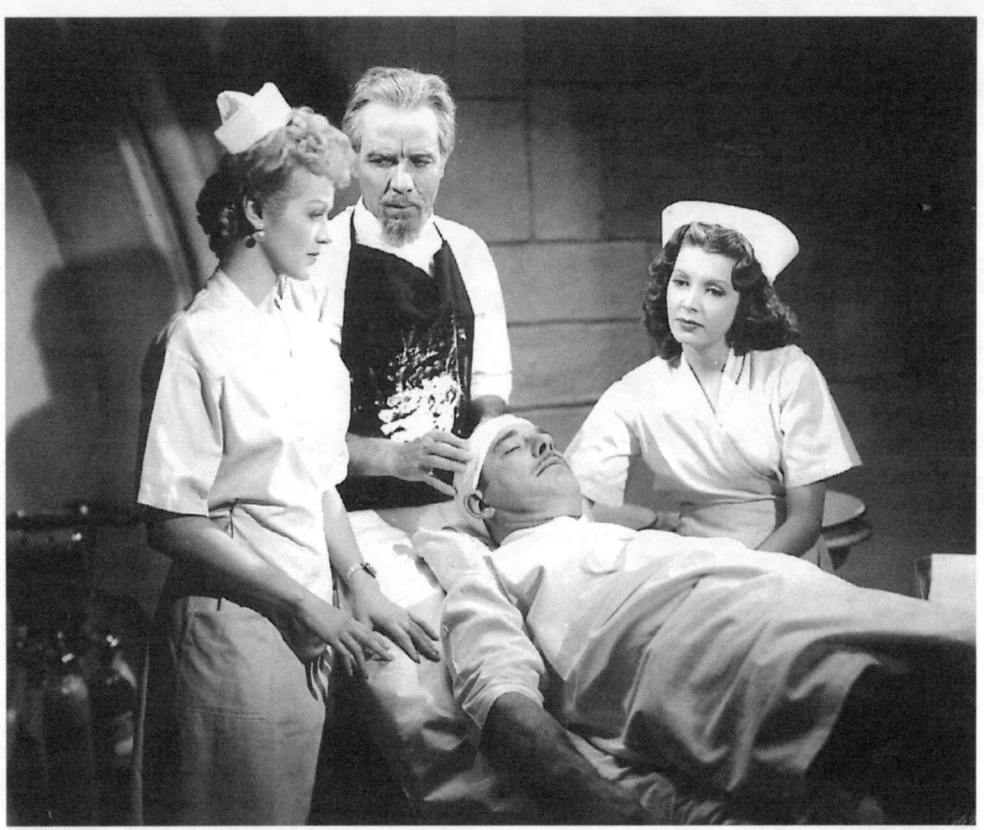

Dr. Edelmann checks Talbot's bandages after an operation to cure his illness, in *House of Dracula.*

If Chaney was a *lovely* man, he was also a very *lonely* man, just as Talbot's condition isolated him from the rest of the world. Reginald LeBorg, director of *The Mummy's Ghost* and the first three *Inner Sanctum* mysteries with Chaney, told Wheeler Winston Dixon in *The Films of Reginald LeBorg* (The Scarecrow Press, Inc. Metuchen, N.J. & London, 1992, page 94) that Chaney "...wanted me to be his pal. But I'm not a drinker. And he invited me to sit and drink, and I could sit a little bit but that's all. And he invited me home to meet his wife and drink. And I couldn't do it." Chaney seemed almost compulsive about sharing company with others. He loved to invite struggling young actors to his home, just as he enjoyed displaying his culinary talents in his dressing room during lunch break by inviting his co-stars from *House of Frankenstein* to sample his delicious meals—and join him in a nip or two.

Chaney's wife Patricia shielded her husband from the notoriety of his alcoholism, just as the gypsy Maleva had shielded Talbot from his curse of lycanthropy. As Don Smith observes in his *Lon Chaney, Jr.* (page 189), Patsy "...stood by him through all their trials and protected him till the end—and beyond. My impression is that Patsy developed all the coping strategies common to wives of alcoholics. She was, in essence, his caretaker and possibly a surrogate mother." Her job may have been made more difficult by Chaney often admitting to his addiction, just as Talbot revealed his lycanthropy to others in the hope they would cure him. And just as Larry was skeptical of Dr. Niemann's ulterior motives in effecting a cure, so too was Chaney distrustful of women, a trait that may have stemmed from his learning that his mother swallowed a vial of bicarbonate of mercury in an unsuccessful suicide attempt (an abandonment, in Lon's mind) that permanently damaged her vocal cords and ended her career as a singer.

Three years after Larry Talbot leaped into the sea in *House of Dracula,* Lon Chaney, Jr., repeated his mother's rash act with his own suicide attempt during the filming of *Abbott & Costello Meet Frankenstein.* As described in Don Smith's fascinating biography (page 103), "...Lon almost died before the film was released. On the evening of April 22, 1948, following a serious argument with Patsy, Lon took 40 sleeping pills and retreated into his truck to die. His son Ron discovered the unconscious actor, who was rushed to Van Nuys Receiving Hospital in Burbank. Upon admittance, he was listed in critical condition, but in time rallied and reunited with his distraught wife." Was this, too, a cry for help? In addition to this blatant attempt to end his life, Chaney's perpetual drinking, as in the case of many alcoholics, may also have been a strong death wish.

Lon's loss of a contract after *House of Dracula*, the rigors and insecurities associated with freelancing, his alcoholism and the embarrassments it caused him spiraled Chaney into severe depressions, far greater than those he "reenacted" as Larry Talbot. After a "live" telecast as the Frankenstein Monster on the January 18, 1952 airing of *Tales of Tomorrow*, Chaney, upon learning of his disastrous drunken performance, was so distraught that he went into a depression that crippled him for weeks. Like Larry Talbot, Lon had the sensitivity to be regretful and ashamed of his binges and unprofessionalism.

In *The Wolf Man*, Sir John Talbot explains to his son that the definition of Lycanthrope is "the good and evil in every man's soul—in this case, evil takes the shape of an animal." Robert Louis Stevenson years earlier distinctly separated these two traits in his famous novella *The Strange Case of Dr. Jekyll and Mr. Hyde*. The same theme appears in *House of Dracula*, first as Talbot's Wolf Man and then as Edelmann's transformation from Jekyll to Hyde. In each, good men—victims if you will—become evil, with their appearances altered to reflect their bestial natures.

As Lon Chaney's demons ran rampant, they too created a physical change in the victimized actor. Chaney's appearance became not hirsute, but bloated with drastically diseased vital organs. His alcohol- and smoke-damaged vocal cords issued far worse than a growl—the once smooth voice now becoming gravelly and harsh until it could speak no more. Reginald LeBorg in an interview with Bernie O'Heir in *Cinemacabre* (Number 7, Fall 1988) commented on Chaney's deteriorating appearance within the thirteen years since he had first directed him in *The Mummy's Ghost* (1944) to *The Black Sleep*: "...in his body there was about twenty-five years' difference. With Chaney, I could see that he was dying because his voice was different and his face was bloated and he was drinking quite a bit. He knew he was going, and he didn't care anymore." And in Tom Weaver's interview with Sam Sherman in *Filmfax,* (Number 27, June/July, 1991, page 88), the low-budget producer relates how Chaney kept repeating to his friend, Denver Dixon, during the filming of *Dracula vs. Frankenstein*, "...I want to die now. There's nothing left for me; I just want to die." Sounds like a line from *House of Frankenstein* and *House of Dracula*, doesn't it?

It is only natural, of course, that we all age. Some of us do it more gracefully than others. Lon Chaney, Jr., "through no fault of his own," as his gypsy protector Maleva was prone to say was one of those "others." All too often, we seem to take an unhealthy

Talbot remembers Edelmann's words, "you must do it for me," and fires. Edelmann smiles serenely and sinks to the floor, leaving Larry to deal with the fury-ridden Monster, from *House of Dracula.*

interest in the weaknesses, scandals, and ultimate downfalls of actors we had once admired, perhaps to justify our own insecurities. (In writing this chapter, I too am guilty of perpetuating this charge.) But because of the thrills he generated for his horror-film fans and the entertainment values he provided for audiences in general, perhaps we can remember him not as the cancer-ridden, alcohol-ravaged invalid of his twilight years, but rather as he appeared near the climax of *House of Dracula*, standing tall and straight as Larry Talbot, shoulders back and looking proud, knowing that the demons that had once possessed him had been dispersed forever. After all, isn't it the man's talented characterizations as an actor that attracted us to Lon Chaney, Jr. in the first place?

House of Frankenstein

CREDITS: Producer: Paul Malvern; Executive Producer: Joseph Gershenson; Director: Erle C. Kenton; Story: Curt Siodmak; Screenplay: Edward T. Lowe; Photography: George Robinson; Editor: Philip Cahn; Art Direction: John B. Goodman and Martin Obzina; Music: Hans J. Salter; Sound Director: Bernard B. Brown; Set Decorations: A. J. Gilmore and Russell A. Gausman; Gowns: Vera West; Special Photography: John P. Fulton; Make-up: Jack P. Pierce and Otto Lederer; Camera Operator: Eddie Cohen; Hair Dresser: Carla Hadley; Wardrobe: Leroy Hommedieu; A Universal Picture released December 15, 1944 in black and white; Running Time: 70 minutes

CAST: Boris Karloff (Dr. Gustav Niemann); Lon Chaney (Larry Talbot); John Carradine (Count Dracula); Anne Gwynne (Rita Hussman); Peter Coe (Carl Hussman); Lionel Atwill (Inspector Arnz); George Zucco (Professor Bruno Lampini); Elena Verdugo (Ilonka); J. Carrol Naish (Daniel); Glenn Strange (Frankenstein's Monster); Sig Ruman (Burgomaster Hussman); William Edmunds (Fejos); Michael Mark (Strauss); Frank Reicher (Ullman)

House of Dracula
CREDITS: Producer: Paul Malvern; Executive Producer: Joe Gershenson; Director: Erle C. Kenton; Story: George Bricker and Dwight V. Babcock; Screenplay Edward T. Lowe; Cinematographer: George Robinson; Editor: Russell Schoengarth; Art Directors: John B. Goodman and Martin Obzina; Musical Director: Edgar Fairchild; Sound: Jess Moulin and Bernard B. Brown; Set Decorators: Russell A. Gausman and Arthur D. Leddy; Gowns: Vera West; Make-up: Jack P. Pierce; Hair Stylist: Carmen Dirigo; Special Photography Effects: John P. Fulton; A Universal Picture released December 21, 1945 in black and white; Running Time: 67 minutes

CAST: Lon Chaney (Lawrence Talbot); John Carradine (Count Dracula); Martha O'Driscoll (Miliza Morelle); Lionel Atwill (Inspector Holtz); Onslow Stevens (Dr. Edelmann); Jane Adams (Nina); Glenn Strange (Frankenstein's Monster); Ludwig Stossel (Siegfried); Skelton Knaggs (Steinmuhl); Joseph E. Bernard (Brahms); Dick Dickinson and Harry Lamont (villagers); Fred Cordova and Carey Harrison (gendarmes)

Acknowledgment: Once again, I am grateful for the editing and suggestions provided by my daughter, Laura Parnum.

WEIRD WOMAN (1944)

by Bryan Senn

"Man's struggle upward from his dark past is the struggle of reason against superstition."—Lon Chaney, Jr. as Professor Norman Reed.

In June of 1943, Universal bought the rights to use the *Inner Sanctum* name from publishers Simon and Schuster, Inc. Under the guiding hand of low-end producer Ben Pivar, the studio planned to release two *Inner Sanctum* films a year, each starring their new golden boy of terror (and "Master Character Creator" as the studio PR department so grandiosely named him), Lon Chaney, Jr. What resulted were six more-or-less desultory pictures in a tiresome and disappointing series that stretched from December 1943 with the release of *Calling Dr. Death* to December 1945 with the final entry, *Pillow of Death.* In between, the studio crammed four more features: *Weird Woman, Dead Man's Eyes*, *The Frozen Ghost*, and *Strange Confession.*

The second in the series, *Weird Woman* has traditionally been thought of as the best of the bunch (rather faint praise, actually). It's an appellation the film doesn't really deserve, however, since one of the entries (*Dead Man's Eyes*) is at least as good, and *two* others (*Strange Confession* and *Pillow of Death*) are decidedly better. Perhaps it's the fact that the film's predecessor, *Calling Dr. Death*, was simply so dull that anything that followed immediately after looked good by comparison. Or maybe *Weird Woman* has attained such a (modestly) elevated status because it is the sole *Inner Sanctum* film which carries a (semi)supernatural theme. God help those pictures which pass themselves off as "horror" (as the *Inner Sanctum* series did) but fail to present the devoted genre fan with some kind of monster or preternatural trick or two.

Professor Norman Reed (Lon Chaney, Jr.) returns to Monroe College from his research trip to "the islands" with a new book (entitled *Superstition Versus Reason and Fact*) *and* a new wife, Paula (Anne Gwynne). The daughter of a deceased archeologist, Paula has been raised by her native nurse, a voodoo high priestess. Norman's mundane small-town newlywed idyll is soon shattered, however, when he discovers his wife practicing her protective "white magic."

After forcing Paula to burn all her voodoo paraphernalia in an attempt to overcome her "silly superstitions," things begin to go horribly wrong for Norman. An old flame (Evelyn Ankers), who's bitter over Norman's surprise marriage, uses deceit to induce a colleague (Ralph Morgan) to commit suicide and then intimates that Norman is responsible. Ilona also orchestrates a co-ed (Lois Collier) into accusing Norman of "taking advantage of her" while goading the girl's beau (Phil Brown—later Luke Skywalker's kindly uncle in *Star Wars*) into attacking Norman, resulting in the accidental death of the hotheaded boy. Ilona also begins terrorizing Paula with voodoo death chants played over the phone.

Finally, the suicide's bitter widow, Evelyn (Elizabeth Russell), discovers that it was Ilona rather than Norman who was behind her husband's death. She and Norman formulate a plan to trap her. Showing Ilona a voodoo doll and telling her of a mysterious dream in which her dead husband claims "the woman who lied" will die in thirteen days at exactly one minute past midnight, Evelyn plants the seed of fear in Ilona's mind.

As the days go by, Ilona becomes more and more terrified until finally, just before midnight on the last day, she breaks down and confesses to Evelyn, pleading with her to destroy the evil doll. It's already been reduced to ashes, says Norman and several others, as they step from the other room to confront the guilty woman. "You tricked me!" cries Ilona and dashes out the upper story window to make her escape across a vine-covered arbor. Racing across the top, the slats give way and she plunges through, only to end up swinging from a vine wrapped about her neck—dead. The time: one minute past midnight.

The film starts promisingly enough as Paula hurries fearfully down a dark, forbidding street while the wind blows violently and howls ominously. The production quickly becomes terribly set-bound, however, and on rather uninteresting sets at that. Most of the "action" (talk, actually) takes place in standard 1940s offices or living rooms. The only intriguing backdrop is a rather cramped graveyard set which Paula and Norman simply walk through on one occasion.

Reginald LeBorg's straightforward direction does little to augment the scenes, though he occasionally does come up with a minor flourish. For instance, after the suggestion has been planted with Ilona that she will die in 13 days, LeBorg (aided by editor Milton Carruth) utilizes a compact and effective montage sequence to show her mounting fear reflected in a series of seemingly ordinary events: a radio commercial announcing "remember only 8 more days left to get your...," a theater poster advertising the play "The Lady Lies" noting "LAST 7 DAYS," or Ilona opening up a package of yarn to find a card printed with "6 SKEINS YARN." For the most part, however, LeBorg makes do with the usual round of mundane angles and pedestrian staging. (To be fair, it must be noted that the director was allowed very little preparation time. According to LeBorg, he received the script on Friday and was told to start shooting a week from Monday.) Fortunately, cinematographer Virgil Miller provides effective lighting which at times generates some much-needed macabre mood, particularly with select low-key illumination at the proper moments.

For the voodoo fans, the main ceremonial sequence (a flashback to the island ritual at which Norman first met Paula) is a major disappointment, for it looks more like a genteel luau than a frenzied voodoo rite. Though Paula ominously labels it "The Dance of Death," sarong-wearing native girls pathetically stomp their feet and clap and wave their hands in an innocuously choreographed (and not very *well*, as several of these dancers can't seem to keep on the same rhythm) motion, making this "weird pagan ritual" look like low-rent nightclub filler.

The *Weird Woman* scripters obviously failed to do their homework, for they cast their voodoo ceremony in a decidedly Polynesian slant (thinking, perhaps, that voodoo came from someplace "safe" like Hawaii rather than the seedier and more dangerous Caribbean). The drummers wear leis and flowers in their hair and worship the god "Kahuna-Anna-Anna" (a new one for the voodoo pantheon). Perhaps, as yet another stroke of Hollywood racism, the filmmakers chose to portray the voodoo homeland as populated by people no more exotic than well-tanned whites.

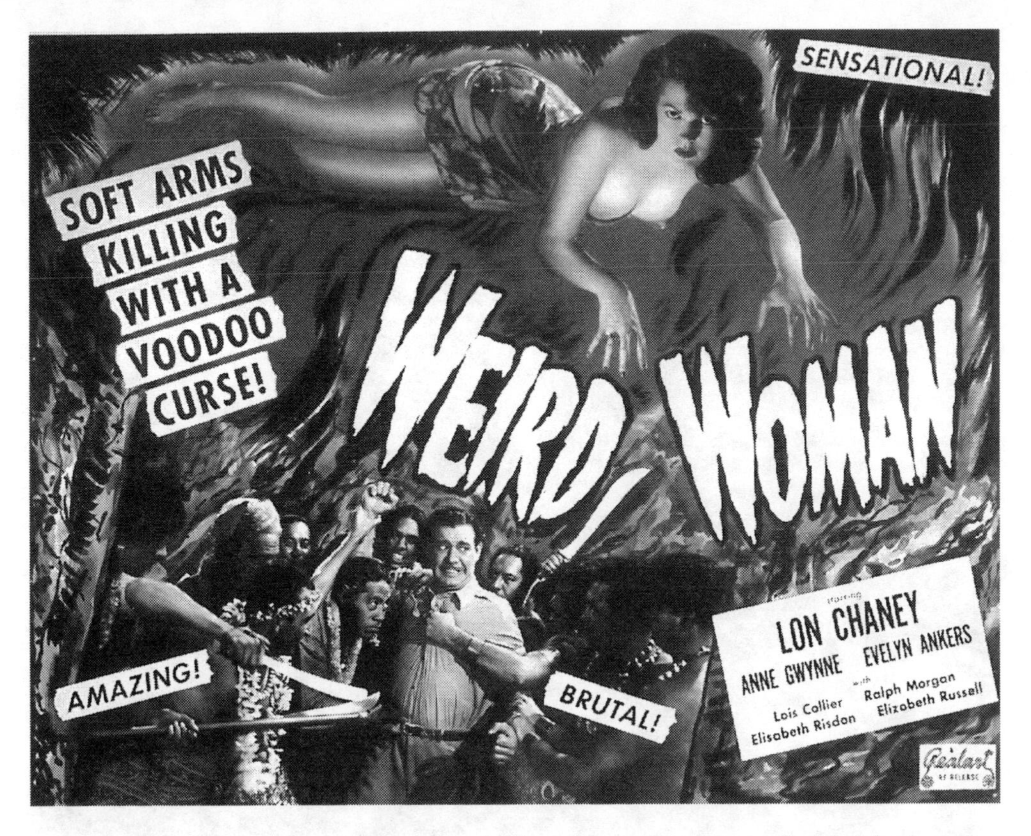

"I believe," stated Lon Chaney, Jr. in the *Weird Woman* pressbook, "that voodoo merely is the untutored savage's realization of the power of auto-suggestion." While such an articulate pronouncement from such an "untutored" actor like Chaney, Jr. seems unlikely (and probably leapt straight from the pen of a well-educated PR writer rather than from the actor's mouth), it accurately reflects the demeaning attitude commonly held by Americans toward the Voudoun religion and its practitioners (the "untutored savages").

> "I liked Lon in those *Inner Sanctum* mysteries. It's hard to act when you're covered with hair like a werewolf. But the *Inner Sanctum*s gave him a chance to act and he proved he could do it."—Glenn Strange (frequent Chaney co-star).

> "An unexciting actor—a pall of dull sincerity hung over him—Chaney created characters that were more to be pitied than respected, more cringing than aggressive, more plebeian than aristocratic. If ever a star lacked charisma, it was Chaney, Jr."—Arthur Lennig (author of *The Count*).

No matter to which camp one subscribes, it's dreadfully apparent that in *Weird Woman*, Lon Chaney, Jr. was woefully miscast. With his rather puffy face (looking just this side of jowly) and saddlebags under the eyes, no pencil-thin mustache can transform him into a B-grade Charles Boyer. But more important than Chaney's physical (mis)attributes are his less tangible traits. When a love-struck co-ed coos, "He's so

For the voodoo fans, the main ceremonial sequence (a flashback to the island ritual at which Norman first met Paula) is a major disappointment, for it looks more like a genteel luau than a frenzied voodoo rite.

brilliant... there's something so *dynamic* about him," the viewer can't help but give a sardonic snort. Chaney comes off as just the opposite of "dynamic," appearing as a rather dull and pedantic pretender who's betrayed by his unsubtle mannerisms and blue-collar speech patterns. Far from the "mental giant" one character labels him, Chaney's Norman only really seems to be in his element when he brutally manhandles an attacking student.

Chaney's (lost) cause isn't helped by the demands placed upon him by Scott Darling's unlikely script. Particularly awful is the hushed voice-over narration in which he shares his "thoughts" with the audience. *Sotto voce*, Chaney injects little inflection into the often obtuse and melodramatic dialogue (e.g. "The so-called phenomena of mysticism and sorcery are brought about by fear; fear, insulating countless millions, making them believe because they're afraid not to believe"). As Chaney's banal and toneless voice whispers its words on the soundtrack, his dramatic facial expressions (straining desperately to appear pensive and thoughtful) simply make it look as if he's battling a bout of intestinal trouble.

"When [Chaney] did the *Inner Sanctum* pictures," observed director Reginald LeBorg in *Cinemacabre* magazine, "he played them in very fine clothes... He didn't want to be a ghoul, but unfortunately he was typed and he wasn't suave enough for the *Inner Sanctums*. The pictures didn't cost much money [about $150,000 with a 10-12 day shooting schedule, according to LeBorg], so they made money, but if you had a William Powell doing them, it would have been a much better situation. But with Chaney, he never achieved that elegance that you had to have."

Chaney's co-star, Anne Gwynne, concurred: "He was wrong for the role in *Weird Woman* —in the picture, both Evelyn Ankers and Lois Collier are mad about him, but he's my husband. I think of Lon as a character heavy, like he was in *Frontier Badmen*, or as a monster. It seems strange that he would be in this type of part. I just didn't feel he was the leading-man type" (from *It Came From Weaver Five*, by Tom Weaver).

This is not to say that Lon Chaney, Jr., was a bad actor. Far from it, in the right role he performed admirably—even, at times, in this ill-fated *Inner Sanctum* series. Though for the most part Chaney failed to live up to the urbane characterizations handed him throughout most of the *Inner Sanctum*s, he seemed to have finally hit his stride in the last two, giving relatively good performances in both *Strange Confession* and *Pillow of Death*. (Of course, it helped that these two roles didn't require him to be impossibly suave, and that these pictures dropped the awful stream-of-consciousness narration which plagued the rest of the entries.)

In *Strange Confession* he played a more or less regular guy, rather naïve, who's trampled by forces larger than himself (much like his Dan McCormick/*Man Made Monster* and Larry Talbot/*Wolf Man* portrayals). In addition, *Strange Confession* (a remake of the 1934 Claude Rains vehicle, *The Man Who Reclaimed His Head*) possesses such a wonderfully tragic story that it far outshines the rest of the *Inner Sanctums*' tepid tales to become the series' best film.

Pillow of Death, besides sporting a welcome haunted house/graveyard atmosphere sadly absent from the rest of the series, focuses more on the intriguing supporting characters than on Chaney himself, who gives his best (and briefest) *Inner Sanctum* performance by simply not straining so hard to be sophisticated.

In *Weird Woman*, Chaney's lack of charisma was such that his co-stars couldn't help but shine—simply out of contrast. In fact, apart from the lead, *Weird Woman* is a particularly well-acted film. Elisabeth Risdon (as Grace) brings to her part of Norman's friend and colleague a natural humor (commenting, "Ilona, there's something about your smile right now that makes me think of Jack the Ripper," with just the right touch of sardonic veracity), while Elizabeth Russell, as the ambitious and bitterly hateful widow, nearly drips with venom at the proper moments.

Anne Gwynne is quite good in the poorly written part of Paula. Her sincerity overcomes the condescending attitude the script and characters exhibit toward her (Norman thinking of her as a "superstitious child" or calling her [to her very *face*] a "poor, frightened, strange little child"). Gwynne brings a likable innocence to her role, and her almost hysterical fear at hearing the "death chant" makes the viewer believe that *she* truly believes. Even when the screenplay forces her to pull that old chestnut—the fainting spell—we actually believe that she fainted out of fear.

In the pivotal role of Ilona, Evelyn Ankers makes a stylish villainess. Her natural poise and charm renders Ilona's vile machinations that much more heinous. Surprisingly (since most actors *love* playing the villain), Ankers was not pleased with her role. "*Weird Woman* was my first 'heavy' part," recalled the actress, "and not of my own choosing. This was a new field for me and I found it very difficult to feel comfortable or convincing. Reggie LeBorg, the director, sensed something was wrong, and on the first day, after each scene, asked 'Evie, what's the problem? It's not believable.' I

Weird Woman **director Reginald LeBorg and Chaney, Jr. [Photofest]**

answered, 'I know why—I'm miscast. I don't feel a bit mean and I don't want to hurt Anne [Gwynne] because she's my best girlfriend.' He answered, 'Well, this time forget all that. Think of something mean she must have said or done to you and try it again.' He then would say 'Action!' and I would sort of squint or narrow my eyes, even attempt to flare my nostrils in desperation—trying to work myself up to appearing evil—then turn my head and look Anne in the eye threateningly. Bang, we would become hysterical with laughter, and so would the whole company watching us. This happened time and time again, until we were absolutely exhausted. It was not only ridiculous but also costly in time as well as money, not to mention poor Reggie's patience. We felt so sorry for him, even when he tried to get angry with us, which only made it worse. How we ever finished that picture, I'll never know. Universal got the message and never cast me as a villainess again." (Quoted in *Forties Film Talk*, by Doug McClelland.)

Ankers and Chaney, though paired together in a number of films (including *The Wolf Man*, 1941; *The Ghost of Frankenstein*, 1942; *Son of Dracula*, 1943; and *The Frozen Ghost*, 1945), apparently loathed one another. "He didn't like her," stated Patsy Chaney, the actor's second wife, in *Filmfax* magazine. "He called her 'Shankers'—Evelyn Shankers."

"I have nothing but glowing things to say about Boris Karloff," related Ankers' co-star and best friend, Anne Gwynne, "and only praise for Bela Lugosi, but Lon Chaney was something else, although we actually got along fine together. But... he would pull practical jokes on people—and they did become quite cruel. He never bothered me at all—it was Evelyn who incurred his wrath. They worked together more often, and yet

Anne Gwynne, Chaney, Jr., and Evelyn Ankers in *Weird Woman*.

they couldn't stand each other, sort of like the way Jon Hall and Maria Montez never got along." (This mutual *detestation* society became so bad that at one time Chaney even picked a fight with Ankers' husband, Richard Denning, at a Universal press party.)

In her introduction to Doug McClelland's *The Golden Age of B Movies*, Evelyn Ankers herself recounts the genesis of Chaney's animosity toward her: "Just before I started [*The Wolf Man*], the front office called me in to tell me they liked my work and were rewarding me with a plush, new dressing room which I would share with Anne Gwynne, also under contract to Universal. Naturally I was thrilled. On the first day of shooting, Lon Chaney, Jr., my leading man, said to me, 'So you're the gal who swiped my dressing room. You took it away from Broderick Crawford and me—I think that was a hell of a thing to do!' Since I was going to have to work with this man (over and over again, as it turned out), I agreed. When I asked the front office about it, they told me Lon had been warned that this would happen if he didn't stop 'misbehaving.' Soon after, I found out just what 'misbehaving' meant. Someone told me that every Friday or Saturday night, Lon and Brod Crawford would take bottles into their dressing room, get loaded, and then somehow manage to hang the furniture from the ceiling and brawl. On Monday, the cleaning crew was treated to a sight resembling a World War II battlefield."

Surprisingly, *Weird Woman* garnered some rather favorable reviews at the time of release. *The New York Herald Tribune*'s Otis L. Guernsey, Jr., called it "a neat little murder tale all souped up with black magic... Universal has produced it with more taste and effort than is usual with a thriller of this type."

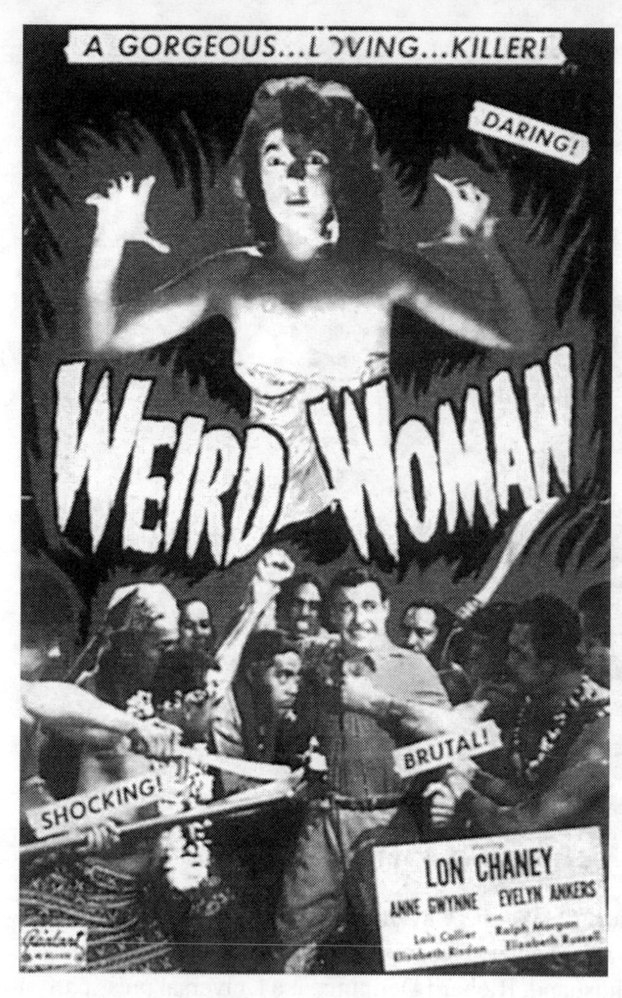

Though *Variety*'s "Walt" labeled it "a standard dual supporter and okay for the secondary and nabe houses," he went on to award it moderate praise: "Picture hits slow pace in early reels to establish characters and foundation for the series of mysterious events, after which it gains momentum and fairly fast clip through directorial efforts of Reginald LeBorg." Walt also felt that "Chaney, Miss Gwynne and Miss Ankers combine adequately for the three leads."

The reviewer for the *Motion Picture Exhibitor* also singled out the cast (including Lon Chaney, Jr.): "Chaney, Gwynne and Ankers handle their assignments ably as does director LeBorg. The story and presentation pace are good."

Not everyone liked the picture, however. *Harrison's Reports*: "Discriminating audiences will find it tiresome, and even the most ardent followers of this type of entertainment may find it but mildly interesting. Moreover, it is a slow-moving, moody entertainment."

At *The New York Times*, Bosley Crowther merely exclaimed, "Boy, is it dull!"

More recent assessments have also been mixed. Though saying little about the production itself (apart from the usual synopsis), Doug McClelland in *The Golden Age of B Movies* claimed that *Weird Woman* "stood out among Universal's fright flicks," while a more astute Calvin Thomas Beck (in *Heroes of the Horrors*) called *Weird Woman* a "disappointing production" and "the weakest segment of the entire [*Inner Sanctum*] series."

Universal Horrors authors Michael Brunas, John Brunas, and Tom Weaver, however, found *Weird Woman* to be "an absolute joy, outclassing the other films in the series for its sheer audaciousness alone. Brenda Weisberg's mildly hysterical screenplay has all the veracity of a Carol Burnett skit and is almost as funny." Of Chaney, the authors noted that "once again, Chaney is laughably miscast as a broody intellectual."

In his groundbreaking work, *An Illustrated History of the Horror Film*, Carlos Clarens had nothing good to say about the *Inner Sanctum* series (or Chaney himself): "In all of these [*Inner Sanctums*], Chaney revealed himself as a monotonous actor of rather narrow range, possessing neither the voice and skill of Karloff nor the demonic persuasion of Lugosi, and his rash of films were themselves mechanical, uninventive, and hopelessly serialized in flavor."

Incredibly, in *The Films of Reginald LeBorg* Wheeler Winston Dixon asserted that "Seen today, the film holds up extremely well, and indeed surpasses [*Burn, Witch, Burn*], which now seems flashy and superficial."(!) Dixon did allow, however, that "Chaney is a trifle hard to accept as an intellectual, but the other cast members are uniformly excellent."

Weird Woman is based on the novel *Conjure Wife* by Fritz Leiber, Jr. The story was adapted twice more to the screen (plus once on television for the series *Moment of Fear*, which is Leiber's own personal favorite of the adaptations), first in 1961 as *Burn, Witch, Burn* and then in 1980 as an (uncredited) comic variation called *Witches' Brew*. Of all the versions, *Burn, Witch, Burn* stands head and shoulders above the rest. *Weird Woman* not only pales in comparison to the intelligent and enthralling *Burn, Witch, Burn*, but it turns absolutely transparent.

Even so, despite a horribly miscast lead, uneven scripting, and indifferent direction, *Weird Woman* still offers up a relatively painless 63-minute diversion—thanks mostly to the film's fine supporting cast.

Regarding Lon Chaney, Jr., director Reginald LeBorg summed it up: "He was a complicated man with possibilities that were never realized. But he was all right with me. He wasn't the greatest actor in the world, but he was a good, solid guy. He had his personal problems, but then so does everybody."

CREDITS: Director: Reginald LeBorg; Associate Producer: Oliver Drake; Screenplay: Brenda Weisberg; From the novel *Conjure Wife* by Fritz Leiber, Jr.; Adaptation by W. Scott Darling; Director of Photography: Virgil Miller; Musical Director: Paul Sawtell; Art Directors: John B. Goodman and Richard Riedel; Director of Sound: Bernard B. Brown; Technician: William Hedgcock; Set Decorations: R. A. Gausman and A. J. Gilmore; Film Editor: Milton Carruth; Gowns: Vera West; Special Photography: John P. Fulton; An *Inner Sanctum* Mystery produced by arrangement with Simon and Schuster, Inc., Publishers; Released April 14, 1944 by Universal; 63 minutes

CAST: Lon Chaney (Professor Norman Reed); Anne Gwynne (Paula Clayton Reed); Evelyn Ankers (Ilona Carr); Ralph Morgan (Professor Millard Sawtelle); Elisabeth Risdon (Grace Gunnison); Lois Collier (Margaret Mercer); Elizabeth Russell (Evelyn Sawtelle); Harry Hayden (Professor Septimus Carr)

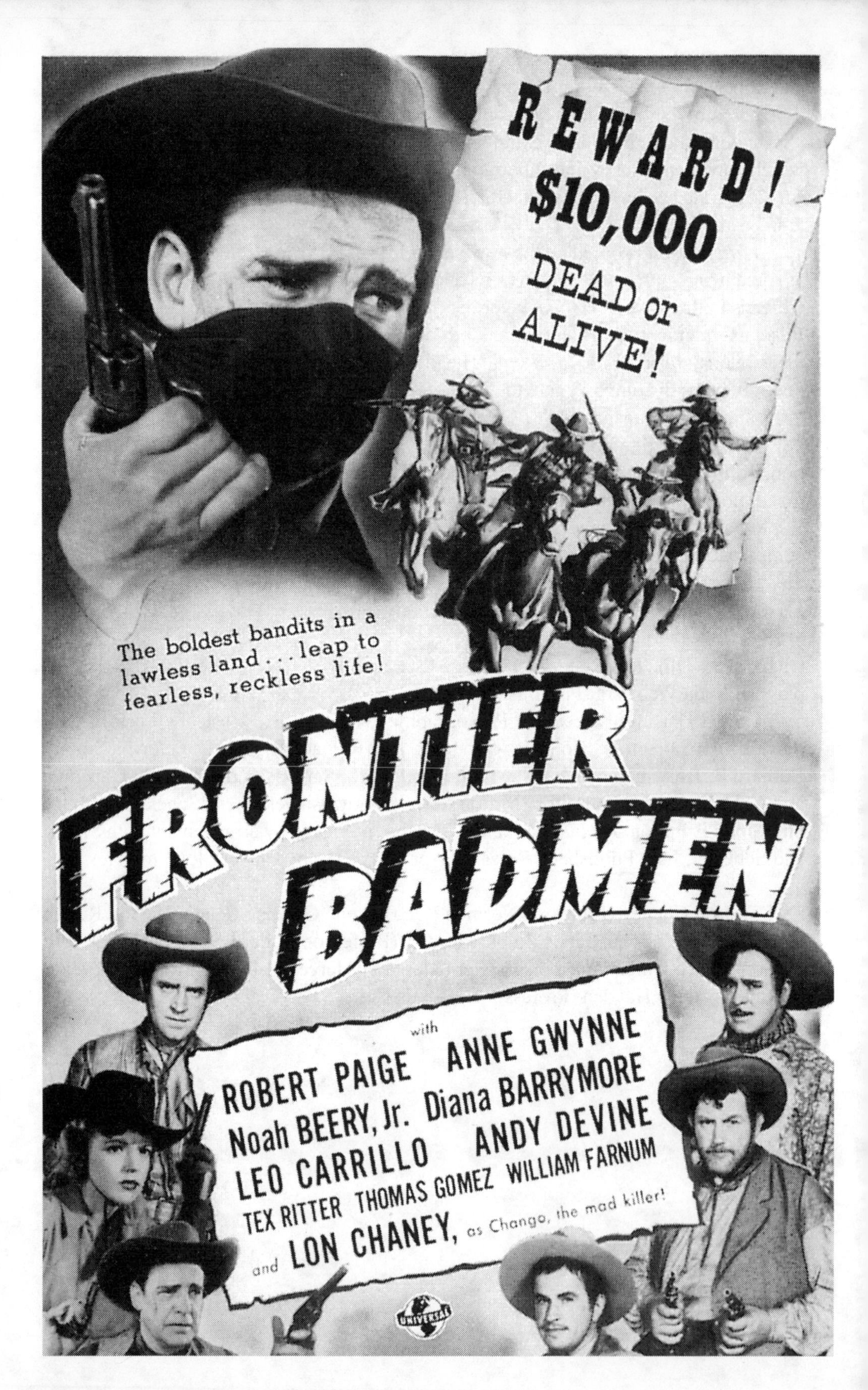
REWARD!
$10,000
DEAD or
ALIVE!
The boldest bandits in a
lawless land . . . leap to
fearless, reckless life!
FRONTIER
BADMEN
with
ROBERT PAIGE ANNE GWYNNE
Noah BEERY, Jr. Diana BARRYMORE
LEO CARRILLO ANDY DEVINE
TEX RITTER THOMAS GOMEZ WILLIAM FARNUM
and LON CHANEY, as Chango, the mad killer!
UNIVERSAL

LON CHANEY, JR.
TALL IN THE SADDLE
by C. Courtney Joyner

If Zane Grey were trying to imagine a good origin for a Western character, he might have looked to Lon Chaney, Jr. as an example: stillborn until his panicked father forced life into his body by dunking him in a frozen lake, hitting the road as a boy to make his own way picking fruit, learning how to handle a shotgun, trapping line, and skinner's knife with skill, and yet having the sensitivity to master sign language so he could speak to his deaf-mute grandparents.

With an Oklahoma twang that never left his voice, his natural love of the outdoors, and his ability with horses and guns, Lon Chaney, Jr. seemed destined for Western movies. Like a man of the West, he had good humor, a way with a drink, and lifelong loyalty to his friends.

Although he is best remembered by fans for his horror work, over forty of Chaney's one hundred and seventy-one films were Westerns, and include one of the finest ever made, *High Noon*.

But Fred Zinnemann's classic was a long way off for Creighton Chaney on August 28, 1930, when news of his father's death made worldwide headlines. Lon, Sr. died secure in the knowledge that he had destroyed any interest his son might have had in the movies. Of course, he was wrong. And soon the younger Chaney was struggling his way into the movies as Hollywood was trying to perfect its new Vitaphone voice.

One thing had not changed since the silent days: Westerns were the studios' bread and butter. They were quick and cheap to make, and there was a ready audience who would flock to everything from major productions like Wesley Ruggle's 1931 *Cimarron* to poverty row quickies and serials being ground out at the rate of one a week by outfits like Lone Star, Mascot, and Monogram.

Along with his early costar John Wayne, Lon Chaney, Jr. first hit the trail in Gower Gulch.

In 1932, RKO studios put young Chaney under contract at a salary of two hundred dollars a week. After supporting bits in *Bird of Paradise* and *Girl Crazy*, the studio took a chance and gave Chaney the lead in the Western serial, *The Last Frontier.*

Seen today, *The Last Frontier* is on par with most poverty row shoot 'em ups of the period: silent film-style cowboy action interrupted by static dialogue. In fact, with all the ridin' and shootin', who needed to sweat a story or performances? Certainly not ex-stuntman/director Spencer Gordon Bennett who would direct fifty-two serials and countless programmers in his career, including Alex Gordon's *The Atomic Submarine*. Under Bennett's hurry-up guidance, all Chaney could do was plow through the dialogue and action scenes as quickly as possible without killing himself.

Chaney's performance in the serial has been rightly criticized. As a sincere "Clark Kent" style newspaper editor by day and the dashing, outlaw-busting Ghost by night, he's out of his depth. And yet, is he any worse than the dozens of other stiff-backed

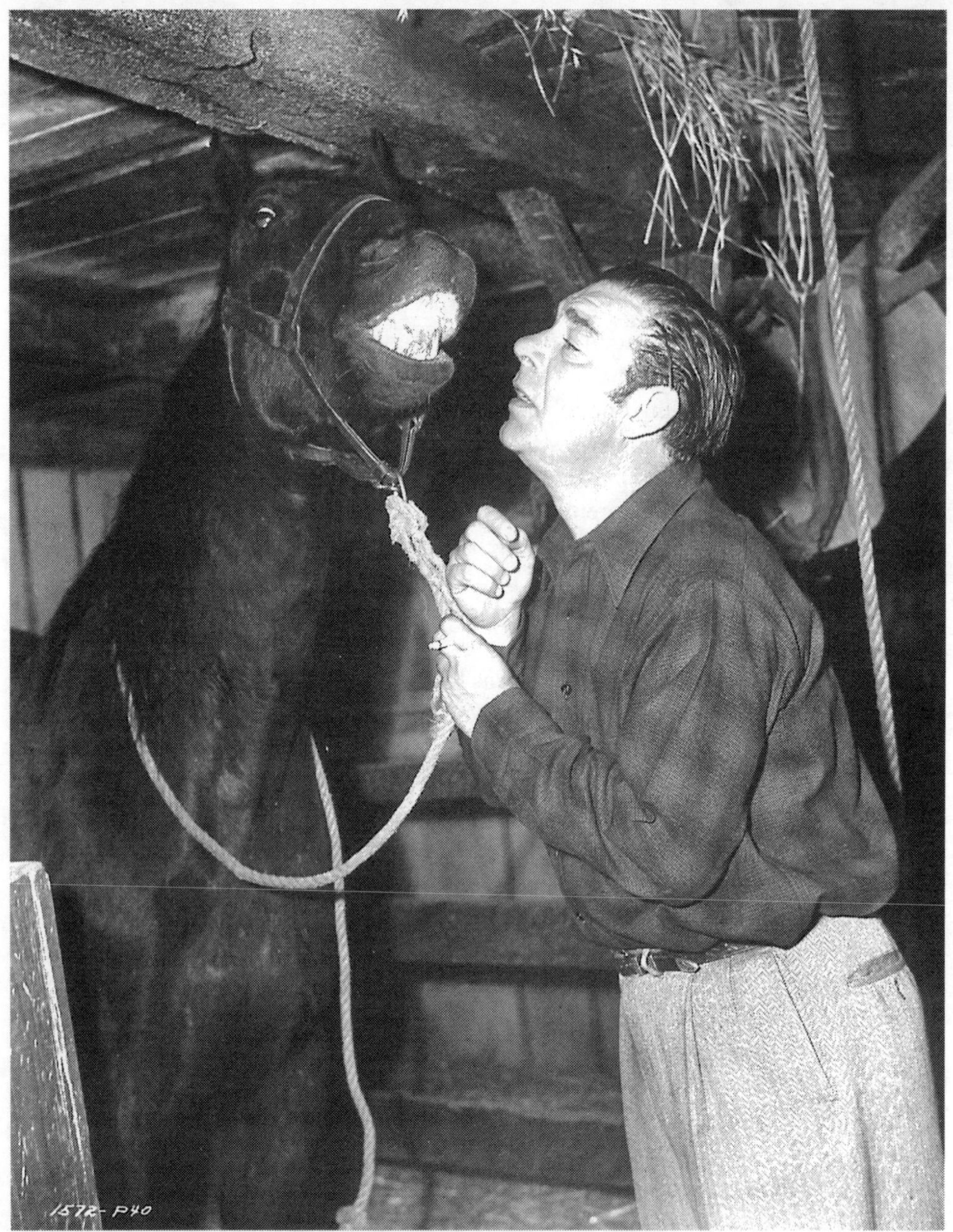

Lon Chaney, Jr. would make a name for himself as a strong Western character actor, throughout his entire movie career. [Photofest]

cowpokes who were playing the leads in low-budget quickies? Not really, and in retrospect it's fun to see the fresh-faced Chaney before he grew into his more mature persona of the 1940s.

RKO's response to Chaney's leading man effort was to put him in a series of supporting roles including two Tom Keene sagas, *Scarlet River* and *Son of the Border*, shot in 1933. Both films were written by Harold Shumate, who would also script Chaney's 1941 Western *Badlands of Dakota*, and feature nice character work for Lon opposite the square-jawed Keene.

Lon acquits himself pretty well in the two Keene films. He plays the heavy in both, really his first time as a Western villain, and still manages to underscore his performances with bits of dimwitted humor that he would use to great advantage as Lennie and his later character work in the 1950s.

As Lon's career progressed, cowboy star Tom Keene shuffled between RKO, Paramount, and Monogram in the '30s and '40s before heading for the last roundup as a member of Ed Wood's stock company.

The early 1930s was a time for Lon to cut his teeth, much like John Wayne, his costar in Nat Levine's Mascot serial *The Three Musketeers.* An odd take on the Dumas story, it tells the tale of three friends who join the Foreign Legion rather than Malady's Guards. Their adventures unfold in typically slapdash Mascot fashion, high on energy if nothing else.

Although Lon dies in the first chapter, it's interesting to note this role as his only work with John Wayne. Despite Lon's being cast in Western after Western and working with regular Wayne directors like Burt Kennedy, this is the only time the two men would share the screen.

While Mascot continued to grind out serials with Wayne or future Chaney costar Bela Lugosi, Nat Levine was busy negotiating a sale of the company to Consolidated Labs boss Herbert J. Yates. Yates merged Mascot, Monogram, and Majestic pictures, christened the company Republic, and made Levine his executive producer. Up first on Levine's slate were two Westerns showcasing their singing discovery Gene Autry, with Lon Chaney, Jr. riding right along as a bad guy.

The Old Corral and *The Singing Cowboy* are classic Autry vehicles, with that peculiar mix of modern gangsters zipping around in convertibles, Gene saving the day on horseback, and those amazing tunes (co-written by *The Mummy's Curse* producer Oliver Drake). But these maiden Republic efforts are important in gauging Lon's career, since they show a beginning of continuity in the actor's professional life. Although typecast, he was returning to work for a producer who obviously appreciated him. Also, Lon was starting to relax in front of the camera, no doubt helped along by the sure direction of Republic's ace Joe Kane.

Lon looked on his years in Gower Gulch as paying his dues and later reflected, "Now I knew what Dad meant when he said 'I've taken the bumps.' Well, I'd taken them. I did every possible tough bit in pictures. I had to do stuntwork to live. I've bulldogged steers, fallen off and gotten knocked off cliffs, ridden horses into rivers, driven prairie schooners up and down hills—everything."

It was around this time that Chaney divorced Dorothy, the mother of his two sons, and married model Patsy Beck. Patsy would remain Mrs. Chaney until Lon's death in 1973.

Lon hit the trail at the end of 1936 for the infamous Sam Katzman in the Tom Tyler vehicle *Cheyenne Rides Again.* Produced by Katzman's Victory Pictures and directed by Robert Hill, who would helm Universal's *Flash Gordon's Trip to Mars,* the film features Lon in another menacing cowhand part. The film's sole interest today is to see Lon and Tom Tyler —both future Kharis'—sharing scenes without their mummy wrappings.

After all the quickies, Lon would soon be in demand on larger scale films after winning a contract with 20th Century-Fox. Although some of Lon's parts were bits and featured support in Charlie Chan or Sonja Henie vehicles, the Fox contract gave Lon his first chance to work with veteran director Allan Dwan. Dwan, who would cast Lon, Jr. in two Westerns, had a long history with the Chaney family: "I picked up a new property man at Universal who was quite a nice guy. He used to come around with funny teeth in his mouth and weird make-ups... I said to him, 'What the hell is this? Do you want to get in front of the lens?' He said, yes. He was a property man because he had to make a living. So I put him to work (as an actor)... and he caught on. And that was the start of Lon Chaney (Sr.)."

After thirty-two movies, Lon, Jr. ended his Fox contract with the Technicolor masterwork *Jesse James*, starring Tyrone Power and Henry Fonda as the notorious bandits. As a bearded member of Jesse's gang, Lon makes a strong impression. His aggressive physicality and brooding features had always worked for his outlaw portrayals, but captured by George Barne's brilliant cinematography, Lon had never looked better (or more menacing).

Turning in one of the strongest performances in the picture is Lon's friend John Carradine. His portrayal of Jesse's assassin, Bob Ford, stands as a highlight in the veteran actor's long career. This was the fourth film in which Lon and Carradine were cast together. The two would co-star a dozen times over the years, in everything from *The Mummy's Ghost* to *Hillbillys in a Haunted House*, but *Jesse James* is the qualitative high water mark.

Jesse James remains a movie classic and is the finest production Lon was associated with before *Of Mice and Men*. It was the first film in which he was involved that was nominated for Academy Awards and, although his role is brief, it was the start of a career-long pattern of consistently excellent character work in top Hollywood productions. While Lon's later horror films jumped about wildly in terms of budget and quality, his Westerns (even the cheapest ones) were always the product of prominent producers and featured name casts.

In the months preceding *Of Mice and Men*, Lon made his first film for Cecil B. DeMille and returned to work for Alan Dwan. 1939's *Union Pacific* was DeMille's massive follow-up to his hugely successful Western *The Plainsman* of 1936, and is considered by many to be his finest Western. *Stagecoach* author Ernest Haycox's novel *The Trouble Shooter* was the basis for this retelling of the construction of the first intercontinental rail lines. With a cast including Joel McCrea, Robert Preston, Barbara Stanwyck, and Brian Donlevy, Lon was again making his mark a million miles away from poverty row. Despite the small role, DeMille took notice of Lon and used him in a more substantial part in another epic a year later.

Lon then jumped from Paramount back to 20th Century-Fox and Allan Dwan for the Randolph Scott vehicle *Frontier Marshal* One of Hollywood's strongest retellings of the legend surrounding Wyatt Earp, and predating John Ford's classic *My Darling Clementine* by seven years, *Frontier Marshal* boasts a solid script and excellent acting from Scott as Earp and Cesar Romero as Doc Holliday. Lon lends support as Pringle, one of the town ruffians. John Carradine is on hand as a baddie modeled after Ike Clanton and makes a strong impression.

Author Brian Garfield, in his excellent *Western Films*, calls *Frontier Marshal* "highly satisfactory with all the traditional myths solidly in place. At the time of its release it suffered from competition from the slew of blockbuster Westerns that brought the genre out of the doldrums in 1939: *Union Pacific, Man of Conquest, Stagecoach,* and *Jesse James*. But in retrospect, *Frontier Marshal* stands up well against all of them."

Cecil B. DeMille must have had Lennie on his mind when he cast Lon in the giant-scale *Northwest Mounted Police* (1940).

Of the films Garfield cites, Lon appears in three. Over and over Hollywood's best were asking Lon to hit the trail as part of their Western stock companies, but John Steinbeck's masterful creation Lennie Small loomed in the young actor's future, forever changing his life.

Cecil B. DeMille must have had Lennie on his mind when he cast Lon in the giant-scale *Northwest Mounted Police* (1940). A manhunt story set against the background of the Matis revolt in 1880s' Canada, Lon's character provides much of the film's comic relief.

Chaney, Jr.'s first Western on his Universal contract was *Riders of Death Valley.*

Despite a French accent, Lon's Shorty is very much in the Lennie mold without the tragic overtones. In one scene, after being told his wife has just had a baby, a joyously confused Shorty runs to her bedside with the news that *he's* given birth. It's a funny moment, but this film was the start of Lennie typecasting for Lon and a style of acting he would be forced to return to again and again.

The first of three films Lon would make with Gary Cooper, the sprawling DeMille production was one of the year's most popular releases and won an Academy Award for film editing. And it was another endorsement of Lon for big-budget action films that led naturally to MGM's all-star production, *Billy the Kid.*

Directed by David Miller (who would score with his 1962 Kirk Douglas Western *Lonely Are the Brave*), the film stars Robert Taylor and Brian Donlevy and is about as historically accurate as a Monogram kiddie matinee special, but done with MGM gloss. Lon does one more solid turn as an outlaw, and added another A picture to his credits.

The period immediately following *Of Mice and Men* was a strange one for Lon. He had given a shattering performance in a film that was nominated for an Oscar as Best Picture of the Year but lost to *Gone With the Wind*, and yet he found himself back giving support to top Hollywood names, rather than standing equally alongside them.

But the tide was to turn again for Lon, Jr. The biggest B factory of them all came knocking with a contract and, finally, stardom.

In order to properly assess Lon's Westerns made during his five years at Universal, it's important that we understand the status of the studio and the position of the contract player. Always considered the "runt of the litter" of the major studios, Universal had a long history of financial problems and when "Uncle" Carl Laemmle sold out the family interest in 1937 to J. Cheever Cowdin and Charles Rogers, the studio was on the verge of collapse.

Rogers and Cowdin had a plan, and it brought Universal back to life and remained the studio policy throughout the war years: make as many movies for as low a price as possible. Unlike Warner Brothers or MGM, Universal had no big stars under exclusive contract. Abbott and Costello were an exception, but even their hugely popular films were made quickly and according to strict budget guidelines. To the front office, movies were simply product to be delivered and the studio was one more factory working to meet a wartime demand.

This was the situation when Lon Chaney, Jr. signed with the company in 1941. Even after Lon struck box office gold as Larry Talbot, Universal worked out his contract by casting him in everything from Olsen and Johnson comedies to the *Inner Sanctums* for a total of thirty-two movies in less than five years.

Although it seems a waste that Lon was never given a role in the studio's few bigger productions, like 1942's *The Spoilers* or *Pittsburgh*, he shines in the four Westerns and two serials he made during his contract days.

Lon's first Western assignment on his contract was the 1941 serial, *Riders of Death Valley*. Now considered a "super serial," *Riders* is a beautifully photographed (by Jerome Ash and William Sickner) and well written example of the heights the form could reach when everyone involved really put forth the effort.

Setting *Riders* apart from the hack work of most serials are the genial performances. Dick Foran uses his affable charm to make hero Dick Benton more than the usual cowpoke looking out for the pretty heroine (Jeane Kelly). Buck Jones is along to supply some surprising deadpan humor, needling pal Foran every chance he gets.

Opposing our heroes is the excellent Charles Bickford who wants control of Miss Kelly's mine. But it's Lon Chaney, the muscle of Bickford's gang, who steals the acting honors. As Butch, Lon gives an open and comfortable performance. He tosses away his lines in a relaxed, smiling manner and projects a nice vulnerability that's quite a relief from the usual black hat villain stuff required of most serials.

After paying his dues, Lon must have felt a twinge of *deja-vu* to be playing a second banana in another serial, particularly to his *Of Mice and Men* co-star Bickford. But if he did, it didn't stop him from delivering a fine rough and tumble characterization. Butch is the kind of B role Lon could do in his sleep, and it's to his credit that he gives it his all.

Lon followed his stint in the fifteen-chapter serial with a turn as real-life outlaw Jack McCall in director Alfred E. Green's *Badlands of Dakota*.

The first film to pair Lon and lifelong pal Broderick Crawford, *Badlands* is an example of the multi-character Western that brought together various historical figures for a fanciful story, often with a complete disregard for the facts. In this case, the characters include McCall, Wild Bill Hickock (Richard Dix), General Custer (Addison Richards), and Calamity Jane (Frances Farmer).

The wide-open town of Deadwood is the setting as these famous Westerners are embroiled in a conflict between brothers Crawford and Robert Stack. Lon's McCall is a brute, and a good foil for the white hats that surround him. It's a solid performance in a film brimming with them, particularly the personally troubled Farmer who's dead-on as Calamity Jane.

Lon barely had time to swap his chaps for a lumber jacket when he was paired again with Brod Crawford for *North to the Klondike*, directed by old pro Erle C. Kenton.

Lon barely had time to swap his chaps for a lumber jacket when he was paired again with Brod Crawford for *North to the Klondike*, directed by old pro Erle C. Kenton. *Klondike* is an assembly-line job, put together quickly to take advantage of the box office (and the left over sets) of *The Spoilers*, the classic Rex Beach story that Universal had just remade with John Wayne and Randolph Scott.

Dismissed as a poor cousin to the larger film, *North to the Klondike* actually has a good deal to recommend it. "Inspired" by a Jack London tale, it's the old "gold fever up North" story but helped along greatly by Lon's and Crawford's burly performances. These two look completely at home trading snarls and punches with one another. You can almost smell the whiskey in the air when they finally go at it, and their brawl is a well staged and energetic set piece.

Behind the camera, Erle Kenton guides the action with clean economy. As a journeyman director, Kenton's career would be peppered with triumphs like 1932's *Island of Lost Souls*. This was the first of four films Kenton would make with Lon, and the only non-horror film. Soon they would be collaborating on *The Ghost of Frankenstein, House of Frankenstein*, and *House of Dracula*

Two more horror veterans were credited with the film's screenplay. 1950s' horror maven William Castle adapted the piece from Jack London and George Bricker penned the dialogue. Bricker later banged out the scripts for *House of Horrors* and *The Brute*

You can almost smell the whiskey in the air when Lon and Brod finally go at it, and their brawl is a well staged and energetic set piece, in *North to the Klondike.*

Man. On a final horror note, economy minded Universal would put Lon through his paces on these sets again, as Kharis in the climax of *The Mummy's Ghost* (1944). But all that was to come. Lon wrapped *Klondike* while he studied a new script called *Destiny* and reported to Jack Pierce for make-up tests.

An Autumn moon hung in the sky foretelling the actor's future, and when he hit the trail again the following year, it was as a bonafide leading man.

"Men of valor! Deeds of daring! No quarter asked... none given... as dauntless riders blaze the mail trail to the West!" So proclaimed the ad lines for Lon's fifteen-chapter *Overland Mail*, released in 1942.

Even though it was one more serial for Lon, this time he was cast as the hero, battling it out with a gang of varmints led by Noah Beery, Sr. Cowboy Jim Lane is a stock man of action part, but Lon carries it off well, and it's nice to see him give the beatings rather than take them.

Lon makes a fine and believable hero, but note should be made of B Queen Helen Parrish as the perennial daughter seeking Lon's help to save Dad's stage line. Miss Parrish was always an appealing presence, often in Republic Westerns. Along for his fifth film with Lon was Noah Beery, Jr., the homespun good guy who was forever a sidekick before coming into his own in the 1970s as James Garner's father on *The Rockford Files*.

Don Terry, Chaney, Jr., and Helen Parrish in *Overland Mail.*

While producer-director Ford Beebe does his best, *Overland Mail*'s action scenes are not very well staged, and in a serial this is a deadly flaw. Later this same year, Beebe would make an impression as director of the wonderfully suspenseful *Night Monster* as well as producing *Son of Dracula* before directing Lon again in a vastly superior Western.

A slew of horrors, including *The Mummy's Tomb* and *Frankenstein Meets the Wolf Man,* occupied Lon before he stepped in front of Ford Beebe's cameras for *Frontier Badmen* in 1943. When he did, it was as the nastiest villain he had yet played.

Frontier Badmen is the best Western Lon made during his contract period. He was at his height of popularity as a horror star and much was made of his appearing in the film, and the studio seems to have spent a little more production money than usual to support his status.

A straight action tale of cattlemen fighting corruption along the Chisholm Trail, *Badmen* features a typical Universal cast of the period: Robert Paige, Noah Beery, Jr.,

Thomas Gomez, and Lon's pal Andy Devine. This time the strong-willed girl is played by Diana Barrymore, the tragic daughter of John. All of the players in front of and behind the camera were pros who knew how to deliver the goods, and Lon responded to this assignment by dominating every scene in which he appears. His handling of the role of Chango elevates *Badmen* into something special.

Lon bristles with energy, even when kicking back and smiling as he remembers his latest killing. As was usual for this time, Lon was given special billing as "Chango—The Mad Killer!" and many of the posters featured him with his face masked, perhaps to emphasize a mystery/horror angle to his presence.

This time director Ford Beebe helps with the film's energy level. An ex-publicity flack who'd been with Universal since 1913, Beebe redeems himself after some of the clumsy action in *Overland Mail* by staging an exciting cattle stampede and several shoot-outs. Cameraman William Sickner also contributes first-rate work.

During the shooting, Diana Barrymore was accidentally hurt by Lon when he shoved her out of the way of some gunfire and she twisted her ankle. Despite the mishap, Miss

4 MEN AGAINST A NATION!
...writing their crimson history in blood and gun smoke!
UNIVERSAL presents
THE DALTONS RIDE AGAIN
with
ALAN CURTIS LON CHANEY
KENT TAYLOR NOAH BEERY, Jr.
MARTHA O'DRISCOLL JESS BARKER
THOMAS GOMEZ JOHN LITEL
Original Screenplay by Roy Chanslor and Paul Gangelin Additional Dialogue by Henry Blankfort
Directed by RAY TAYLOR Produced by HOWARD WELSCH
UNIVERSAL

Noah Beery, Jr., Alan Curtis, Kent Taylor, and Lon Chaney on a rampage in *The Daltons Ride Again.*

Barrymore liked Lon and makes special note of him in her autobiography *Too Much, Too Soon.* Many of Lon's strongest friendships were forged during his Universal period and, just as he was the son of a film legend, some of his friends were the second generation sons and daughters of famous acting families like Miss Barrymore, Brod Crawford, and Noah Beery, Jr.

If *Frontier Badmen* showed how a programmer could be elevated, Lon's last Western on his contract, *The Daltons Ride Again,* is strictly business as usual. Shot in sixteen days by Ray Taylor, the film is a rehash rather than a remake of Universal's 1940 *When the Daltons Rode.*

Lon is cast alongside Kent Taylor, Alan Curtis, and Noah Beery, Jr. as the Dalton brothers and the script follows them as they rob banks and are eventually brought down in Coffeyville, Kansas. The film turns the boys into standard movie outlaws, a contrast to the character-driven approach of the 1940 original.

Lon had put on some weight in his last few films, notably *Pillow of Death*, and the *Daltons* pressbook claims he shed thirty pounds before starting the shoot. Although it adds to his rough appearance, if the diet was just for this movie it hardly seemed worth it. *The Daltons Ride Again* was formula stuff for the bottom of double bills, but Lon still gave it his all.

In many ways *The Daltons Ride Again* is a good summing up of Lon's Universal period. He did his best to shine in films that were made on the assembly line, whether good, bad, or indifferent. A John Ford was not on board to guide him. Like Lon himself, the men writing and directing were contractees doing their best with little money or time.

In many ways *The Daltons Ride Again* is a good summing up of Lon's Universal period.

While none of Universal's Westerns Lon appeared in are on the level of an *Ox Bow Incident* (1943), taken as fast-paced entertainment, they hold up well. With their multi-character plots of double crosses and constant gun play, these films truly define the term "horse opera" and are great examples of the kind of action films America hungered for during World War II. Lon Chaney was an important part of the formula that made these movies work, and without his efforts they would have surely suffered.

Lon's contract, along with almost the entire Universal stock company, was terminated in 1945 and he began to freelance again. It would be three years before he'd make another Western, but when Lon reported to work at Paramount for the Pine-Thomas production *Albuquerque* in 1948, he was met by a young publicist who would have a great impact on his last active years.

A. C. Lyles had been cranking out publicity items for Pine-Thomas productions almost as fast as the producing team was cranking out movies. Dubbed the "Two Dollar Bills" in the columns (actually planted by Lyles himself), William Pine and William Thomas had been producing low-budget pictures since the forties, but were moving on to bigger adventure films and Westerns. Lyles, a protégé of Paramount president Adolph Zukor, went to work for the team and met Lon Chaney. They became fast friends while shooting *Albuquerque*, and Lyles would make Lon a member of his stock company when he was producing years later.

Albuquerque, adapted from a novel by Luke Short, finds drifter Randolph Scott stumbling into the middle of a range war between youngster Russell Hayden and his uncle, played by George Cleveland. Lon is the crooked Sheriff who tries to straddle both sides of the fence. As always, Lon projects a smooth charm for the rogue lawman before exploding with temper.

It's a solid little Western, well directed by journeyman Ray Enright who had helmed the remake of *The Spoilers* at Universal. But the real plus factors of the film are the behind-the-scenes friendships that Lon cemented that led to a continuous string of movies in the 1960s.

Lon wouldn't saddle up again until 1951, but a great deal was happening to the actor off the screen. He had attempted suicide in 1948 and already his heavy drinking and smoking were causing a marked physical change. His face was craggier than before, and deep lines were beginning to form. His gruff voice seemed to drop an octave and was perennially smoky and whiskey-burned.

It was these changes in Lon's appearance that made him a good casting choice for roles many years older than his actual age. Still physically imposing, Lon could now play muscled villains or beaten, older men depending upon the script. His range as an actor broadened in the 1950s with a remarkably diverse body of work.

Inside Straight (1951) was Lon's return to MGM after *Billy the Kid.* While *Billy* was elevated kid stuff, at least it had more entertainment value than this tale of gamblers in 1870s' San Francisco. Lon dominates the early part of the film as Shocker, a miner who helps a young orphan (Claude Jarmon of *The Yearling*) before he grows into adulthood as the most notorious gambler in the country.

Lon enjoyed children and always worked well with them and this film is no exception. But *Inside Straight* fails primarily because of the unsympathetic casting of Warner Brothers heavy David Brian in the lead. Also in the cast is Barry Sullivan as a card sharp. Sullivan and Lon would be reunited in the '60s in several films for A. C. Lyles.

Lon went immediately from a humdrum film to one that remains underrated. Produced by James Cagney's brother William, *Only the Valiant* is a gritty Western that features Lon in a fine role among a star-studded cast: Gregory Peck, Gig Young, Ward Bond, Neville Brand, and Michael Ansara. Well directed by Gordon Douglas of *Them!* fame and beautifully shot by Lionel Lindon, the film is one of Lon's best of the '50s.

Peck portrays a by-the-book Cavalry officer who assigns an inexperienced Lieutenant a dangerous mission in Indian territory. The Lieutenant is killed, and Peck, racked by guilt, takes on the mission himself with the troopers who despise him for his supposed cowardice.

Lon plays an Arab soldier who is so consumed with hatred for Peck that he attacks him every chance he gets. Lon's Trooper Kebussyan is a wild, physical role and the actor is up to the challenge. In one of his finest scenes, the Arab is confined to the stockade where he is going out of his mind, then explodes in a rage and bends back the window bars to escape, only to be beaten down in tears.

This aggressive role is the kind in which Lon often excelled and one couldn't imagine anyone doing it better. Ironically, he almost didn't play the part at all. Michael Ansara recently related his experience on the film (which was his screen debut): "William Cagney wanted me to play the part that Lon ended up with, but Gordon Douglas decided I'd do better in the Indian role."

Ansara does so well as the Apache that he was later cast as the lead in the television series *Broken Arrow*. But what did the young actor think being in such experienced company his first time out?

"I was in awe, frankly. I mean, I had seen these guys in movies when I was a kid. Lon Chaney in particular, he was The Wolf Man, how can you beat that? But Lon was very nice to me, knew that I was nervous. They all were. Peck even gave me a puppy that I named Valiant in honor of the picture! Guys like Lon Chaney and Ward Bond were of the old school. Real pros who knew what they were doing and I admired them very much. And I learned from them."

With its script by Edmund H. North, who would later share an Academy Award with Francis Coppola for writing *Patton*, *Only the Valiant* is a small film with big ambitions. Lon's next Western, *The Bushwhackers* (1952), was a return to his B programmer days.

Produced by Jack Broder for Realart, *Bushwhackers* takes an old page from *Shane* and *The Gunfighter* in its story of a Confederate soldier who has put down his gun only to be forced back to violence to take on a band of outlaws. John Ireland plays the soldier and Lawrence Tierney the leader of the outlaws, but it's Lon who dominates the film.

In his first truly aged performance, Lon plays a land baron who's crippled with arthritis but still able to bark orders to his hired guns who do his bidding. With his head and hands frozen into place, Lon exudes dramatic energy and easily walks away with the acting honors.

Associate producer on the film was young Herman Cohen, who would make his mark with such horror films as *I Was a Teenage Werewolf* and *Horrors of the Black Museum*. In a personal interview, Cohen recalled working with Lon. "The first time was actually on *Bride of the Gorilla* (1951), which was also for Broder/Realart. Broder had made a lot of money reissuing Lon's old Universal pictures, and so when I suggested Lon for these films, Broder was all for it. The main thing about Lon was that he was always very professional, you know? Whatever he had to do, he did. Of course we never mentioned his dad, because he had that all of his life. But these were low-budget films, made very fast, and Lon was always prepared, always ready to go. And believe me, I've worked with some actors who are never ready to shoot so I know how valuable a pro like Lon could be."

Lawrence Tierney remembers Lon and the film in a more critical light: "I liked Lon. He was a good guy, quiet. But I always hated the picture. I played a miserable bastard who was always hiding behind trees and I didn't enjoy it at all."

The one technical footnote of interest about the film was that it was an early writing effort of Tom Gries who would later write and direct the excellent Western *Will Penny* (1968) starring Charlton Heston.

The Bushwhackers remains a minor item, but Lon's next Western has stood the test of time as a true masterpiece and is among the best films ever made.

From its opening image of Lee Van Cleef leaning against a rock on an open range, as the strums of Tex Ritter's guitar fill the soundtrack, *High Noon* is a model of restraint and economy. The film is stunning in the clarity of its dramatic structure as we live the same ninety minutes the characters live waiting for the noon train—and death—to arrive in the small town of Hadleyville.

Carl Foreman's story of Marshal Will Kane (Gary Cooper) and his struggle to rally a community around him to help fight off a band of killers is the stuff of cinema legend. But the film could have been made as a noisy, guns a-blazin' Western instead of the intense, quiet study of fear that it is.

At the center of the film is Gary Cooper's studied performance as the lawman, but it is the work of the cast around him that drives the story of cowardice home. Otto Kruger, Thomas Mitchell, and Henry Morgan all shine as the town folk, but it's Lon Chaney's sympathetic turn as the old marshal who'd like to help but cannot that is the standout performance.

With a flowing mustache, gray hair, and arthritic hands, Lon plays Martin Howe not as a coward but as a man who's had enough of an unappreciated life. When he tells Gary Cooper what it really means to be a lawman in the West, there's no trace of bitterness in his voice, only the experience of a man who walked the streets at high noon himself and knows that *nobody* gives a damn if you die for your community or not.

It's a masterful characterization. Lon projects Howe's age with the soft inflection of his voice, coming across perfectly as Cooper's mentor, despite the fact that he was only forty-five at the time and Cooper was five years older. According to the notes in director Fred Zinnemann's script, it was Lon's voice and under playing that won him the part over contenders Victor McLaglen and Jay C. Flippen.

High Noon was nominated for six Academy Awards, including Best Picture, and won four. Zinnemann's direction, Floyd Crosby's stark images, and the haunting Dimitri Tiomkin score combined to make the film what it is: a prime example of filmmaking art. And Lon Chaney was one of the artists who brought it into being.

High Noon benefited Lon in many ways, not the least of which was the start of his relationship with Stanley Kramer who would cast him in two more films. Lon would ride the wave of his excellent work in the film for several years, but none of the Westerns in which he appeared would ever come close to the quality of the Zinnemann film.

Springfield Rifle is just the kind of '50's shoot-'em-up that *High Noon* was not. Although it also stars Gary Cooper, its story of Confederate spies and illegal horse trading gets so convoluted that by midpoint the film is merely tiresome. This is a shame, since Lon contributes a full, lusty performance as an outlaw who thinks he smells a rat in Gary Cooper. Lon and Cooper finally brawl, with Cooper lashing Lon's backside with a knife.

It is fun to contrast Lon's roles in the two Cooper films. Shot almost back-to-back, Lon's transformation from the arthritic, beaten Martin Howe to the fast riding horse thief of *Springfield Rifle* reminds us of just what a versatile actor he was. Unfortunately, there's little else to derive from the film which is directed in mediocre fashion by Andre (*House of Wax)* de Toth.

The Battles of Chief Pontiac (1952) brought Lon back to work for producer Jack Broder and his associate, Herman Cohen. Shot quickly by the talented Felix Fiest, Lon rises to the occasion by turning in a studied performance as the legendary Indian Chief. It was a role he cherished and Cohen remembers his enthusiasm for it. "I really wanted Lon for *Pontiac*, and I got to know him well when we went on location in Rapid City, South Dakota. We were working with the Sioux tribe, and Lon wanted to get to know the Indians. He really thought he was Pontiac! (laughs) The Indians had an encampment at location, and Lon had a hotel room, but many nights Lon would spend at the campsite, listening to the stories of the old timers because he wanted to get a feel for the tribe. And they loved him, used to laugh with him all the time. You know, he was a very funny man. He had that deep voice and was very commanding, but he was unassuming. Of course he was a boozer, but I never saw him drunk in the three films we made together.

Battles of Chief Pontiac is not a major work, but it is a colorful action film and Chaney, Jr. makes a dignified Pontiac.

Hell, John Wayne used to drink too. But Lon was a hell of a nice guy and a good actor and he could do so much more beyond the horror films."

Battles of Chief Pontiac is not a major work, but it is a colorful action film and Lon makes a dignified Pontiac. Screenwriter Jack DeWit would address Native American concerns again when he wrote *A Man Called Horse* in 1970.

1954 was a busy year for Lon as he returned to Warner Brothers to work for the great Michael Curtiz in *The Boy from Oklahoma*. Designed as a vehicle for Will Rogers, Jr., it's a leisurely, backporch tale of a shy, Destry-like lawman who takes a town in hand with humor instead of gun play.

The Boy from Oklahoma captures the spirit of many of the films that starred Will, Sr. with Lon adding to the comedy in a bawdy performance as a town drunk. It's an inconsequential film, but it does show Lon in a rare comedy role without a hint of dark shading. It also shows a lighter side to director Curtiz, who made a number of musicals and comedies in his career but was most famous for *Casablanca* and *Angels With Dirty Faces*.

Lon chucked the comedy and went for full-tilt villainy in his last collaboration with Allan Dwan, *Passion* (1954). A silly story of Cornel Wilde teaming with his dead wife's twin sister (Yvonne De Carlo) to find a band of killers, the film features Lon as a Mexican bandit.

Passion is a melodramatic throwback to Dwan's silent work like *Robin Hood* (1922) with every emotion on screen at high pitch. Lon contributes the best moments in a splendid knife fight with Wilde. It's the kind of brutal, tough display that Lon always did well and it's fun to see him doing this action scene himself while Cornel Wilde is obviously doubled.

Producer-actor Earl Lyon brought Lon in on his Lippert Production *The Silver Star* in 1955 to help draw comparisons between his film and *High Noon*. This tough Western about the problems of a newly elected sheriff is nowhere near the Stanley Kramer classic, but it's a finely tuned little film. Lon portrays the old sheriff who's beaten out of his job and seeks revenge, an interesting combination of Martin Howe and his psychotic roles.

The Silver Star and *The Bushwhackers* were Lon's least significant Westerns after his Universal period, but both films utilized his talents well and backed him with strong casts. *Bushwhackers* certainly falls into the B category because of its screenplay, but *The Silver Star* has higher aspirations and should be recognized as such.

Lon went before the cameras a second time for Andre de Toth in *The Indian Fighter* (1955) costarring with Kirk Douglas and Walter Matthau. De Toth is back in form here, and armed with a screenplay by the legendary Ben Hecht (*Scarface* and *Spellbound*), delivers a top-drawer adventure film.

Lon and Matthau play settlers who deal liquor to the Indians in exchange for gold nuggets the tribe is mining on their land. Lon's character is a drunk and a liar who shoots his mouth off at every opportunity to tell of his bravery when dealing with the Indians, when in fact he's afraid of them.

Lon comes through with a robust interpretation, in keeping with the tone of the film and the star performance by Kirk Douglas. His excellent work was singled out in many reviews and the film was a major success for United Artists (helped along, no doubt, by a small nude scene for starlet Elsa Martinelli).

Although nowhere near *The Indian Fighter* in terms of budget or script, *Daniel Boone—Trail Blazer* (1956) is a nice, juvenile version of history that gave Lon the chance to play another Indian. Lon is one of the few actors who played roles showing both sides of the Native American problem, as both Indian Chief and bigoted frontiersman.

A Mexican co-production, *Daniel Boone* was one of the last releases by Republic Pictures where Lon had mixed it up with Gene Autry in the company's first films. While Herbert Yates' Republic would fade into the sunset, Lon would keep on riding from one dusty Western street to another. In fact, his next film was a throwback to his days at Universal with Abbott and Costello and Olsen and Johnson.

Pardners, directed by Norman Taurog, was a Martin and Lewis spoof that found Lon frustrated in his attempts to kill Jerry. Lon plays straight man to the spastic Lewis well, but he's really just along for the ride as an outlaw. The film is remembered today for its unusual ending where Dean and Jerry break character and tell the audience that they'll never split up as a team as long as the public wants to see them in the movies. They split the following year.

During the '50s and '60s, Lon kept himself very busy in Westerns on television. *Have Gun, Will Travel*, *Wagon Train*, and many others cast him as villain and victim. One in particular is worth noting: an episode of *The Rifleman* entitled "Gunfire" has Lon playing a cool, sadistic outlaw locked up in the town jail. While waiting for his gang to break him out, Lon does his best to psychologically torment Sheriff Paul Fix. It's a pleasure to watch these two going at it, each one topping the other with a new threat. Richard Donner, who would become the dean of large-scale action films like *Lethal Weapon* and *Maverick*, directed the show.

Lon Chaney, Jr. plays a man condemned to die in "Cage at McNaab," an episode of television's *Have Gun, Will Travel.* [Photofest]

Money, Women, and Guns (1958) was a typically slick Jock Mahoney Western in color and 'scope. Universal seemed to be making films like this by the yard in the 1950s, with beautiful photography and good musical scores, but interchangeable scripts and leading men. This was actually more detective story than Western with Mahoney hired to find the killer of an old prospector who has left a fortune to his children.

Lon's supporting work in the film is on par with the production: solid and professional. After this Universal Western, Lon would move over to Paramount for his long run with A. C. Lyles. Lon was heavier and his days as a rough riding cowboy were

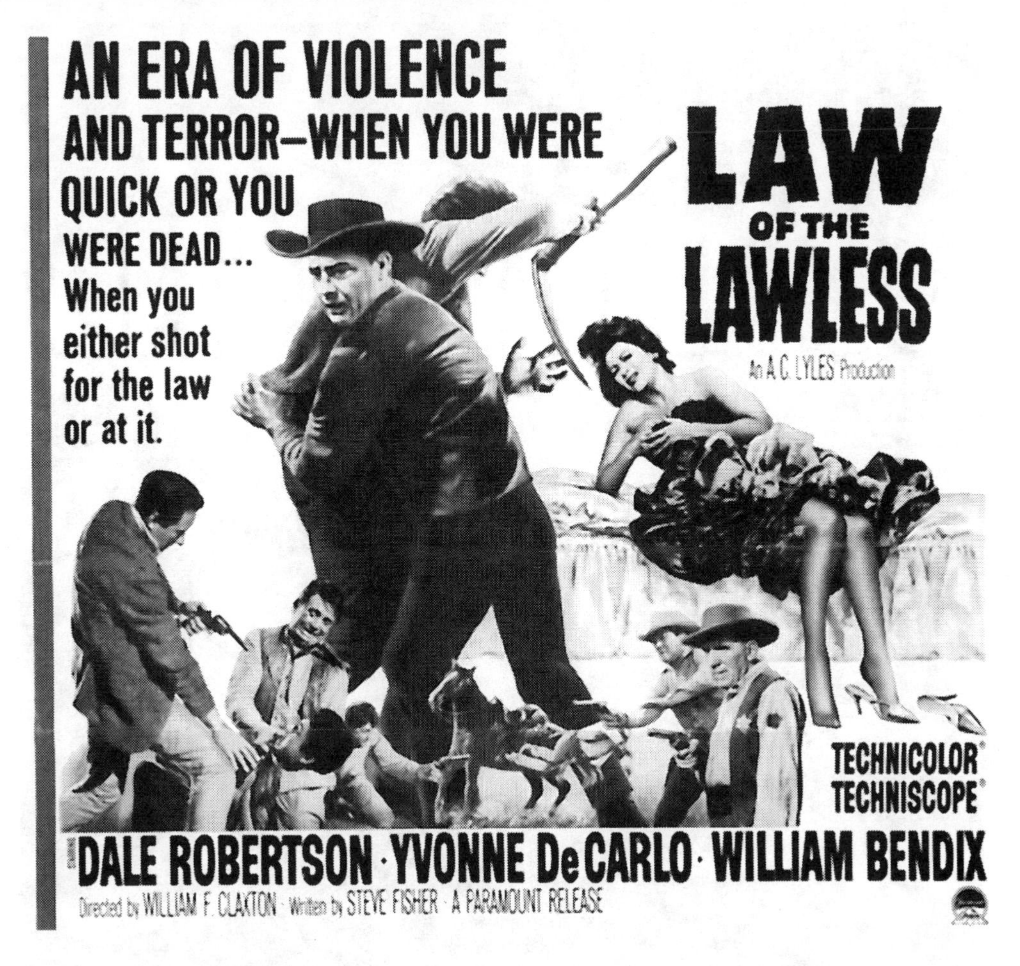

pretty much over. From now on he'd usually find himself tending the bar or the chuck wagon, but, when he had to spring into violent action, he could still deliver the goods.

Lon's first for Lyles, *Law of the Lawless* (1964), was not a particularly good role but the film is a model for all the others that were to follow. Lyles used not only scores of veteran actors, some past their prime, but turned the directing duties over to the likes of Republic Pictures regular R. G. Springsteen and Western work horse Lesley Selander. Most of the screenplays were written by Steve Fisher who wrote Bogart's most vicious film, *Dead Reckoning* (1947). It was a reunion of pros doing their jobs quickly and well, and Lon fit right in.

Lyles recalled his first Western to me in this way: "*Law of the Lawless* was almost like a pilot to a television series. It was an experiment to see if I could do a picture like this on a strict budget, and we did and it was very successful and so it led to all the others."

The "others" tend to vary in quality, but none are less than enjoyable for the casts alone. Between 1964 and 1968 Lon appeared in Lyles' *Stage to Thunder Rock*, *Young Fury*, *Black Spurs*, *Town Tamer*, *Apache Uprising*, *Johnny Reno*, and *Buckskin*. Some of the films found Lon in support, while others were simply character cameos. In a *Filmfax* interview, Patsy Chaney recalled that Lon, "loved (doing) them and he liked A. C. Lyles. He was a good friend of ours. Lon worked on them anywhere from one to six weeks."

Three of the films stand out in regard to Lon's work: *Stage to Thunder Rock* (1964), *Apache Uprising* (1966), and *Buckskin* (1968). These particular films allowed Lon to demonstrate range that other roles he was playing at this time did not.

Stage to Thunder Rock stands as arguably the best of the Lyles productions simply because of Barry Sullivan's performance as a lawman transporting a prisoner (Ralph Taeger) to jail. Lon plays Parker, the manager of the way station where the characters hole up waiting for the stagecoach to take them to Thunder Rock.

The film is best described as *The Petrified Forest Goes West*, as Taeger taunts his captors, especially Lon. His Parker is a weak man, whose sense of failure in himself has estranged his wife (the excellent Anne Seymour) and daughter. Lon's sad eyes and tortured expression bring Parker vividly to life and he is matched by Sullivan's excellent underplaying as the wounded Marshal.

While *Stage*'s Parker is weak, *Apache Uprising*'s Charlie Russell is a humorous opposite. Lon makes Russell a sly, tough, hard drinkin' old buzzard of a stage driver

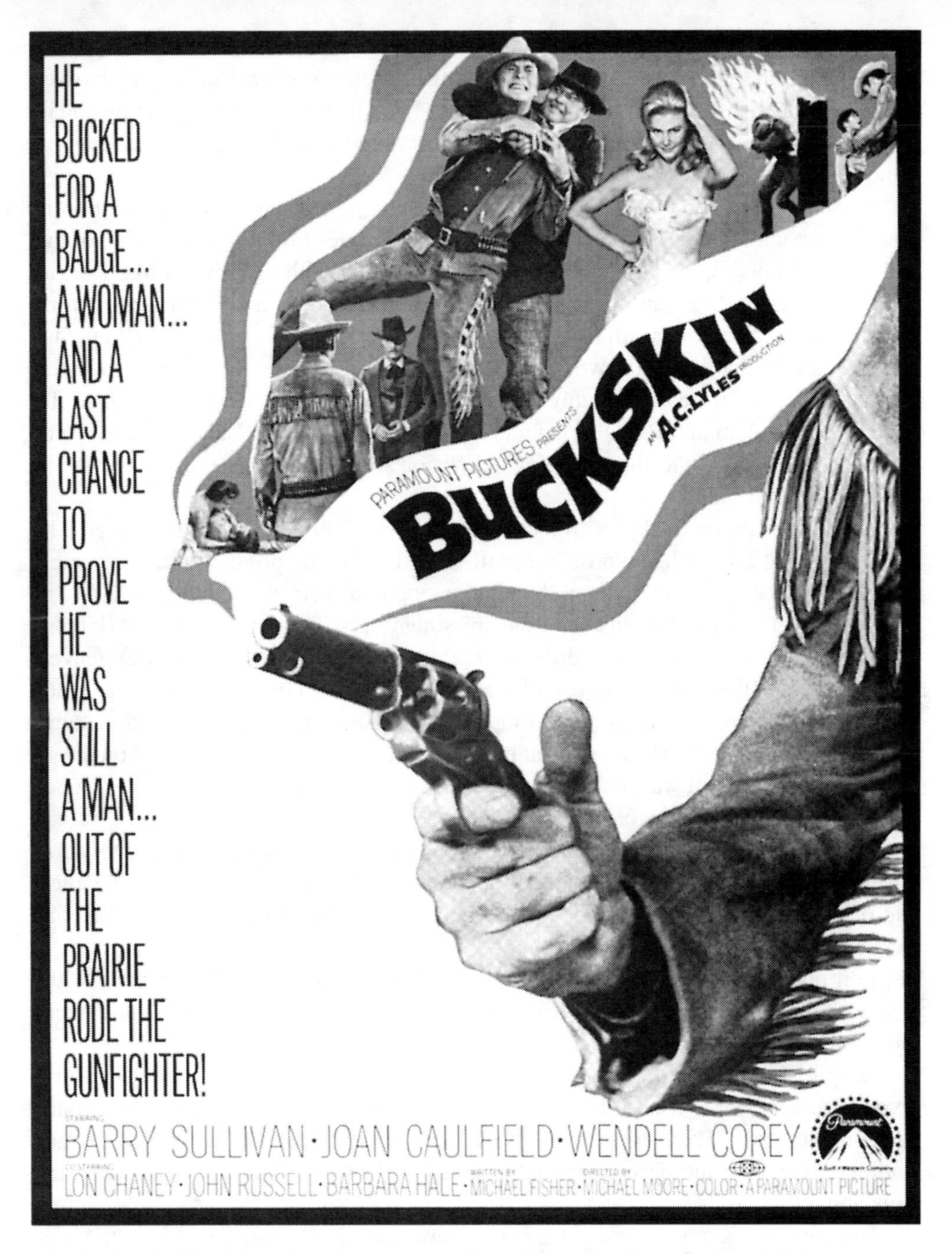

who isn't afraid of Apaches or young punk outlaws. As Russell, Lon brightens every scene whether he's having a laugh about Arthur Hunnicut's hangover or confronting psychotic DeForrest Kelley in the climax.

Lon's last role for Lyles, *Buckskin* (1968), seems to meld the best of his supporting work into one role. As the crooked Sheriff in the pocket of gambler Wendell Corey, Lon plays his scenes as a man at the end of his rope. He's a panicked fool who can still order a killing to solve problems and he dies bloody at the end.

Lon doesn't look well in *Buckskin*. His face is puffy and he's gone from merely paunchy to fat. And yet, when hero Barry Sullivan attacks Lon's character in the street, it is still Lon in there doing all the rough stuff himself. Director Robert Gist worked with Lon around this time and remembered that, "Lon loved any physical acting and he was damn good at it. When he got in there, he worked. And I mean hard, like a coal miner."

It's a tribute to Lon that despite illness, he maintained the old school code of doing your best no matter what the personal cost. The A. C. Lyles films are a reflection of that code. Lon is good in the films because he was working with old friends like Richard Arlen and Barton MacLane doing what he dearly loved—to act. After almost forty years in the saddle, he was still in demand and a man can't ask for much more than that.

The late Richard Jaeckel worked with Lon in *Town Tamer* (1965) and said this about Chaney: "Lon was a good guy who always knew his lines, knew his business. I'd sit and listen to him and Pat O'Brien and Richard Arlen swap old actor stories. I only worked with Lon on that film and a few television shows, but whenever I saw him, he treated me like a friend."

The final word on the Lyles films should go to A. C. himself: "It's true I used a lot of drinkers, but I never had a problem (with them holding up production). I remember on one film, and Lon was in there, they had enough guys [from the cast] in A. A. that they actually held a meeting in one of the dressing rooms! They had a quorum! (laughs) But these fellows were part of a different era, kind of like the characters they played. Whenever I'd call up Lon, he'd just tell me to send the script on over and he was ready to go. We were great buddies and I thought he was a fabulous guy and an absolute professional all the way. He knew what he was doing from the moment he got on the set until we wrapped and I was honored to have him in my pictures because he was a good friend. And a damn fine actor."

Lon's final Western was a major film in every way. Adapted from the E. L. Doctorow novel by writer-director Burt Kennedy, *Welcome to Hard Times* (1968) is a darkly violent tale of redemption starring Henry Fonda, Janice Rule, Warren Oates, Aldo Ray, and Keenan Wynn.

Lon plays Avery, the bartender of the Hard Times saloon, and falls prey to the psychotic Man from Bodie (Aldo Ray) who goes on a killing rampage as the citizens look on helplessly, including Sheriff Fonda.

Despite thirteenth billing, Lon has a good deal of screen time and steals the film's pivotal moment. Sick of all the killing, Lon confronts Fonda in his office to demand something be done. That's when he realizes that Fonda is afraid like everyone else. Lon studies the lawman, and shakes his head with a tired, "Hell, you're nothing but a coward. How about that."

Director Burt Kennedy thought Lon was perfect casting for the part: "Lon had been in front of the cameras for a long time when I finally worked with him. He really put over that feeling of helplessness. I thought he was just great."

He is great in the film, although it's sad to see the physical contrast between the sixty-two-year-old Lon and his *Jesse James* co-star Fonda, who was sixty-three. Lon's life and times read on his face and frame, and like a Remington painting, his very image in the film evokes the harsh realities of the old West.

Lon's final screen death in a Western has him raising a whiskey toast to the villain of the piece before being beaten to the floor. In some ways, he could have been toasting himself. He'd been on both sides of the law, ridden with the posse and been gunned down by them. He'd been hero and heavy, worked on the dregs and the classics. Now all he wanted was a little peace for himself and his fellow Hard Timers. He'd earned it.

Lon continued acting for Al Adamson and a few other others until his death, but his days on the open range and dusty streets were over. Still, he ended his Western career at MGM giving a top performance in a film he could respect. It's a fitting caveat.

One of the shames of Lon's last years was that he wasn't cast in Sam Peckinpah's *The Wild Bunch* in 1969. Lon was considered for the role of Harrigan, the bloodthirsty railroad agent who puts up the bounty to bring The Bunch back dead or alive. Albert Dekker was cast instead. Yet, Peckinpah might have been saying it for Lon's Western work when he wrote this line in his legendary film, "He was a good man who played his string out to the end."

Playing out your string is what men of the West did. And Oklahoma-born Lon Chaney, Jr. was a man of the West.

NOTES

1. Calvin T. Beck, *Heroes of the Horrors* (New York: Collier Books, 1975), p. 231
2. Peter Bogdonavich, *Who the Devil Made It* (New York: Alfred A. Knopf, 1997), p. 66

SOURCES

Beck, Calvin. *Heroes of the Horrors*, New York: Collier Books, 1975
Bogdonavich, Peter. *Who the Devil Made It*, New York: Alfred A. Knopf, 1997
Eyles, Allen. *The Western*, London: The Tantivy Press, 1975
Garfield, Brian. *Western Films: A Complete Guide*, New York: Rawson Associates, 1982
Hardy, Phil. *The Overlook Encyclopedia of Western Movies*, New York: The Overlook Press, 1995
Miller, Don. *B Movies*, New York: Ballentine Books, 1987
Smith, Don. *Lon Chaney, Jr. Horror Star*, North Carolina: McFarland and Co., 1996
Walker, John. Ed. *Halliwell's Filmgoer's Companion,* London: Harper Collins, 1993

Variety Movie Guide: 1994. London: Hamlyn Press, 1994
Videohound's Golden Movie Retreiver. New York: Visible Ink, 1997

ACKNOWLEDGMENTS

There are a number of people who helped me tremendously in preparing this tiny piece of the Lon Chaney, Jr. saga.

For their personal memories I'd like to thank A. C. Lyles, Michael Ansara, Burt Kennedy, Herman Cohen, and particularly Richard Jaeckel. Despite a crippling illness, Mr. Jaeckel was kind enough to share his thoughts on *Town Tamer*. He passed away on June 13, 1997.

For help with materials, a major tip of the hat must go to Eric Hoffman who supplied all of the Universal and A. C. Lyles pressbooks. Chris Chaffin was invaluable in digging up copies of the films and kept the post office busy sending them to me, and Bob Bates was a great emergency source of information.

Finally, my sincere thanks to Gary and Susan Svehla for allowing me to be a part of this terrific project. A Lon, Jr. fan couldn't ask for anything better.

STRANGE CONFESSION (1945)

by Michael H. Price and Kerry Gammill

Lon Chaney, Jr., had ascended to the "A" list of genre actors far too late to be accorded the dignity—artistic or commercial—that his industry had once briefly shown Boris Karloff, Bela Lugosi, and Peter Lorre.

Chaney had become in 1941 only the fourth leading man in American cinema to find his career defined and limited by Gothic horror and science-fantasy. He shared with Lugosi, Karloff, and Lorre a playful sense of humor that underscored the prevailing grimmer business, but unlike those Gray Eminences he usually came across as a guy-next-door sort. And his emotions were always worn on the outside; he seemed incapable of hiding them. The face that showed so clearly the torture and despair of a soul in immeasurable pain, emanated joy with equal intensity. The result was a kind of pathos that few actors ever have achieved.

So decisive was Chaney's horror-film typecasting, however, that even today, many people are astonished to learn of his similarly effective track record in Westerns, comedies, and crime pictures. And the half-dozen movies that should have placed him among the preeminent film noir players—most notably, *Strange Confession*—have never been acknowledged as belonging among the noir canon, simply because Universal Pictures mismarketed them from the outset as horror programmers.

Chaney's father had sidestepped this pitfall by defying typecasting to gain popular acceptance as a versatile character/leading man. But Junior's star had risen at the beginning of a shabbier new cycle for science-fantasy and the supernatural—one that treasured the Chaney name more so than it appreciated the actor for himself.

The elder Chaney, after all, had enjoyed his share of hits that qualify as spookers, and a decade after his death the name had remained bankable—especially if son Creighton should carry on as Lon, Jr., a show-business birthright he had assumed in 1935.

And so it happened that Universal Pictures became so dead-set on selling Junior as a horror star, that the big studio seemed hardly to care in what caliber of pictures, or in what ill-matched role, it placed him—just so long as the casting-to-type remained in force.

The Wolf Man (1941) is a top-shelf picture by practically any measure. It allowed Chaney the plum role of the tormented Larry Talbot, which he developed into a painstakingly sustained performance over the course of an otherwise deteriorating cycle of sequels-within-sequels (1943's *Frankenstein Meets the Wolf Man*, 1944's *House of Frankenstein,* 1945's *House of Dracula*, and a surprisingly strong wind-up with 1948's *Abbott and Costello Meet Frankenstein*). But Chaney fares better as Talbot—athletic and dashing if boyishly awkward, and by turns ebullient and subdued—than he does with Talbot's transformation into the title character: A werewolf is by definition diseased, and Chaney's Wolf Man seems anything but.

In *Strange Confession*, Chaney seems more himself, more the pleasant-natured middle-American householder and devoted husband/father, than in any other role assigned him.

Likewise, Chaney's Monster in *The Ghost of Frankenstein* (1942) and his vampire in *Son of Dracula* (1943) are altogether too robust, however intimidating, by comparison with the Karloff and Lugosi standards. Chaney's Kharis, the Egyptian proto-zombie of Universal's gratuitous and repetitive *The Mummy's Tomb/Ghost/Curse* (1942-44-44), is scarcely even an acting role and could have been played by practically anyone else. Only *Man Made Monster* (1941), the film that cinched Chaney's genre identity along with *The Wolf Man*, seems wholly tailored to its star player: an easygoing, too-trusting Everyman with an unusual talent, sickened to a monstrous state by Big Science and Bad Medicine.

It could be, under the circumstances, that the timid little *Inner Sanctum* series of 1943-45 was the best thing that happened to Chaney all during his confinement at Universal. For all the penury of budget, over-obvious writing, peculiarities of casting, and indifferent creative vision that afflicted the *Sanctum*s, Chaney appears throughout to be stretching his dramatic reach and grasping an attitude that should have led to his acceptance within the greater film noir cycle. The development of noir, after all, paralleled Chaney's years as a B-movie bogeyman, and a cross-pollination should have occurred. The film noir purists might turn up their noses at such a notion, but if so then their ig*noir*ance is showing.

For the *Sanctum*s have plenty in common with such acknowledged lesser classics of noir as *Detour* (1946), *The Devil Thumbs a Ride* (1947), and *Behind Locked Doors* (1946)—from their appropriately modest production values, to their combination of

Mary (Brenda Joyce) speaks hopefully of a better life—frankly defining it in terms of more money—although Jeff Carter (Chaney, Jr.) is doing the best he can.

random misfortune and calculated manipulation, to the hapless schmoes whose eager-to-please nature strands them somewhere between heroism and antiheroism. Chaney nailed this variety of portrayal in the *Inner Sanctums* and could have graduated as easily as not to something like the Robert Mitchum part in 1946's *The Locket* (working artist, driven over the brink by a conniving woman) or the Victor Mature role in 1947's *Kiss of Death* (reformed crook-turned-family man, torn between the law and the lawless).

The hoodoo motif of *Weird Woman* notwithstanding, the *Inner Sanctum* features are grounded in real-world psychological concerns: sexual possessiveness and illicit medical priorities rage all through *Calling Dr. Death* (1943), *Dead Man's Eyes* and *Weird Woman* (both 1944), and *The Frozen Ghost*, *Strange Confession*, and *Pillow of Death* (all 1945). But Universal's horror agenda, reinforced by top billing for Chaney, prevented these slight productions from reaching the customers who would embrace the greater range of psychological melodramas (the likes of *Jealousy* and *Guest in the House*) that proliferated during World War II and beyond. Worse yet, the loyal horror-movie audience found the *Sanctum* series a bait-and-switch letdown: nary a monster in sight.

Strange Confession is unique among the Chaney films, and notably so among the *Sanctums*, which were made on the quick-and-cheap to tie in loosely with a radio serial and a line of mystery novels. (Lew Landers' 1948 film *Inner Sanctum*, starring Charles Russell and Mary Beth Hughes, is connected in name only.)

Roger Graham (J. Carrol Naish) tries to take away Carter's life. Toady Stevens (Milburn Stone) looks on.

In *Strange Confession*, Chaney seems more himself, more the pleasant-natured middle-American householder and devoted husband/father, than in any other role assigned him. Although the performance takes place only four years after *The Wolf Man*, Junior looks noticeably older despite the rejuvenating effect of a thick hairpiece; his appetite for strong drink, an accepted fact of life among his colleagues, has begun to take a toll.

Chaney's natural rapport with animals had been demonstrated as early as *Man Made Monster*, in that film's rambunctious and tender-hearted scenes with Corky, the trained dog. He also had developed a closeness with Moose, the Universal Studios German Shepherd who appeared in many behind-the-scenes photos with Chaney.

This tenderness carries over to the on-camera relationship with Gregory Muradian, the child actor who plays Chaney's high-spirited son in *Strange Confession*. It is surprising to realize that this is one of the few times that Chaney played a father or shared any screen time with a youngster. Although the dialogue is sometimes stilted and Chaney's delivery is not always convincing, the paternal affection seems genuine. Chaney's torments and final breakdown are all the more devastating for that quality.

Confession is likewise unusual in that it boasts a distinguished origin in the legitimate theatre; had Universal only re-secured its permission to adapt from this source, the film might have remained in circulation. But more on that later.

As a remake of Edward Ludwig's *The Man Who Reclaimed His Head* (Universal; 1934), *Strange Confession* is also a curiously de-politicized—given the climate of war—

Carter seizes a machete from a mantelpiece display and undertakes to "reclaim his head."

version of the 1932 antiwar play by Jean Bart. Claude Rains had starred in both the stage and screen productions, playing a pacifist writer whose ideas (and whose wife) are appropriated by a war-profiteering publisher. Rains' character retaliates with the symbolic gesture of lopping off the interloper's head.

Strange Confession sidesteps the opportunity to commit propaganda—and what a fine stab at the Third Reich it would have made!—and instead re-invents the writer character as a humanitarian chemist, dedicated to healing a suffering world. This is Chaney's role, and he plays it with enough benevolence and indignation to compare favorably with the Rains version. The military-industrial sellout publisher of the original (played by Lionel Atwill in the '34 film) becomes a profits-conscious pharmaceuticals manufacturer, one of J. Carrol Naish's oilier portrayals.

In a truer-to-life twist on Hollywood's mad-doctor formula, screenwriter M. Coats Webster catches Chaney, as scientist Jeff Carter, in the act of rebelling against bossman Roger Graham's (Naish) suggestion that he hasten research on a new medication, the better to cash in on a prevailing ailment. Carter, who has tolerated Graham's habit of claiming his scientists' breakthroughs as his own, resigns in disgust. Graham has Carter blacklisted, and Carter must settle for work as a neighborhood pharmacist.

But Carter continues his research in private, crowding a makeshift laboratory into the bathroom of his family's boarding-house flat. His wife, Mary (Brenda Joyce), is patient with him, but only just, and it seems their preschooler son, Tommy (Gregory Muradian), is chiefly what keeps them together. She speaks hopefully of a better life—frankly defining it in terms of more money.

So when Graham approaches Carter with a write-your-own-ticket offer to reclaim his old job, Carter accepts under pressure from the Missus. Graham first assigns his flunky, Stevens (Milburn Stone), to prowl through Carter's unrefined research notes and then, finding himself lusting after Carter's wife, arranges for the scientist to travel abroad in search of a crucial ingredient.

Graham also hastens Carter's premature discoveries into production, developing a moneymaking product that proves useless in the face of an epidemic. Among the victims of the disease is Carter's son. Returning to find his household torn apart, Carter confronts Graham: "You've taken everything in my life away from me!" Carter seizes a machete from a mantelpiece display and undertakes to "reclaim his head." The tale is related in relentless flashback, book-ended by framing sequences where a distraught Carter displays his grisly trophy (discreetly off-camera) as a prelude to delivering the confession.

The sad-eyed longing and soft-spoken manner that the recording artist Garland Jeffries remarked in "Lon Chaney," a 1972 tribute-song memorializing Junior, are very much in evidence in *Strange Confession*. Although a more boisterous manner asserted itself in his screen presence as early as the 1950s, as Chaney's voice roughened and his burly physique sagged, *Strange Confession* captures the actor in some little-noticed prime of mature vigor—poised for better things that were not forthcoming.

Chaney was hardly the first star to experience this unfortunate syndrome; witness the extreme highs and lows of Bela Lugosi, or the careers of so many silent-screen leads who lapsed into type-driven character work with the arrival of the talkies. Nor was Chaney the last; his pattern has repeated itself in the careers of such major talents as Rod Steiger, Mickey Rourke, and Frederic Forrest, who like Chaney have done the honorable thing and kept working at whatever opportunity.

Most of the *Inner Sanctums* have remained on view via television syndication. but until an ambitious package-deal video edition came about in June of 1997, they were long conspicuously missing from the MCA/Universal Home Video Catalogue.

"We had held off on the *Inner Sanctums*," explains MCA/Universal spokesman Evan Fong, "because it would have been awkward to release only five of them and omit *Strange Confession*." Peculiarly, the MCA/Universal press release inaccurately describes *Strange Confession* as having to do with an idealistic writer and an unscrupulous publisher.

It took some doing, long overdue, for Universal to regain control of its own production of *Strange Confession*. The film had been shelved by court order following an early-1950s Realart theatrical reissue under the proxy title *The Missing Head*. Seems the estate of playwright Jean Bart (professional name of Marie Antoinette Sarlabous) objected to the remake, charging an unauthorized adaptation "with inordinate dramatic liberties." The screenwriting credit on *Confession* acknowledges only "a composition by Jean Bart," neglecting to cite the celebrated Broadway production of *The Man Who Reclaimed His Head* or the Jean Bart–Samuel Ornitz screenplay of 1934. The settlement lay in the film's withdrawal, and the 1997 video reissue required a re-negotiation of story rights that originally had been secured during the big studio's Depression-era heyday. Not to say that copies of *Confession* had not proliferated on bootleg video.

But pirated video images are only a stop-gap measure, a means of seeing—sort of—motion pictures that otherwise have been obscured by long-defunct litigation, rights-holders' stinginess, or plain oversight. And among three different bootleggers' cassettes of *Strange Confession*, all viewed in preparation for the present volume, not one does justice by the movie. Amateurish telecine transfers reduce the film's textured layers of gray to an unintended high-contrast level. Sound quality is compromised by too much or too little volume and a high-end "hiss." And generations lost in tape duplication—copies of copies of copies—leave the image fluttering or falling apart at precisely the worst moments to break the viewer's concentration. Watching a film under such conditions is a great deal like watching a baseball game through a cobweb-covered knothole in the stadium fence. Even the least of the Universals, after all, wants seeing in a form near its original presentation. Practically all the studio's pictures boast that burnished "Universal feel," and Ben Pivar's B-as-in-budget outfit recaptured a measure of the Depression years' Universal style right on through the '40s.

Brenda Joyce, as Chaney's more or less devoted wife, is perhaps the truest film noir element in *Strange Confession*: the quietly demanding (as opposed to predatory) *femme fatale* stereotype whose insistence maneuvers the protagonist into a ruinous compromise. J. Carrol Naish is every inch the glad-handing, backstabbing big-shot. Lloyd Bridges contributes sturdy support as a loyal and irreverent colleague to Chaney, and Milburn Stone is a weasel and a half as Naish's snooping yes-man.

Mary Gordon, the Scots-born actress so beloved as Sherlock Holmes' screen-and-radio housekeeper, lends a bittersweet quality to the proceedings as the spirited Irish servant who must break some tragic news to Chaney. For comic relief in an otherwise forbidding little picture, Jack Norton shows up in his stock-in-trade role, the perpetual souse.

Director John Hoffman had been a visual effects artist before a brief hitch in the director's chair, and after *The Crimson Canary* (1945), a truer low-grade noir set in the jazz-nightclub demimonde, and *The Wreck of the Hesperus* (1948), *The Lone Wolf and His Lady* (1949), and *I Killed Geronimo* (1950), he settled in more lastingly as a film editor.

Hoffman exhibits little in the way of distinctive technique but allows Chaney a free rein, and the star seems proud enough to be carrying his own vehicle—his own series, for that matter—that he affects a controlled, soulful performance.

CREDITS: Producer: Ben Pivar; Director: John Hoffman; Screenplay: M. Coats Webster, after a Play by Jean Bart; Cinematographer: Maury Gertsman, A.S.C.; Music Director: Frank Skinner; Art Directors: John B. Goodman and Abraham Grossman; Director of Sound: Bernard B. Brown; Technician: Jess Moulin; Set Decorators: Russell A. Gausman and Andrew Gilmore; Film Editor: Russell Schoengarth; Dialogue Director: Willard Holland; Gowns: Vera West

CAST: Lon Chaney (Jeff Carter); J. Carrol Naish (Roger Graham); Brenda Joyce (Mary Carter); Lloyd Bridges (Dave); Milburn Stone (Stevens); George Chandler (Harper); Mary Gordon (Mrs. O'Connor); Wilton Graff (Brandon); Francis McDonald (Hernandez); Gregory Muradian (Tommy Carter); Jack Norton (Drunken Boarder); Addison Richards (Dr. Williams); Christian Rub (Mr. Moore)

It's a grand
New Idea for FUN!

UNIVERSAL-INTERNATIONAL presents

BUD
ABBOTT
and
LOU COSTELLO
meet
FRANKENSTEIN

WITH

The Wolfman PLAYED BY LON CHANEY

Dracula PLAYED BY BELA LUGOSI

The Monster PLAYED BY GLENN STRANGE

LENORE AUBERT · JANE RANDOLPH

Original Screenplay by Robert Lees, Frederic Rinaldo, John Grant

DIRECTED BY CHAS T. BARTON · PRODUCED BY ROBERT ARTHUR

Universal International

ABBOTT AND COSTELLO MEET FRANKENSTEIN (1948)

by Susan Svehla

FADE IN
STOCK SHOT - LONDON - NIGHT
MED. SHOT - INT. LONDON HOTEL ROOM - NIGHT
LAWRENCE TALBOT (WOLF MAN) is in an extreme state of aggravation. He tosses his cigarette away and CAMERA PANS HIM over to the phone, where he lifts the receiver.

And away we go as Bud Abbott, Lou Costello, Bela Lugosi, Glenn Strange, and Lon Chaney, Jr., rise from the graveyard of stalled movie careers to once again conquer hearts and Hollywood in the "Universally" loved *Abbott and Costello Meet Frankenstein.*

Movie studios, much like everything else, were dominated by behind-the-scenes politics and Universal-International was no exception. According to Greg Mank in the *Universal Filmscripts Series*, Universal-International honchos wanted to distance themselves from what they considered the crass comedy of Abbott and Costello and the low-brow horror films for which Universal had become known. Fortunately for moviegoers, the scent of dollars overcame the bigwigs' delicate sensibilities and *A&C Meet Frankenstein* went into production with the working title of *The Brain of Frankenstein*, scripted by Frederic Rinaldo, Robert Lees, and John Grant.

With an impressive list of supporting roles under his belt, Lon Chaney, Jr. was a vital member of the Universal stock company. As such he was no stranger to comedy and, although it is an accepted fact he wasn't given a chance to be very funny in films, he made a great straight man for the likes of The Ritz Brothers in *Life Begins in College* (Fox, 1937) and Abbott and Costello in Universal's 1945 *Here Come the Co-Eds* where Chaney portrays an evil wrestler, The Masked Marvel, out to foil the duo's plan to save a girls' school. Chaney hammed it up good-naturedly with Lou Costello in their first appearance together.

In 1947 Chaney would join fellow horror icon Peter Lorre in the big-budgeted Bob Hope burlesque *My Favorite Brunette* (Paramount). *Brunette* would be one of Hope's best films and offered sweet roles for the delightfully devilish Lorre and the stalwart Lon Chaney. Chaney and Lorre as thugs menacing the imperiled Hope seemed happy lampooning their oft-typecast screen personas; Lorre as tough guy mad-man and Chaney as the slow-witted thug. Chaney would once again enact a Lennie-type character, managing to play it straight as the capricious Hope tried to wriggle his way out of Chaney's

Chaney's bad-guy with a heart of gold cracked walnuts in the crook of his elbow, cheerfully munching away as mayhem reigned around Bob Hope in *My Favorite Brunette.*

clutches. Chaney's bad-guy with a heart of gold was portrayed as so strong he cracked walnuts in the crook of his elbow, cheerfully munching away as mayhem reigned. *Variety*, in their review of the film, would note, "Lon Chaney, as a muscular and moronic sanitarium guard rates for a risible replica of imbecility." Next up for Chaney would be a return engagement with Abbott and Costello, whose popularity seemed to be on the wane. Universal-International hoped to rally the once mega-popular duo by merging them with Universal's other formerly prominent cash cow, the Universal monsters.

Abbott and Costello Meet Frankenstein marked the end of the trio of terror as Frankenstein, Dracula, and The Wolf Man would conclude their horrific reign with a regal dignity denied them in the previous Universal monster rallies such as *House of Dracula* and *House of Frankenstein*.

Lugosi would once again be his debonair self as Count Dracula while Lon Chaney was back as the tortured Larry Talbot, a role he was born to play.

From the beginning the Larry Talbot role in *The Wolf Man* seemed custom made for the tall, chiseled-featured actor. Chaney had been blessed with rough good looks and cleaned up real nice. However, there was always an underlying sadness in his face and eyes that made Chaney the doppleganger of the doomed Larry Talbot. Called unexpressive by many critics, they obviously haven't stared deeply into those eyes that reflected a sadness that cut to the core.

One can only imagine the poignant life of this young man. Torn from his unstable mother, shunted between homes, competing not only with his father's ego but Chaney

Lon Chaney, Jr. and Lou Costello laugh it up on the set.

Sr's. incredible talent, Chaney, Jr. threw himself to the mercy of vicious critics when he bravely took those first tentative steps in trying to fill his father's immense shoes. But the lure of Hollywood is great and, like others before and since, he succumbed to its seduction.

The tragedy of the Talbot character was made-to-order tug-at-the-heartstrings material and the scripters of *A&C Meet Frankenstein* put it too good use turning the tortured Wolf Man into the film's hero.

As our film begins Big Ben tolls in the background; the camera pans over foggy London town. Suddenly wooden blinds jerk open and we see a pair of haunted eyes peering into the misty night. The man, Larry Talbot (Chaney), places a frenzied telephone call as director Charles T. Barton highlights Chaney's troubled face. "It's terribly important."

The call is eventually received by the pleasant but dim-witted Wilbur (Lou Costello), working at an express office.

"The moon is full here and I haven't much time... Listen closely. I'm flying out of here at dawn. Under no circumstances must those crates be delivered until I arrive... Understand. Under no..." Moonlight madness once more strikes the unfortunate Larry Talbot and Chaney gleefully tears up the screen for his final appearance as the Wolf Man.

"Look Mister, this is no time to be gargling your throat.—Who is this, anyhow..." Wilbur slams down the phone. "The nerve of some people!"

Costello and Chaney engage in a game of catch the moron as the poor Wolf Man tries to pounce upon the unwary Wilbur.

Wilbur doesn't know what to make of Talbot's strange warning but soon forgets as other matters arise. He and partner Chick (Bud Abbott) deliver two forbidding crates to McDougal's House of Horrors but they are tossed in the slammer when the exhibits, Dracula (Lugosi) and Frankenstein (Glenn Strange), walk off into the night. Of course nobody will believe the frantic Wilbur who insists he's seen the grisly duo. Wilbur and Chick think they have been bailed out of jail by Wilbur's drop-dead gorgeous girlfriend Sandra (Lenore Aubert) who, when she says she loves him for his mind, really means it! Sandra is in a satanic league with Count Dracula and together they plan to place a malleable brain into the weakened Frankenstein monster. When Chick asks the voluptuous Sandra, "I'd still like to know what he's got that I haven't got," Sandra replies, "Brains."

But they have actually been bailed out by insurance investigator Joan Raymond (Jane Randolph as the token love interest—her romance would be with the barely noticeable Charles Bradstreet as Sandra's assistant) who is convinced she can make Wilbur lead her to the missing exhibits.

Talbot catches up with Wilbur and Chick in their hotel where he has taken a room across the hall. Looking a trifle more haggard than he did in *The Wolf Man*, Chaney still possessed the appealing good looks that helped carve him a niche in Hollywood. He shows up the hotel in a spiffy looking suit with a white handkerchief jauntily sticking out of his pocket. He resembles a well-to-do gangster rather than a lycanthrophic detective chasing the elusive vampire king.

"I'm a baaaad boy!"

Chaney's demeanor is sad and haunted when as Talbot he tells Wilbur and Chick he cannot go to the police with his story. "No. I would have to tell them who I am—and why I know what I know. The moon will be up any moment. I've no time to explain. Quick!... Lock me in. Hurry!" Chaney rushes past Wilbur, hurriedly thrusting him aside. He tosses his hat onto a chair, removes his coat, and rubs his chest as though he can already feel the beginning of the change. "Remember, no matter what you hear, don't let me out." Of course things don't end there as Wilbur and the Wolf Man engage in a game of catch the moron as the poor Wolf Man tries to pounce upon the unwary Wilbur who, through a series of sight gags, manages to remain unharmed.

As adults watching this film we marvel at the fact the monsters never caught their oblivious prey. Like the poor old Mummy, the monsters had to pace themselves so they wouldn't catch their co-star victim and end the film before its time.

While portraying Larry Talbot, Chaney would switch between tormented soul and raving madman, and this is before he turned into the wolf! One minute he would be wringing his hands at his predicament and the next he would have poor old Wilbur by the lapels shaking the living daylights out of him.

The next morning Wilbur and Chick enter Talbot's room. "What a binge you must have been on last night," Chick notes as they spy the disheveled Talbot lying face down in the shambles. While this could have been a sly commentary on the rowdy lifestyle of Chaney, the scene was actually in the script.

Wilbur is a little disappointed in their new friend. "And I thought you were such a nice man! Look at you. You look awful." And Chaney did look awful. His hair was

The Wolf Man tries to attack Wilbur but manages to get caught in a bush where Wilbur lands a well-placed kick on his behind.

splayed out over his forehead and he looked as though he had been on one long bender. Again the similarities between the real Lon Chaney and fictional Larry Talbot unwittingly cross paths.

The ensemble attends a masquerade enabling Chick, who is conveniently armed with a wolfman mask, to be confused with the real Wolf Man who has attacked the nasty old McDougal (Frank Ferguson). Wilbur also mistakes the Wolf Man for Chick and slaps the monster about, thinking his friend is fooling around. The poor old Wolf Man is not used to such treatment from the average Joe. He tries to attack Wilbur but manages to get caught in a bush where Wilbur lands a well-placed kick on the behind of the enraged Wolf Man. Wilbur quickly realizes his error and takes off for greener pastures only to wind up under the spell of Dracula.

A typical Universal mob gathers and begins to hunt for Chick although Talbot thinks they are after him. He and Chick unite and head toward Sandra's island where Joan, Sandra, and Wilbur have all been taken by Dracula. Sandra is ready to proceed with the operation, but just before making an incision on the still conscious Wilbur, she is stopped by Talbot and Chick. Unfortunately, Talbot once again changes into the Wolf Man. He begins to chase Dracula while Wilbur and Chick try to evade the really ticked off Frankenstein Monster.

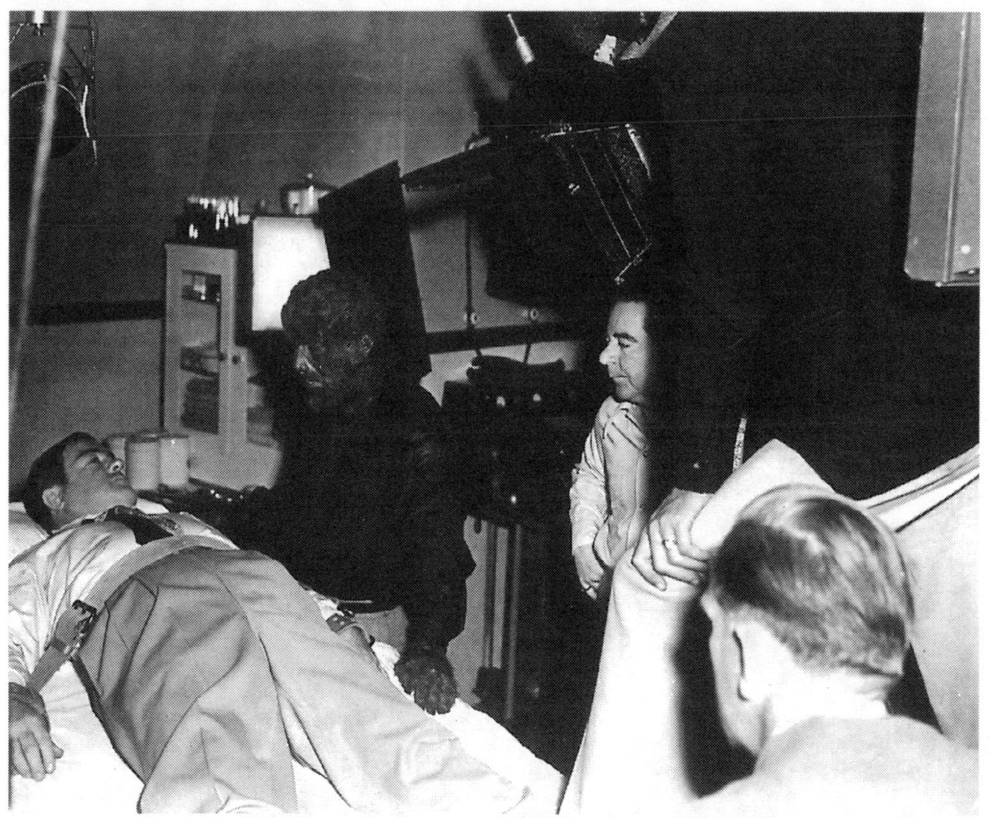

The Wolf Man confronts an immobile Wilbur as the crew looks on.

Between the two titans of terror, Chaney as the Wolf Man seems to have the upper hand, or paw as it may be, since Dracula is the one on the defensive. Their battle royale winds through the halls of the old dark house before ending on a balcony where Dracula tries to escape by turning into a bat. The Wolf Man makes a desperate grab for the escaping vampire and manages to grasp him, causing both to plunge onto the rocky shoreline below. A dramatic end for the damned Larry Talbot.

Abbott and Costello were well-known for their off-screen antics while filming and *A&C Meet Frankenstein* is no exception. In Greg Mank's introduction in *The Universal Filmscripts Series* (MagicImage, Absecon, NJ, 1990) director Charles B. Barton notes, "we never had any trouble with Lon or Bela or Glenn. The 'monsters' were as sweet as little babies. Isn't that wonderful? God, they were great." While it seems the "monsters" indulged in their fair share of offscreen tomfoolery, they were their typically professional selves onscreen. It would have been easy to mug or parody the now aging miscreants but Chaney and Lugosi managed (probably with great difficulty) to keep their villains on the horrific straight and narrow. Reportedly Glenn Strange had a more difficult time keeping a straight face when they shot the scene in which Costello sits on the lap of the Frankenstein Monster. In the *Filmscripts Series* Bud Abbott, Jr. remembers, "The scene was going great but all of a sudden Glenn Strange, who was portraying the monster, burst out with a fit of laughter. After several takes, all that Glenn Strange would have to do is look at Lou and he would crack up. Lou didn't help much, for once he knew he had Strange going, he would invent new ways to make him laugh!"

Did you hear the one about the Burgomeister's daughter? Together again, the Frankenstein Monster (Glenn Strange) and the Wolf Man.

Abbott and Costello Meet Frankenstein is very much an ensemble piece. No one actually steals the show, although everyone turns in a wonderfully energetic performance. Lugosi, Strange, and Chaney seem to be enjoying partying with the clown princes of comedy and, for their part, Abbott and Costello seem to respect the credentials of the monster men. Lon was third billed under Abbott and Costello and has the most screen time of the big three monsters. His hangdog expression would suit him well as he tried to convince Wilbur and Chick of the danger they were in and the need to stop the evil Dracula.

While filming the sequence where the Monster picks up Sandra and throws her through a window, the stunt backfired and Glenn Strange broke his ankle. Lon Chaney gallantly volunteered to put on the well-remembered Frankenstein makeup and finished the scene tossing a stuntwoman though the glass. With make-up king Jack Pierce pitched on the junk heap by the Universal moguls, new make-up mavens Bud Westmore and Jack Kevan developed lighter and more comfortable make-up for the pancake weary monster men, although Chaney still got the worst of it having to endure the involved transformation scenes.

In their review of the film *Variety* opined, "Abbott and Costello work with less of their standard routines than usual, but keep the fun at high level. Bela Lugosi as Dracula; Glenn Strange, the Monster; and Lon Chaney, the Wolf Man, bulwark the chills and thrills."

Chaney's downfall, like Judy Garland's, would be dramatically recorded on film for all the world to see. *A&C Meet Frankenstein* would be his last starring role in a major production. His subsequent film work would cast him as a world weary character actor, his handsome face morphing into a rugged, troubled countenance—although one feels the grizzly bear exterior masked the heart of a teddy bear. Lon Chaney, Jr. belonged to a breed of men no longer considered "politically correct." Cussin', drinkin', carousin', and brawlin' were their forte and it's too bad they are all gone. We could use a few charming scoundrels in our by-the-book lives.

Mixing horror and comedy seemed a match made in heaven, although the results are usually far from angelic. *Abbott and Costello Meet Frankenstein* is one of the pleasant exceptions and few films following this opus would get it right until Mel Brooks' *Young Frankenstein.*

Chaney would venture into comedy once again, joining Bob Hope in 1954's *Casanova's Big Night* from Paramount. The cast was filled with horror alumni such as Basil Rathbone, Vincent Price, and John Carradine who, along with Chaney, had a grand old time mugging with the ever over-the-top Hope. Dean Martin and Jerry Lewis had replaced Abbott and Costello as box-office gold and Chaney appeared with them in their Western/comedy *Pardners* (Paramount, 1956) as an outlaw confounded by the rambunctious Lewis.

The final comedy (and quite a few critics would justifiably argue with that term) Chaney appeared in would be *Hillbillys in a Haunted House* where he joined his old chums John Carradine and Basil Rathbone in this country music/spy/ghost story. Reviled by fans and critics alike, I must confess enjoying this film tremendously as a kid.

Lon Chaney, Jr. contributed immensely to films as a Hollywood character actor, but that elusive stardom always seemed to slip out of his desperate grasp. It's a shame his inner demons kept him from enjoying the niche he carved for himself, but he could take pleasure in the fact the Wolf Man was still alive and well in 1948's *Abbott and Costello Meet Frankenstein.*

CREDITS: Producer: Robert Arthur; Director: Charles T. Barton; Screenplay: Robert Lees, Frederic I. Rinaldo, John Grant; Photography: Charles Van Enger; Art Direction: Bernard Herzbrun, Hilyard Brown; Editor: Frank Gross; Sound: Leslie I. Carey, Robert Pritchard; Set Decoration: Russell A. Gausman, Oliver Emert; Make-up: Bud Westmore, Jack Kevan; Music: Frank Skinner; Universal-International; 1948; 90 minutes

CAST: Bud Abbott (Chick); Lou Costello (Wilbur); Lon Chaney (Lawrence Talbot); Bela Lugosi (Count Dracula); Glenn Strange (Frankenstein's Monster); Lenore Aubert (Dr. Sandra Mornay); Jane Randolph (Joan Raymond); Frank Ferguson (Mr. McDougal); Charles Bradstreet (Dr. Stevens); Howard Negley (Mel Harris); Vincent Price (The Invisible Man)

BRIDE OF THE GORILLA (1951) *THE DEVIL'S MESSENGER* (1962)

by David H. Smith

It was a different world for Lon Chaney, Jr. in 1951. His Universal leading man heyday behind him, Chaney was freelancing in features from United Artists to Warner Brothers, with stops at all studios in between. His development as a reliable character actor was in full swing, and only a year later he would earn his greatest accolades in a decade for *High Noon* (United Artists).

But horror films had fallen out of favor with the studios, their box office returns becoming ever lower as the unconditional surrenders of Germany and Japan were signed and veterans returned home. Chaney's marquee value as the man behind the Wolf Man's yak hairs and the Mummy's gauze had decreased to almost nil.

The key to survival was adaptability. Writer Curt Siodmak (b. 1902), the German émigré who had penned so many of the Universal horror programmers, would find only sporadic work outside the genre, at least until its rebirth with the fifties paranoia of nuclear Armageddon and outsized denizens from other worlds. Writing everything from costume melodramas (*Frisco Sal*) to spy thrillers (*Berlin Express*) to jungle adventure (*Tarzan's Magic Fountain*), Siodmak nevertheless began to envy his older brother's success as a film director.

Robert Siodmak (1900-1973) had begun to accrue quite a number of positive reviews for his atmospheric psychological thrillers (*Phantom Lady, The Suspect*), for casting against type (musical actors Deanna Durbin and Gene Kelly in the noir *Christmas Holiday*), and for drawing strong performances out of Hollywood newcomers (Burt Lancaster in *The Killers*). Even as the forties horror boom was waning and Curt's career seemed to stall, Robert's was on the rise. But the younger Siodmak had a plan.

"Men are seldom really good, They are so little sympathetic.
What man thinks of changing himself so as to suit his wife?"
—Anthony Trollope, *Phineas Redux* (1874), ch. 3

"I wanted to show my brother Robert I could direct," Siodmak said in an interview. "I wrote [*Bride of the Gorilla*] on speculation, because I wanted to direct something." And to stack the deck in his favor as much as possible, Siodmak saw to it that Chaney—whose Larry Talbot had garnered the scriptwriter his best notices—would figure prominently in his directing debut. However, Chaney, Siodmak's one-time trump card, would instead get virtually lost in the shuffle.

As Police Commissioner Taro, Chaney's first appearance doesn't come until 15 minutes into *Bride of the Gorilla*.

Aside from the horror boom gone bust, so too had Chaney's earnest, youthful features. Alcohol and depression had withered his face, making him far more suitable for secondary roles. In *Bride of the Gorilla*, a story that only a few years before would have fairly screamed for Chaney in the lead, the actor was instead given a decidedly minor role as a jungle policeman. The billing was good, the part was minor, but, though his performance was adequate, Chaney was nonetheless horribly miscast.

As Police Commissioner Taro, Chaney's first appearance doesn't come until 15 minutes into *Bride of the Gorilla*. He presides over the inquest looking into the mysterious death of rubber plantation owner Klaas van Gelder (Paul Cavanagh). Smoking cigarettes and taking his glasses on and off, Chaney questions plantation foreman Barney Chavez (Raymond Burr) about an argument he had had with the deceased earlier, but it leads to nothing. Siodmak's direction is crude; at one point, as the local doctor (Tom Conway) comes toward the seated Chaney, he completely blocks the dead man's widow (Barbara Payton)—she, in turn, deliberately moves stage left to place herself in the camera eye.

The inquest at a close, Taro muses on his situation. "I sometimes feel as though I don't even speak my own people's language. Since I became an official I seem to be standing outside their code of law." Chaney's enunciation is stiff and awkward, the words spoken as though the actor was speaking a second, unfamiliar language.

This argot may have been Siodmak's invention, but it's hard to tell even where *Bride of the Gorilla* is supposed to take place. The prominent clues of latex harvesting and indigenous gorillas are at odds with one another. Natural rubber comes from the *Hevea brasiliensis* tree in Brazil and, although the tree had been cultivated in many tropical countries in Asia by the early fifties, it was nowhere close to West Africa where gorillas live.

Furthering the confusion, the local natives whisper in Spanish but have exotically outré names, are all black, and Chaney even claims to be one of them. From such evidence, it is likely the role was written with someone else in mind, with Chaney first cast in the foreman's part hoping to capitalize on his thematically similar Wolf Man character, but someone (possibly Siodmak himself) had second thoughts.

From her first appearance, dancing alone, the camera tracing a path from her espadrilles up her shapely legs, Barbara Payton (1927-1967) oozes sexuality as the beautiful widow. With her full lips and hourglass figure, the air heavy with humidity and pheromones, no one could begrudge the sweaty Burr (or at least his character) his lust. It may be that Siodmak recognized the unlikelihood of her taking up with the bloated, middle-aged Chaney (though her May-December marriage to the cuckolded Paul Cavanagh [1895-1964] is just as unlikely) and rethought the casting.

Given his intense and ominous eyes and hulking figure, Burr (1917-1993) may not have been the best alternative, but he is somewhat more plausible. A pity, though, that Payton never looks at him with anything faintly resembling desire, even after her subsequent marriage to him. She seems indifferent to all the attention paid her throughout.

With the dialogue as it is, instead of Chaney, a far more logical choice to play the commissioner would have been cast member Woody Strode (b. 1914). A former star end in the Canadian Football League and professional wrestler, Strode would later find fame in John Ford's *Sergeant Rutledge* (1960). But such a cast revamping would have left Chaney the odd man out, and Siodmak stood by his guns.

Later in *Bride of the Gorilla*, Chaney mulls over the dilemma facing him and talks with Conway about his outsider status: "You know, doctor, I was born in this little town.... I sometimes regret that I went to university then returned to this jungle with its superstitions. It only served to confuse me."

"You never impressed me that way, Taro," Conway says.

"How can I help being confused?" Chaney agonizes. "My native mind is filled with these superstitions; my legal mind was developed through books written by people without emotion."

"Yes, but justice must detach itself from emotion," Conway reminds him.

"Well, that I realize," he says condescendingly. "But I know that Barney Chavez murdered Van Gelder. I know it emotionally. I should arrest that man and charge him with murder."

Playing devil's advocate, Conway asks, "Why don't you?"

"The case I have is not tight enough to get a conviction," Chaney sighs. Chaney goes on to predict the jungle itself will mete out punishment to the guilty in the form of a demon, a roundabout explanation of the shaggy metamorphosis Burr believes himself to be undergoing.

Burr's character, already carrying on an affair with his boss's wife, nonchalantly standing by to watch the man get bitten by an opportune snake, is hardly the sympathetic fellow Larry Talbot was. When the old native housekeeper (Gisela Werbisek) chances upon the "murder" scene, she vows to avenge her master's death by brewing a weird potion from an "illegal evil tree" and casting a spell over Burr's character.

Barbara Payton, Lon Chaney, Jr., and Tom Conway in *Bride of the Gorilla.*

While touching on the ideas of voodoo and the power of suggestion, Siodmak's script fails to follow through on an important plot point. Though Siodmak has acknowledged in interviews it was his aim to make a psychological thriller rather than a woolly *Wolf Man* cheat, he nevertheless insured comparison with the potion business (as opposed to an ancient gypsy curse), the power of suggestion affecting the change.

However noble Siodmak's intentions, it has to be guilt alone that causes Burr's character to imagine himself becoming a jungle beast. Though suspicious, he remains ignorant throughout *Bride of the Gorilla* of the old woman's spiking his drink with any transmuting potion.

Siodmak's pride in shooting the film in only seven days is reasonable, but the ending is ambiguous—is Barbara Payton's "heroine" dead or merely unconscious?—and there really isn't anyone to root for anyway among the wishy-washy supporting cast (the doctor admits he loves her himself; Taro never comes to terms with his unself-confidence) and the adulterous leads.

Bride of the Gorilla has found little critical admiration over the years, and Chaney's miscasting aggravates quite a number of reviewers. The seventh issue of *Castle of Frankenstein* allowed it was a "fair jungle 'Were-thing' melodrama," but *The Horror Film*'s James J. Mulay one-upped that review by calling it "an amusingly bad horror film" and "extremely silly."

James O'Neill, in *Terror On Tape*, sighed, "This dopey Z flick wastes a good cast in embarrassing roles." Similar sentiments were echoed in the seventh issue of

Monsterscene, wherein Frank Kurtz said, "Veteran actors like Burr, Chaney, Cavanagh and Tom Conway elevate the production above a typical B-flick."

Michael Brunas summed up Chaney's then-career in *Scarlet Street* #23, calling him "egregiously miscast" in *Bride of the Gorilla*. He concluded, "The career of hard-drinking Chaney was just sputtering along at this time; the actor was no longer Universal's top horror personality and had not yet found his niche as a Hollywood character actor."

Bill Warren labeled *Bride of the Gorilla* as being "quite bad" in *Keep Watching The Skies!*'s retrospective on *The Magnetic Monster* (1953), Siodmak's directing follow-up. While lauding Siodmak's power of the pen, Warren pointed out that, with this, "almost perversely, the worst film [Siodmak] wrote he also directed."

Other, shallow critics tried to latch onto the nonexistent connection between Chaney's Wolf Man and Burr's gorilla, using Siodmak as a mortise. It's not that *Bride of the Gorilla* is derivative—so are most science-fantasy movies, even the best. In fact, in this genre connoisseurship is a specialty of the house; for true believers, spotting all the steals and arcana is part of the fun. But *Bride of the Gorilla* doesn't really work up its derivations into any kind of style; it doesn't build into something radically new.

Cruel to many and brief for most, Hollywood life treated Curt Siodmak fairly well. Although he isn't half as famous as his creations, he certainly has fared better than some of the actors he put words in the mouths of along the way. Thespians such as Barbara Payton and Tom Conway (1904-1967) eventually became icons of superstar burnout—tales from the down side of fame.

Siodmak persevered, however, but his directing skills never came close to equaling his power with the pen. After forming A-Men Productions with producer Ivan Tors (1916-1983) and actor Richard Carlson (1912-1977) in 1953, Siodmak again took up the director's reins for *The Magnetic Monster*, handing them off to Carlson for the company's follow-up *Riders To The Stars* (1954). Siodmak then sojourned to Brazil under Universal's auspices to make *Curucu, Beast of the Amazon* (1956) and the risible *Love Slaves of the Amazons* (1957), both of them garish, color-drenched Amazon corn. Even the participation of accomplished actors (like Beverly Garland and Eduardo Cianelli) and the plum of location photography were unable to camouflage the movies' inadequacies.

But Siodmak's and Chaney's professional relationship would come full circle by the close of the decade.

"There was given to me a thorn in the flesh, the messenger of Satan to buffet me."—2 Corinthians 12:7

After the failed union of Hammer Films in England and Columbia Pictures Corporation to market a U.S. *Frankenstein* TV series with his scripts and direction, Curt Siodmak returned to Europe for *13 Demon Street*, made by Herts-Lion International in co-production with Svensk Filmindustri. Siodmak wrote and, in Stockholm's Nordisk ToneFilm motion picture studio, directed a number of episodes for the proposed television series, a spooky anthology program a la *Twilight Zone* and, to a lesser degree, *Alfred Hitchcock Presents*. Chaney was cast as the mysterious "host" by his old friend, not only for his reliability, but in the hope that network executives, looking back with moistened eye at the great films and the no-longer-with-us actors of the "golden age" of horror, would recognize his name and snap the series up.

Chaney, hired to do only the introductory and closing moments of each episode, was required to little more than lurk about a shadowy house (the title address) and bemoan his immortal fate. Disheveled and wearing a coarse sackcloth shirt, Chaney was evidently supposed to be (though never definitively identified as) the "Wandering Jew," a popular topic in literature as an archetype borrowed from Christianity (though running a distant second to Faust). Best known through mainstream works like Eugene Sue's *The Wandering Jew* or Walter M. Miller's *Canticle For Liebowitz*, the Wandering Jew, cursed by Jesus to live forever (Matthew 16:28 and John 21:22), has also been the subject of poetry by Percy Bysshe Shelley and stories by Nathaniel Hawthorne. Other, lesser appropriations of the legend include everything from a series of men's adventure novels (Barry Sadler's *Casca: The Eternal Mercenary*) to supernatural comic book heroes (DC Comics' *The Phantom Stranger*). The story of the Wandering Jew has been translated to film several times, from obscure silent films in 1905 and 1923, to a Yiddish remake of the latter in the thirties, to even a Soviet interpretation of the legend in 1931, and an Italian one in 1947.

The president of Herts-Lion, however, was less than sure about the marketability of his wares even as they emerged from the film lab. Kenneth Herts contacted film editor and sometime director Herbert L. Strock (b. 1918), then working at Warner Brothers, to evaluate the early episodes of *13 Demon Street*. Watching them at home, Strock's own children laughed at their crudity and non-scariness, and Strock was forthright with Herts when asked his opinion.

From feelers put out to the three major networks, Herts realized the idea of a weekly TV show was a lost cause, and was desperate to at least recoup costs with a theatrical release. He insisted Strock go to Sweden and salvage what he could. As if that weren't enough, Strock was instructed to cast minor actress Karen Kadler in a pivotal role in the revised film. With virtually no money left in the budget, but with considerable ingenuity, Strock reconfigured three of the savable episodes into one feature film, again hosted by Chaney, now promoted to playing Satan himself (though never formally introduced as such). In October 1962, more than two years after the last clapsticks sounded, *The Devil's Messenger* was finally released.

Siodmak was, of course, the odd man out in all of this (bizarrely, it was Strock who directed A-Men Productions' third feature). According to Siodmak, Herts-Lion showed *13 Demon Street* to CBS but the network begged off. Rival NBC came out with *Thriller*, hosted by Boris Karloff (1887-1969), six months after that in September 1960. Siodmak, in a 1984 *Fangoria* interview with Tom Weaver and John Brunas, thought this was more than coincidental. (Hubbell Robinson was *Thriller*'s executive producer and was the originator of the concept; earlier, he had produced *Climax, Studio One*, and *Playhouse 90*, and worked on the *Startime* series for Dumont as far back as 1950. By 1960, he was already a high-level network executive; with such a pedigree such chicanery is very unlikely.)

Strock, forced by nepotism to use Kadler (she was Herts' wife at the time), gave it all he could. "We had what I would call a half-assed crew," Strock told Weaver and Brunas in a *Fangoria* interview from 1983. "Everything was done for spit and chewing gum. It was no fun." Such self-effacements notwithstanding, *The Devil's Messenger*—especially with Strock's inserts and Chaney's new role—is a tidy little thriller with much to offer.

The movie's credits play out against a cityscape, continuing as the camera traces a cartoon path below ground to the shadowy waiting room of hell. There, behind an academic desk, Chaney sits in a dark short-sleeved shirt and tie; like some malevolent Brooklyn butcher, he thumbs through a Rolodex and barks "Next!" to the line of confused-looking people lingering in the shadows.

Chaney clearly relishes the part, smiling wickedly as he consigns each of them in turn to the off-camera abyss. With the intermittent laughter of an unseen demon welcoming each new resident, Strock's tinhorn vision of hell is oddly just as effective as the multimillion-dollar *mise en scenes* of Clive Barker's *Hellraiser* movies of the eighties and all their trammels and tenterhooks.

When a suitably named suicide named Satanya (Karen Kadler) is called forward, the Devil rethinks his usual punishment (in Milton's *Paradise Lost*, suicides were described as being turned into withered trees pecked by harpies) in favor of using her as his messenger. If she succeeds in her assignments, the Devil promises to take her case before a special tribunal. "Actually what you'll be doing is delivering to your society up there a passport," he tells Satanya. "A ticket—one-way, of course—for them to join our society down here. We try very hard to make it easy for them to join us. It's like a big country club," at first a hilarious, but later strangely thought-provoking, metaphor.

Already Strock's overhaul shows considerable imagination, taking inspiration not only from Scripture but from some of Western civilization's most influential literature, like *Paradise Lost* (1667) and *Dante's Inferno*. By calling her his "messenger," the Devil is pulling a reverse on God's angels. Angels are frequently mentioned in the Bible, mostly in the role of messengers from God to mankind. Their appearances on Earth seem to have been in human form. In the Old Testament books of Job, Ezekiel, and Daniel, as well as in the Apocryphal Book of Tobin, angels play significant roles. In the Book of Job, the leading demon, Satan, is also introduced. But it is not until the New Testament that Satan is portrayed, under the name Lucifer, as the first of the fallen angels.

Curiously, in the Bible the term "angel" translates Hebrew and Greek words meaning "messenger."

Satanya is instructed first to deliver a camera to New York photographer Donald Powell (John Crawford), who, while vacationing in New England, uses it to take a picture of an enigmatic woman leaving an isolated cottage. Enraged by her disregard of his attention, he accidentally strangles her. Haunted by guilt, when the photo (minus the girl) of the cottage turns up in a gallery showing, Powell imagines he sees the girl still approaching him on the walkway.

Pleased by her successful delivery, the Devil greets Satanya's return ("The beautiful Devil's messenger," he purrs), dispelling her notions that he manipulates the outcome. "People ruin their own lives," he pooh-poohs. "All we do is help them a bit."

The Devil has Satanya deliver a pickax to a Norwegian miner, who chips out a block of ice from a subterranean glacier containing the frozen body of a beautiful prehistoric woman. The paleontologist called in to examine the find becomes obsessed by the woman's icy beauty, to the point of murdering colleagues for fear they will defrost her, revealing her nakedness and drowning her (!) in the thawing process.

Again, while intentionally done or not, Strock's reclamation of Siodmak's work borrowed from a literary classic. In Dante's *Divine Comedy* (1321?), as Dante Alighieri's *Commedia* is generally known, angels appear as both messengers and guardians, and Satan is vividly portrayed frozen in a block of ice.

The whole idea of Satanya as the devil's messenger mirrors the Biblical intent of angels and intermixes the role of demons. In the Old Testament the functions of angels are to worship God and attend on Him, standing ready to do His will. They appear unsummoned, perform their appointed task and vanish—just like Satanya.

At the same time, demons have been described as malevolent spirits having supernatural powers and dedicated to destruction. They were winged and, like Satanya, traveled to the uttermost limits of the Earth, always at night. They had the power to see, while at the same time remaining invisible (like Satanya), and were committed to a cruel conspiracy against the human race.

For the third and final story, Satanya returns to hell for her assignment. The Devil contemplates a medium's crystal ball (wherein Chaney's face, inverted and distorted in the reflection, brings to mind actor David Hoffman peering out of its spherical depths at the outset of Chaney's *Inner Sanctum* films at Universal in the forties). "The crystal ball is the toy of the devil," he muses, sending an understandably enthusiastic Satanya to deliver the glass globe which will bring about the downfall of the man who spurned her in life and drove her to suicidal despair.

After the third episode (more laden with contrivance than the others), Satanya confronts the Devil. With her former lover sputtering denials beside her, Satanya demands the Devil fulfill his part of their bargain by convening a tribunal to decide her damnation (as if hell were ruled by committee). Here, at the finale, the Devil bids the two of them deliver one last item, an envelope. "We've selected both of you to help us annex Earth as part of our domain," he proclaims. Asked what the envelope contains, the Devil tells them, "It's our greatest achievement. It assures us of more territory. Space. We've been overcrowded here for years. That envelope contains a formula."

"What is it?" Satanya asks. "What do we do with it?"

Breaking the fourth wall, the Devil turns and points at the camera (and thus the audience), saying, "Deliver it to them. They'll know what to do with it." He cackles wickedly. "They'll play hell with it! That formula is a 500 megaton bomb!" Over his fade out laughter, stock footage of nuclear mushroom clouds plays out, a single black cat wandering over the rubble of a decimated civilization.

Once more, Strock's renovation shows a decidedly classical bent. The opening sentences of Richard Bovet's *Pandemonium* (1684) provide a typical description of Satan's power and purpose: "Since the defection of the Fallen Angels from the first rectitude, or state of sublime Happiness and Glory... the indefatigable Enemy of Souls hath been restless in his Attempts to advance his own Infernal Dominion..." With a single megaton (MT) the equivalent of a one-million-ton TNT explosion (bombs with a yield of roughly 60 MT have been tested, though most nuclear devices today have a yield of less than one MT), the Devil's plan would seem to have some credibility.

Chaney, his teeth glinting like Chiclets in the dim studio light, is totally believable as the Devil. Without the usual trappings of horns, hooves, and Vandyke beards, Chaney is altogether convincing in a part that *pro forma* called for his physical antithesis. Although his new scenes were likely shot in only a day or two, Chaney still delivers one of his best but unjustly ignored performances. Barking commands like a drill sergeant, whispering enticements for revenge, tittering at his own perverse plans, Chaney seems to be having naught but devilishly good fun.

The *Castle of Frankenstein 1967 Annual* reviewed *The Devil's Messenger* as an "interesting but minor 3-part grade-B fantasy meller... but stories are underdeveloped and novel idea is defeated by lack of imagination." Still, the writer extolled Chaney's contribution to it, calling him "wonderful as leering Satan plotting downfall of humanity."

Steven H. Scheuer, in *Movies on TV and Videocassette*, bemoaned the "hazy plot" and "poor production values." Ed Naha entered *The Devil's Messenger* in his encyclopedic *Horrors! From Screen To Scream* as "a low-budgeted *Twilight Zone* imitation that never gets off the ground.... Imaginative at times but mostly a mammoth bore."

In *Terror On Tape*, author James O'Neill disparaged Chaney as much as the film itself, calling *The Devil's Messenger* "awesomely inept" and "murky and dull," with "a puffy Chaney [looking] like he may have been soused through most of it and probably was."

Strock may have felt hamstrung by Herts' insistence on using wife Karen Kadler in the lead, but the attractive brunette made this, her last film, an adequate bid for a limited genre immortality. She appears in the three stories only briefly, superimposed over the Siodmak-shot footage, to make her deliveries. After making her screen debut in *Francis Joins the WACs* (1954) alongside genre favorites Julia Adams (b. 1928), Mara Corday (b. 1932), and Allison Hayes (1930-1977), Kadler made only a handful of movies. She was billed tenth (as Karyne Kadler) in Roger Corman's seminal *It Conquered the World* (1956), playing a member of the team of space scientists whose satellite is hijacked by a conical visitor from Venus. Kenneth Herts had been production supervisor for *The Beatniks* (1960) which starred Kadler, where the two met.

Other faces in *The Devil's Messenger* are tougher to recognize. John Crawford, who played the photographer in the first episode, had been in movies since the mid-forties, playing mostly in serials (*Radar Patrol vs. Spy King, The Invisible Monster, Zombies of the Stratosphere*) and B-films (*The Phantom of 42nd Street, Serpent of the Nile*). After this, Crawford went on to become a semi-regular fixture in genre films, from *Captain Sindbad* [sic] and *Jason and the Argonauts*, both in 1963, to *The Severed*

Arm (1973) and *The Boogens* (1981). Aside from parts in bigger-budgeted films like *The Longest Day* (1962), *The Greatest Story Ever Told* (1965), and *The Towering Inferno* (1974), Crawford earned his most lasting fame as Sheriff Ep Bridges on *The Waltons* TV show from 1972 to 1981.

Ninth-billed Jan Blomberg chose to leave *The Devil's Messenger* off his resume, evidently to boast he made his film debut in 1964 in a minor film (*All These Women*) directed by Ingmar Bergman. It was little help, however; by 1970, Blomberg was starring in questionable fare like *What Are You Doing After The Orgy?*, and after that he was confined mostly to Swedish television.

As a production/release company, Herts-Lion had only marginal success. Although it lucked into the Croatian *Ersatz* (*The Substitute*) in 1961 (which won the Academy Award for Adapted Story), the company's only other notable release seems to have been the Japanese science fiction film *Denso Ningen* (1960). Originally a wide-screen color release, a straitened Herts-Lion, unable to finance a theatrical release, sold it directly to U.S. television, cropped and in black-and-white, as *The Secret of the Telegian*. Kenneth Herts himself wrote and directed the hysterically overhyped *Daughter of the Sun God* ("Virgin Sacrifice! Ritualistic Love! Awesome Death! Strange Drama!") in 1962, but that was it for Herts-Lion.

Curt Siodmak felt betrayed by the company. "They took three of the [*13 Demon Street*] shows, put 'em together, put a frame around it and put Herbert Strock's name on it as director," the writer/director said in 1984. "They never mentioned me, but I'm glad of that. I never saw it. Actually, some of those episodes did come out okay. I think they were better than the *Thriller*s in story values." After this debacle, Siodmak's only other turns in the director's chair were *Liebesspiel im Schnee* (1966) and *Ski Fever* (1969).

If durability is any measure of filmmaking greatness, Curt Siodmak can indeed lay claim. Working away from the glare, he survived more than 40 years in show business to see his movies become touchstones and, finally, to see his behind-the-scenes efforts get some deserved accolades. Siodmak's allegiance to Lon Chaney, Jr. over those years, despite his publicized misgivings over the actor's alcoholism and alleged homosexuality, resulted in two very serviceable thrillers.

While poor casting may have subdued Chaney in *Bride of the Gorilla*, and radical reshooting may have made Siodmak's association with *The Devil's Messenger* tenuous at best, both films show a progressively dissipated journeyman actor unafraid to take risks, and still capable of coming through in a pinch—the results of a master writer/director with a sense of loyalty uncommon in Tinseltown.

Bride of the Gorilla
CREDITS: Producer: Jack Broder; Director: Curt Siodmak; Writer: Curt Siodmak; Director of Photography: Charles Van Enger, A.S.C.; Editorial Supervision: Francis D. Lyon, A.C.E.; Music: Raoul Kraushaar; Art Director: P. Frank Sylos; Men's Wardrobe: Elmer Ellsworth; Women's Wardrobe: Betty Zackin; Assistant to the Producer: Herman Cohen; Associate Producers: Edward Leven and Adrian Weiss; Set Decorator: Edward G. Boyle; Assistant Director: Richard Dixon; Hairdresser: Ann Kirk; Sound: Bud Myers; Make-up: Gus Norin; Special Effects: Lee Zavitz; copyrighted 1951 by Jack Broder

Productions, Inc.; distributed by Realart Pictures Inc.; released in 1951 with a running time of 64 minutes

CAST: Barbara Payton (Dina Van Gelder); Lon Chaney (Commissioner Taro); Raymond Burr (Barney Chavez); Tom Conway (Dr. Viet); Paul Cavanagh (Klaas Van Gelder); Gisela Webisek (Al-long); Carol Varga (Mme. Van Heusen); Paul Maxey (Van Heusen); Woody Strode (Nedo); Martin Garralaga (Native); Felippa Rock (Stella Van Heusen); Ray Corrigan (Gorilla)

The Devil's Messenger
CREDITS: Producer: Kenneth Herts; Director: Herbert L. Strock; Writer: Leo Guild; Director of Photography: William Troiano; Sound: Rod Sutton; Production Manager: Jack Shnell; Assistant Director: David McDonald; Music: Alfred Gwynn; Art Director: Robert J. Herts; Titles and Opticals: C.F.I.; copyrighted 1961 by Herts-Lion International Corp.; released in October 1962 with a running time of 71 minutes

CAST: Lon Chaney; Michael Hinn; Ralph Brown; John Crawford; Bert Johnson; Chalmers Goodlin; Gunnel Brostrom; Tammy Newmara; Jan Blomberg; Ingrid Bedoya; Eve Hossner; "and introducing Karen Kadler as Satanya"

13 Demon Street
CREDITS: Originator: Curt Siodmak; Production Manager: Lars Werner; Camera: Max Wilen; Editor: C. O. Skeppstedt; Art Direction: Bibi Lindstrom; Wardrobe: Sigyn Sahlin; Sound: Olle Bohlin; Music: Len Fors; Producers: Gustaf Unger, Ken Herts, Leo Guild; Writer/Director: Curt Siodmak; a Herts-Lion production (no copyright date); released by Crosby/Brown Productions

CAST: Lon Chaney

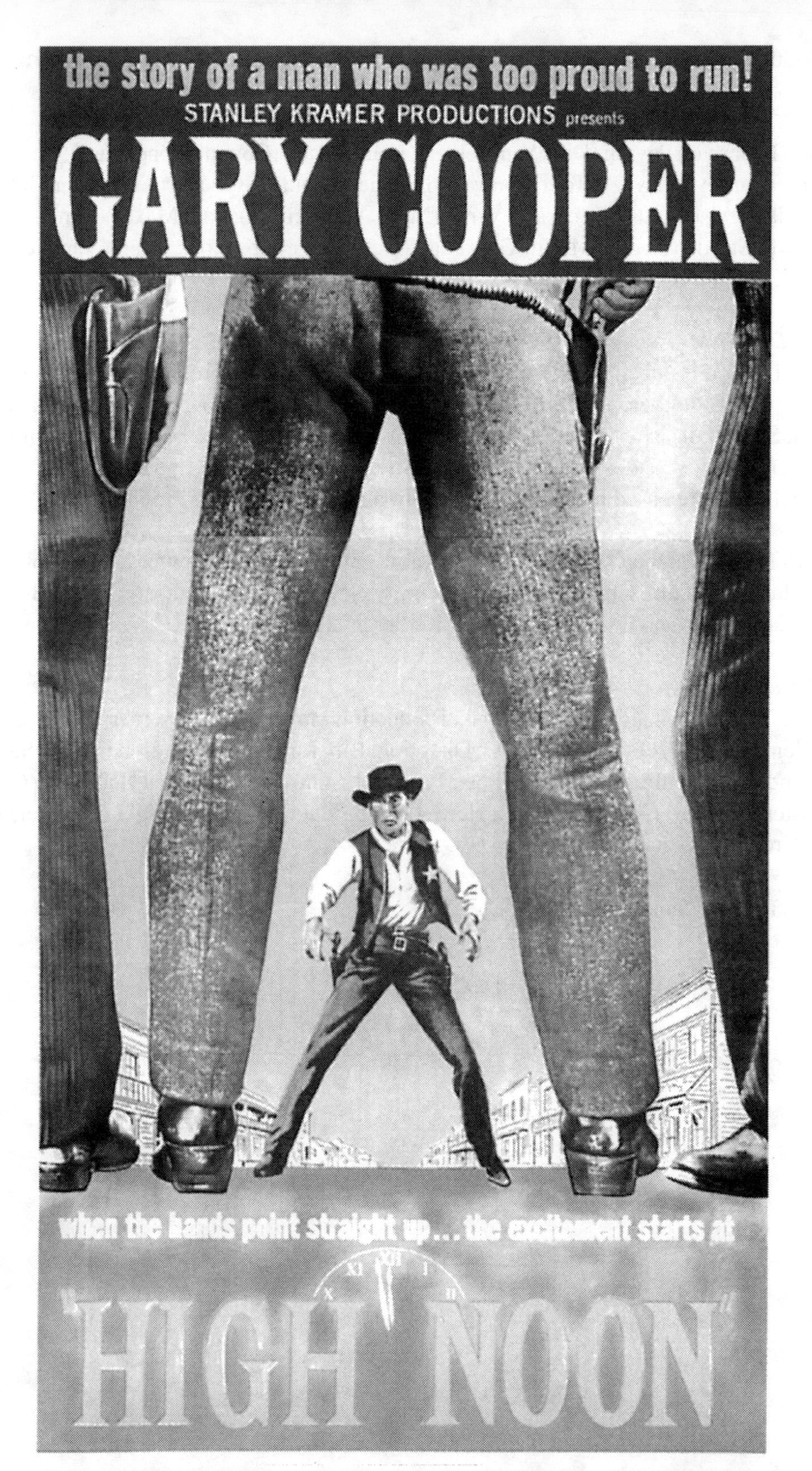

STANLEY KRAMER PRODUCTIONS presents GARY COOPER in "HIGH NOON"
with THOMAS MITCHELL · LLOYD BRIDGES · KATY JURADO · GRACE KELLY · OTTO KRUGER
Lon Chaney · Henry Morgan · DIRECTED BY FRED ZINNEMANN · Screen Play by Carl Foreman · Music Composed and Directed by Dimitri Tiomkin · Director of Photography Floyd Crosby, A.S.C. · RELEASED THRU UNITED ARTISTS

HIGH NOON (1952)

by Cindy Ruth Collins

In 1952, Lon Chaney, Jr. appeared in a different kind of monster movie: a film about monsters of cowardice and self-interest lurking behind the facade of friendship.

Though set as a Western, the original trailer marketed the film as a "Masterpiece of Suspense." And though Chaney received seventh billing, the trailer's first vignette (following the iconographic shot of Gary Cooper standing very small and alone on a dry deserted street) showed Chaney cynically instructing Cooper on the citizens' lack of commitment to law and order.

Despite the brevity of his role, Chaney had one of the most crucial moments near the film's climax, a moment in which the Marshal's childhood hero Mart Howe (Chaney) tells the Marshal (Gary Cooper) to turn tail and run out of town while there is yet time.

The film, of course, is the Western classic, *High Noon.*

For those unacquainted with the plot, *High Noon*'s director, Fred Zinnemann, provides a succinct summary in materials he prepared for publicity:

> The entire action of the film "High Noon" occurs within an hour and a half on a hot summer Sunday in 1865, in a small western town. It dramatizes the futile efforts of the town marshal, (Gary Cooper), to organize a posse in order to oppose a dreaded outlaw [Frank Miller] who is about to arrive on the noon train. The townspeople fail to support the marshal in this crisis. In the end he is forced to fight four gunmen all by himself. He finally kills three of the outlaws; the fourth is shot by his young bride.

What Zinnemann's words do not tell us is that the main character, Will Kane, Marshal of Hadleyville, not only must face "a dreaded outlaw," but an outlaw whom he sent to hang five years earlier and who swore to return... to kill him. The three surviving members of the killer's gang have reunited for the event and await the killer's arrival at the Hadleyville train stop. And the entire town feels the tension inherent in their presence. However, Will Kane not only must face these four deadly killers, he must also face the moral dilemma of choosing, on his wedding day, between "love and duty"—a dilemma underscored by the film's Oscar-winning theme song.[1] In essence, Kane must decide between running off with his bride to start a life without the badge and gun, or facing the newly paroled killer due to arrive in town on the noon train. Even worse, as the song's title ("Do Not Forsake Me Oh My Darlin'") hints, if Kane faces the killer, his Quaker bride, Amy (Grace Kelly), has promised *to* forsake him.

Neither Zinnemann's words nor the song reveals, however, that the citizens do not merely "fail to support him" *en masse*; but one by one, as Kane canvasses his friends for help against the killer and his reunited gang, each friend individually turns his back on Kane, or (for one logical reason or another) tells him to leave town. Only a young teen and an old one-eyed drunk, both of whom Kane refuses to send to almost certain death, volunteer their assistance.

In the end, as Zinnemann indicates, the townsfolk force Kane to face these four desperate men alone. Or almost alone. In one of the film's most dramatic moments, Kane's bride rushes back into town from the train stop just as the first shots ring out from the gunfight—and violates her religious principles of non-violence by helping her husband kill the *two* remaining killers.

Some thirty minutes before this ending, though, Will Kane's entire world had already been turned upside down, when his lifelong friend Mart Howe—suffering from arthritis and probably acting out of genuine concern for Kane's well-being—refused to face the killers with him. Regardless of Howe's handicap or his motives, Kane is "staggered" by Howe's refusal, as Fred Zinnemann notes on his script. And Chaney's understated performance as Howe, quietly conveying a flat air of hopelessness and despair, increases the film's mounting tension to fever pitch.

The question remains, though: how was horror icon Lon Chaney cast for this small, but potent, role as the defeated, world-weary ex-Marshal?

Toward the back of the director's shooting script, Zinnemann placed several pages of handwritten notes, listing each actor or actress considered for each role. Some of the choices and near-choices prove interesting. For example, "Tamblyn" (presumably Russ) was considered for, but did not win, what I believe to be the role of the brave fourteen-year-old who begs Kane to let him help. And Lee Van Cleef (noted as "Van Cleve") remains the solitary listing for the silent gunman Colby, who opens the film waiting for his two cohorts on a lonely hilltop.

The list with which we are most concerned, the one for Lon Chaney's role, demonstrates just exactly how high producer Stanley Kramer, initial co-producer/scriptwriter Carl Foreman, and the director aimed in their casting:

Howe:
John Dierkes
3) Bart McLane
2) Paul McVey
1/) Lon Chaney→FLAT VOICE![2]
1) McLaglen
Jay Flippen?
Jas Barton
Joe Sawyer?
Art Smith?

Unfamiliar names? Perhaps. Unfamiliar faces? Perhaps not. Most of these men specialized in character roles that billed them sixth or seventh—give or take a few spots up, or about twenty spots down, in the credits! Most were in a veritable multitude of films.

A few years before *High Noon*, **John Dierkes** appeared as Ross in Orson Welles' rendering of *Macbeth*—Shakespeare's tale of witches, ghosts, madness, and murder. In 1951, the year *High Noon* was cast, he gave a great performance as Jim Conlin the Tall Soldier in the mainstream classic, *Red Badge of Courage*, and in the same year, appeared lower on the bill in another classic, Howard Hawks' science fiction thriller, *The Thing from Another World.* Despite these credits, Dierkes does not appear to have been seriously considered for the role of Mart Howe. Perhaps, at 43, he was just a bit *too* young—or perhaps Kramer, Foreman, and Zinnemann had some mystical foreknowledge (!) that only a few years later, he would play Jacob, the notorious caretaker who knows how to drive a stake through a werewolf's heart, in Edgar Ulmer's bizarre vampire/werewolf/Dr. Jekyll movie *The Daughter of Dr. Jekyll* (1957)... which incidentally filled out the double-bill for another Chaney picture, *The Cyclops* (1957).

Bart McLane (better known as Barton MacLane) *did* receive fairly serious consideration for the role of Mart Howe. His was an ubiquitous face in films—appearing in about two hundred of them, "mainly at Warner Brothers, and most often as a heavy."[3] In addition to having last billing in the Marx Brothers' first film, MacLane appeared throughout his career in several of the same films as Lon Chaney: as Inspector Walgreen in the Chaney vehicle *The Mummy's Ghost* (1944), as Big Tom Stone in *Law of the Lawless* (1964), and as James Fennimore Fell in *Town Tamer* (1965). MacLane, however, is perhaps best remembered by a wide audience for his small, effective roles in some John Huston/Humphrey Bogart films—particularly as the hard cop who wants nothing more than to arrest Sam Spade in *The Maltese Falcon* (1941), and as the conman McCormick, who refuses to pay his laborers (and is willing to break a bottle over their heads for it), in the beginning of *Treasure of the Sierra Madre* (1948).

Paul McVey received even more serious consideration for the role of Howe than MacLane did. Billed between thirteenth and thirty-second, McVey had appeared in *Drums Along the Mohawk* (1939), *Stagecoach* (1939), Peter Lorre's vehicle *Stranger on the Third Floor* (1940), the ape brain-transplant movie *The Monster and the Girl* (1941)—and would go on to appear in Alan Ladd's classic *Shane* (1953). Perhaps most curious, though, is a stint at Monogram, where he tended to play much higher on the bill.

Lon Chaney. The pressbook for *High Noon* states that Hollywood initially gave the son of the legendary "Man of a Thousand Faces" only "bit parts" and that "finally Chaney was typed in heavy roles. Hoping to broaden his scope, he forsook films to play 'Lennie' in the Pacific Coast stage run of *Of Mice and Men* in 1939. The popular film role followed." Of course, contrary to publicity, not all of Chaney's early roles were "bit parts." In fact, in one of his earliest Westerns, *Scarlet River* (1933), he receives and earns third billing (as Creighton Chaney), for the role of foreman Jeff Todd. Curiously, too, the pressbook stops its bio after Chaney's first starring role and fails to mention his years of large and leading roles at the Universal monster factory.

Presumably, though, it was his character roles and particularly his experience in Westerns that placed Chaney's name on the casting list for *High Noon.* Chaney had played in many Westerns, both before and after becoming a star at Universal. Prior to *The Wolf Man* (1941), he had appeared as a heavy in the 1936 Gene Autry vehicles *The Singing Cowboy* and *The Old Corral;* he had lost his contract with Fox over heavy drinking during the filming of the Tyrone Power/Henry Fonda classic *Jesse James* (1939);

and in his last Western before signing with Universal, Chaney again played a heavy in MGM's *Billy the Kid* (1941).

Universal, apparently recognizing Chaney's talent in the genre, also placed him in several Western films and serials, including *Riders of Death Valley* (1941), *Badlands of Dakota* (1941), *Overland Mail* (1942), *Frontier Badmen* (1943), and *The Daltons Ride Again* (1945). Most recently, he had played in *The Bushwhackers* (1952), a non-Universal Western.

The casting note for **McLaglen** almost certainly refers to Victor McLaglen. There is a long-shot chance that it could refer to one of Victor's brothers or his son Andrew, though most of the brothers had not made a film in years, and Andrew, at 31, was far too young for the role. Victor McLaglen, of course, had long been a favorite actor of John Ford's who starred him alongside Boris Karloff in *The Lost Patrol* (1934), directed him to a Best Actor Oscar in *The Informer* (1935), and had recently featured him in the John Wayne Westerns *She Wore a Yellow Ribbon* (1949) and *Rio Grande* (1950). Of all the actors not cast as Howe, McLaglen was probably the most grateful: that year Ford would again direct him to an Oscar, this one for Best Supporting Actor, in the John Wayne classic *The Quiet Man* (1952).

Of the four remaining actors on the list, three received only modest nods for the role of Howe, while the fourth (James Barton) does not appear to have been seriously considered. Prior to the casting for *High Noon*, **Jay Flippen** had received fourth billing as the hardened criminal T-Dub in Nicholas Ray's seminal film *They Live By Night* (1949), and would soon go on to play Sheriff Singer in Marlon Brando's groundbreaking classic, *The Wild One* (1953). Though **James Barton** had played everything from drunken Irishmen to Kit Carson, he devoted much of his time between 1950 and 1951 to musicals starring the likes of Betty Grable, Mitzi Gaynor, and Bing Crosby. **Joe Sawyer** had played a police sergeant in the Cagney/Bogart gangster film *The Roaring Twenties* (1939), a military sergeant in *Sergeant York* (1941), and had appeared in a couple of Abbott and Costello features. And **Art Smith** had played in many Westerns, with titles such as *Moon over Montana* (1946), *Trail to Mexico* (1946), *Six Gun Serenade* (1947), and most recently *The Painted Hills* (1951) to his credit.

This cast list reveals that the production team strongly committed itself to getting quality performances in the character roles. According to *Photoplay* (June 1952), "No expense was spared in the casting" for *High Noon.* "Important players willingly accepted smaller roles in order to play under Kramer's banner."[4] And in fact, the producers hired an Oscar-winning actor, Thomas Mitchell, for a role no larger than Chaney's, and apparently considered another Oscar winner for the role that Chaney got. Mart Howe is on screen for a total of about five minutes. Yet Chaney won this role over an entire field of highly skilled character actors.

Since Zinnemann numbers both McLaglen and Chaney "first" for the part, the battle for Mart Howe was clearly fought between the two actors who had repeatedly starred in films themselves. At 64, McLaglen was much closer in age to the character than the 45-year-old Chaney was. Still, the production team obviously believed that the younger actor (younger, in fact, than Cooper himself) could convincingly pull off the portrayal of a much older man. Though the pressbook makes no mention of Chaney's monster roles, his monsters had required him to act under heavy make-up and transform himself completely. Apparently more important than the monsters, though, was his role in *The Bushwhackers* (1952). In his Chaney biography, Don G. Smith indicates that according

Will Kane (Gary Cooper) asks his mentor Martin Howe (Chaney, Jr.) for assistance in the Western classic *High Noon*.

to *The Bushwhackers'* pressbook, Chaney's performance as the elderly and arthritic Mr. Taylor drew Stanley Kramer's attention to Chaney for the role of the elderly and arthritic Mart Howe in *High Noon*. Fred Zinnemann, though, seemed to find Chaney's "flat voice" his most impressive characteristic, as the director excitedly notes on his shooting script. And in fact Leonard Maltin observes in his *High Noon* documentary that the actor's flat voice perfectly conveys the character's "world-weary" cynicism.

Still, we must ask whether Chaney won the role over McLaglen head-on or by default. Was Victor McLaglen already slated for *The Quiet Man* and unavailable for *High Noon*?

Actually, McLaglen had been informally slated for *The Quiet Man* since 1944. Ever since the 1930s, director John Ford had wanted to make this film about an Irish-born American returning to Irish village life, and he wanted McLaglen in the role of the brother. But for years, the director had run into trouble with the financing. In fact, according to Tag Gallagher, Ford filmed *Rio Grande* (1950) with the purpose of getting money for *The Quiet Man*—and also of "warming up O'Hara, Wayne, and McLaglen for the Irish movie" (p. 257). Ford finally went to Ireland in 1950 to shoot locations, then returned with his cast to shoot the film from June to August 1951.

Meanwhile Fred Zinnemann finalized his contract for *High Noon* with Stanley Kramer in July 1951, after having first been approached by Kramer in June 1950. By this time, McLaglen had already begun shooting the Ford picture in Ireland. Since there are no dates attached to Zinnemann's casting notes, however, it is difficult to determine whether he wrote these notes before or after finalizing his contract in July, and whether these are actors that he sought to contact or actors who had actually read for the part.

Still, if Kramer, Foreman, and Zinnemann had truly wanted McLaglen (and McLaglen had sought the role), the shooting schedule for *The Quiet Man* would not likely have interfered seriously with the shooting schedule for *High Noon*. Unless McLaglen still needed to shoot a number of scenes at the studio, he could have returned from Ireland in August and begun the shooting on *High Noon* in September—and if necessary, the production team could possibly have pushed back the shooting of Howe's scenes to a little later in September than they shot the scenes with Chaney.

Though we do not know for certain whether McLaglen's filming of *The Quiet Man* kept him from playing Mart Howe or whether Chaney beat him outright for the role, we do know that Kramer and Zinnemann were well satisfied with Chaney and felt no need to go out of their way to acquire McLaglen. This fact—plus Zinnemann's excited note about Chaney's voice—indicates that it really was Chaney that they wanted in the part.

By the time that Lon Chaney shot his scenes (September 7-12, 1951), several subtle but significant changes had already been made to his character. In the wedding sequence, where Howe first appears, he receives material that had originally belonged to Thomas Mitchell's character in writer Carl Foreman's script.

When Mayor Joe Henderson (Mitchell), the Marshal's Best Man, bursts in to the Marshal's office declaring the honeymoon "officially over," Foreman's script would have him add as a second thought, "A man's entitled to some privacy on his wedding day." In the film, however, that line is dropped, and Mart Howe speaks in counterpoint to Henderson's intrusion: "That's no way to treat a man on his wedding day." This small change establishes greater consistency within the two characters: Howe shows concern for Kane, while Henderson remains full of himself... as he will later on when he tells the townsfolk in the church not to support the Marshal's quest for a posse, for Hadleyville cannot economically or politically afford a gunfight on its streets.

Howe also indicates concern for Kane in a section of the wedding sequence that remained unchanged. When Sam Fuller (Henry Morgan) tells Will that he can't see him giving up the badge to run a store, Howe affirms Amy's statement "I can," by adding "So can I. And a good thing too." Though Zinnemann notes that Howe "betrays" Kane with this statement, the perception of betrayal at this point could come only from Kane's perspective. In reality, Howe here implies the belief that he elaborates on later when Kane begs him to join the posse: that it's better to get out of law enforcement than to waste one's life fighting villains for little thanks and an ignoble death. Howe sees Kane's marriage as an opportunity for Will to escape a lousy job, not as a sentence to an unexciting life, as Fuller does. In fact, the film shows Howe beaming as his friend resigns the badge moments after his wedding.

Later on in the wedding sequence, when news arrives that Frank Miller's three gunmen are waiting at the depot for Miller's noon return, Howe most likely loses hope that Kane can leave the job. Still, he whisks Will and Amy out of the Marshal's office and quickly gets them out of town. In the Foreman script, the Marshal "climbs up into the buckboard" after Mart Howe "has already unhitched the two horses and turned them to the street." Henderson then "slaps one of the horses on the rump."

In the film, though, Howe—not Henderson—hits the horses... and then rubs his mangled, arthritic knuckles in pain. Not only does this action, which again changes the script, establish consistency in Howe's desire to get Will out of the business, but it also establishes the ex-Marshal's honesty with Kane when he later claims arthritis as a reason not to fight the badmen alongside his friend.

These changes show early in the film that of all the characters who will later refuse Kane help, Howe at least will not lie or try to weasel his way out. Throughout these early scenes, the picture emerges of a man who no longer has the physical ability to help enforce the law, and also of a man so fed up with law enforcement that he wants his friend out of it, looming threat or not. And we see all this about an hour before Kane appears at Howe's home, trying to convince the former Marshal to assist him once again; that is, we have a sense of Howe's disability and disillusionment, long before he refuses to wear the badge again.

One of the more intriguing changes is the movement of Chaney's main scene from first in the sequence of Kane's visits to his friends to last. In the shooting script, the Marshal seeks help in the saloon and meets with derision, sees the note "fluttering" on his office door, then finally goes himself to look for the friends he had sent for. His first stop, Zinnemann notes, will be "to Howe." And when he leaves Howe's home stunned, the clock face shows 11:26.

In the film, however, the clock shows 11:44, sixteen minutes before high noon. Once again, Chaney receives material that originally belonged to Thomas Mitchell. In the script, Mitchell's much noisier, more kinetic scene—the big scene in the church—ends at 11:44. In the film, though, Kane has already met with Henderson's blatant hypocrisy at the church, not to mention Fuller's rank cowardice behind the curtains of his home, by the time he reaches Howe. Making Howe's refusal the final one makes it the *ultimate* refusal, the refusal of Kane's fellow lawman—and worst of all, an *honest* refusal by his childhood hero, not motivated by greed or cowardice but by concern for Kane and the conviction that dying for the sake of law enforcement is nothing more than dying for a "tin star," that "it's all for nothing." Mart Howe's honesty apparently hurts Will Kane far more than everybody else's lies and self-interest.

With Chaney's scene taking the place of Mitchell's in the sequence, the climax of refusals becomes far quieter—and far more intense. As Zinnemann noted on his script when the scene was still slated to end at 11:26: "Even this man didn't come." The switch in sequence allows the film to build chronologically to this sense of Kane's utter abandonment.

Director Fred Zinnemann changed a considerable amount of dialogue within this scene as well, adding dramatic tension to Howe's refusal.[5]

Throughout the script, Fred Zinnemann edited and tightened up scriptwriter Carl Foreman's original dialogue. For example, in the scene where Will and Amy argue over his decision to stay in Hadleyville and face the threat, and Will tells her that perhaps there won't be any trouble, Zinnemann changes Amy's response from "You don't believe that... Where there are guns, there'll always be trouble" to the more forceful, less editorial "You know there'll be trouble." The director's changes in this scene consistently add strength to her character, making her appear not as a begging bride but as a determined woman, as strong (despite her pretty face) as her husband.

This characteristic of Zinnemann's—to make the dialogue more terse, more strong, more hard-boiled if you will—carries on throughout the script and on into Chaney's scene. And somewhere between Zinnemann's editing and the shooting of this scene on Friday, September 7, the dialogue changed slightly again, becoming more vernacular, and less literary or "writerly." Presumably, some of these latter changes involved Chaney's own contribution to the part. Let's take a look at the progress of Chaney's dialogue, from script to screen.

Mart Howe's scene with Will Kane hinges on Howe's three short speeches: the speech on what being a lawman is really like, the speech on law and order (which was featured so prominently in the film's trailer), and the speech on why Howe would not go down to the depot with his friend.

In the first, Foreman has Howe answer his friend's exclamation "Mart, you been a lawman all your life" with the embittered response:

> It's a rotten life. You risk your skin catching killers and the juries let them go so they can come back and shoot at you again. If you're honest, you're poor your whole life, and in the end you wind up dying all alone in a dirty street, or some stinking alley. For what? For nothing. A tin star...

In his script, though, Zinnemann scratches out "It's a rotten life" and changes it to the far more bitterly ironic statement "Yeah—my whole life—a great life" (which is again changed on film to repeat the "Yeah," as if Howe were musing about how awful it is to be a lawman). The director also drops the "stinking alley," thus focusing on the sort of death that Kane will die that afternoon (death "in a dirty street") if he does not succeed against the Miller gang.

In the film version, though, we hear these lines:

> Yeah... Yeah, all my life. It's a great life. You risk your skin catchin' killers and the juries turn 'em loose so they can come back and shoot at you again. If you're honest, you're poor your whole life, and in the end you end up dyin' all alone on some dirty street. For what? For nothin'. For a tin star.

Here, the juries no longer so passively let the killers go; they actively "turn 'em loose." This line pointedly states what Howe more verbosely argues in dialogue which Zinnemann scratched out from the original script: "When they gave him that silly sentence, I knew this day would come. I've been waiting for it."

In the "law and order" speech, Zinnemann's changes make Howe sound less like a man fishing for a way to express himself and more like a man who knows his own mind. To the Marshal's statement that "The Judge left town. Harvey's quit. I'm having trouble getting deputies," the script has Howe respond:

> It figures... It's all happened too sudden. People kind of got to talk themselves into law and order before they do anything about it... Maybe because deep down they got no use for it. I don't know.

"Seems like a man that already had busted knuckles didn't need arthritis too, don't it?"

Obviously, the "kind of got to" and the "I don't know" indicate that Howe isn't really too sure himself. Zinnemann, though, changes "kind of got to" to "have" (a change which the film renders "gotta"), showing that he does know. Even more significantly, Zinnemann scratches out "Maybe because deep down they got no use for it. I don't know" and substitutes "They don't care. They really don't care." This change, curiously enough, echoes Foreman's setting description for the exterior of Mart Howe's house:

> EXT. MART HOWE'S HOUSE. It is a small house, rather shabby in appearance, as if its owner is unwilling or unable to keep its paint and trim and flower beds in order, or perhaps *just doesn't care.* (Emphasis added)

Was Zinnemann perhaps inspired by Foreman's description to give Howe this more convincing line, the film's statement that they "just don't care"? In the shooting script, Zinnemann notes to himself that he needs to "TALK TO CHANEY RE: TALK THEMSELVES 'INTO LAW AND ORDER'." What he needed to speak with Chaney about (whether it was changes to the script, changes to Chaney's approach, or whatever) we will probably never know. But clearly Zinnemann knew the importance of these new lines for the character.

What we do know is that after all the changes had been made, the film version of Howe's speech sounds as follows:

> It figures. It all happened too sudden. People gotta talk themselves into law and order before they do anything about it, maybe because down deep they don't care. They just don't care.... Get out, Will... get out.

In the film, obviously, Foreman's original line and Zinnemann's alteration merge, retaining the forcefulness that Zinnemann contributes, yet still retaining Foreman's cadence. The change, of course, becomes Chaney's signature line in the film, the line which publicity used to help draw viewers into the theaters.

Finally, when Kane asks Howe if he will go "down to that station" with him, Foreman's script has Howe respond:

> No...
> You know how I feel about you, but I won't go with you, and I won't be with you.
> (he looks at his twisted fingers)
> Seems like a man that already had busted knuckles didn't need arthritis, too, don't it?
> (he shrugs hopelessly)
> No... I couldn't do anything for you. You'd be worried about me. You'd get yourself killed worrying about me. It's too one-sided the way it is...

This time, Fred Zinnemann makes only one formal edit to Foreman's script, omitting the repetitive "and I won't be with you," thus making the line more concise and to the point. Yet in the film version, we hear:

> Nah. You know how I feel about you, but I ain't goin' with you. Seems like a man with busted knuckles didn't need arthritis too, don't it? Nah, I couldn't do nothin' for you. You'd be worryin' about me. You'd get yourself killed worryin' about me. It's too one-sided like it is.

Foreman and Zinnemann occasionally toss colloquialisms into the script, but nothing in the script or its revision indicates that either writer could have created the ungrammatical eloquence of these simple lines. Foreman's script is often too grammatical and too wordy. Zinnemann generally makes the dialogue more intense and to the point, though not often more colloquial. But the changes in this speech have the earmarks of an actor's ear for dialogue—an actor's understanding of the speech patterns for the character he is playing. More likely than not, Lon Chaney himself is responsible for the final changes to this piece of dialogue.

And what a piece of dialogue it is. To every other character's self-interest, Howe claims an interest in Kane himself. We know Howe is not lying about the arthritis and

Chaney gives one of several excellent character performances in the film, and *High Noon* is all the stronger for it.

that Kane may well worry about him in the midst of the gunfight. We know also that Kane has exhausted his options, but that even with exhausted options, he will not let the drunk and the boy fight alongside him.

So why does Kane insist on approaching Howe? Has his boyhood worship of Mart Howe blinded him to the man's disability? Does he wish Howe to relive the glory of the past with him, even though this man is physically incapable of doing so? The film never answers these questions, but it does use two characters to underscore the problem.

Johnny, the hero-worshipping boy who is not afraid to face Frank Miller, provides us a glimpse of the youthful Will Kane who worshipped Mart Howe. Considering the power of youthful impressions, it may well be impossible for Kane to see Howe any differently than Johnny sees him—as the all-powerful lawman. Kane's survival against the four badmen, of course, can only solidify Johnny's worship of him.

An entirely different picture begins to emerge for us, however, when Kane drops his badge in the dust and rides out of Hadleyville disgusted. While his marriage to Amy may provide him the love and emotional sustenance he needs to avoid cynicism, the hypocrisy of his "friends" has shaken him so badly that he may find it impossible to trust anyone outside his marriage. The thoroughly disillusioned Mart Howe, in other words, may provide us a foreshadowing of the future Will Kane. One can only wonder if some twenty years hence, a broken-down Will Kane will counsel the lawman Johnny that "People gotta talk themselves into law and order" and that "it's all for nothin"—with Johnny, of course, so blinded by his youthful impressions that he cannot recognize the debilities of his hero or his hero's love in telling him what he does not want to hear.

In spite of a rocky political climate (the film was picketed as "un-American" after Carl Foreman had proved uncooperative in the McCarthy hearings), *High Noon* received excellent reviews from newspapers and magazines, and a warm response within the industry; played to packed houses, and took numerous awards.

The reviewer for *Photoplay* called the film "The best of its kind." Bosley Crowther wrote for *The New York Times* that *High Noon* "does honor to the western and elevates the medium of films." The *Movieland* correspondent recommended "the picture as exciting adult entertainment."

Exhibitors, too, heartily endorsed the film after witnessing a screening at the National Variety Clubs Convention. A few of their endorsements, included in the pressbook, read: "Oklahoma will love HIGH NOON and Gary Cooper. One of the best produced action westerns I have ever seen" (Morris Lowenstein President, Oklahoma Theatre Owners Association); "HIGH NOON deserves and will get my best playing time" (Eph Scharininsky, Souther Theatre Co.); "The industry needs more pictures like HIGH NOON. Stanley Kramer produced the best western Cooper made in years" (S. L. Oakley; Sam Landrum, Jefferson Amusement Co.); "All exhibitors who saw HIGH NOON today at Variety Club convention here unanimous in praise. United Artists has sure box office winner" (Paul Sperling, Nevada Theatres); "200 exhibitors can't be wrong. They all like HIGH NOON screened for them at Variety convention" (Herman H. Hunt, Hunt Theatres, Cincinnati, Ohio).

Two hundred exhibitors were not wrong. According to snippings Fred Zinnemann saved from *Variety*, *High Noon* looked "to bring in a socko $44,000 or close to the Mayfair" in Philadelphia; was "shooting for fancy $36,000 at State-Lake" in Chicago; looked "to hit socko $51,000, playing in four theaters and pacing the city" of Los Angeles; and "took first place nationally in August, according to reports from VARIETY correspondents in some 25 representative key cities." This gritty, black-and-white Western, made on a budget of only $786,600.01 and shot in 28 days during September 1951, was the eighth-highest grosser of 1952, raking in what was then a formidable $3,400,000.

It received four Oscars (Best Actor, Best Editing, Best Score, Best Song), was nominated for the Best Picture and Best Director Oscars, and was picked as Best Picture by the New York Film Critic's Circle. In addition, it was chosen as "one of the 'Ten Best' in the FILM DAILY annual poll," and earned the Silver Spurs Award from the City of Reno as "the outstanding Western motion picture released during 1952." Fred Zinnemann took home the coveted Director's Guild award and was "honored by the press with a Page One Award in Movies" by the Newspaper Guild of New York.[6]

Within a couple of years, the film had so entered the popular consciousness that Gimbels advertised its Saturday hours (apparently alone among major New York City department stores) as comparable to Cooper's standing alone against the bad guys in *High Noon*; and one newspaper cartoon parodied the Middle East situation in the mid-1950s by showing a lone defender of the peace heading toward a shoot-out at "Nasser & Co." Not surprisingly, the film was re-released only four years after its first run, and drew an unprecedented four million viewers when WRCA-TV broadcast the film in 1958.[7]

Of course, with all this hoopla, Lon Chaney's small role tended to get lost in the shuffle. He did his part, gave a solid performance in a quiet role, and contributed to the overall impact of the film. Some reviewers even noticed. *Photoplay* listed Chaney as one member of a "strong supporting cast," and a *New York Times* review noted:

> "Excellent support is supplied by Thomas Mitchell, as a town leader; Lloyd Bridges as a disgruntled young deputy, vengeful at being ignored in the selection of a successor to Cooper as marshal; Katy Jurado, as a twi-

> light character who had been loved successively by MacDonald, Cooper and Bridges; Otto Kruger as a Judge, and Lon Chaney and Henry Morgan, as friends of Cooper's unwilling to join the posse. The character bits have an authenticity that contribute materially to the effectiveness of the story."

Chaney, as the reviewer states, gives one of several excellent character performances in the film, and *High Noon* is all the stronger for it.

Thankfully, Chaney's performance in *High Noon* so impressed Stanley Kramer that Kramer hired him twice more for character parts: as Robert Mitchum's alcoholic father in *Not As a Stranger* (1955) and as a man who steps forward to talk a mob down from a lynching in *The Defiant Ones* (1958)—both solid films in a period when Chaney performed in fewer and fewer of them. And some forty years after directing the film, Fred Zinnemann wrote that he was "lucky to have excellent actors" in *High Noon*, Lon Chaney among them.[8]

In the final analysis, Chaney fans, whether they enjoy Westerns or not, can take pride in Chaney's appearance in *High Noon.* Lon Chaney overcame strong competition to get the role of Howe and makes an excellent contribution to the creation of a true classic. Perhaps most importantly, the film gives Chaney the acting legitimacy that he always sought, showing conclusively that not only could he hold his own in the same frame with mainstream heavyweights such as Gary Cooper, but he could actually shine. Mart Howe may not be Lon Chaney, Jr.'s best-remembered role, but Chaney's Howe did help make *High Noon* one of America's greatest films.

CREDITS: Producer: Stanley Kramer; Director: Fred Zinnemann; Screenplay: Carl Foreman (based on the story "The Tin Star" by John W. Cunningham); Cinematographer: Floyd Crosby; Music: Dimitri Tiomkin; Editors: Elmo Williams, Herry Gerstad; Production Director: Rudolph Sternad; Art Director: Ben Hayne; Set Director: Emmett Emerson; Music/Lyrics: "Do Not Forsake Me, Oh My Darlin'," Dimitri Tiomkin, Ned Washington.

CAST: Gary Cooper (Will Kane); Grace Kelly (Amy Kane); Thomas Mitchell (Jonas Henderson); Lloyd Bridges (Harvey Pell); Katy Jurado (Helen Ramirez); Otto Kruger (Percy Mettrick); Lon Chaney (Martin Howe); Henry Morgan (Sam Fuller); Ian MacDonald (Frank Miller); Eve McVeagh (Mildred Fuller); Harry Shannon (Cooper); Lee Van Cleef (Jack Colby); Robert Wilke (James Pierce); Sheb Wooley (Ben Miller); Tom London (Sam); Ted Stanhope (Station Master); Larry J. Blake (Gillis); William "Bill" Phillips (Barber); Jeanne Blackford (Mrs. Henderson); James Millican (Baker); Cliff Clark (Weaver); Ralph Reed (Johnny); William Newell (Drunk); Lucien Prival (Bartender); Guy Beach (Fred); Howland Chamberlin (Hotel Clerk); Morgan Farley (Minister); Virginia Christine (Mrs. Simpson); Paul Dubov (Scott); Jack Elam (Charlie); Harry Harvey (Coy); Tim Graham (Sawyer); Nolan Leary (Lewis); Tom Greenway (Ezra); Dick Elliott (Kibbee); John Doucette (Trumbull)

[1] The lyrics to the film's theme song provide the scenario over the opening credits and later serve as a sort of Greek Chorus commentary on the action throughout the film. Sung from the

Marshal's point of view, the song tells his bride that he must not forsake his duty ("Although you're grievin', I can't be leavin', Until I shoot Frank Miller dead"), but at the same time begs her not to leave on the noon train.

[2] It is difficult to decipher the numbering notation next to Chaney's name. It appears to read "1/"; I am assuming that this numbering places Chaney first in consideration for the role, particularly since Zinnemann also notes his vocal qualifications and Chaney did play Mart Howe in the film.

[3] Ephraim Katz, *The Film Encyclopedia*, p. 874.

[4] Zinnemann's papers reveal that a total of $54,975.41 went to "Cast and Bits" (after Cooper's $100,000 salary). Despite what seems, even by 1951 standards, to be a rather *small* expense on the character roles, the casting list for Mart Howe is extraordinarily strong.

[5] In both Leonard Maltin's short documentary on *The Making of High Noon* and in his own autobiography, Fred Zinnemann mentions Stanley Kramer's work on the script, but takes no writing credit for himself. However, the shooting script, on which the revisions we will discuss appear, contains handwritten revisions which seem to be in the same hand as other notes which Zinnemann unquestionably made. My assumption is that Zinnemann himself wrote these revisions—and thus wrote many of the film's most memorable lines, not only in Chaney's dialogue but throughout the movie.

[6] All quotes here are taken from Fred Zinnemann's correspondence.

[7] All of these materials are from clippings that Fred Zinnemann saved. The editorial cartoon also appears in the director's autobiography, p. 110.

[8] Zinnemann autobiography, p. 100.

Sources: Publicity materials, contracts, financial information, correspondence, clippings, and heavily annotated shooting script donated by the director to the Academy Library (The Academy of Motion Picture Arts and Sciences Center for Film Studies) as part of the Fred Zinnemann Collection; *The Motion Picture Guide* by Robert Nash and Stanley Ralph Ross, Cinebooks, 1985-1987; *Lon Chaney, Jr.: Horror Film Star, 1906-1973* by Don G. Smith, McFarland, 1996; *The Film Encyclopedia*, 2nd ed., by Ephraim Katz, HarperPerennial, 1994; *John Wayne: American* by Randy Roberts and James S. Olson, The Free Press, 1995; *John Ford: The Man and His Films* by Tag Gallagher, University of California Press, 1986; *About John Ford* by Lindsay Anderson, McGraw-Hill, 1983; *Duke: The Life and Times of John Wayne*, by Donald Shepherd and Robert Slatzer with Dave Grayson, Doubleday, 1985; *The Making of High Noon* by Leonard Maltin, short documentary included with 40th Anniversary Edition videotape of *High Noon*, Republic Home Video, 1992; *A Life in the Movies: An Autobiography* by Fred Zinnemann, Scribner's, 1992.

The author would like to thank Leonard Maltin for his help in pointing her toward the Fred Zinnemann Collection, and the late Fred Zinnemann for so graciously donating his papers to the Academy Library.

BIG HOUSE, U.S.A. (1955)

by David J. Hogan

By 1955 Lon Chaney, Jr.'s best asset was his face: craggy, deeply lined across the forehead and from nose to mouth, small eyes undercut by dramatic pouches. His head was large, his neck thick. Although Chaney was now nearly fifty years old, his hair had not thinned, so despite his lived-in, undeniably weary aspect, and despite a body that had been thickened by countless gallons of bourbon consumed since the mid-thirties, on the screen he exuded strength and the intriguing possibility of violence. His raspy growl of a voice was the final, perfect complement to his appearance. You look at his face in a film from this period and you understand that, whichever character Chaney is playing, he is not a fellow to be trifled with.

Chaney's career had become curiously dichotomous by the mid-fifties, bringing him leads in *Indestructible Man* (1956) and other minor, cheaply made pictures, and showy supporting roles in films as diverse as *High Noon* (1952) and *A Lion is in the Streets* (1953). One of Chaney's best roles from the period is a small supporting one in a superior Bob Hope vehicle, *Casanova's Big Night* (1954). In it, Chaney plays a ragged, bearded prisoner imprisoned with Hope in a dank dungeon. Each time Hope mounts an elaborate escape through a labyrinth of passages and tunnels, he ends up back in the dungeon, where the demented Chaney is ecstatic to see him.

Chaney's characterization is hilarious, yet the part is just another variation on the Lennie role he had played so memorably on Broadway and in the 1939 Lewis Milestone/Eugene Solow adaptation of Steinbeck's *Of Mice and Men*. In that film, Chaney proved himself a performer of depth and power, a star character actor who brought insight and poignancy to the innocent, simpleminded giant who dreams of one day living with his friend George on a farm of their own. The Lennie character (and, more to the point, Chaney's interpretation) almost instantly became folklore, and was frequently parodied by other actors and even cartoon characters. Given Hollywood's love of the self-referential, that Chaney himself would eventually do takeoffs of Lennie was inevitable. (He did so most pointedly in another Hope comedy, *My Favorite Brunette*, 1946, and echoes of the character haunt various Chaney performances that came later, including the Groton role in his final film, the execrable *Dracula vs. Frankenstein*, 1971.)

Chaney had been freelancing since 1946, when Universal dropped him from its contract roster. He had been a key player in the horror boom of the forties, and earned enormous amounts of money for the studio. But although a talented actor, Chaney also was a limited one, with neither the range nor the looks that might have allowed him to become a leading man or farceur. When the horror cycle petered out in the mid-forties, Universal wanted no more of the man it had built into a major horror star. (Chaney's last great horror performance, as the Wolf Man in Universal-International's *Abbott and Costello Meet Frankenstein*, 1948, was set up on a freelance, work-for-hire basis.)

Chaney worked steadily after leaving Universal, but without the weight of a studio behind him, and without the guaranteed paycheck that came with contract-player status, he suffered the insecurity known to any unaffiliated movie actor—insecurity magnified for him because of his high-profile (if ghettoized) former stardom. His predicament was worsened by ongoing strife with his second wife, Patsy. (However, Chaney and the former Patsy Beck, a redheaded, onetime photographers' model, were married from 1937 until Lon's death in 1973.)

In April of 1948 Lon swallowed forty sleeping pills in a suicide attempt, then secreted himself in his truck. He was discovered by his son, Ron, and rushed to Van Nuys Receiving Hospital in Burbank, where he gradually recovered. He carried on in films good, bad, and indifferent until the end of his life.

Big House, U.S.A. is a crime thriller produced by Bel-Air Productions for 1955 release by United Artists. It was Chaney's 121st film. Cast as a hulking, taciturn convict named Alamo Smith, Chaney was the fifth-billed member of a potent tough-guy lineup: Broderick Crawford, Ralph Meeker, Reed Hadley, William Talman, and Charles Bronson. Chaney had not been top-billed in a picture since *Sixteen Fathoms Deep*, a Monogram adventure released in 1948. The enduring, lucrative stardom of which Chaney may have dreamed was not going to materialize. Although he would make thirty-five films after 1955, he would receive top billing in only nine of them. But he remained a more-than-competent working actor, and his name was never without marquee value. When he was cast by producer Aubrey Schenck in *Big House, U.S.A.*, Schenck wasn't doing him a favor. Chaney was hired because he had a following and because he was good at his craft.

Although absorbing and toughly competent, *Big House, U.S.A.* seems like two-thirds of one movie and one-third of another. In the first third, a boy who has run away from a summer camp at Colorado's Royal Gorge National Park is discovered in the wild by an apparently sympathetic hiker. But the hiker is an extortionist who demands a $200,000 ransom from the boy's wealthy father. The money is delivered, but in the meantime the boy has accidentally fallen to his death. The extortionist is later captured on his way out of the park, a portion of the money hidden in his truck. Where is the rest?

The film's middle third is the antithesis of the documentary-style, on-location adventure of the first portion; instead, we join the by-now-convicted extortionist at Cascabel Island prison, in a claustrophobic cell he shares with four other cons. The film becomes an ensemble piece at this point, with Meeker's extortionist, Jerry Barker, now just one of a number of strong personalities. The others despise their new cellmate (the suspicion, never proved, is that Barker murdered the boy). But the cons are keenly interested in the remainder of the ransom, which, they are convinced, remains hidden somewhere in the vastness of the park.

In the story's final third we return to the milieu and visual style of the first. The extortionist becomes an unwilling member of a jailbreak and is forced to lead the others through the wilderness to his cache of loot. But the authorities have tracked the cons' movements, and the climactic discovery of the ransom is interrupted by gunfire and capture.

Big House, U.S.A. takes obvious structural cues from Raoul Walsh's *White Heat* (1949), a much better film that, although similarly "divided" into three acts—crime, prison, escape and retribution—has the personality of James Cagney to hold it all together. Walsh's picture does not become an ensemble piece once Cagney's Cody Jarrett arrives in prison, and even Edmond O'Brien, a powerful actor in his own right, remains subordinate to Cagney, who dominates every frame.

Ralph Meeker would prove in another 1955 release, *Kiss Me Deadly*, that he, too, was capable of carrying a picture by the force of his personality. Unfortunately, once Jerry Barker arrives at Cascabel, Meeker is absorbed by and ultimately subordinated to the other actors, particularly Broderick Crawford. It's not merely the structure, then, that makes *Big House, U.S.A.* seem like two movies, but the fact that the script and direction force our attention away from the Barker character. Of course, for viewers interested in Chaney, Crawford, and other actors, that's not entirely a bad thing. Still, we are not allowed to explore our legitimate fascination with Barker—an unfortunate dramatic shortcoming.

The first image in *Big House, U.S.A.* is a closeup of a hand gripping a revolver, barrel to the sky. The trigger is pulled, the gun jerks, and we see that the weapon is a starter pistol being used to begin a foot race of boys at summer camp. One of those boys is Danny Lambert (Peter Votrian), and the revolver has suggested the violence, if not the particulars, of his fate. From the beginning, though, we are ambivalent about the boy. One subtly clever aspect of John C. Higgins' script is that Danny, although clearly a victim, is not entirely sympathetic: he's skinny and rather unprepossessing, an asthma sufferer given to whining, and with a fear of needles that drives him into the woods when the camp's attractive young nurse (Randy Farr) attempts to give him an injection to quell an asthma attack.

Well, okay, so the kid's kind of a pain in the ass, but it's still too bad he's lost in the woods. When the kindly hiker comes along, Danny seems to be in good hands, and we relax. But as the man and boy walk together, the apparent rescuer becomes evasive about returning the boy to the camp. By the time he climbs with Danny to a rickety fire tower and leaves him there, we're worried. Pain in the ass or not, Danny's just a kid, and something funny is going on here.

The boy's accidental plunge through a rotted railing is shocking, and if his death makes us feel remorseful for having thought badly of him, it does nothing at all to affect the demeanor of Barker, who discovers the accident after setting the extortion plot in motion. Barker regards the body with mild interest. He doesn't curse, he doesn't frown, he barely blinks. Emotionless, he gathers the boy in his arms, walks to the edge of a yawning precipice, and tosses the painfully frail corpse into thin air. You witness this heartless pragmatism with a sort of open-mouthed disbelief, and you realize that this movie isn't going to be pulling its punches.

Director Howard W. Koch and cinematographer Gordon Avil emphasized the rough immensity of Royal Gorge—its peaks, escarpments, and essential isolation. No sound stage ever fills in for an exterior and the film has no process shots. (A single matte shot, a distant view of the island prison, is so-so.) The outdoor lighting is even and high-key, calling to mind the much-imitated, quasi-documentary look established by a trio of 1948 releases, *The Naked City, Call Northside 777*, and *Force of Evil.* The directors of those pictures (Jules Dassin, Henry Hathaway, and Abraham Polonsky, respectively) chose the visual approach for artistic reasons; Koch for budgetary ones. Regardless, the first third of *Big House, U.S.A.* is as potent and realistically explicated as the best crime thrillers of the period.

The unforgiving nature of the Royal Gorge natural landscape is reflected by Paul Dunlap's portentous score, and by Barker and nurse Emily Evans (Farr), the latter an attractive, seemingly innocent blonde who once worked for a physician whom Barker tried to blackmail. Although she was not involved in the blackmail scheme, she was later fired because of an "irregularity" in the doctor's narcotics cabinet. She subsequently hooked up with Barker, became his partner in a variety of petty extortion schemes, and tipped him off to the presence at the summer camp of Danny. In an effective, if obvious, irony, this "angel of mercy" is no angel at all.

Barker is captured at an exit checkpoint after claiming to have been fishing in a lake that the park service had purposely poisoned the year before. Suspicious rangers find a handgun in the back of Barker's truck, and later discover that Barker is carrying greenbacks with serial numbers matching those of bills that comprised some of the ransom.

Voice-over narration (initially by Roy Roberts, who plays the park's chief ranger; and subsequently by Reed Hadley, cast as FBI agent James Madden) dryly informs us of Barker's background—shoplifter, bigamist, petty mobster—and telescopes Barker's trial. Because Danny's body was never found, and because no physical evidence links Barker to the boy, "the Iceman" (as he is dubbed by reporters) is tried and convicted for extortion only, and sentenced to imprisonment for one to five years.

The film treads familiar territory once Barker arrives at Cascabel. As in countless prison movies that had come before, Barker's cellmates are a colorful mix of unpleasant "types": kingfish Rollo Lamar (Broderick Crawford), a self-consciously erudite schemer who looks at Barker the way Fred C. Dobbs looked at a vein of gold; Machine Gun Mason (William Talman), a cold-blooded, pale-eyed contract killer; Alamo Smith (Lon Chaney), a cynical but soft-spoken giant who occupies himself by fashioning nudie figures from soap; and Benny Kelly (Charles Bronson), an intimidatingly muscled young tough whose dislike for Barker is ferocious and immediate.

The Iceman has arrived at a propitious moment, for Lamar and the others have completed an escape tunnel that begins inside a workroom boiler. During one surreptitious look-see at the set-up, a hapless con named Dibsy is trapped inside the boiler and scalded to death. Director Howard Koch once again refuses to spare us: the victim's face fills the frame, eyes bulging with fright and pain, features contorted in a scream nobody can hear, the deathly steam enveloping him like a shroud.

The group's escape is effected via the tunnel, then along a damp culvert, and finally into the ocean. When Rollo's cobbled-together "scuba gear" goes bad part way through his swim, he is rescued by Bronson's Benny Kelly. Once on board a waiting boat, the exhausted Benny collapses on deck and sleeps. Rollo hands Mason (Talman) a heavy hammer and instructs him to bash in Benny's head. When Alamo (Chaney) protests, Rollo kills him and orders his body dumped overboard. Mason subsequently does his work with the hammer, then takes the blowtorch Rollo has handed him and burns away Benny's face and fingertips. (We view this act only peripherally, but when the boat's skipper, played by Jan Merlin, happens to look back from the pilot house to Mason's labors, the expression on his face tells us more than Koch could ever have shown.)

The charred body is dressed in Barker's uniform (which also is singed by the torch) and pushed overboard. The linchpin of Rollo's clumsy scheme is his faith that the authorities will assume the getaway boat exploded and burned at sea, killing Barker. (The business with the blowtorch, plus the earlier death of Dibsy in the boiler, are variations of one of the more celebrated sequences in Jules Dassin's *Brute Force*, 1947, in which a squealer trapped by cons against a prison furnace is dispatched by blowtorches.)

Chaney was the fifth-billed member of a potent tough-guy lineup: Broderick Crawford, Ralph Meeker, Reed Hadley, William Talman, and Charles Bronson. [Photofest]

Barker can barely believe the stupidness of Rollo's idea, but the trick seems to have worked when a later radio broadcast announces that two bodies retrieved from the ocean have been identified as those of Alamo Smith and Jerry Barker. Rollo congratulates himself for his cleverness, but of course the radio broadcast is a ploy by the authorities, who know full well that the burned body is not Barker's. Further, a small army of FBI agents and park rangers stakes out the Royal Gorge Park, awaiting Barker's return.

Once led to the buried loot, Rollo knocks Barker cold and greedily digs for his prize. When the authorities announce their presence, Mason pulls a revolver and tries to shoot it out, only to be perforated like a Swiss cheese by agent Madden's M-1 carbine. It's a kinetic, violent demise: Madden's heavy slugs punch patterns into the timber and literally blow Mason's body into the air. Reminding ourselves once again that the film was released in 1955, this sequence is rough stuff.

In a regrettably anticlimactic conclusion, Rollo puts up his hands and surrenders, and Barker does not wake up until the whole confrontation has ended. Agent Madden's concluding narration informs us that Rollo and Barker were later condemned to die in the gas chamber, and that nurse Emily Evans received a sentence of twenty years to life.

Although dramatically flawed, John Higgins' script proceeds with a metronomic logic, establishing the authorities' careful, unglamorous investigation as a counterpoint to Barker's and Rollo's less-carefully executed activities. The park rangers graciously cooperate with the FBI; tourists and park employees are carefully questioned; every vehicle leaving the park is stopped and searched; and the Colorado National Guard fans out amidst the peaks and scrub in a fruitless search for the boy's body.

As in countless prison movies that had come before, Barker's cellmates are a colorful mix of unpleasant "types."

The "police procedural" was refined by Jack Webb's *Dragnet* radio (and later television) series, from which *Big House* takes its style of plot explication and characterization; stone-faced Reed Hadley, for instance, is very much in the Joe Friday mold: competent, matter-of-fact, unassumingly relentless. The Jack Webb style also is apparent in the film's treatment of the criminals, who are dogged and professional (if not nearly so bright as they assume themselves to be), each with individualistic quirks.

Chaney's role as Alamo Smith did not give the actor a great deal of dialogue, but what there is is juicily amusing. When the prison guards note that the (steam-cooked) Dibsy is missing, Alamo laments, "Everybody around here's missin', but nobody misses *us*." Alamo doesn't give a good goddamn about Dibsy, but he's certainly unhappy about his own plight.

Because Alamo's nudie carvings have established the con's preoccupation with women, it's no surprise that, just prior to going underwater, Alamo advises a skeptical Barker, "Just pull the water into your arms, like a dame. You'll manage!" But as Alamo himself prepares to take the plunge, he notes, "I'm beginning to appreciate the delights of our good old cell."

Once on board the boat, Alamo observes as Rollo attempts to resuscitate Barker, who has swallowed some water. "Look at the good Samaritan," Alamo says sourly, "fattening the golden goose."

These and Chaney's other pieces of dialogue are made more piquant by the actor's rough rasp of a voice, and by his enormous physical presence, which seem to carry more potential for menace even than Bronson's sleekly muscled Benny. In an apt metaphor given Chaney's love of the outdoors, Alamo is a bear of a man: quiescent when undisturbed but a holy terror when aroused. Protesting Benny's murder, he picks up the spitting blowtorch and angrily advances on Rollo, who has to put two bullets into Alamo's chest in order to stop him.

There's something likable about Alamo. You get the sense that, although a "border killer, narcotics smuggler, wetback killer," he's a regular guy who'd be pleasant to hang out with. The two of you could fish or hunt or just sit around, neither of you saying much, and liking it that way. This unlikely feeling exists because we've seen the actor play sympathetic fellows in other films but, more to the point, because of something in Chaney himself—his weary but kind eyes; his deep rumble of a laugh; the easy, unselfconscious way he moves his big body. Chaney had by this time become a great character actor not simply because he could manage blocking and the convincing delivery of dialogue, but because he had a unique, unexpectedly complex *presence.* No matter what the role by this stage of his career, Chaney would effortlessly, perhaps unconsciously, invest the character with a sense of history, of having lived—lived hard, sometimes regretfully, but with grit and perseverance. That history is written in every line of Alamo's face, every flicker of his gaze, every time he opens his mouth to speak.

Bel-Air Productions was an independent film company founded in 1952 by Aubrey Schenck, Howard W. Koch, and Edwin Zabel. The company's existence was predicated on a deal with United Artists, which agreed to distribute three pictures that Bel-Air would bring in at pre-determined costs, each featuring a star with whom UA was comfortable. The first Bel-Air production, *War Paint* (1953), is typical of the company's product: an action-filled, modestly budgeted genre picture directed by a competent Hollywood veteran (Lesley Selander); featuring a B-plus leading man (Robert Stack) and a capable supporting cast (Joan Taylor, Charles McGraw, Peter Graves). At 89 minutes, it could be played off separately or as half of a double bill.

War Paint and the two Bel-Air productions that followed were moneymakers, so the deal with UA was extended—good news for Schenck, Koch, and Zabel, and for exhibitors, too. The studio system was showing serious cracks by the mid-fifties, and production companies like Bel-Air, whether tied to a studio or completely independent, were becoming increasingly important. While in-studio production units concentrated on A product intended to combat television, the independents provided an increasing number of programmers that were virtually guaranteed to make money, and offset losses incurred by big-budget flops.

Bel-Air's story man and leading light was Aubrey Schenck, a relative of legendary 20th Century-Fox co-founder and production executive Joe Schenck. Aubrey was born in 1908 and earned a law degree at Cornell. He worked as an attorney at 20th Century-Fox in New York from 1932 to 1939, and also was an assistant to Fox's New York-based president, Spyros Skouras. In time, Schenck became interested in the nuts-and-bolts aspects of the business, and relocated to Hollywood, where he learned the craft of editing and began to refine his gift for sure-fire story ideas. His first film as producer was *Shock* (1946), a Vincent Price vehicle directed by Alfred Werker, and based on Schenck's original story.

Howard W. Koch (not to be confused with *Casablanca* co-scripter Howard Koch) was born in 1916. He began his film career working as a booker for Universal in New York, and subsequently became a film librarian at Fox in Hollywood. He achieved second assistant director status on *The Keys to the Kingdom* (1944), and filled that role on *Shock.* His knack for keeping things moving on the set was noticed by Schenck, who promoted Koch to assistant director and took him along when he moved to Eagle-Lion in 1947. Koch later followed Schenck to Universal, and also worked as an assistant director at MGM.

Schenck's tenure with Eagle-Lion hooked him up with producer Edward Small, one of the sharpest operators in Hollywood. Schenck produced a pair of Small pictures that rank among the greatest of all films noir, Anthony Mann's *T-Men* (1947) and *Raw Deal* (1948; uncredited). The former, like *Big House, U.S.A.*, was scripted by John C. Higgins, who co-wrote the latter.

Schenck's talents were matched by his confidence. He had worked successfully with Small, and also had come out unscathed in dealings with two other sharpies, producers Sam Briskin and Sol Lesser. Comfortable with his flair for production and story, and with Koch's on-set expertise, Schenck lay the groundwork for Bel-Air.

The third Bel-Air partner was Edwin Zabel, the head buyer for Fox theaters on the west coast. Zabel had the contacts necessary to book Bel-Air's pictures into top Fox theaters; equally important, he provided the cash flow needed to keep the company going between projects.

Big House, U.S.A. was shot in three weeks for $102,000, of which $3,500 went to pay Chaney. Another $5,000, for a complete and recorded score, was paid to composer Paul Dunlap, one of two Bel-Air "house" composers (Les Baxter was the other). Cast and crew spent fourteen days on location at Canon City, Colorado—rugged country in which the outdoorsy Chaney felt very much at home. (In 1948 director Crane Wilbur and famed cinematographer John Alton had brought a crew to the same location to shoot a prison thriller, *Canon City*.)

Koch, who had made his directorial debut on the 1954 Bel-Air production *Shield for Murder* (co-directed with star Edmond O'Brien), went solo on *Big House.* He turned in a taut, focused job, allowing the story to tell itself and avoiding gratuitous visual tricks that are endemic in pictures by novice directors. The semi-documentary approach was a congenial one for Koch because it did not demand that he push himself beyond his limits. He directed other films, but none with the blunt force of *Big House, U.S.A.*

Koch was not unfamiliar with Lon Chaney. The men had met in 1951, during casting of *Across the Wide Missouri*, produced at MGM when Koch was working at the studio as an assistant director. (Chaney auditioned for the role of a trapper that ultimately went to MGM contract player James Whitmore.) Koch was fond of Chaney, and visited him more than once at his modest beachfront home, where the big actor happily prepared steaks, chicken, and his famous homemade chili. In 1990 Koch told interviewer Jack Gourlay, "As an actor, Lon was believable and frightening when he should be, and he was strong. I loved him."

Cast and crew worked efficiently during the shoot of *Big House, U.S.A.*, although Chaney's drinking meant that his performance became variable after lunch. He was not a closet drinker, however. To the contrary, as early as 1942 he freely advised directors to get what they could from him before one p.m.

Broderick Crawford, like Chaney, a big man with an enormous appetite for alcohol, was more problematic on-set. The former Academy Award winner (*All the King's Men*, 1949) enjoyed his vodka, but did not give directors the courtesy of waiting until after lunch to become unpredictable. Howard Koch recalled Crawford "gave us some problems" during the *Big House* shoot. Compounding the difficulty was the friendship of

Crawford and Chaney, which dated back to Chaney's stepping into Crawford's "Lennie" role on Broadway in 1937, and which often manifested itself on film sets as practical jokes and mock-serious brawls. These were usually all in fun, but bystanders were alarmed to witness the two enormous men swinging and kicking at one another. Producers, of course, could only look at the clock and tear their hair out. (In 1942 Lon and Brod appeared together in an ironically titled short, *Keeping Fit*.)

Koch and Schenck must have felt the *Big House* set was positively awash in alcohol. In 1995 Schenck told historian Tom Weaver, "Lon Chaney—well, he drank too much and I think it killed him in the end. On *Big House, U.S.A.*, you know how many drinkers I had there? There was Brod Crawford, who was always soused but never missed a line; there was Bill Talman, who drank; Lon Chaney; and Ralph Meeker, who kept up with the rest of 'em." Schenck added, "Chaney was a sweet guy, provided he knew where he was at the moment."

Big House top billing was shared by Ralph Meeker and Broderick Crawford. Meeker was for a brief time one of the most promising actors on Broadway and in Hollywood. He was born in 1920 and educated at Northwestern. He undertook his stage career in Chicago in 1943, came to Broadway two years later, and gained national attention in June 1949, after taking over the Stanley Kowalski role from Marlon Brando in the original Broadway production of Tennessee Williams' *A Streetcar Named Desire*. Another stage triumph, as the seductive drifter in William Inge's *Picnic*, followed in 1953 (the 1955 film role went to William Holden). Meeker made his movie debut in *Teresa* (1951), a minor but well-meaning drama about the readjustment of returning World War II veterans.

Although very much a tough-guy type, Meeker was considerably more talented than his muscular physique and cold good looks may have suggested. He is excellent as a shell-shocked G.I. in *Shadow in the Sky* (1952), and as a troubled boxer in *Glory Alley* (1952). He's especially enjoyable as a wiseacre rookie cycle cop in *Code Two* (1953), a slick little B-picture directed by Fred Wilcox. The big time beckoned with a strong supporting role as a no-good Union deserter in Anthony Mann's *The Naked Spur* (1953), in which Meeker co-starred with James Stewart, Robert Ryan, and Janet Leigh. A good performance as a killer, opposite Barbara Stanwyck, in *Jeopardy* (1953) led to top billing as unprincipled private dick Mike Hammer in the aforementioned *Kiss Me Deadly*, one of the best and most startlingly innovative films of the fifties. But despite Robert Aldrich's fiercely aggressive direction, A. I. Bezzerides' apocalyptically metaphoric script, and Meeker's pluperfect playing of Hammer, *Kiss Me Deadly* was raked by critics and did not live up to box-office expectations. *Big House, U.S.A.* was released the same year, and functioned to downgrade Meeker's status, establishing him as a star of B-movies and a reliable supporting actor in A productions. He worked sporadically on Broadway and other stage venues until 1971.

Meeker's body thickened as he grew older, and health problems slurred his speech, but he continued to give tough, credible performances in films, including Stanley Kubrick's *Paths of Glory* (1957; excellent as one of the doomed soldiers), Jack Garfein's *Something Wild* (1961; an odd rumination on urban loneliness), Aldrich's *The Dirty Dozen* (1967), Roger Corman's *The St. Valentine's Day Massacre* (1967; as Bugs Moran), Gordon Douglas' *The Detective* (1968; as a corrupt cop), John Frankenheimer's *I Walk the Line* (1970; as a moonshiner at odds with sheriff Gregory Peck), Sidney Lumet's *The Anderson Tapes* (1971), and William Richert's *Winter Kills* (1979).

In 1976 Meeker found himself being eaten alive by a giant rat in Bert I. Gordon's *Food of the Gods*—sufficiently dispiriting, no doubt, to move the actor and his wife to produce a film of their own, *My Boys Are Good Boys* (1978), an interesting melodrama about teenagers who hold up an armored car; Meeker also starred in the picture. His final film, *Without Warning*, was released in 1980. Meeker died of heart failure in 1988.

As suggested, he is ideal as "the Iceman," imbuing the role with a chilly shrewdness that makes him, in the end, a considerably more disquieting character than the film's other, more overtly villainous figures.

Thick-set Broderick Crawford (1911-86) came from a theatrical family: his father was vaudevillian Lester Crawford and his mother was Helen Broderick, a very popular stage actress and comedienne. Following three weeks at Harvard, Crawford struggled to begin an acting career. He found work in radio in the early thirties, and conquered Broadway with his performance as Lennie in the 1937 production of *Of Mice and Men*. He came to Hollywood the same year and was promptly squandered, playing thuggish fellows in a variety of dramas and comedies until 1949, when he gave an electrifying performance as Willie Stark in Robert Rossen's adaptation of Robert Penn Warren's novel of unprincipled Southern politics, *All the King's Men*. Crawford earned a well-deserved Oscar for his work, and was for a few years thereafter one of Columbia's golden boys, gaining top billing and giving fine performances in pictures as diverse as *Born Yesterday* (1950; repeating the stage role he had assumed from Paul Douglas), *The Mob* (1951), *Scandal Sheet* (1952; as a ruthless tabloid publisher), Fritz Lang's *Human Desire* (1954), *Down Three Dark Streets* (1954), and Federico Fellini's *Il Bidone* (1955; released in the United States in 1964 as *The Swindle*).

Not easily cast in leads, Crawford turned to television in 1955 to star in *Highway Patrol*, a popular but very cheaply made cop show produced by Ziv for syndication until 1959. The show continued in reruns for decades, and tarnished Crawford's reputation as a film actor, not least because he spent numberless episodes merely barking orders from behind a desk or while crouched behind a squad car. He traveled to Europe, where he starred and co-starred in film dramas and costume spectaculars throughout the sixties. He starred also in two other television series, *King of Diamonds* (1961-62) and *The Interns* (1970).

Late in his career Crawford gave a game performance as the eccentric director of the FBI in Larry Cohen's disjointed, very cheaply produced *The Private Files of J. Edgar Hoover* (1977). His final film, George Roy Hill's *A Little Romance* (1979), is a good one and brought Crawford a bright cameo role as himself. As Rollo Lamar in *Big House,* he's typically engaging, and while some of his dialogue is clever ("Welcome to the wormy aristocracy of Cascabel Island Prison," he says to Barker by way of introduction), other lines awkwardly force Rollo's presumed erudition down our throats ("I'm not deprecatin' ya," he tells Barker later). Regardless, you believe that Rollo is both sharp and tough enough to command this bunch of nasty lugs.

William Talman (1915-68) is best known to generations of TV watchers as district attorney Hamilton Burger, who was unable to win a case against defense attorney Perry Mason. An unhandsome, very masculine type with a high forehead and pale, piercing eyes, Talman is highly regarded by noir fans for his unsettling performance as the murderous title character in Ida Lupino's *The Hitch-Hiker* (1953). He is effective also in Richard Fleischer's underrated *Armored Car Robbery* (1950; in which he ends up chopped to bits in the propeller of an airplane), and in John H. Auer's *City that Never Sleeps* (1953).

While still in his fifties Talman became terminally ill. He had been a heavy smoker for decades, and he bravely consented to do a public service spot for television in which he looks straight into the camera, introduces himself, and then pronounces, "I've got lung cancer." The remainder of the spot is the dying actor's exhortation not to begin the cigarette habit.

As the killer Mason, Talman is nearly as icy as "the Iceman," with the added character flaw of pure redneck meanness. Talman had one of the most intimidating stares in movie history, so it's particularly funny late in the film when Rollo orders Mason to remove the hook from a fish that has been landed from the side of the boat. "Take out the hook?" Mason exclaims. Clearly a city boy, he gives the fish a wary look, and protests, "It's got *teeth*!"

For Charles Bronson, of course, international stardom awaited, though at this moment in his career that pinnacle was about a dozen years in the future. He was born in 1920 and joined his father and some of his 14 siblings in the Pennsylvania coal mines at age sixteen. He was a tail gunner during World War II and subsequently studied art, set design, and acting in Philadelphia. In Hollywood from 1951 (where he was billed early on as Charles Buchinski or Buchinsky), his tough countenance and muscled frame restricted him to roles as thugs, lunkheads, and American Indians. By 1958 he had snagged the lead in Roger Corman's energetic *Machine Gun Kelly*, and starred in a TV series, *Man with a Camera*. His supporting roles became more prominent as the sixties progressed, e.g., *The Magnificent Seven* (1960) and *The Dirty Dozen* (1967). Late in the decade Bronson traveled to Europe, where he became a sensation with audiences who regarded him as the epitome of the best and worst of the American character: tough, violent, self-reliant, roughly sexual. An American film (directed by an Englishman, Michael Winner), *Death Wish* (1974), solidified his domestic stardom, which Bronson has not relinquished even in semi-retirement.

The young Bronson is at his most intimidating as Benny Kelly, who seems a creature composed mainly of pumped-up muscle and brute emotion. It's an attention-getting performance.

The remainder of the players demonstrate Bel-Air's knack for effective casting. Established horror stars filled out the cast of the company's later *The Black Sleep* (1956); similarly, tough-guy types bring added grit and realism to *Big House, U.S.A.* Reed Hadley, a TV star thanks to *Racket Squad* (1951-53) and *Public Defender* (1953-54), was an old hand at playing cops and other upright authority figures. (He also had narrated the aforementioned *T-Men*.) Agent Madden has no personality at all, which is probably what Koch wanted. Madden is, simply, an unsmiling avenger.

Roy Roberts, too, usually played cops, though as Ranger Erickson, he's a bit more avuncular than usual. Husky Robert Bray, appearing in *Big House* as one of the rangers who nails Barker at the checkpoint, nearly always was cast as a hard guy, sometimes noble, sometimes not. His best role is as the patient bus driver in Joshua Logan's *Bus Stop* (1956), but casual viewers are most apt to recognize him from his 1967-68 stint on the *Lassie* TV series. Like Ralph Meeker, Bray played Mike Hammer, in *My Gun is Quick* (1958), a low-budget trifle that skates by on the appeal of Bray and female costars Whitney Blake and Pamela Duncan. Bray's *Big House* role is small, but his natural screen presence and easy acting style are effective, and you wish he had more screen time.

Willis Bouchey, cast as little Danny's frantic father, was another actor who specialized in authority figures, playing innumerable doctors, lawyers, sheriffs, and executives in film and on TV. Science-fiction fans recall him as the physician who "certifies" the desperate family at the conclusion of Ray Milland's *Panic in Year Zero* (1962). As Danny's father, he's a perfect picture of misery and apprehension, and has a marvelous scene immediately following Barker's capture, when he confronts the extortionist in Erickson's office. He looks at Barker the way an animal regards something utterly alien, then his features shift and he speaks, softly at first, and then with fury: "I paid you the money. Where's my boy? *Where's my boy*?"

Jan Merlin, appearing in a bit as the boat skipper, had co-starred as Solar Guard trainee Roger Manning on TV's *Tom Corbett, Space Cadet* (1950-55). For the remainder of his onscreen career, Merlin was inevitably cast as a tough punk, most notably opposite Nick Adams and Marla English in William Witney's *A Strange Adventure* (1956). He became an Emmy-winning soap opera writer in the seventies. Although Merlin has a line or two in *Big House*, his best moment is the aforementioned look of astonished revulsion his face registers after seeing Mason turn the blowtorch on Benny.

The film's only featured actress, Randy Farr, had virtually no screen career at all. *Big House, U.S.A.* is her only film, and she apparently never worked in television. Farr was good looking but rather too sharp-featured to be cast in traditional leads. She registers nicely as Nurse Evans, playing it cool at first, acquiring that telltale shifty look early in her questioning by Madden, then breaking down completely and 'fessing up. The most successful aspect of her performance is that it arouses no sympathy at all.

The blunt unpleasantness of *Big House, U.S.A.* did not endear the movie to critics. The *Monthly Film Bulletin*, representing the prissy faction, described the characters as "so brutal as to anaesthetize all sympathy, and their savagery is minutely explored... in a manner that leaves one shocked yet disinterested. The playing is indifferent, and the film as a whole singularly distasteful." Howard Thompson, writing in *The New York Times,* dismissed the picture as "an idea for a good crime melodrama gone wrong... steeped in bloody, sadistic prison commotion."

Leave it to the ever-pragmatic *Variety* to recognize the picture's assets; reviewer "Brog" said the film provides "a fair amount of entertainment. Plenty of violence is featured throughout in some rather chilling scenes, but fits the tough characters with which the story deals." The reviewer added that Ralph Meeker turned in "a good job... [and that] Crawford, Talman, Chaney, and Bronson also are okay heavies."

Like other Bel-Air releases, *Big House, U.S.A.* turned a profit and allowed subsequent productions. Horror fans enjoy *The Black Sleep* (written by Bel-Air mainstay John C. Higgins) and *Frankenstein—1970* (1958); male viewers cannot resist *Hot Cars* (1956; starring luscious Joi Lansing), *Untamed Youth* (1957; starring that "platinum powerhouse," Mamie Van Doren, and scripted by Higgins), or *The Girl in Black Stockings* (1957; a lurid thriller featuring Van Doren *and* Anne Bancroft and Marie Windsor). In 1958 Schenck and Koch assisted William Castle with production details on Castle's first independent production, *Macabre*. The pair took no screen credit but did wrangle a piece of the profits.

Bel-Air was dissolved following *Born Reckless* (1959), another vehicle for Mamie Van Doren. Schenck and Koch continued as partners, however, producing *Miami Un-*

dercover, a syndicated cop series starring actor/game-show host Lee Bowman and ex-boxer Rocky Graziano. The show managed just a single season's worth of production, in 1961.

Schenck stepped up briefly to bigger productions, including *Up Periscope* (1959), then returned to more modest films, such as *Robinson Crusoe on Mars* (1964; scripted by Higgins), *Kill a Dragon* (1967), and his last, *Daughters of Satan* (1972; scripted by Higgins).

Things panned out very nicely for Howard W. Koch, post Bel-Air. As a solo he did a great deal of episodic television for Warner Bros. and Desilu, directing installments of *Hawaiian Eye*, *Maverick*, *Cheyenne*, and a two-part episode of *The Untouchables*, "Unhired Assassin," which later was edited to feature length and telecast as *A Gun for Zangara*. In 1961, when Frank Sinatra struck a production deal with United Artists, the star hired Koch as vice-president in charge of production, on UA's recommendation. Koch's 1961-64 tenure with Sinatra Enterprises produced *Come Blow Your Horn* (1963), *Robin and the Seven Hoods* (1964), and other commercially successful films, plus one bona fide masterpiece, John Frankenheimer's *The Manchurian Candidate* (1962).

Koch's success with Sinatra led to his 1964 appointment as Paramount's head of production, a post he held for two years. He returned to independent production in 1966 and enjoyed more success: *The Odd Couple* (1968), *Plaza Suite* (1971), *Once is Not Enough* (1975), and one of the biggest "sleeper" hits of the nineties, *Ghost* (1990). He returned to directing in 1973, with *Badge 373*. Throughout his long, savvy career, Koch has established himself as a rarity: a Hollywood nice-guy who displays fairness, decency, and kindness. Today he is one of the best-liked people in the industry.

The portion of Lon Chaney's life and career that followed *Big House, U.S.A.* will be described elsewhere in this book. Here, it's appropriate to note that the alarming physical changes that began to manifest themselves in the late forties were Chaney's curse and, in a way, his salvation. Always rugged, Chaney eventually became burly and tree-like, with that marvelously furrowed face and drinker's voice we contemplated at the beginning of this chapter. He achieved a metamorphosis from hopeful leading man to top-notch character actor. Chaney did honest work in *Big House, U.S.A.*, and deserves the highest compliment any viewer of the film can offer: he gave life to Alamo Smith.

CREDITS: Producer: Aubrey Schenck; Director: Howard W. Koch; Screenplay: John C. Higgins; Story: George George and George Slavin; Cinematographer: Gordon Avil; Production Designer: Charles D. Hall; Editor: John F. Schreyer; Music: Paul Dunlap; Costumer: George A. Thompson; Running Time: 82 minutes; A Bel-Air Production; copyrighted by Camden Productions, Inc.; released by United Artists, 1955

CAST: Broderick Crawford (Rollo Lamar); Ralph Meeker (Jerry "the Iceman" Barker); Reed Hadley (FBI Agent James Madden); William Talman ("Machine Gun" Mason); Lon Chaney (Alamo Smith); Charles Bronson (Benny Kelly); Randy Farr (Nurse Emily Evans); Roy Roberts (Chief Ranger Erickson); Willis B. Bouchey (Robertson Lambert); Peter Votrian (Danny Lambert); Robert Bray (Ranger McCormick); Jan Merlin (Skipper)

Sources: Gourlay, Jack. "Lon Chaney, Jr. Part Two," *Filmfax* #21, July 1990; Smith, Don G. *Lon Chaney, Jr.: Horror Film Star, 1906-1973.* McFarland, 1996; Weaver, Tom. *It Came from Weaver Five*, McFarland, 1996

I DIED A THOUSAND TIMES (1955)
INDESTRUCTIBLE MAN (1956)
by Michael H. Price

The popular image of Lon Chaney, Jr., during the 1950s and '60s is that of a high-profile artist in inexorable decline, incapable of sustained performance and reduced to self-franchised pageantry in lieu of any "real" acting. Has anyone out there actually bothered lately to reconsider the man's final two decades of work? Or is it just too convenient to accept the conventional "wisdom" of the status quo and avoid forming one's own opinions?

Nearer the truth is the reality of the Hollywood stereotype system, which unthinkingly reduced Chaney to a craggy face, a gruff voice, and a "scary guy" reputation rather than rise to the challenge of matching the artist with the right roles. When cast fittingly, as in Jack Hill's phantasmagorical *Spider Baby* (1968), Chaney met the occasion with as effective a combination of menace and poignancy as he had ever shown in his younger days. When simply saddled with a role of little dimension, such as the grudge-bearing predatory Cajun in *The Alligator People* (1959), Chaney's noble generosity of spirit kicked in to make more of the assignment than was written.

Even within the confines of Chaney's forced specialty fields of supernatural horror and science-fantasy, there were opportunities that the larger studios' anti-visionaries overlooked: if Larry Talbot, Chaney's recurring Wolf Man character from 1941 through 1948, was supposed to be immortal, then why not a later-in-life sequel to show how Talbot had borne up under his curse into the 1960s? (The nearest anyone came to that notion was a gimmicky episode of the teleseries *Route 66* called "Lizard's Leg and Owlet's Wing," with Chaney and Boris Karloff playing themselves, more or less, and Peter Lorre playing a hybrid of himself and Bela Lugosi. Go figure.)

During his days of stardom—narrowly defined—at Universal Pictures in the 1940s, Chaney had demonstrated his preferences for living as a devoted family man and for carousing with chums among the movie business's blue-collar ranks, rather than for schmoozing with the Hollywood elite. He paid for this maverick streak with diminished opportunities as the post-WWII period began and the now-struggling big studios closed ranks and reorganized.

But Chaney's resolve to keep working paid off in the quantity of roles if not in their quality. Aided by the postwar rise of the independent production companies and the growing influence of lesser producers who remembered his early work fondly, Chaney graced approximately as many pictures after 1948 (and the capper to his tenure as a

***I Died a Thousand Times* is a remake of Raoul Walsh's *High Sierra* (1941), with Jack Palance as a holdup artist forced to deal with a gang of punks. Chaney appears as Palance's mentor, a terminally ill criminal mastermind known as Big Mack. [Photofest]**

Universal horror star, with *Abbott & Costello Meet Frankenstein*) as he had during 1932-48.

And if he couldn't land a fitting showcase role in just one good picture, then Chaney was artist enough to weave a couple of roles into a miniature body of work. Such an oddity is the curiously matched combo of Stuart Heisler's *I Died a Thousand Times* (1955) and Jack Pollexfen's *Indestructible Man* (1956)—films that probably shouldn't even be mentioned in the same breath, if not for Chaney's portrayal of a boss mobster in each.

Chaney's characters in *I Died a Thousand Times* and *Indestructible Man* are opposite sides of a coin. Each is, in its way, suggestive of the film noir style that Chaney had tentatively approached in his *Inner Sanctum* series of peculiar mysteries during the 1940s.

I Died a Thousand Times is a remake of Raoul Walsh's *High Sierra* (1941), with Jack Palance inheriting the Humphrey Bogart role of a veteran holdup artist forced to deal with a gang of wet-eared punks—and winding up like an animal at bay in the foothills of the Sierras. Chaney contributes an extended cameo as Palance's mentor, a terminally ill criminal mastermind known as Big Mack. Despite little time onscreen, Chaney looms over the picture like a frustrated guardian angel to Palance, leaving the indelible impression of a mentor whose stabilizing influence has become sadly irrelevant in the face of a meaner-spirited new breed of criminal.

"Butcher" Benton could just as easily have been Big Mack, betrayed by his gang and railroaded onto Death Row, only to rise again to exact retribution, in *Indestructible Man*.

Indestructible Man is an asphalt-jungle takeoff on the *Frankenstein* myth, faintly echoing Chaney's 1941 vehicle *Man Made Monster* and Michael Curtiz' *The Walking Dead* (1936), with Boris Karloff as a wrongly executed innocent who comes back from beyond. Chaney serves *Indestructible Man* as Charles "Butcher" Benton, an executed mobster brought back to life as a mute (but still cunning) instrument of his own vengeance. A prison-cell prologue establishes Benton as the same variety of Old School racketeer as Big Mack.

The films—one a name-brand, mass-audience production from Warner Bros., the other a Poverty Row indie aimed at Allied Artists' bread-and-butter drive-in theater trade—were issued so close together during late 1955/early 1956 as to leave the impression of variations on a theme, at least for those moviegoers who declined to discriminate between the genres and the classes of studio.

For "Butcher" Benton could just as easily have been Big Mack, betrayed by his gang and railroaded onto Death Row, only to rise again to exact a grisly retribution. Each character comes across as a fatherly presence of tremendous pride and indignation, each on his last legs in one respect or another, and each determined to leave a monument to his passing. For Big Mack, one last spectacular heist will suffice—even if he must orchestrate it from his deathbed. For "Butcher" Benton, the heist has already been performed to satisfaction, the loot hidden away; all that remains is to foil the executioner, do away with a disloyal lawyer (Ross Elliott) and two turncoat henchmen (Marvin Ellis and Kenneth Terrell), and reclaim a stolen fortune.

Which seems like a tall order, but Benton's last words—spoken to harrowing effect among Chaney's few lines of dialogue—tell us to expect precisely that outlandish development. Benton is merely putting up a defiant front, of course. But he has not reckoned with the interference of a renegade scientist (played by Robert Shayne), who will claim Benton's body shortly after the death sentence has been carried out.

Having treated the corpse to test an irradiating process that might lead to a cure for cancer, Shayne finds his experiment has unexpectedly re-animated the "Butcher" and rendered him practically invulnerable. Chaney is memorably expressive in what becomes, for the balance of the picture, essentially a silent-movie role; a voice-over from a hard-boiled police lieutenant (Casey Adams) explains that Benton's vocal apparatus has been destroyed. Benton seems genuinely surprised to find himself back among the living. Shayne's reaction is, by contrast, disappointingly matter-of-fact.

Reluctant to become an experiment, Benton kills the doctor and an assistant and commences his rampage. Director Jack Pollexfen captured considerable footage of Chaney's face in extreme close-up, and these studies are inserted with annoying constancy throughout *Indestructible Man*—presumably to emphasize "Butcher" Benton's rage.

But the emphasis is unnecessary. Chaney's very presence is performance enough, and though he often said he disliked memorizing dialogue, he clearly was not hesitant to work hard to make a wordless role expressive. From the moment of the character's resurrection, the actor does vastly more than just "look scary."

Benton is a walking horror, all right, but our sympathies are squarely with Chaney as he sets out to destroy the slimy underlings who had set him up for a fall. Chaney confounds our expectations, however, when Benton begins attacking innocent people, and by the time he finds himself cornered in a sewer tunnel—close to his hidden loot, but under siege by cops with flame-throwers—he has become a figure of genuine emotional and physical repulsion.

Pollexfen allows Chaney a few minutes in horrific make-up, after Benton has been mutilated by the flames, but the appearance is secondary to Chaney's immersion in character. The big death scene is inappropriately impersonal: a high-voltage shock, suffered while fleeing through a municipal power station. But then, perhaps Big Mack would have liked to go out with such a bang.

One splendidly directed early scene has Shayne prattling on about the revival of what, to him, is merely a new lab animal—but the camera is trained unwaveringly on Chaney. "Butcher" Benton's shifting expressions inform us that he is absorbing every word, every suggestion of what his rebirth might mean, and in rapid order he moves from clinical disorientation, to an awareness of his new situation, to an understanding that he has cheated the executioner, after all, and can get on with squaring things with his betrayers. Scientific breakthroughs be damned.

Pollexfen, a prolific producer/director/screenwriter who specialized in horror and high-adventure pictures during the 1950s, was seldom as nuanced a storyteller as that laboratory scene might suggest. It is a genuinely cinematic moment in a film that, otherwise, plays out in a flat, semidocumentary style as Chaney goes about his business of search-and-destroy. Casey Adams' dry narration lends *Indestructible Man* rather a *Dragnet*-type sensibility, leavened by Adams' lifelike romantic attraction to Benton's moll (played by Marian Carr), a stripper who radiates a surprising innocence. Albert Glasser's old-fashioned orchestral score recalls the "house style" of Universal Pictures in the

1940s, alternating bombastic passages with sentimental strains.

If *I Died a Thousand Times* represented an ambitious literary exercise for original novelist and screenwriter W. R. Burnett, then *Indestructible Man* must be the big-screen equivalent of a disposable paperback novel for its scenarists, Vy Russell and Sue Bradford. Chaney cannot have but rankled at the irony of lapsing from the dignity of *I Died a Thousand Times*, however small the role, to the indignity of star billing in a shabby number like *Indestructible Man*.

The late writer/director Al Adamson, who many years later would exploit Chaney (along with contemporaries J. Carrol Naish and Angelo Rossitto) in the lurid *Dracula vs. Frankenstein* (1971), once offered a reasonable defense for such practices: "It's not as though we were trying to abuse these guys or detract from their value. We loved them for what they were, and we tried to give back some of the joy they'd given us, with their earlier pictures. It's not our fault we were incapable of making films as good as these guys deserved."

For work is work, and Chaney seems never to have perceived himself as any kind of star but rather as a working actor. If the measure of a movie lies in the effort put forth to make it work, then Chaney almost single-handedly made *Indestructible Man* a better picture than it has any business being.

A bizarre afterthought: the kinship between *I Died a Thousand Times* and *Indestructible Man* has never reflected more sharply than in Allan Dwan's *Most Dangerous Man Alive* (1961), which effectively fuses into a single role the Jack Palance character from *I Died a Thousand Times* and the Chaney character from *Indestructible Man*.

In *Most Dangerous Man Alive*, fugitive from justice, Ron Randell, receives a dose of bad chemistry that renders him impervious to harm, and the inevitable rampage winds up with the killer at bay in the fringes of a mountain range. Somebody *must* have seen those Chaney and Palance pictures back-to-back, just the way they were first inadvertently released.

I Died a Thousand Times
CREDITS: Producer: Willis Goldbeck; Director: Stuart Heisler; Screenplay: W. R. Burnett, from his novel *High Sierra* and his collaborative (with John Huston) 1941 screenplay; Cinematographer: Ted D. McCord, A.S.C.; Musical Score: David Buttolph; Orchestrators: Gus Levene and Maurice de Packh; Sound: Charles Lang; Art Director: Edward Carrere; Set Decorator: William L. Kuehl; Make-up: Gordon Bau; Film Editor: Clarence Kolster; Costumer: Moss Mabry; Dialogue Supervisor: Eugene Busch; Assistant Director: Chuck Hansen; Second Unit Director: Russ Saunders; Second Unit Assistant: Al Alleborn; Second Unit Cinematographer: Edwin DuPar

CAST: Jack Palance (Roy Earle); Lon Chaney (Big Mack); Shelley Winters (Marie Garson); Lori Nelson (Velma); Lee Marvin (Babe); Earl Holliman (Red); Gonzales Gonzales (Chico); Howard St. John (Doc Banton); Ralph Moody (Pa); Olive Carey (Ma)

Indestructible Man
CREDITS: Producer/Director: Jack Pollexfen; Screenplay: Sue Bradford and Vy Russell; Cinematographer: John Russell, Jr., A.S.C.; Musical Director: Albert Glasser; Art Director: Theobold Holsopple; Production Manager: Chris Beute; Film Editor: Fred Feitshans, Jr.

CAST: Lon Chaney (Charles "Butcher" Benton); Casey Adams (Detective Lt. Dick Chasen); Robert Shayne (Professor Bradshaw); Marian Carr (Eva Martin); Ross Elliott (Paul Lowe); Marvin Ellis (Squeamy Ellis); Stuart Randall (Police Captain); Kenneth Terrell (Joe Marcella)

THE CYCLOPS (1957)

by David H. Smith

"Tell us, pray, what devil
This melancholy is, which can transform
Men into monsters."
—John Ford, *The Lady's Trial*, III.i

Strange things can happen after death swoops down and pulls someone away. Since absence no doubt makes the heart grow fonder, there is a postmortem tendency to gloss over the shortcomings of the departed—an impulse, natural or otherwise, to find nobility in their flaws, to excuse their faults, if only to make the taste of death a little more palatable.

Fans of Lon Chaney, Jr. know this is true because of the retroactive praise heaped on much of his diverse television and film work made after the 1946 merger of Universal Pictures with the independent studio International Pictures. With the reorganization came the new executives' edict that all B film units (the horror films, the B Westerns, and the serials) would be shut down immediately and absolutely no B or cheap films were to be produced.

Chaney was among those in the old regime's stable of contract stars who were swiftly herded out the Universal City gate. For the next decade, Chaney did not so much eke out a living in character roles as he would prove his thespian mettle working for a variety of studios in a variety of films and—much to his detractors' chagrin—in a variety of roles.

Instead of being taken for granted as the temperamental "star" of the forties, the fifties kept Chaney busy honing his talents playing characters in Westerns and other mainstream films. Aside from his outstanding turn as the arthritic former lawman in *High Noon* (1952), he played a variety of lovable drunks, funny sidekicks, town characters, crooks, and the inevitable "Lennie" types. A few of the films were good, some were not, and most are forgotten but by his fans today. But Chaney was always in there trying, and beginning to win the admiration of critics.

By 1957, horror and monster films—the oldies, released in the *Shock* and *Son of Shock* packages from Universal and by other studios to television—had once again become popular fare. A whole new generation of kids was seeing Chaney for the first time, and their parents were enjoying him all over again.

"They're all on television now," said Chaney of his past glories. "I get more mail now than when those pictures were made."

Exploitation producers were not oblivious to the reborn marquee value of Chaney's name. Flying in the face of the cliché "opportunity knocks only once," producers fairly beat down the actor's door. They inveigled him with pinchbeck scripts that variously rewrote Edgar Allan Poe (*Manfish*), revived the venerable theme of a mad scientist and his monster (*Indestructible Man*), or re-engineered a tawdry assembly line of man-made creatures (*The Black Sleep*).

But the fifties was first and foremost the era of the mankind-versus-giant-monsters film, epitomized (though not conceptualized) by film auteur Bert I. Gordon. Born in Kenosha, Wisconsin on September 24, 1922, Gordon is regarded by nostalgic middle-agers as a creative genius and, ignorantly, by others as a tiresome dilettante. Educated at the University of Wisconsin, Gordon was a producer of television commercials and worked as the production supervisor (1951-3) of the CBS television series *Racket Squad*, starring Reed Hadley (1911-1974), before making his co-directing debut (with Tom Gries) in 1954.

Said debut, *Serpent Island*, a voodoo thriller starring Sonny Tufts (1911-1970), was deemed too excruciatingly awful for theatrical release and was immediately sold to television. Gries (1922-1977), the producer of *Donovan's Brain* (1953), would move on to a successful career as a television director, mostly with episodes of *The Rat Patrol* and *Voyage to the Bottom of the Sea*, occasionally returning to the big screen with Charlton Heston dramas in the sixties and Charles Bronson thrillers in the seventies.

Undeterred, Gordon pushed on alone to helm the desultory *King Dinosaur* the following year. Inspired by the 1952 re-release of the 1933 original *King Kong* (hence the title), it was the first film in Gordon's factotum career in the genre as the story- and scriptwriter, producer, director, and special visual effects technician. Whereas the major studios had access to ultra-powered, triple-head process projectors, the economically inventive Gordon made do with comparatively primitive stationary mattes and rear projection.

The drive-in crowd would ultimately embrace Gordon's tales of humans against mutated nature (or mutated men), despite the movies' grainy and out of focus effects, and their glaringly obvious process scenes. Many of the major studios, even with their superior equipment and teams of technicians, would have been daunted by such effects-laden scenarios. Gordon's "ghostly" superimposed effects, achieved with the nominal collaboration of his co-producer wife Flora, became synonymous with the genre, and were just as noticeable and notorious then as they are today. His initials became his calling card.

It is with Chaney and *The Cyclops*, probably filmed in late 1955 or in 1956, that Gordon would get his first real chance to show his stuff with a cast of "name" actors. In the French film magazine *Fantastyka*, Gordon recalled Chaney as an unhappy man, living in the shadow of his more successful father, but professional throughout. Working from his own bravura script, Gordon recast Homer's *The Odyssey* in the mold of a fifties' jungle adventure, and his choice of literary source material was an excellent one. No one can argue there is something particularly vital in Homer's 2,700-year-old tale, which provided Western culture with its first novel, its first extended epic, and, of course, its first odyssey.

The dangers faced during Odysseus' journey home from the Trojan wars have been passed on from generation to generation: the rival cataclysms offered by Scylla and Charybdis, the alluring temptations of the Sirens and Circe, and the cannibalism of the Cyclops. What Western quest has not followed a path similar to Odysseus', one strewn with tests and failures, lures and obstacles, destiny mixing with bewildering freedom? Stretching the point, it can even be seen as an allegory of Lon Chaney's own life and career.

Chaney, Jr., James Craig, and Gloria Talbott star in *The Cyclops*.

Homer looms over literature like a meddling god from Olympus, making his presence felt in Dante, Shakespeare, Tennyson, Joyce—even in *Star Trek* and comic books. Gordon sought to incorporate the most vivid and eidetic aspect of *The Odyssey*—the adventure with the Cyclops—into a screenplay involving modern man's greed, a lost love, human redemption, all backed by a radioactive *raison d'être*.

In Greek mythology, the Cyclopes were a race of gigantic one-eyed beings, their name meaning "circle-eyed." Divine craftsmen, they were the forgers of Zeus's thunderbolt and are also credited with building ancient walled cities such as Tiryns in Greece. In Homer's epic, when the wanderer Odysseus visited Sicily, he found the Cyclops Polyphemus both inhospitable and cruel—Polyphemus ate six members of his crew, and out of courtesy offered to eat Odysseus last. The resourceful adventurer got the giant drunk and blinded his one eye with the heated point of a stake. However, the Cyclops almost managed to sink the ship of Odysseus by hurling a gigantic rock into the sea.

Without citing his literary source—or even mentioning the word "Cyclops" in the film proper—the ingenious Gordon managed a nifty homage. Homer's heroes were heroic, but they were all different. There was Achilles, the fearless hothead; the courageous and disciplined Hector; and the wily, imaginative Odysseus. Even the heroines of Homer's imagination—from the intelligent, patient Penelope to the tragic Helen—were melded into a single character for *The Cyclops*.

Billed fourth, Chaney was cast as Martin Melville, a stock manipulator whose shady background first arouses the suspicion of the governor (Vincent Padula) of the Mexican

Tom Drake, Chaney, Jr., and Craig discuss their deteriorating situation.

state of Guayjorm. Susan Winter (Gloria Talbott) has mounted an expedition into the wilds of Mexico in search of her missing fiancé, whose plane disappeared in the desolate Tarahumare Mountains three years before.

Denied permission to explore the remote region, Susan rejoins her fellow expeditionists at a sidewalk cafe: Marty, bacteriologist Russ Bradford (James Craig), and pilot Lee Brand (Tom Drake). With unscripted gusto, Marty plows through a plateful of enchiladas as the four discuss the situation. Washing it down with a bottle of *cerveza*, Marty agrees with the others that they ignore the magistrate's enjoinder and continue anyway.

At the landing field, the strapping Marty knocks their intended escort (Manuel Lopez) unconscious with one punch, and the four fly off in Lee's single-engine plane. Marty's reasons for partially financing Susan's search of the remote region are far from altruistic: he believes the area they plan to reconnoiter, because the geological formation is perfect for it, is laden with precious uranium.

In 1789, the German chemist (and coincidentally named) Martin Klaproth discovered the chemical element uranium. For approximately 150 years following that, uranium was to have some of the most wide-reaching effects of any element in history. Above all, it would be put to use in nuclear reactors and atomic weapons.

Uranium is widely dispersed in the Earth's crust, though not in large quantities. The United States has large deposits of uranium as does Canada—a major supplier of the element. Australia has rich uranium deposits in its Northern Territory, and South Africa has also been a chief supplier.

In correspondence with Sue F. Gagner, public relations manager with the United States Nuclear Regulatory Commission, she revealed the Belgian Congo and Portugal also supplied the U.S. with uranium in the early days of the atomic age, but the NRC does not know whether Mexico has uranium reserves or has been a supplier of uranium. Because much of Mexico has not yet been adequately surveyed, even more than 40 years after *The Cyclops* was made, it is believed significant new discoveries could be forthcoming as new exploration techniques are developed.

Furthering the prescience of Gordon's script, Marty's airborne scintillation method of detecting radioactive material on the ground is still viable today, although, according to the NRC, we do not know how effective such detectors would be at detecting uranium underground.

Sitting in the front of the plane, Marty tells Lee of his plans once he locates the mother lode. Realizing the Mexican government won't license him to take it out, Marty will content himself with filing a claim and floating a stock issue.

"There's only two kinds of people," Marty philosophizes. "Those that get rich, and the suckers that furnish the money."

The pilot asks, almost rhetorically, "Which side are you on?"

With Chaney's most impish grin, Marty replies, "Do I look like a sucker?" With that one line, it's as though Chaney was talking to himself, ruminating on the conflicting impulses that fueled his best work. It is Chaney the character actor at his very best, dogged by the inherent need to prove himself to the critics, with any luck before his abusive lifestyle claimed him.

Just as Russ doubts his senses when he sees a large animal below, Marty panics as dangerous downdrafts begin to buffet the plane with turbulence. Despite pleadings to stay calm, Marty knocks Lee out with a rabbit punch and grabs the yoke himself, sending the plane into a steep dive. Russ desperately fights for control from the rear of the cockpit, while Susan revives the inordinately glass-jawed Lee in time to resume flying.

They make a dead-stick landing and set up camp (everybody forgets about Marty's panic attack and pugilism). Almost immediately, Marty's scintillator registers high concentrations of radioactive ore. Russ bursts Marty's bubble by suggesting it might be something other than uranium triggering the meter, but Marty won't hear of it. When Susan and Russ go off on their own to search for her missing fiancé, Marty urges Lee to fly him back alone to civilization posthaste so he can file his claim.

Meanwhile, Susan and Russ encounter a giant hawk devouring an equally humongous gopher. When they hear the plane's engine start to rev up, they run back and confiscate the ignition key to prevent the possibility of their being marooned. Of course, Lee and Marty wouldn't have gotten too far anyway, inasmuch as the plane's wheels were still chocked.

After encountering a gigantic tarantula (it chirrs like a Jew's-harp) and cowering before the donnybrook between a monitor lizard the size of a school bus and an equally outsized iguana, Russ gets hold of a blood sample from one of the wounded combatants and analyzes it under the microscope he's conveniently packed.

The behavior of the reptilian blood cells amazes Russ: "The secret of continuous, limitless multiplication of living cells in ordinary animals," he beams, the ultimate fifties dimbulb scientist wondering what could be affecting the local animal life even as Marty's scintillator clicks away.

Despite his near-constant trepidation, Marty here becomes the voice of reason, wondering if they too will be mutated. Despite urging to depart, Russ decides they will remain to search for Susan's missing fiancé. " I realize you have to look for him," he tells her, "whether you find him or not."

With deaf ears turned to his pleading, Marty is left to shove his hands deep into his pockets and assume a hangdog look. The next morning, Susan finds part of the wreckage of her beau's plane, then turns and screams as the camera P.O.V. descends on her.

The three men roll out of their pup tents and trail her to the familiar fifties science fiction confines of Bronson Caverns. They find Susan dazed but unhurt, even as a 25-foot bald giant (Duncan "Dean" Parkin) blocks their escape with a papier-mâché boulder. One side of his face disfigured by an enormous cyst, his remaining eye bulges from its socket as he studies his tiny captives. He roars gutturally, with no evidence of comprehending their entreaties.

Making themselves as comfortable as possible, the four settle in for the long haul. While the others sleep, Marty sneaks the one revolver they bothered to pack from Russ' backpack. In the morning, just as it seems Susan is making headway in communicating with their captor, Marty opens fire. Enraged by the bullets' sting, the giant reaches in and pins Marty to the cave wall, killing him (offscreen).

The giant is distracted by a giant snake (a nonindigenous South American boa) slithering by, which he tussles with long enough for his three remaining captives to make their escape. Dispensing with the snake, the giant chases them back to their plane. The one-eyed monstrosity blocks their makeshift runway, so Russ decides to act as a decoy, leading him away.

On a ridge, Russ climbs just out of the giant's reach. Russ hefts a convenient spear, wraps some underbrush around its tip, and sets it aflame with his Zippo. In an outrageously grisly scene (especially for the fifties), Russ plunges the fiery lance into the Cyclops' single orb; with blood gushing, the giant screams in mortal agony.

Russ returns to the plane, and they take off, just missing the blinded giant's flailing hands. Susan has come to terms with her fiancé's fate, realizing the tiny scar over his right eye was affected by the radiation in the region. In his three years of seclusion, the mysterious ore had mutated his features and his mind beyond hope. As they ascend, the giant lays dead on the ground.

Perfunctory as the film sounds with its incorporation of the standard by-the-numbers science fiction clichés—radiation, monsters, lectures, etc.—Gordon's ideas and writing show profound imagination. Nowadays, the idea of a radioactive region affecting the indigenous fauna is hardly as farfetched as once thought.

In April 1986, Chernobyl's No. 4 reactor exploded, releasing radiation 200 times that of the atomic bomb dropped on Nagasaki, Japan. Scientists studying wildlife in contaminated areas around Chernobyl have reported that voles are thriving on radioactive pollution. "These are the most contaminated animals I've seen anywhere," Ron Chesser of the University of Georgia (U.S.) said, observing that, although a species of the rodent is mutating at an "incredible rate," it is breeding healthily and producing ever-stronger offspring.

Scientists have also found mice there with twice the usual number of chromosomes, acorns as big as watermelons, and leaves from oak trees a foot wide. Sadly, for the people who live and work in the area around Chernobyl, biologists have noticed immune system problems, shorter life spans, and increased evidence of cancer.

Martin Melville (Chaney, Jr.) desperately seeks uranium.

For Bert I. Gordon, *The Cyclops* represented his first real triumph. After the critical drubbing heaped on *King Dinosaur* (it too quickly sold to television), enough positive word-of-mouth of *The Cyclops* circulated in Tinseltown to get him noticed by moguls James H. Nicholson and Samuel Z. Arkoff over at American International Pictures, who would release most of Gordon's films for the next 20 years.

In reviews then and since, Chaney's performance, though cut short by his character's demise, was singled out on a few occasions.

"Kove.," in *Variety*, thought *The Cyclops* was only for the "easily entertained," but conceded it had a "cast of good actors."

Bill Warren, in *Keep Watching The Skies!,* saw Chaney as the film's salvation: "As usual when left to his own devices, Lon Chaney goes way over the top, but in so doing

Bert I. Gordon's *The Cyclops* is not a Lon Chaney, Jr. film per se, but it nonetheless features another of the actor's fine character performances of the era.

provides the only entertainment to be had from the actors, who actually are of a slightly higher caliber than usual for Gordon."

In *Sleaze Creatures*, author D. Earl Worth could not differentiate between Chaney the man and Chaney's character, writing, "In the showiest human part, Lon Chaney was drunk as usual, but had much dialogue in the outing—most of it gassy diatribes."

Glenn L. Damato, in the fifth issue of *Movie Club*, liked everybody in *The Cyclops*, saying, "Performances in this shocker were better than average.... Lon Chaney gives a fun performance as shady Martin Melville. In fact, most of his '50s horror films were fun (unlike his contemporary, Boris Karloff)."

Lawrence McCallum commended the movie for "characterizations [delving] a bit more deeply than usual" in the "slimy slithering seventeenth issue" of *Scary Monsters*. McCallum further recognized "The various elements of *The Cyclops* were soon recycled to greater effect in [the] visually striking by humanly interesting [sic] *The Amazing Colossal Man*" released only two months later.

David Quinlan, impressed by the literacy of the ideas and the dialogue, was able to perceive the shine behind the unpolished product in *The Illustrated Guide to Film Directors*, stating, "Gordon has such lovely ideas, in fact, that one wonders what he might do if someone actually gave him sufficient money to see them properly brought to the screen."

Tom Weaver, in the first *Starlog Science-Fiction Video Magazine*, found *The Cyclops* "a few small notches above most of Gordon's similar efforts: this time he has a

The men roll out of their pup tents and trail Susan to the familiar fifties science fiction confines of Bronson Caverns.

fairly strong and attractive cast, an impressive title monster and some better-than-average special effects." In the end, though, Weaver thought Chaney was "hopelessly hammy as the clumsy con man."

That was still better than Steven R. Johnson's hilariously pretentious take on *The Cyclops* in the second issue of *Delirious*. There, Johnson saw the name of Chaney's character as a play on the author of *Moby Dick*, Herman Melville, likening uranium to the "modern man's white whale." Johnson goes on to draw further analogies about "divided conscience" and "the elevation of the cyclops' ruined soul," before bestowing his blessing on "the unity of the three survivors."

In a similarly toplofty vein, Lawrence McCallum struck again in the eighth issue of *The Scream Factory*: "The last shot is of the massive, disfigured corpse, now peaceful in death. Perhaps we should think of how often people are twisted by dreams of wealth and personal triumph, becoming hideous parodies of what they once were."

Neither of Chaney's male co-stars, while adequate here, ever came to much in the industry. Both James Craig (1912-1985) and Tom Drake (1918-1982) toiled on the edges of stardom throughout their respective careers, playing everything from bits to leads in films ranging from a Karloff-Lugosi thriller to "Lassie" movies to gangster melodramas. In fan circles, Craig has earned a strange notoriety in recent years for his leading role as an overworked NASA technician-cum-mad botanist in *The Double Garden* (c1970), an obscure U.S./Japanese co-production boasting unwieldy dialogue and a vapid storyline ascribed to the legendary Ed Wood (1922-1978). It was posthumously released on video, misleadingly retitled *The Revenge of Dr. X*. Never outgrowing his "boy next door" image of the forties, Drake would twice reunite with Chaney, first in the catchpenny *House of the Black Death* in 1965, briefly donning a gorilla mask to enact his role as the title real estate's resident werewolf, and later in the hackneyed low-budget *Johnny Reno* (1966).

Duncan Parkin (b. 1930) was a next door neighbor to "special make-up" artist Jack H. Young. His muscular physique earned him the titular role. "I did the whole show as a 'good time' frolic and a favor to Jack," he shrugged in an interview nearly 40 years later. Parkin's pretend battle with "Consuela," a 20-foot anaconda in *The Cyclops*, very nearly resulted in his strangulation when she started to constrict and had to be beaten off him, souring his outlook on the whole acting profession. His only other screen role was in a similarly gigantic getup in *War of the Colossal Beast* in 1958. Voice-over artist Paul Frees dubbed all of Parkin's bellows and growls in both movies.

As the heroine, Gloria Talbott (b. 1931) would earn screen immortality the year after *The Cyclops* was released, becoming the "I" in the genre classic *I Married A Monster From Outer Space*. A busy actress on television as well during this period, she enjoyed the spotlight with prime roles in *Daughter of Dr. Jekyll* (1957) and *The Leech Woman* (1960). Largely retired since 1966, she emerged for a bit in *Attack of the B-Movie Monster* in 1985. Her memories of her Cyclopean co-stars, particularly Chaney, are fond, even though she did not share their mutual fondness for the bottle.

Behind the scenes, Bert I. Gordon stocked his staff with professionals to give the movie the edge it needed to succeed. Gordon had heard composer Albert Glasser's portentous score for the Philippine-made *Huk!* (1956) and immediately signed him on to score all his films. The association was a happy one, with Glasser contributing vibrant music soundtracks to *The Amazing Colossal Man, Beginning of the End* (1957), *War of the Colossal Beast, Earth vs. the Spider* (1958), *Attack of the Puppet People* (1958), and *Tormented* (1960).

Not so happy was Gordon's relationship with veteran cinematographer Ira H. Morgan, whose career extended back to 1918 and silent features. Publicity photos and insider reports from the forties show Chaney was always especially gracious to anyone in the industry who had worked with his father, and *The Cyclops* made for another reunion of sorts—Morgan had been the director of photography for *Tell It To Marines* (1927), one of the few films the senior Chaney had made sans special make-up. The fifties found Morgan working almost exclusively for low-budget producer Sam Katzman (1901-1973), acting as the cinematographer for the second Superman serial and several Johnny Weissmuller "Jungle Jim" features. Gordon had to shoot much of *The Cyclops* himself because Morgan refused to film into the lengthening shadows of twilight time with Tri-X, a brand new fast-speed film. *The Cyclops* would be Morgan's last assignment.

The Cyclops was paired with the aforementioned *Daughter of Dr. Jekyll* for an exploitatively terrific double-bill to be distributed by RKO. However, when studio owner Howard Hughes sold the assets of the company to General Tire about this time, the movie field was abandoned in favor of television. When most of the key employees were shown the door, it must have delighted Chaney, who had watched helplessly as his contract with RKO had expired in 1935, making for several lean years. Both features languished until Allied Artists, formerly Monogram (the studio that banked on its Bela Lugosi ne'er-do-well mad doctor thrillers to compete with Chaney's slick Universal fare the decade before), picked them up for distribution.

The same month *The Cyclops* opened in theaters, Universal released *Man of a Thousand Faces*, a treacly and inaccurate biography of the senior Chaney starring James Cagney (1899-1986). The younger Lon had sold his father's life story to Universal in 1955 in the hope he himself might essay the role, but saw that hope quashed almost immediately. Handsome Roger Smith (b.1932), the future husband of sex symbol Ann-Margret, played the junior Chaney in it, at the fatuous finale accepting his father's prized make-up kit on the elder man's deathbed.

His fortunes changing with audiences' renewed interest in horror films and the work thrown his way, Chaney bought a new home about this time overlooking the San Fernando Valley. He was quoted in a newspaper at the time as saying, "All my life I've wanted to look down on Universal Studios and now at last I can." A rumor also circulated Chaney would make it a point to urinate in his former studio's direction as well.

The use of the Cyclops as a movie monster extends back to 1905, when French film pioneer Georges Melies (1861-1938) made *Ulysses et le Geant Polypheme*; since then, everyone from Kirk Douglas to The Three Stooges has squared off against one. The legend of the Cyclops has been retooled to fit into two different screen voyages of Sinbad, figured into sword-and-sandal epics featuring various sons of Hercules, adapted into epic TV mini-series by both the Italians and the Americans, and even menaced Jayne Mansfield.

Bert I. Gordon's *The Cyclops* is not a Lon Chaney, Jr. film per se, but it nonetheless features another of the actor's fine character performances of the era. One does feel particularly sorry for Marty when he meets his end in the cave, and rather wistful the colorful character is no longer along for the ride.

Whether absentmindedly polishing the chrome finish of his scintillator by the campfire, conniving with the mercenary pilot, sputtering fear of the mutagenic ore he coveted, or simply quaffing an icy brew, Martin Melville and hence Lon Chaney, Jr. is the liveliest aspect of *The Cyclops*. It is irrefutable proof that no matter the budget or the billing, that even with a short running time and despite his premature demise, Chaney could deliver the goods. That alone makes *The Cyclops* worth the relatively short investment of time.

CREDITS: Producer: Bert I. Gordon; Director: Bert I. Gordon; Writer: Bert I. Gordon; Cinematography: Ira H. Morgan; Music: Albert Glasser; Film Editor: Carlos Lodato; Assistant to the Producer: Flora M. Gordon; Associate Producer: Henry Schrage; Aeronautical Supervision: Henry "Hank" Coffin; Animal Sequences: Jim Dannaldson; Assistant Director: Harry L. Fraser; Special Voice Effects: Paul Frees; Technical Effects: Bert I. Gordon; Props: James Harris; Snake Fight Supervision: Ralph D. Helfer; Script Supervisor: Diana N. Loomis; Production Manager: Henry Scrage; Sound Effects: Douglas Thane Stewart; Assistant Director: Ray Taylor, Jr.; Make-up: Carle Taylor; Special Make-up: Jack H. Young; made by B & H Productions, Inc.; distributed by Allied Artists Pictures Corporation; released in July 1957 with a running time of 65 minutes

CAST: Gloria Talbott (Susan Winter); James Craig (Russ Bradford); Tom Drake (Lee Brand); Lon Chaney (Martin Melville); Duncan Parkin (The Cyclops/Bruce Barton); Manuel Lopez (The Policeman); Marlene Ross (The Salesgirl); Vincent Padula (The Governor)

THE ALLIGATOR PEOPLE (1959)

by Dennis Fischer

The Alligator People is to horror movies what Olivia Twain, wife of Mark Twain, was to cursing. As Twain observed about his wife when she tried to swear, "You've got the words right, but you haven't got the tune." In this case, *The Alligator People* was concocted to accompany *Return of the Fly* on a double bill. It was shot in CinemaScope by Fox's resident widescreen horror expert, Karl Struss (who had shot 'scope films for Kurt Neumann). The make-up was created by Ben Nye and Dick Smith (no relation to the later famous Dick Smith of *Altered States, The Exorcist,* and other classics). The make-up work in the film, unfortunately, was not even up to Nye's usual standards, as Nye presents one of the more ludicrous-looking monsters ever to grace the silver screen.

The film's director was the critically neglected Roy Del Ruth, who turned out a number of reasonably entertaining films in his thirty-five-year career. He apprenticed with Mack Sennett as a writer and gag man, and in the early thirties showed promise of becoming a major director (certainly his work was comparable to that of William Wellman). His films then included *Taxi, Blessed Event*, and *Lady Killer*, all classic early Warners movies with adult wit, as well as the first cinematic adaptation of *The Maltese Falcon*. He tried his hand at musicals, but while *Thanks a Million* and *On the Avenue* were sprightly paced, neither was a classic, and such later efforts as *Du Barry Was a Lady, Broadway Rhythm, The West Point Story*, and *On Moonlight Bay* were worse. Already Del Ruth's best work was behind him, though apart from *The Alligator People*, Del Ruth also tackled a couple of other genre pieces, namely the delightful ghost comedy *Topper Returns* and the mediocre *Phantom of the Rue Morgue*.

Two of the film's supposed stars are barely in the film itself. Douglas Kennedy and Bruce Bennett play a pair of psychiatrists who hypnotize Jane Marvin (Beverly Garland) in order to discover what happened during a period that she has mentally blocked out of her mind. To convince the audience that this is an authentic story, they even hook her up to a lie detector before starting, though this is never consulted nor referred to again. Through hypnosis, they discover Jane is actually Joyce Halton Webster, the newlywed wife of Paul Webster (Richard Crane).

The majority of *The Alligator People* is a prolonged flashback which relates Jane/Joyce's story. We see the tale that she relates starting with the newlyweds on a train as they are about to embark on their honeymoon. Paul reveals that he had been in a plane wreck and had been torn and mangled, though he exhibits no signs of any scars. A porter delivers a telegraph and mysteriously Paul gets off at a brief mail stop to make a phone call, never returning to the train which carries Joyce off without him. When she makes it back to the station, he's gone.

Screenwriter Orville Hampton—whose other credits include *The Snake Woman, Jack the Giant Killer*, and a werewolf version of *Beauty and the Beast* (1963)—works constantly to build up feelings of ominous menace. In fact, that's about all his script

Mannon (Chaney, Jr.) meets Jane Marvin (Beverly Garland) who is searching for her husband.

tries to do for the entire length of the film, which contains very little in the way of action or thrills. What's more is that having set up mysteries, Hampton seems to forget about them. (We never find out, for example, what was in Paul's telegram that made him get off the train and leave his wife without a word.) Hampton's main concern is to provide something ominous or motivational in every scene.

Apart from its silly monster, the main reasons *The Alligator People* is remembered is because of two of its cast members. One is Beverly Garland, who tries her hand at playing a typical Gothic horror ingenue but whose specialty is playing tough, competent dames who take no nonsense and try to get on top of every situation. Typically, she indicates her character's intelligence and determination in her performance as Joyce tries to track down her husband's records in his ancestral manse deep in the Louisiana bayou country, where she heads for her husband's plantation.

The other significant cast member is Lon Chaney, who plays his clichéd part of the drunken, one-handed handyman with great gusto, turning one of what could have been his later dull typical roles into a performance to relish. He brings a liveliness to the movie that it desperately needs. His character of Mannon, a drunken lout who has it in for 'gators, may not be a complex individual, but Chaney makes it clear that he tackles his interests with a passion, whether it be consuming booze or shooting at alligators.

When the two are together, it sparks such memorable dialogue as:

Mannon: You ever been in the bayou country before?
Joyce: It's so wild... so primitive....
Mannon: Yeah... and deadly.

What it is not is subtle. Even better is Mannon's speech explaining his antipathy to his reptilian brethren: "Eeeh! Dirty, stinkin', slimy 'gators! Yuh bit my hand off, didn't yuh? I'm gonna spend the rest of my life killin' 'gators!" To prove his resolve, Mannon can't resist taking his pistol out to blast away joyfully.

When Joyce gets to the plantation, she meets the aloof Mrs. Henry Hawthorne (Frieda Inescort) who bows to the conventions of "Southern hospitality" while indicating that she wishes to be anything but hospitable: "While you're a guest for one night only," she informs Joyce, "I must insist on one thing... under no circumstances will you leave your room." You can bet that makes Joyce feel right at home.

Joyce asks the black housemaid Lou Ann for information, but Lou Ann isn't any more helpful than her mistress: "This is a troubled house," she darkly intones. "Real, deep, big trouble. Like the ol' conjure woman in the big bayou says, Miz Hawthorne, she deal with the Evil One. She got big sorrow. Jus' like you get if you stay here."

However, despite the sinister implications, it is later revealed that there is no reason for Lou Ann to associate Mrs. Hawthorne with Satan. It's just another ominous red herring designed to throw viewers off the scent.

When it comes to being sinister, few practitioners are better at it than George Macready was. Macready (*My Name is Julia Ross, Alias Nick Beal, Seven Days in May, Daughter of the Mind, The Return of Count Yorga, Paths of Glory* among many other distinguished credits) plays Dr. Mark Sinclair, who, following the conventions of the horror film, is conducting mysterious experiments at the big house, or at least in a lab nearby, and is the real heavy of the piece. He and Mrs. Hawthorne agonize over the sudden reappearance of Mrs. Webster; however, Mrs. Webster isn't the only thing on-hand with an unexpected appearance.

When I interviewed her, Beverly Garland indicated to me that the atypically timid Jane Marvin in *The Alligator People* was one of her favorite roles. "That was fun," she said. "I just thought it was funny and wonderful. I thought it was well done; I thought it was great to do. I really like to do movies, and I always have, that are downright dirty and muddy and you look like the wrath of God and nobody gives a damn. I like that. I remember doing a television show set in the Sahara desert and we're dying of thirst, and we were filthy and had no make-up... I thought it was a great week. I *loved* it!"

Concerning her horror icon co-star in the film, she said, "Lon Chaney, Jr. was a fun, wonderful guy. He would sit there and tell you all about his father and all the things he had learned. He had fabulous stories about his dad. I really liked him and I was very impressed with him."

"Dirty, stinkin', slimy 'gators! I'm gonna spend the rest of my life killin' 'gators!"

The film develops some unintentional comedy when the monster, in the process of transformation, appears in a lab with what looks like a urinal over his head. Recalls Garland, "Some of the urinals on the heads bit was cut out. When I opened the door to go into his laboratory the first time, you see me; there were a lot of men walking up and down the aisle, and when you see the film, there *weren't* a lot of men walking up and down the aisles. I guess (somebody) thought they all looked like they had urinals on their heads also, so they cut it out and you didn't see them. Because I'll tell you something, I broke up.

"It was very hard for them to find something to put over these people's heads, they only had one alligator head, and that was being used, so to have all these men turning into alligators and waiting for the serum, they didn't know what to do with their heads, and they didn't have any more alligator heads, so they had to make something that would work with this big snout, and alligators have a fairly large head and this snout, so this white thing... (they wore) looked like a white urinal. I tell you when I opened the door and saw all these white urinals walking up and down the side... We had to go to lunch. I could not stop laughing. It was so funny."

As if the spectacle of a toilet-faced patient was not enough, director Roy Del Ruth has two well-muscled orderlies struggling to give a patient an injection. Dr. Sinclair comes in and says, "You didn't have to hit him!" One of the orderlies then turns and responds, "Quickest, simplest way, doctor."

"But these are people, you don't handle them like animals," rejoins Sinclair. "When he comes to, give him some additional hydrospray therapy." (Translation: throw some water on him!)

That night we get our first look at an alligator person, after the film is about half over. Paul Webster comes in, sits at the piano downstairs and plays; he has some kind of scaly make-up on his face. Having established that Joyce has been locked in her room, Del Ruth mysteriously allows her to open the door and investigate. Apparently, realizing that the scene is not very suspenseful, Del Ruth adds another ominous voice-over for Joyce to reveal her thoughts to us: "I couldn't rid myself of the premonition that each step was taking me closer to the true secret contained in the shadowy house." Perhaps Joyce is considering taking up a career as a romantic novelist.

Anyway, she espies her husband and yet does not recognize him. He dashes out, leaving behind muddy footprints and wet piano keys. Why only his extremities are wet is left unclear—perhaps it is meant to suggest that he lives out in the swamp, but then why isn't the rest of him damp? It simply becomes one more ominous touch, allowing Joyce to confront Mrs. Hawthorne with the questions, "And another thing, who was playing the piano in the house last night? In the dark? Someone who left *wet footprints* on the carpet?" (Or possibly Joyce could just be subtly indicating to Mrs. Hawthorne that it wasn't she who made the mess.)

The next morning Dr. Sinclair drives up in an amphibious vehicle, which seems like such a neat device that it is a shame that it is never used or seen again. He simply explains to Joyce, "That's my swamp buggy. I need it to get around."

Back in his lab, Sinclair eagerly tells his assistant, "The cobalt bomb; it arrived today," as if he were a kid awaiting the prize from some mailed-in-boxtops. Sinclair reveals that he plans to combine gamma rays from the cobalt with X-rays in an effort to cure the ailing Paul, and proceeds to set up his X-ray machine.

Mrs. Hawthorne is frustrated and upset that Joyce has failed to depart on the morning train as she wished her to do. She agreed to put up Joyce largely because another train would not be arriving until then, but clearly does not want Joyce for a guest. When Joyce accuses her of possibly hurting Paul, she finally admits that she is Paul's mother.

Not long after, Paul reappears to check with his mother to see if Joyce has gone, but he runs into Joyce instead. Fleeing from his fiancée, he dashes off across the swamp with Joyce in rapid pursuit. Unfortunately, Del Ruth's attempt to build up any tension in this sequence is dissipated by such touches as having Joyce step across a patently phony alligator along the way. While the environment is not depicted as being particularly

inhospitable, suddenly we learn that Joyce's dress is ripped and torn, though there appears to be an absence of brambles and branches that might have torn it.

Chaney gets his other big scene when he hears Joyce cry out. He arrives just in time to "save" her from a snake, which is shown as coiled and ready to strike in close-up, but it is already crawling away when seen in long shot. Since it is raining, inhospitable, and dangerous, Mannon takes Joyce to his little cabin in the swamp, where he starts sampling some of his home-made hooch, a touch that seems to nod at Chaney's own well-noted problems with alcohol.

"You ought to get them wet things off," he tells her leeringly. Mannon makes a pretense at being a gentleman by wrapping a blanket around her, but once her arms are immobilized, he begins kissing her. When she screams, he punches her and knocks her out. Like a boy with a new Christmas present, he eagerly begins to unwrap her when Paul comes in and they get into a knock-down, drag-out fight. Paul triumphs, carrying Joyce to safety.

This earns the enmity of Mannon, who swears, "I'll kill ya, alligator man, just like I would any four-legged 'gator!" Chaney's ripe, over-the-top performance is richly suited to this clichéd role.

The filmmakers make an unsuccessful run at poignancy as Paul returns to his mother and inquires, "Why didn't he just let me die?" in a gruff voice that indicates he is undergoing additional changes. Mrs. Hawthorne has an abrupt change of heart and asks Paul to finally inform his wife as to what has transpired.

Meanwhile, Sinclair's experiments are not going well. He has to quiet one of his reluctant patients with a sun-lamp (doesn't heat make reptiles more active, not less active?) because they are turning into cold-blooded reptiles. Joyce comes across his experiments and quickly puts two and two together, noting that the patients are turning into alligators. "In effect, you could say that," an unfazed Sinclair sinisterly concedes. He finally reveals the thought process, the motivation, behind this bizarre experiment.

Impressed with the effects of hydrocortisone on simple organisms such as reptiles, some of which can regenerate lost limbs, Sinclair has been attempting to combine the two species to give humans the same ability. Paul became a subject following his plane

crash. "There was scarcely a bone in his body that wasn't broken," Sinclair declares, though the question of why Mannon, with his missing hand, was never made a patient is never raised.

Joyce tries to reassure her despairing husband. "It doesn't make any difference. I'm your wife and I love you," she tells her scaly hubby. Paul, however, refuses to spend the rest of his life looking like an alligator bag and insists that Sinclair proceed with his new procedure, hoping that the combined gamma and X-rays will provide a miracle cure. He is so impatient that he insists there be no further testing and the experiment be conducted at once.

Sinclair prepares the experiment, warning, "The controls and the timing must be precise. When you are dealing with radioactivity and millions of volts of energy, the slightest deviation from standard—even a few seconds of excess—and anything might happen." But then, how accurate can you expect a scientist to be when he shows Joyce two charts and says, "Here's something intriguing: two similar muscular charts. You might take them for the same animal, but as you know, this is a man, and this is an alligator."

However, Sinclair is not depicted as your basic mad scientist. His intentions are honorable and his desire to help mankind and Paul in particular appears to be genuine. He tells Paul just before he is about to throw the switch, "I'll never be able to tell you how sorry I am."

"Don't blame yourself," replies Webster. "I certainly don't. Who could know everything? You're not God, Mark."

"I feel as if I've been playing at it, and been punished," returns Sinclair, echoing the old horror cliché of "there are some things man was not meant to know."

"Forget it," replies Webster, offering a form of absolution.

But once more, the plans of mice and men, or make that gators and goofballs, end badly. A drunken, enraged Mannon bursts in just as Paul is being exposed to the ray during a crucial period in which he should not be exposed for more than 30 seconds. Insisting that he will get that "two-legged 'gator," Mannon smashes the controls, knocking Sinclair aside, and in an ultimate bit of clumsiness, manages to electrocute himself on the power grid.

Paul, having received an overdose of the ray, regresses further into reptilian state. His body now is completely scaly and his human head is now replaced with an alligator head, complete with an elongated, toothy snout. Rather than scary or horrifying, the Wyle E. Coyote–like croc-man seems simply ridiculous, though he does make for some memorable imagery.

Unfortunately, there is not much else, apart from Garland, Macready, and Chaney's performances that make this mostly mediocre movie memorable. It tries to thrill and fails badly. It wants to be creepy, but lacks any true sense of atmosphere. Its script is filled with ominous and arch dialogue, but can't escape the tedium of the plotting. All throughout there are half-hearted touches that echo other, better movies.

In the weak climax, Joyce screams at the transformed Paul (echoing the revelation scene of *The Fly*, also shot by Karl Struss), while Mrs. Hawthorne simply faints. (Fainting dowagers are quite common in many old horror films.) Rejected, Paul dashes out into the swamp, while Joyce once more chases after him. The house containing Sinclair and Mrs. Hawthorne suddenly explodes.

Paul does not notice his physical transformation until he sees his reflection in some swamp water, though one would think that his two-foot facial extension would be as plain as, well, the nose on his face. Del Ruth tries to add another thrill by showing his alligator man wrestling with a real alligator, but it only serves to remind how inadequate the make-up really is. (The part was at this point taken over by stunt man Boyd Stockman.) There's an attempt at ambiguity as Paul stumbles into some quicksand and goes under (a la one of the Mummy movies) without struggling, as if resigned to his fate or simply uncertain what to do. (He certainly might have lost some intelligence in the transformation, but even a gator can work his way out of a swamp.) Ms. Garland is left screaming, "Nooooo!" and we can certainly sympathize.

There is a final return to the framing story of the two psychiatrists discussing the case. In typical movie fashion, they state the obvious and tell each other what they both already know for the benefit of the slower members of the audience.

McGregor: This girl has lived through a horrible experience, true or not, but she has made a satisfactory adjustment. She lives a normal, useful, happy life by completely suppressing it.

Lorimer: It's obvious. Anxiety, neurosis, and amnesia suppression. You didn't need to tell me that.

Apart from reassuring that audience that the heroine turned out fine even if she must repress horrible memories and her husband was turned into an alligator person, these two characters serve no other purpose than to pad out the running time. At the end, they simply decide not to inform or make Jane/Joyce aware of the memories she is suppressing.

The Alligator People tries hard to achieve a sense of foreboding, but it fails miserably. Instead, it meanders around, killing time trying to set up a few big set-pieces which it fumbles badly. The climax is especially weak when all the alligator people are simultaneously revealed and destroyed before additional costly make-ups would be required, keeping budget costs down. What delights now is the film's strained seriousness, which can be taken as acceptable or amusing depending on one's inclinations, but for the most part, it will quickly slip back into the primordial ooze from which it arose, its most notable aspect being the bits of scenery-chewing it offered Chaney during the swamplands of his career. Ahead was only throat cancer, depriving Chaney of his full-voiced expression, and continued decline due to alcoholism, as well as the nadir of such awful epics as *Dr. Terror's Gallery of Horrors* and *Dracula vs. Frankenstein*, both of which would rank high on the lists of the worst horror films ever made.

CREDITS: Director: Roy Del Ruth; Producer: Jack Leewood; Screenplay: Orville H. Hampton; Story: Orville H. Hampton and Charles O'Neal; Art Director: John Mansbridge and Lyle R. Wheeler; Set Decoration: Walker M. Scott and Joseph Kish; Photography: Karl Struss; Special Effects: Fred Etcheverry; Editor: Harry Gerstad; Music: Irving Gertz; Sound: W. Donald Flick; Sound Effects: Arthur J. Cornell; Make-up: Ben Nye and Dick Smith; Costume Supervision: William McCrary and Ollie Hughes; Hairstyles: Eve Newing; Script Supervisor: Mary Coleman; Assistant Director: H. E. Mendelson; An Associated Producers Production for 20th Century-Fox; CinemaScope; 74 minutes; Released July 16, 1959 on a double bill with *Return of the Fly*

CAST: Beverly Garland (Jane Marvin); George Macready (Dr. Mark Sinclair); Lon Chaney (Mannon); Richard Crane (Paul Webster); Frieda Inescort (Mrs. Henry Hawthorne); Bruce Bennett (Dr. Erik Lorimer); Douglas Kennedy (Dr. Wayne McGregor); Vince Townsend Jr. (Toby); Ruby Goodwin (Lou Ann); Bill Bradley (Patient #6); Dudley Dickerson (Porter); Hal K. Dawson (Conductor); John Merrick and Lee Warren (Male Nurses); Boyd Stockman (Alligator Man)

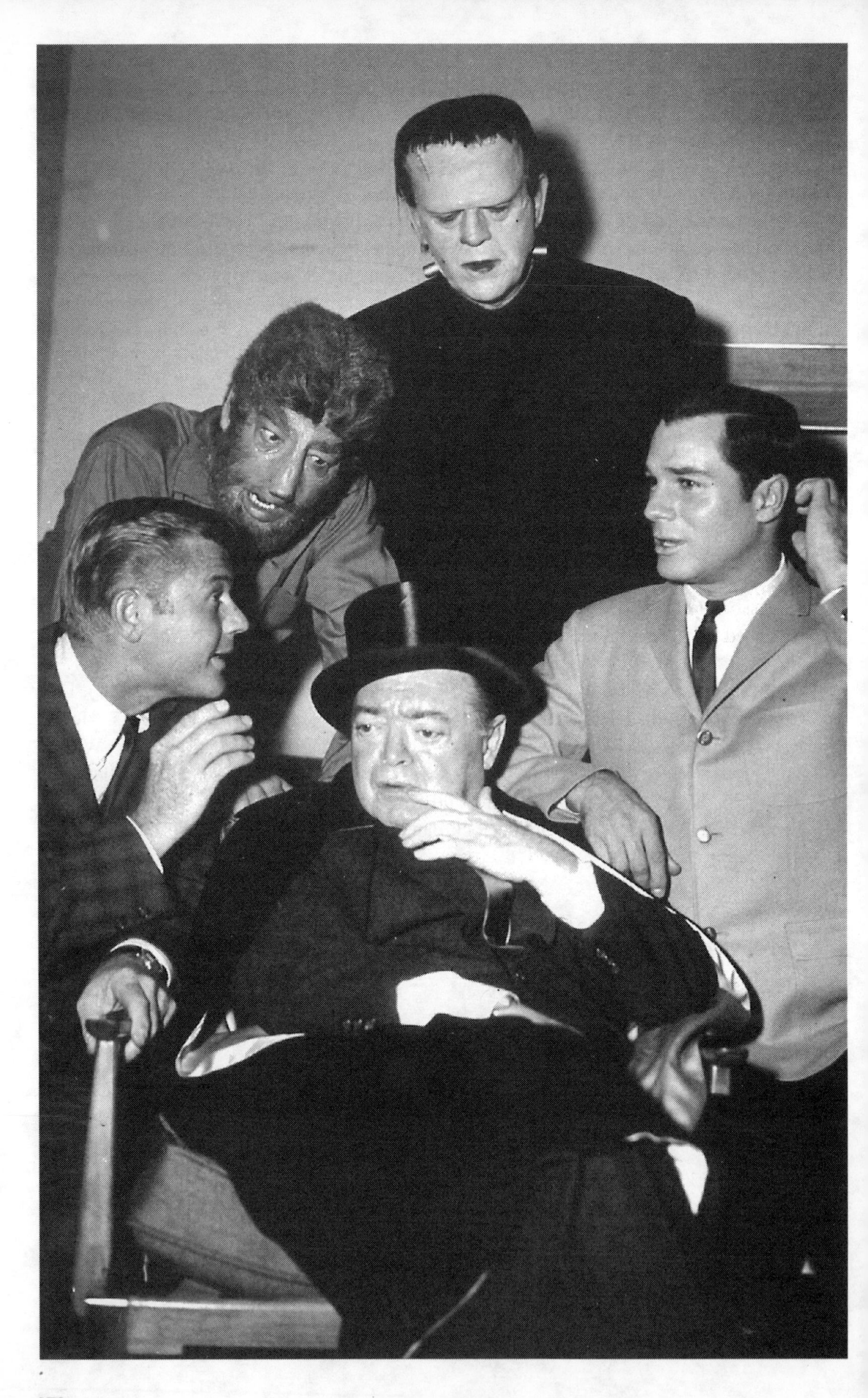

ROUTE 66 "LIZARD'S LEG AND OWLET'S WING" (1962)

by Gary J. Svehla

In October of 1962 the horrors of the real world greatly outnumbered the chills on the screen. I had been a fan of horror movies since my father Richard took me to see my first monster movie in 1957, when I was seven years old. I was hooked for life, and in those more innocent times, a youngster could see horror/fantasy/science fiction movies and not be traumatized for life (although my increasingly violent fears forced my mother to ban me from seeing horror films for a full year—1959—thus denying me the privilege of seeing such Hammer classics as *The Mummy* and *The Hound of the Baskervilles* in the theater).

However, as I was devouring the Hammer Gothics and the American-made monster-romp cheapies in the neighborhood theaters, I was beginning to be introduced to the horror classics of the 1930s via late-night weekend television—and names such as Boris Karloff, Bela Lugosi, Lon Chaney, Jr. stood just as tall in my mind as the more current Peter Cushing and Christopher Lee. By the time I was twelve, in 1962, I was a true connoisseur of the cinema of the macabre and was only one year away from publishing my first crude issue of *Midnight Marquee*.

But while I found my sessions with horror cinema to be cozy and comforting, as well as exhilarating, I was totally overwhelmed by the fears that the Nuclear Generation had wrought: at school we had "duck and tuck" drills in the event of a nuclear attack. Fall-out shelters were advertised and advocated nationally, and the realization that the world might end at any moment was to be a general fact of modern life for many years to come.

But things became really scary near Halloween of 1962—the Cuban Missile Crisis was upon us, a dramatic showdown between Russian and the United States over the presence of nuclear missiles in Cuba, photos revealing they were aimed toward America. President Kennedy imposed an immediate embargo—nothing went into Cuba until the missiles were dismantled and removed. Would Russia fight their way out or back down to Western pressure!? For pride's sake, in my mind at least, it seemed Russia would surely destroy the planet before backing down! For almost a week the fate of humankind hung in the balance with the imminent fear of total nuclear devastation a reality to this 12 year old. I prayed every night that the world would not be destroyed and my thoughts at Junior High during the day were filled with images of instant, painful/painless (?) death. Living in Baltimore, a major urban center located only one hour away from the nation's capital, I understood we would definitely feel the full brunt of a nuclear

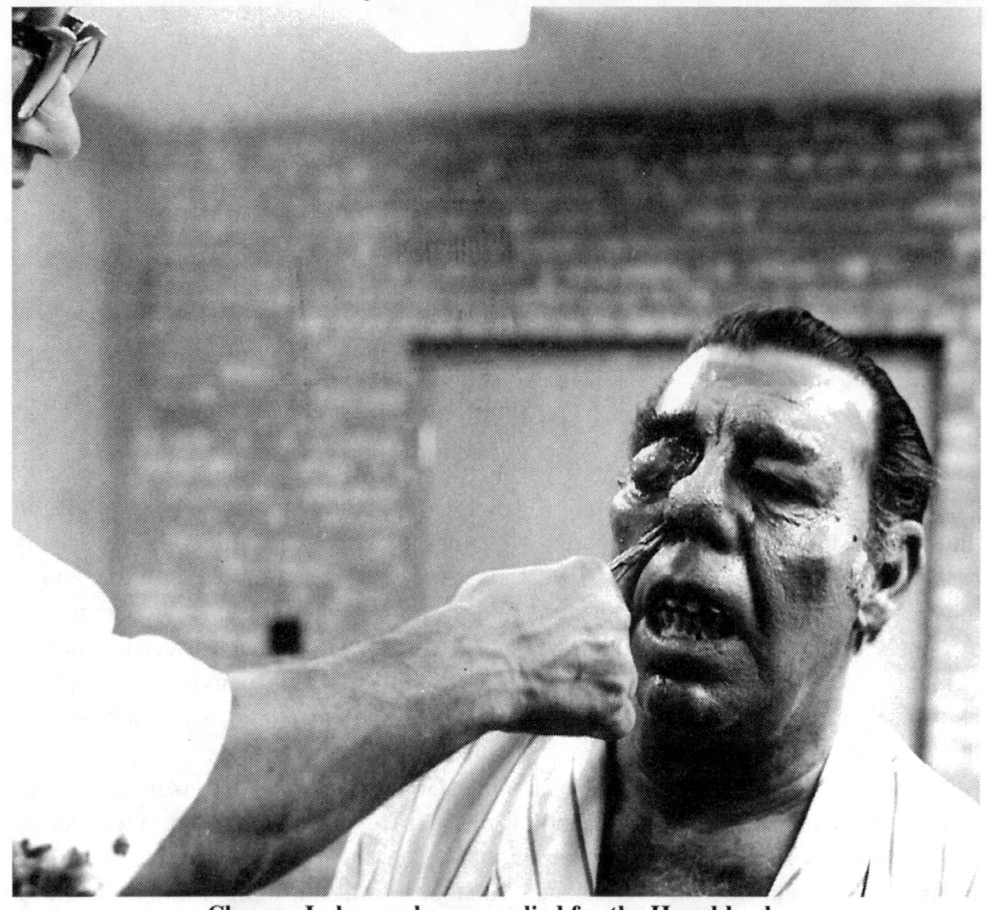

Chaney, Jr. has make-up applied for the Hunchback.

war. For that week I truly believed the end of the world was upon us, that I might be dead before last period ended at Herring Run Junior High, before I would reach the safety of my brown-shingled home in northeast Baltimore. So cinematic horrors became something of a safety cushion, artistic expression I sought out for protection and hope. Monsters and those monster icon horror stars were my salvation. Nuclear war was insidious and ungodly; monsters were my friends.

Oh God, I soon prayed, please don't let the world end until after next week's *Route 66* because the Special Guest Stars were to be none other than Boris Karloff, Lon Chaney, and Peter Lorre! Let me see Boris Karloff and Lon Chaney first! That became my supposed last wish.

Fortunately, the Russians backed down and the ready-to-boil-over Cold War suddenly cooled, but *Route 66* appeared as scheduled, and my dream to see Karloff and Chaney in a current television series became a reality.

Route 66 was a CBS hour-long drama series that aired Fridays at 8:30 p.m. from 1960 to 1964. The series, generally adult oriented, concerned the free-spirited Tod Stiles (Martin Milner) and Buz Murdock (George Maharis, who left the series during the third season) who traveled the U.S. in Tod's Corvette looking for adventure and the meaning of life (Tod came from a wealthy background while Buz was a product of New York's Hell's Kitchen). If the series were done a few years later, Tod and Buz may very well have been cast as long-haired "freaks" on the back of a Harley drifting from coast to coast in search of personal freedoms. But the Hippie era was still half a decade away. Interestingly enough, Tod and Buz's motivation was essentially the same, drifting, directionless, seeking out temporary part-time jobs, following the vast American highway system to wherever it would lead them. The anthology series was filmed on-location, crisscrossing the United States, featuring major Hollywood guest stars every episode.

In October 1962, Tod and Buz ventured into part-time hotel work at Chicago's O'Hare Inn, about to confront the secretive Peter Lorre, Boris Karloff, and Lon Chaney in the episode "Lizard's Leg and Owlet's Wing."

Besides proving to be a marvelous vehicle for declining star Lon Chaney, it would prove to be the final time that Lon Chaney appeared together with either Karloff or Lorre professionally and it bid a touching farewell to the classic horror generation and its special icons.

The pre-title sequence is marvelously rendered and features a dynamic Lon Chaney rekindling the old creative fires. In a little boy's darkened bedroom, the imposing figure of the Hunchback of Notre Dame quietly descends upon the sleeping child as ominous music builds in the background. Lumbering through the night shadows, the hunchback approaches the child, his arm extended, his menacing hand approaching the sleeping boy's head. The monster touches the boy's head, gently patting it, the fiend's face surprisingly erupting into a big smile.

The little boy peacefully awakens: "Hello, Grandpa!"

"Hi, Sonny-boy!" the old fiend gleefully erupts. "I didn't want to wake you up. I only wanted to give you a great big hug and kiss before I went to bed."

"Did you scare 'em?" the excited child asks.

"You bet your life I scared 'em," Chaney proudly brags, receiving a warm embrace from his grandson. "Now you just go to sleep."

The mood of this sequence is tense, surprising, and heartwarming; it takes the typical horror film trappings (the innocent, sleeping victim, the dark, a horrible-looking monster, spooky music, and threatening, clutching hands) and turns them on their ear. Seeing the Hunchback's serious expression erupt into a loving smile only illustrates the creative power that Lon Chaney still possessed.

Remember the time 1962: American International was just beginning their Poe series and the comedy horror *The Raven*, starring Boris Karloff and Peter Lorre, was still a year away. Chaney's return to American International in *The Haunted Palace* was also over a year away. Karloff was working on the American TV series *Thriller* and hadn't made any horror features since the Richard Gordon–produced English titles such as *Corridors of Blood* (made in 1958 but not released until 1962) and *The Haunted Strangler* (1958). Lon Chaney had passed from the exploitative American B movies of the late fifties (*The Black Sleep*, 1956; *Indestructible Man*, 1956; *The Cyclops*, 1957) to playing supporting roles in mainstream movies (*The Defiant Ones*, 1958) and oddball foreign cheapies such as the Mexican *The Face of the Screaming Werewolf*, 1959. Thus, by 1962 Peter Lorre was not appearing in any type of genre work, Karloff was out of features and was hosting a horror/crime drama TV series, and Lon Chaney was working quite steadily as a supporting character actor, his leading man image having dimmed some time ago.

Therefore, the intent of this *Route 66* episode was to remind current television audiences of these former icons of the sinister from a generation past and to contrast the old-style methods of screen horror to the emerging modern horror style, the style best illustrated by Alfred Hitchcock's surprise hit of 1960, *Psycho*, which featured a human monster devoid of make-up or Gothic trappings. Could the old monsters still cut it?—the script appears to be asking.

The horrormeisters speak by conference call and agree to meet in Chicago, at the O'Hare Inn incognito (the script's assumption being that the sight of such horror movie stars would panic the average citizen who would be unable to separate screen persona from real life entity), using their surname as their last names—and reversing the letters (so that Karloff becomes Mr. Sirob, Lorre becomes Mr. Retep, and Chaney becomes Mr. Nol). To further protect their motive and identities, they would be attending a conference of the Society for the Prevention of Gerenuks.

It seems that Boris Karloff, according to the script, has jumped ship and now believes only in the modern view of horror: "I've read your prospectus... I find it psychologically unsound in today's market."

Spokesperson Peter Lorre, defending the position of both himself and of Lon Chaney, still believes in the older tradition of creating cinematic horror: "Boris, what frightened them then, in the dark ages, still frightens them now!" chimes back Lorre. "People don't change, Boris. Fear is born into people. Witch doctors, voodoo priests, zombies, ghosts, ghouls, vampires, monsters—and don't you sell them short, Boris."

Boris, maintaining his dignity, asserts, "Old hat, my dear boy. I'm told that business is so bad that the witch doctors in Africa are asking for relief parcels. We'll need to come to a final and unanimous decision!" Thus, the need for the meeting, and also to attend is a Mrs. Baxter (Martita Hunt from Hammer's *Brides of Dracula*), a financial/legal adviser.

Interestingly enough, even though Lorre, Karloff, and Chaney portray themselves using their given screen names, in reality they are playing the everyday personas that their fans wish them to be—professional actors preoccupied about the most effective ways to terrify a new generation of monster fanatics, audiences who are now being frightened by psychopaths, atomic mutations, and terrors from outer space. This script plays directly to the hard-core fan of cinematic horror and the old icons more than rise to the occasion of entertaining us one more time.

To tie-in to the *Route 66* premise, Tod and Buz have applied for positions at the O'Hare Inn as hotel liaisons, kitchen expediters, banquet trouble-shooters. The romantically inclined young men are most interested in a convention of 40 executive secretaries, all curvy females, staying at the hotel, to which Buz is assigned. The jealous and disappointed Tod is assigned to the convention for the Society of the Prevention of Gerenuks, hosted by our lovable older fossils (all males). The plot revolves around Tod trying to get Buz to help to set him up with a few eligible females, but Buz is so enamored with his responsibility that his puppy-dog stares only see female and he forgets his old buddy.

From here on, the show is played mainly for irony and laughter, especially the opening sequence when Peter Lorre arrives to check in at the hotel wearing a dark overcoat, dark shades, and a big black hat. Without saying a word at first, he grabs the pen out of the hand of the desk clerk, writes his name on a piece of padded paper, and waits. The desk clerk, staring at this strange presence, asks: "Did anyone ever tell you there's a striking resemblance—will you excuse me sir—between you and Peter Lorre!!!"

In deadpan style, Lorre answers matter-of-factly, "That's pretty insulting, isn't it!"

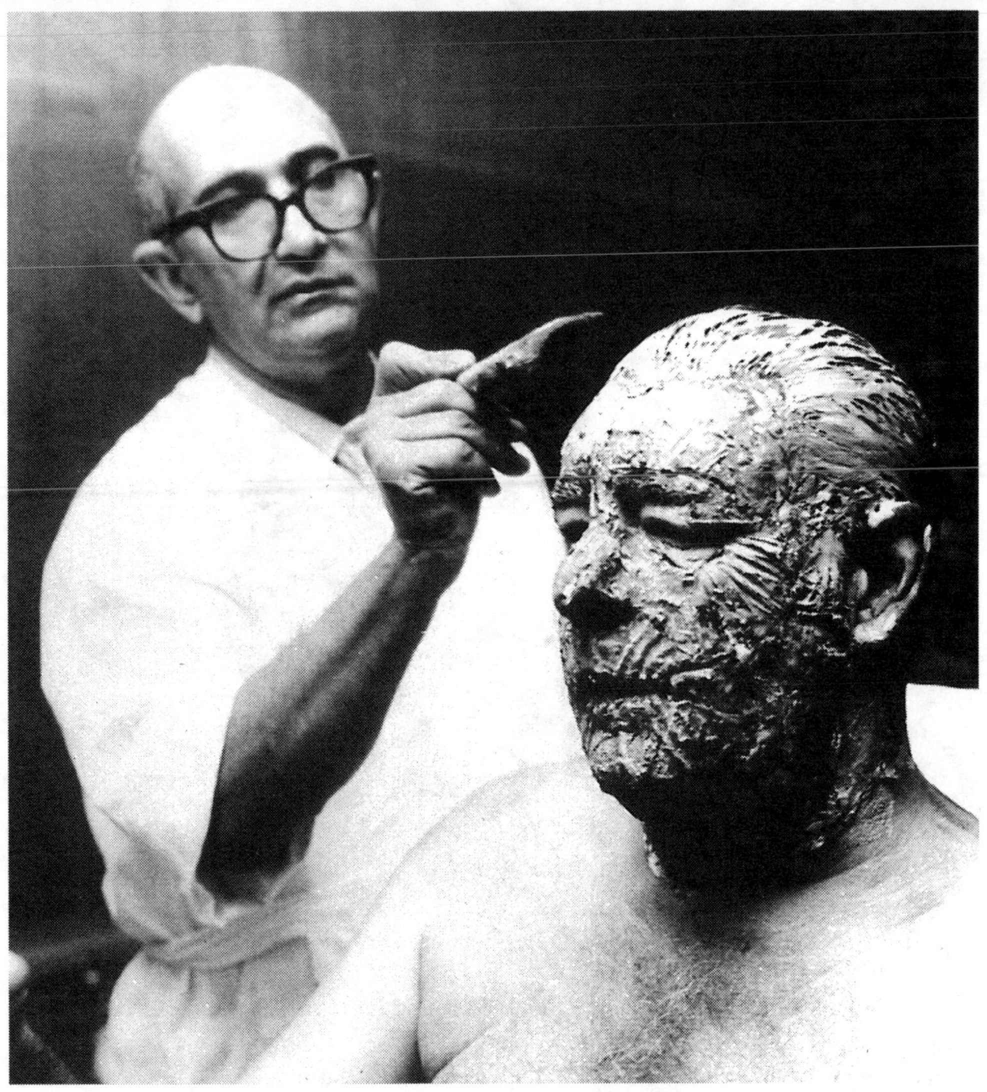

Once again, Chaney is in the make-up chair, this time for the Mummy.

In the major subplot, Buz falls for the sad and lonely Molly Cross (Jeannine Riley), a woman who recently quite her job as executive secretary because she fell in love with her boss, but unfortunately, the boss, Mr. Stevenson, did not feel the same way toward her. However, the all-so-serious convention "boss" Lila (Betsy Jones-Moreland, star of AIP's *The Last Woman on Earth*) has eyes for Buz but Buz only has eyes for Molly. As Lila explains the situation to Buz: "The girls are here to work, to learn, to profit from an exchange of ideas, to advance the status and dignity of the profession of executive secretary." But in her dazed state, Molly is impervious to men, to her job, or to any basic emotion at all. She is distant, lost in her thoughts, alone.

Tod, on the other hand, introduces himself to Lorre, Mr. Retep, who announces "our needs are quite simple," involving a large table, four chairs, locks for the inside of the doors, and one coffin with satin lining and silver handles (but Tod can only acquire a coffin with brush copper handles), the symbol for their society.

Retep asks, "You know about Gerenuks?"

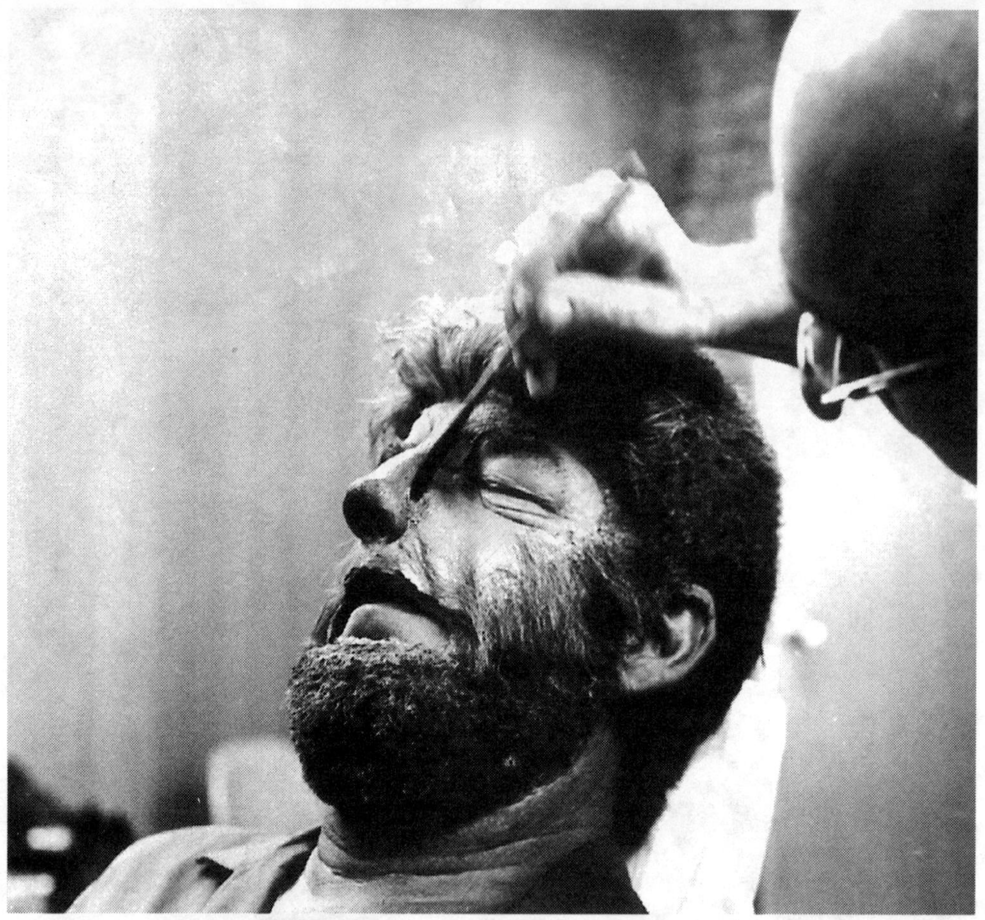

For one final time, Chaney dons the Wolf Man make-up.

Tod, puzzled, answers, "Frankly, no one around here knows what a Gerenuk *is* or *does*—and I'm a Yale man!"

Lorre continues, "That's all right. Don't you speak Somali?"

"I had trouble with the adverbs," the glib Tod snaps back.

Lorre continues, "The explanation is quite simple. Gerenuk comes from a Somali expression and it means an antelope or gazelle, in great danger of becoming extinct. And if that should happen there are black days ahead for humanity. You see the slogan for our society is, if it can happen to the Gerenuk, it can happen to you!"

Stirling Silliphant's script, one of the great television (and movie) screenwriters, is rather pithy and clever, even though the basic situation is corny and as old as the hills. Even snappy dialogue cannot hide the rickety old chestnut plot unfolding before us.

Lon Chaney, after his impressive pre-credit sequence, has minimal dialogue compared to the other two icons, but Chaney's physical acting performance manages to almost steal the show. Boris Karloff is impressive, but he is only portraying an erudite Britisher and his own Karloff persona. Lorre is able to one-up Boris by virtue of his snappy dialogue and well-timed reactions to other people's dialogue and body language. But Chaney is all boyish enthusiasm and is quite energetic in his performance, as will be detailed. Chaney is seen less frequently, but he makes the most of his screen presence and dominates the scenes in which he appears.

For instance, in the initial sequence in Parlor 9, Lorre and Karloff are sitting around the coffin waiting for Chaney to arrive. Chaney is late and Karloff is aggravated. "Time is precious, why isn't he here. I've come all the way from London, Mrs. Baxter from Zurich—it can't be too difficult to fly in from the West Coast!"

Lorre, in his quietly sleazy manner, intones, "Boris, baby, calm down!"; Boris, aware of the new ways of fear, mocks the presence of the coffin. "What a corny piece of theatricality. I thought we agreed to keep our meeting secret. They see us or they don't dare to believe they see us, like a fairy tale, like the Emperor's New Clothes!"

The stuffy Mrs. Baxter, always in agreement with Karloff, states, "A coffin—ridiculous! It's the sort of thing that starts talk. Boris is quite right!"

Tired of waiting, Karloff starts the meeting by stating, "Peter, I am determined not to produce a slate of pictures made in the old way... if we accept the network's offer to star in and produce the most terrifying stories yet produced on television, we must strike out in new directions, a modern sort of horror as it were. We can't rely on hair on our faces, nodules on our foreheads, or any of the old bag of tricks!"

Lorre, waiting for the right moment, secretively knocks on the side of the coffin. Almost immediately, the coffin lid, squeaking as would be expected, begins to slowly open. Lorre smiles, "Mice!"

Lon Chaney, recreating the guise of Kharis the Mummy, rests inside the coffin. Chaney, all seriousness and business, rises and lurches foward, growling.

Mrs. Baxter nonchalantly states, "Oh, there you are."

Chaney registers an immediate look of disappointment. As the meeting continues, with Mrs. Baxter speaking of forming a corporation financed through a Swiss bank, Chaney's keeps shaking his head in the negative, grunting, and depressingly sinking back down into the coffin, his body registering his utter defeat to terrify in the old manner.

"Oh stop this nonsense Lon so we can go to work!" demands Boris.

Chaney, pulling out all the stops by recreating the childlike innocence that was Lennie in 1939's *Of Mice and Men*, rants "they spoiled it" sobbing, banging both fists loudly on the edge of the coffin. His over-the-top spoiled brat interpretation is emotionally effective and simply works. Here the old master is trying to trick the tricksters and comes up disappointed and empty handed.

Lorre reiterates, "Our only business can be to create new monsters. And I don't mean space creeps. Down to earth monsters where people can identify themselves with them."

Again, though he has minimal screen time, Chaney's presence becomes the focus of the entire sequence, his appearance as Kharis (looking more than slightly heavier and puffier in the face than he did twenty years earlier) being the most effective makeup of his three monster appearances in the episode. Chaney becomes the physical extreme to Lorre and Karloff's verbal repartee, and Chaney's ability to tap into that childish angst and rage is both affecting and effective. Sorta like "Lennie Meets the Monsters."

Tod, now understanding the game plan, approaches Lorre and tells him they will work together to create situations here in the hotel whereby the classic monsters get the opportunity to frighten ordinary people (not horror movie stars) to use as the leverage to convince Boris Karloff that the old horror ways are still the best.

Lorre responds, "That's brilliant! Why didn't I think of that, and how come you thought of it!"

Once more around the block for old time's sake—Chaney and Karloff!

With his boyish smile and a giggle, Tod declares, "Nobody's all good, you know!" They both melt into a sea of mutual laughter.

Later, a woman fumbles through her bag looking for a match to light her cigarette when a furry arm and lighter extends from behind a curtain to offer assistance. With bugged-out eyes, the woman reacts to this monstrous sight, screams, and runs away. The joyful Chaney comes bobbing out from behind the curtain, all smiles and laughter. Showing a little of his formerly athletic screen presence, Chaney, as the Wolf Man, runs around a room, hops on the table on all fours, growls, screams, and a roomful of young women faint dead away. However, other terrified women run up to Lorre, see his ordinary face, and still faint dead away. This reaction perplexes the sad-eyed Lorre, producing a stellar sight gag. Chaney, looking around and seeing a roomful of faint-hearted females, is excited and laughs even more boyishly. Chaney pounces up to Lorre and in high spirits declares, "I wish my grandson Lon were here to see this sight. He was starting to not believe in me no more. But if he saw this sight, he'd have a wonderful time." Lorre tells Lon to "beat it" so he can take some photos as proof.

Next up is the broken-hearted Molly, forlorn in love, who phones down to room service for coffee, to be delivered by the Wolf Man. It is in this sequence that Chaney particularly shines. When the beautiful but broken-hearted girl opens the door seeing the monster, she acts nonplused and states: "Please bring it in... I think it's terrible they make you carry such heavy things. You look exhausted," looking directly at the frenzied, lycanthropic Chaney. Working up energy, Lon breathes heavily, snorts, extends his ferocious hands in a menacing manner, growls, and threatens with his body language. "Would you like cream or sugar?" the pretty young secretary asks. Chaney, slowly giving up, begins to whimper and cry and soon bangs his hands against the furniture, loudly. Molly approaches him, bends forward, and kisses his face. Lon begins to build up his rage again, to further release his full arsenal of animalistic barrage, but he soon collapses into self-pity when Molly fails to record any degree of horror or fear. Backing away, sobbing audibly, his entire body heaves in sadness and disappointment. After a few more token growls and howls, he rushes out of the room, embarrassed by his failure to create terror as he always has in the past.

Tearfully walking down deserted hotel corridors, he comes across two women who instantly faint dead away. His sobs becoming transformed into laughter, Chaney gleefully spies another group of people further down the hall. He joyfully charges after them, eliciting the same response: they either run off or faint. Chaney has been vindicated.

Soon Peter Lorre puts his finger on the difference between the styles of Karloff and Chaney: "We might be less regal than he [Karloff] is, but we have more emotion. We *have* more emotion! And what I want is *experience* and not theory!"

Lorre shows the photos of the fainting victims to Karloff and the strongwilled king of horror begins to come around to Lorre's way of thinking. "Not quite, Peter. Remember, there was that one girl in 1114!" referring to Molly Cross and her inability to be frightened.

Lon Chaney restates his frustration: "Hey, you listen to me. Let's take a look at all the facts about these girls I've been frightening. There was this one girl... now you listen to me. there was this one girl. I was actually alone with her in her room, and I was growling. Boris, you know how I can growl. No, she treated me like a charity case! [Sobbing once again] She was sorry for me!" Chaney buries his face in his hands overcome by his seeming impotence.

However Boris immediately remembers the girl he formerly advised in the hotel's auditorium and explains to all. "No wonder you couldn't frighten her. She's completely absorbed in an emotion that's primitive as your pattern of terror—she's in love."

Boris sets up the situation for the final climax. "...you almost convinced me that perhaps the old ways are the best after all, that a new wave—the adult horrors so to speak—may be the wrong technique. But we must be sure—using this girl Molly Cross as the ultimate test. If we can frighten her—a woman in love—we can frighten everybody and anybody!"

A candid shot showing Chaney, Jr. eating in a Chicago restaurant with co-star Conrad Nagel (and notice Peter Lorre hiding in the background).

Thus, in the episode's pivotal sequence, Molly Cross, now reunited with her boss/boyfriend who has flown in to Chicago to see Molly simply on the orders of a quick phone call from Boris Karloff to his office, is enjoying a kiss after proposing to her ("I can always get another fiancée but never another secretary like you!"). Behind her, standing on the stair railing overhead, are the icons in full dress make-up: Peter Lorre in dress top hat and black cape, Lon Chaney as the Wolf Man, and, once again, Boris Karloff as the Frankenstein Monster. (Unfortunately, Karloff's Frankenstein Monster make-up is the weakest of all, appearing to have been a rush job, paling alongside the Wolf Man and Mummy.) Momentarily taking a breath and gazing overhead and seeing the three old monsters, Molly gasps at this sudden horrific vision (to the TV audience it's more heartwarming and nostalgic) and she falls to the floor unconscious. Before running off to hide with Tod's assistance, the police detective in hot pursuit, Boris joyfully says, "That proves it! The old ghosts are the best after all. And the power of all three of us in one picture—can you imagine it? It's almost too ghastly to contemplate!"

In one final sequence, once the coast is clear, Buz and Tod straddle each side of the hideaway door, and the masters of terror make their exits as well deserved curtain calls. Lorre comes out and proudly smiles, as does Karloff as the Frankenstein Monster. And saved for the last exit comes the triumphant Wolf Man, Lon Chaney himself. Chaney enthusiastically shakes Tod's hand and turns and growls at Buz, then playfully laughs and joyfully runs out of the frame. What a playful yet dignified, fitting farewell to Chaney's archival horror film performance.

Lon Chaney faded from Hollywood as a romantic, handsome leading man, ravaged by age and poor health into a baggy-eyed character personality. An actor whose star rose slowly from B Westerns and serial roles in the 1930s to star status for a few short years at Universal in the 1940s, relegated to accepting small roles as his star power faded, yet, his acting ability still perpetuated and probably even grew. Reduced to B and, much later, even Z productions, Lon Chaney remained a working actor his entire career, returning to those beloved Westerns, but also to prestige supporting roles in A productions such as *High Noon* and *The Defiant Ones* during the final decades of both his life and career. Lon Chaney, even after Hollywood forgot him, continued to work and continued to grow and continued to impress with his performances.

And here, on nationwide television, in primetime in October of 1962, Lon Chaney, for the final time, was able to reclaim a little bit of that faded glory by reenacting the role for which he will be long remembered. While "Lizard's Leg and Owlet's Wing" is flawed television (specifically, it is mediocre *Route 66* but inspired Chaney/Karloff/Lorre), it remains wonderfully nostalgic for the horror film aficionado And most importantly, Lon Chaney was able to demonstrate that he was still physically and emotionally able to jump into his werewolf costume and make-up and breathe life into the Wolf Man one more time and not embarrass himself. In fact, Chaney shines and dominates. By miming his physical ability to still encircle a roomful of terrified victims, charge onto tabletops and other pieces of furniture, and tie that physicality to a childlike innocence of character by drawing upon his Lennie role from *Of Mice and Men*, Lon Chaney creates a heightened sense of pathos in his characterization of the Wolf Man.

And for a fleeting moment during the Cuban Missile Crisis of 1962, the sinister mystery man Peter Lorre, the Wolf Man and actor Lon Chaney, and Frankenstein's Monster and beloved Boris Karloff reigned supreme, weaving their cinematic magic once again, and making a frightened 12-year-old forget nuclear annihilation and instead fear the dreaded Pentagram, the sign of the Wolf, and cheer for the old inspired ways of classic horror cinema.

Russia and its modern horrors never stood a chance.

CREDITS: Screenplay: Stirling Silliphant; Director: Robert Gist; Executive Producer: Herbert B. Leonard; Supervising Producer: Leo Davis; Producer: Mort Abrahams; Original Music Composed and Conducted by Nelson Riddle; Orchestrated by Gil Grau; Series Created by Herbert B. Leonard and Stirling Silliphant; Director of Photography: Irving Lippman; Supervising Film Editor: Aaron Nibley; Editor: Marry Coswick; Art Director: John T. McCormack; Costumer: Charles Arrico; Camera Operator: Robert Johannes; Set Decorator: Bill Calvert; Make-up: Abe Haberson; Special Make-up: Ben Lane and Maurice Siederman; A Lancer-Edling Production for Screen Gems; Location filming: Chicago, Illinois, Broadcast October 1962

CAST: Martin Milner (Tod Stiles); George Maharis (Buz Murdock); Peter Lorre (Mr. Retep); Lon Chaney (Mr. Nol); Boris Karloff (Mr. Sirob); Martita Hunt (Mrs. Baxter); Conrad Nagel (Mr. Pavis); Sally Gracie (Beth); Bill Berger (Mr. Stevenson); Jeannine Riley (Molly Cross); Ralph Stanley (Lt. Collins); Betsy Jones-Moreland (Lila)

AFTER 300 YEARS
IN THE GRAVE...
THEY RETURNED
TO REAP
BLOOD HAVOC!
WITCHCRAFT
LON
CHANEY
JACK HEDLEY • JILL DIXON
ROBERT LIPPERT and JACK PARSONS
DON SHARP
HARRY SPALDING

WITCHCRAFT (1964)

by Mark A. Miller

> "Lon Chaney is one of the most talented actors in films today. He has none of the high-class attitude of today's stars; in fact, he is undoubtedly one of the most unassuming men I ever had the pleasure of working with."[1]—Vincent Price

American producer Robert Lippert teamed with British producer Jack Parsons in the 1960s for a handful of low-budget, black and white thrillers. All of them were shot in England, with British casts headlined by fading American stars supplied by Lippert. This strategy, which Lippert previously used with Hammer in the 1950s, helped to ensure distribution in both countries. Through Lippert, Lon Chaney, Jr., at the age of 58, found himself starring in his only British production. It was to be his last horror film of quality.

Fate, fortunately or unfortunately, had rendered Chaney perfectly suited, emotionally and physically, for his role in this film. The movie shines, too, as a monument to the actor's dedication to his craft in the face of debilitating alcoholism, and the isolation and depression that often accompany it. In addition, luck paired Chaney with a talented director, Don Sharp, in a tight, gripping story of witchcraft in a modern setting.

The major horror icons—Boris Karloff, Vincent Price, Peter Cushing, and Christopher Lee—were busy in 1964 and very much in the limelight for their continued unique contributions to the genre. They occupied the upper tier of monsterdom. Chaney, the hard drinking, barrel-chested character actor, labored on the lower tier. None of his brethren, however, could have filled his shoes as Morgan Whitlock in *Witchcraft*. Chaney wears a long, dramatic black cloak for much of the film and constantly waves his gentleman's hat and cane in anger, yet he has the craggy face of a retired construction worker. Consequently, he looks like a mad Victorian trapped in the 1960s. As a human anachronism, Chaney's appearance bridges the past with the present, a theme that permeates this atmospheric chiller and gives it a particularly unsettling ambiance.

Harry Spalding's script for *Witchcraft* is deceptively economic. The author crams plenty of engrossing events into 79 minutes, but it does not become overstuffed because director Don Sharp's strong visual sense of storytelling moves the plot along briskly to its surprising conclusion.

Bill Lanier (Jack Hedley) and his brother Todd (David Weston) are business partners with land developer Myles Forrester (Barry Linehan). Together, they hope to build a large community development on the Laniers' property. Part of the estate, however, contains an ancient burial ground that once belonged to the Whitlock family. As Morgan Whitlock (Chaney) angrily reminds Bill, "The Whitlocks have used that cemetery for 800 years. What right does an upstart like you have to run sewers through their coffins, put buildings over their graves?"

The audience's initial sympathy for the Whitlocks and disdain for the Laniers becomes less and less polarized. When Morgan Whitlock complains to Bill that the bulldozers are destroying his family's grave site, Bill reminds him that the courts have decided in his favor and that Whitlock has had months to move the graves at the Laniers' expense. Also, no one has been buried there for over 100 years. Bill becomes upset that tombstones have been damaged, though, because his partner, Forrester, promised they would be safely removed before excavation.

It quickly becomes evident that the division between the two families is somewhat limited to the older generations. In fact, Bill's brother, Todd, and Morgan's niece, Amy (Diane Clare), are in love. This adds a familiar conflict to the story, but it is an intricate part of the plotting, not an extraneous love interest. Morgan forbids them to be together, and Amy's conflict of loyalty becomes much more complicated than first assumed. A sweet, gentle girl, Amy will provide an unexpected shock much later. Ultimately, her love for Todd contributes to the film's fiery, surprising climax.

Bill finds a chunk of stone in the spoiled graveyard with a circular design like one on his fireplace's hearth at home. He shows it to his grandmother, Malvina (Marie Ney), who is confined to a wheelchair and never leaves her upstairs room in the Lanier mansion. (Oakley Court, next to Bray Studios, was used for the exterior of the mansion.) Malvina gravely tells her grandson that the design is "the Witches' Circle, a pact with the devil." She also reveals that the stone in the fireplace was placed there by the Whitlocks when they owned the mansion. The only other stone like it, she says, was placed on the grave of Vanessa Whitlock, who was condemned as a witch. When Bill jokingly adds that they have nothing to fear because witches were burned at the stake, Malvina offers the unsettling detail that Vanessa was buried alive, not burned.

Malvina's comments prompt even more questions. Why are the Laniers living in the Whitlock mansion? Why is Malvina so upset by the Witches' Circle? What are the implications of Vanessa's having been buried alive? (When Bill removed the stone, moaning sounds could be heard from Vanessa's tomb. He seems to think they were from a howling dog.) One point is obvious to viewers: the centuries-old conflict between the Laniers and the Whitlocks remains as threatening as it is murky.

The uncertainty increases after Vanessa's resurrection in the graveyard reveals that she, indeed, *is* a witch. This dramatic irony (the film's viewers are the only witnesses) is intensified as Todd recounts the family history to Bill's wife, treating the supernatural element as a joke. He discloses that the Laniers' ancestors were the invading Normans who conquered the Anglo-Saxons, took their property, and reduced them to peasant serfs. Even though the two cultures eventually merged, the Normans remained associated with the upper class, the Anglo-Saxons with the middle and lower. According to Todd, in the early 1600s during the witch hunts, the Laniers accused the Whitlocks (Anglo-Saxons) of witchcraft. They had Vanessa Whitlock killed, drove out her kinfolk, and usurped their land. Ever since then, the Whitlocks have made the destruction of the Laniers the focus of their Sabbaths. Todd also mentions that soon it will be May Eve, or Rood Mass, one of the four witches' Sabbaths, when they will gather to make a sacrifice.

Because Todd mentions that the accusation against Vanessa may have been motivated by greed, Bill and Tracy do not take the possibility of witchcraft seriously. By contrast, their visiting aunt, Helen (Viola Keats), feels that they should. This mixture of skepticism and fear with a love interest between the two families, the fact that Morgan

Amy Whitlock (Diane Clare) watches, stunned, as her uncle, Morgan Whitlock (Chaney, Jr.) confronts a bulldozer that is desecrating the Whitlock graveyard.

Whitlock's family was cheated out of the land that will make the Laniers rich, and the viewers' discovery that Vanessa really is a witch, provides a rich framework for the remainder of the story, one that is inherently fascinating and unpredictable because of all these complicated elements.

Vanessa begins her revenge with Forrester, who is directly responsible for the desecration of her grave. He is found mysteriously drowned in his bathtub. Police inspector Baldwin (Victor Brooks) tells the Laniers of his death and mentions that Whitlock has been held for questioning.

Todd invites Amy to stay with them while her uncle (and guardian) is held by the police, but Helen gives her a cold reception and tells Bill that "a Whitlock hasn't slept in this house for 300 years." Todd retorts, "And it's about time one did, just to put a stop to this nonsense." Helen is not deterred: "You know the Whitlocks still belong to the old religion. There's a coven right here. It's common knowledge. I'm only trying to say that there's a coven of 13 right here and the Whitlocks belong to it!" The next day, Helen runs her car off a cliff, an apparent suicide, but Vanessa is really responsible.

Helen's body is entombed in the Lanier crypt beside their mansion. The close proximity of this burial vault to the Laniers' home portrays evil as an insidious intruder. A tunnel leads from the crypt to a walled off portion of the mansion's cellar. It had once been used as a secret route for priests to escape persecution and later served as a chapel

Morgan Whitlock threatens Todd Lanier (David Weston), telling him to stay away from his niece, Amy.

where the Laniers celebrated mass. Long abandoned by them, it is now the hidden setting for the coven's Black Masses. Located directly beneath the Lanier home, it taints where they talk, eat, sleep, and love.

This irony becomes even blacker after Bill and Todd leave the mansion for a London business trip (and nearly have an accident exactly like Helen's). Tracy is left alone to care for Amy (who has become ill) and Malvina. Amy disappears, but from Malvina's upstairs window Tracy spies her entering the tomb. Tracy pursues and is surprised to find the tunnel not only open but also lit by torches. In a sequence reminiscent of one in John Moxey's *Horror Hotel* (1960), Tracy hears chanting and stumbles upon the witches. Secretly peeking at them, she sees ghastly hooded figures form a circle around another hooded witch, who has her back to Tracy. Above them is a horrific altar made of animal bones. Morgan Whitlock stabs something covered in a black cloth on this altar (an animal?) and hands it to the witch standing in the middle of the circle behind him. She finally turns and we see—Amy. Tracy, who has genuinely cared for her, screams uncontrollably, giving herself away, and soon finds herself tied to the sacrificial altar. The next night is the witches' Sabbath. Drugged, Tracy will be their glassy-eyed sacrifice.

From her bedroom window, Malvina has seen Tracy enter the tomb after Amy. Suspecting that Tracy is in danger, she lifts herself out of her wheelchair and tries to climb down the stairs to a telephone, but Vanessa appears and causes her to fall. When Bill and Todd return, they find Malvina alive but rattled. She tells them Tracy is in the tomb.

Horrified, Bill and Todd race through the crypt and discover Tracy just ahead of the coven's arrival for a Black Mass. They escape and so Morgan Whitlock orders his followers to return to their homes. He remains in the tomb, however, with Amy and Vanessa, standing before a flaming cauldron. Morgan accuses Amy of allowing Todd to lead her "away from the old religion. You have disobeyed our priestess." In a chilling, soft whisper that hints of desperation, Amy replies, "That's not true. I am your servant and I respect and worship you."

At the same time, Todd learns from Tracy that she had followed Amy into the tomb earlier and he returns looking for her. "A Lanier returns to die!" Morgan announces with relish. Amy goes into screaming hysterics, fighting her uncle to save Todd. She tips the cauldron onto Vanessa, who embraces her as she, Amy, and Morgan are engulfed by flames. Helpless to save her, Todd watches in agony as his love perishes.

The conflagration quickly spreads to the Lanier mansion, and Bill, Tracy, and Malvina, joined by Todd, look on as the inferno collapses into a spectacular shower of sparks.[2]

Spalding's story avoids the cliché of a happy ending. Instead, *Witchcraft* is a brutally pessimistic treatise on the self-defeat of greed and power. The present, no matter how progressive or innocent, cannot escape the dire consequences of the past: Amy's love for Todd cannot conquer her inherited hatred of his family, and the innocent Laniers of the present cannot escape the sins of the Laniers of the past against the Whitlocks. The harsh, generational hand of Fate taps everyone's shoulder in *Witchcraft*.

Sharp remembers that Spalding's script "needed only minimal re-writes in terms of character or construction. Some adjustments were necessary because of location changes. It was the tightest of tight budgets, and so all locations had to be within thirty minutes of the studio [Shepperton]. If the setting Harry had scripted couldn't be found in the stipulated half hour radius, the setting, and possibly some action, had to be changed."

With art director George Provis, cinematographer Arthur Lavis, and camera operator Len Harris, Don Sharp translates Spalding's script into a moody, visual splendor of shuddery black and white. The atmosphere that they create of light and shadow, gray fog and cold rain underlines the Lanier family's schism of skeptics and believers. Sharp also overlays the modern setting with a Gothic visual style to highlight the centuries-old conflict between the Laniers and Whitlocks. Moreover, this visual quality and Sharp's placement and movement of the camera magnify the tension and fear.

The conflict between the two families, in the present and in the past, is at the heart of the entire picture, and Sharp carefully establishes this from the start. The film opens with a shot of a busy motorway that pans to the Whitlock graveyard, juxtaposing the fast-paced, noisy present with the ancient, silent dead of the past. The credits are shown over various shots of the rural graveyard, a pastoral setting that the modern highway seems to violate. One high-angle shot of a stone cross and a stone casket suggests that that grave will be of significance later. (It is Vanessa's.) The last shot in this sequence is of a destroyed graveyard marker. By connecting the present and the past in this fashion, Sharp creates a subtle uneasiness, a discordant quality that is mysterious, supported by Carlo Martelli's sparse music.[3]

Sharp follows this sequence with a shot of a bulldozer, noisily emerging into view through a heavy, gray fog in the graveyard, and then cuts to a close-up of its blade scooping up tombstones. In this image, modern civilization disrupts the sanctity of the past, with no reverence or respect for it. The man on the bulldozer is faceless in the fog, an indication that this modern, encroaching society lacks personality.

Such locations as the graveyard "were chosen for mood and atmosphere," says Sharp, "and they dictated what the interior sets should be. Once the style was set, everything fell into place—the crypt, for example. The first sketch of it was exactly right. We could not imagine it any other way. The placing of the crypt was important, too. It was seen in POV's [point-of-view shots] from the bedroom window, so a wide-angle lens would have been wrong. We did not, subsequently, want a lot of space around the crypt or other features crowding it. So, again, we went close enough for it to dominate. Somehow I always felt 'This is the right way to do it.' It was instinct. The sets also reveal a lot about the characters living in them. These people would have been out of place in a modern bungalow, as there would have been no link back to the past history of the families. Nor would there have been the contrast between a modern man with his modern machinery and the ancestral memory nurtured by the inhabiting of the old house, the old crypt, and the old graveyard. I doubt if the beliefs of Malvina and the fears of Helen would have worked in, say, a modern apartment."

The resurrection of Vanessa (foreshadowed in the earlier shot of her spoiled grave) is particularly memorable. Sharp uses one continuous movement to capture this. He starts with a medium shot of her sarcophagus, with the stone lid toppled over, and pans to Vanessa's feet. He then tilts up her body to a medium close-up that reveals a beautiful face. This slow build-up to her appearance is effective because viewers are expecting something horrible. (She is approximately 350 years old.) Sharp's direction builds up the realization that horror and death are often packaged in loveliness, which suggests the cunning, devious nature of evil. Welsh actress Yvette Rees, who portrays Vanessa, possesses a unique, frightening beauty that (like Barbara Steele's) is as alluring and erotic as it is difficult to describe. Her large eyes are unforgettable. (According to David Weston, producer Jack Parsons fell madly in love with her during the making of this film, although the passion was not mutual.) In this shot, Vanessa pulls her hood over her head, turns from the camera, and walks away in an icy rain until she is framed by tombstones and a giant stone cross, back lit to throw shadows and reveal her breath in the frigid, wet air. These fearful clouds of steam, streaming from her silhouetted figure, grant her an angry, dominating presence, one that reeks of vengeance given life and inexorable motion. Supporting this impressive image are the sound of the storm's gusty wind and the sight of pelting rain dancing on the tombstones.

Sharp's lack of cutting in such scenes creates a sense of creeping unease through movement of his camera or elements within his frame. His camera takes on a subjective quality that almost forces his audience into the role of participator, rounding corners with no idea what will be waiting in the darkness.

He does this again, starting with a close-up of the Laniers' clock tower chiming midnight. He slowly zooms out to a medium shot and then pans to the mansion. He tilts up to a row of upper windows and gradually zooms in to an extreme close-up of them that dissolves into a medium shot of Helen in bed asleep, as the camera continues to move toward her so that the two shots look like one uninterrupted movement. When Helen is in close-up, the camera pans right to expose a window in the distance as a sudden gust of wind lifts the curtains.

The slow, unbroken nature of this shot suggests a quiet, stealthy intrusion into Helen's bedroom that evokes her vulnerability. What is more, the suggestion is clearly that the

Whitlock points an accusing finger at Todd while Amy helplessly looks on.

audience is taking part in this silent violation. Once Sharp puts viewers off guard with this disturbing notion, he unexpectedly cuts to a close-up of Helen, troubled in her sleep as if feeling a presence. Given Sharp's approach, the off-balanced audience almost feels responsible, which intensifies the shock of the next shot, a close-up of Vanessa standing just inside the flapping curtains. She is still hooded, with the right side of her face totally obscured by shadow.

Sharp quickly cuts between close-ups of Helen and shots of Vanessa approaching her. Vanessa's haunting, high-cheeked face is totally eclipsed by shadow as she moves closer. Then it reappears, much like the moon emerges from behind a cloud, as she moves closer still, a lighting technique that fosters an eerie, anticipatory effect. Sharp next cuts to a two-shot of Vanessa beside the bed, raising her arms toward Helen and then pulling down her covers. He cuts to a close-up of Helen, blinking as she awakens and realizes something is wrong. Sharp wisely resists showing Helen discover Vanessa in a two-shot because their confrontation could not fulfill his audience's expectations after his terrific build-up to this moment. "The audience's imagination," asserts Sharp, "is often more fertile, more full of dread, than the reality a film can achieve." Thus, he leaves the confrontation to the viewers' imaginations by cutting to Bill and Tracy, as they climb the stairs and are suddenly startled by Helen's bloodcurdling scream. Of course, they race to her room to find her in hysterics. Although the witch is gone, Bill finds clay on the floor, evidence that Helen has been "visited."

Sharp's direction of Helen's death the next morning is equally impressive. Instead of using a long, flowing shot, he accentuates the terror of what happens to Helen with

Morgan Whitlock attacks Tracy Lanier (Jill Dixon), his intended sacrifice at the Black Mass.

staccato cuts. Helen drives off and Sharp crosscuts to Bill showing his grandmother the clay he found in Helen's bedroom. "Bill, you must go after her at once," she urgently orders him. "She's in great danger." Sharp cuts back to a shot of Helen behind the wheel, which zooms in to a close-up, and suddenly Helen glimpses something in her rearview mirror. Then Sharp cuts to a close-up of the witch sitting behind her (a tremendous, unexpected shock) with a look of sick satisfaction. Next he cuts back to Helen with large, staring eyes and no fear, obviously in some sort of trance. Then, in a series of long shots, we see Helen's car turn off into a rubbish dump and head toward a rocky cliff. Sharp cuts to a close-up of Helen regaining her senses just before racing over the edge to her death.

This sequence is edited to the beat of a lively death march. It is also evidence that Sharp may effortlessly vary his technique to translate the script's semantics into intrinsically interesting visual terms.

In planning his shots, Sharp explains that he does not "do actual storyboards, but I do use floor plans to work out the shots of each sequence. Early on, weeks before the start of shooting, the art department gives me sketches of the set, with a floor plan showing the suggested layout of the furniture. From this, I work out an approximation of how I will want to shoot it—in other words, make sure that I can stage the scene as I want it to be, given the doors, window, furniture, etc., as in the suggested layout. Quite often this means that part of the proposed set need not be built. Later, a day or two before shooting a sequence, when I am totally saturated by the 'feel' that the film is building up, I work out a detailed list of shots for each day's shooting—a blueprint. If an inspiration comes on the floor—from anyone: actor, cameraman, or me—I can accept it and integrate it into my plan. They like the gratification of instant creativity. I need to know at all times, however, where I am going, not 'How do I get out of this corner?' On tight schedules this helps the crew. Actors also find the method useful."

Sharp points out the irony connected to making good, low-budget films:

> I have sometimes wondered whether *Witchcraft* would have been so effective if I had had more time and money. These constraints forced me to think of the most economically creative ways to shoot. This meant no special effects, no trickery, nothing that would require more time or money. We simply had to put the story on the screen and make the audience believe it. I was lucky to learn valuable lessons of invention through financial constraints.
>
> I was lucky, too, in my DOP [director of photography], Arthur Lavis. He was a man without pretensions. There was never time to spare, so much of the lighting had to be simple. We quickly evolved a method, a style, which allowed for the shock moments to "happen" without any special atmospheric build-up or mood lighting, like the witch's sudden appearance in Helen's car. The mood was there, present from the opening frame of a sequence, and it was up to the actors, the camera, the sets, and the director's creative instinct to communicate—to manipulate, perhaps—the audience. Arthur was more experienced than I was at that time, and I think you have to be experienced to know what you can leave out—to know what is essential and what is merely "decorating the cake."

Camera operator Len Harris, who lensed many Hammer horror films for director Terence Fisher, also receives high praise from Sharp:

> *Witchcraft* was the only time I worked with Len. He was a quiet man, experienced, and quick to appreciate what you were aiming for. He'd give you exactly the set-up you had outlined—but then you'd find him making small adjustments, additions, and he'd say quietly, "Gov, can you have a look at this?" Maybe it was a tracking shot, and I'd ride beside him, watching through the finder while he operated, and would realize how he had strengthened a visual by an adjustment that brought a significant prop into a more dominant foreground position, or increased mood by an adjust-

The Whitlocks prepare for the Black Mass! Left to right: Amy, Morgan, and Vanessa (Yvette Rees).

> ment to the height of the lens during a pan and track. It wasn't just experience. It was a genuine feel for a genre that he loved. He was a nice, modest man.

Don Sharp—also a nice, modest man, generous with praise for co-workers—was born on April 19, 1921, in Hobart, Tasmania, Australia. He left school at age 16 and, he recalls, took a "clerical job in a department handling all government loans—for housing, to farmers, for disaster relief, etc. I was studying at night for accountancy. Not my idea, but through strong pressure from my parents. Then, accidentally, I discovered the local amateur theatre group—and I was hooked! Stage struck. I directed my first play when I was 18."

When he was 19, Sharp joined the Royal Australian Air Force and served in the Far East. After he was demobilized in 1944, he decided not to return to his job in Hobart and began work as an actor. "I worked almost nonstop in theatre in Melbourne and Sydney," recalls Sharp, "and at the same time, pre-TV days, did a huge amount of recorded radio drama, as well as some writing. But I knew I wanted film work. All I managed to get was three days in a documentary."

Sharp moved to London in 1948 and found work in a new play in London's West End. He also acted in recorded dramas for BBC radio. "But I was meeting only closed doors at the film studios. Casting directors didn't answer letters or weren't interviewing new actors. I did get to see one casting director for a film which had an Australian character in it. I was told that research had shown that the average height of an Australian was five feet and ten inches. I was too tall! 'Frustrating' was the word for it."

By 1949 Sharp was sharing a flat with Frank Worth, who had been a combat cameraman during the war and was now an assistant director with a documentary outfit. "Frank wanted to direct," explains Sharp. "I was also sharing a dressing room at the Strand Theatre with Darcy Conyers. Darcy was an in-and-out-of-work actor who wanted to do more with his life."

Out of their shared frustrations and ambitions came the idea of the three of them making a film of their own. "Darcy owned an old boat on the Orwell River in Suffolk," says Sharp, "where we spent occasional weekends sailing. It was the only exploitable asset any of us owned. It had to be the center of the movie." A story evolved of young men returning after the war to restore a sailing boat and establish a boat-building and sailing center. Sharp wrote the screenplay, supported by Worth's technical knowledge. Worth directed, with Conyers and Sharp co-producing and starring in the film. "Getting the money and the distribution was an epic," says Sharp, "but eventually we raised eight thousand pounds and made our supporting feature, with cast and crew all on the same basic wage."

The film, *Ha' Penny Breeze* (1950), went out on circuit release to some pleasant notices, but Sharp was not able to see it. Instead, he spent most of 1950 and 1951 in the hospital with what he describes as "a recurrence of a wartime medical problem." Luckily, *Ha' Penny Breeze* caught the attention of Sir Michael Balcon and John Grierson at Group Three, a company financed by the government to develop and promote new talent. They asked Sharp to join them upon his release from the hospital.

"It proved to be a fascinating set-up and tailor-made for someone with my lack of film know-how," explains Sharp. "Their scheme was to team an experienced producer with a new director, an experienced camera operator with a new DOP, an experienced screenwriter to collaborate with a new writer, and so on. It worked, on the whole, very well. Some fifteen or sixteen films got made." Among the directors who, with Sharp, gained early experience thanks to Group Three were Lewis Gilbert (*Alfie* [1966], *Educating Rita* [1983]), and John Guillerman (*The Blue Max* [1966], *King Kong* [1976]).

Sharp worked on four films with Group Three. In each case, he collaborated with an established screenwriter, and three of their scripts were based on his original stories. "On each film I was also personal assistant to one of their more experienced producers named Herbert Mason," explains Sharp. "So, apart from scripting, I went on the location hunts, sat in on art department discussions with the producer and director, attended casting sessions, learned about budgeting, and saw the daily rushes with the editor and producer. I spent time on the floor watching, asking questions, and learning through the goodwill of the technicians. I sat in on each process from assembly to rough cut to fine cut to effects recording to music sessions to final dub."

From story idea to final show print, Sharp learned about every stage of filmmaking. "Senior technicians, too, were very generous with their time," adds Sharp, "and many evenings, over a couple of drinks after shooting, I'd get very valuable 'tutorials' from an experienced DOP or an editor. During the screening of the dailies with the producer and editor, they would discuss, assess, and criticize the previous day's work, and often Herbert Mason would ask me what I thought. I grew more confident in my appraisal, criticism, and constructive suggestions."

Finally, at the end of the second film Sharp worked on with Group Three, an impressed Mason suggested that Sharp direct. "So, on the next two films, in addition to scripting and being his personal assistant, I directed the second unit. And, once again, I was hooked. I *had* to direct. Nothing else could possibly be so satisfying."

Balcon offered Sharp a staff job at Ealing Studios, but it soon became obvious to him that it would be many years before he might even hope for a chance to direct solo. Grierson advised him not to go to Ealing and, instead, to venture out and find experience on the job. "I took the gamble," says Sharp, "and providentially an opening came up with Howard Thomas, the boss of Associated British Pathe. AB-Pathe made the weekly Pathe newsreel for the cinemas." That was not all that AB-Pathe produced, however. "It was the ideal place for me," says Sharp. "I directed advertising films, documentaries, several dramatized training films for the War Office, and a couple of fiction features for the Children's Film Foundation, all through AB-Pathe. It was a golden opportunity to learn one's craft."

Sharp feels that he was fortunate to "progress through acting to writing to directing. It seems to be an ideal combination. You capture your audience by intriguing them with your story situation and development, and you satisfy them by persuading belief in the characters. A director must have the ability to get the best from these two essential elements. It means cooperation and collaboration. As a director, I've been able to appreciate problems of both writers and actors and be sympathetic to them because I have done both jobs."

By the mid-1950s, Sharp was a busy director, sometimes taking on second unit work. Then, in 1962, he helmed one of Hammer's best horror films, *Kiss of the Vampire* (1962).[4] Sharp translated its routine script into a minor masterpiece of vampire cinema. It remains the film he is most remembered for, although he has directed many excellent films since then, including such genre favorites as *The Face of Fu Manchu* (1965), *Curse of the Fly* (1965, another Lippert/Parsons production and Harry Spalding script), *Rasputin—the Mad Monk* (1965), *The Brides of Fu Manchu* (1966), *Psychomania* (1971), and *Dark Places* (1972).

Sharp explains that "years earlier, Bob Lippert's editor had been Elmo Williams. Elmo was now a production executive with 20th Century-Fox, for whom I had recently worked as second unit director on *Harry Black and the Tiger* [1958, Hugo Fregonese]. Elmo had also seen *Kiss of the Vampire* and recommended me to Lippert. I read the script for *Witchcraft*, I liked it, and I liked the double challenge to make an audience accept the reincarnation of a witch and to do so in a modern setting. Although I was told I must use Lon Chaney, Jr., I also liked that the rest of the casting was down to me."

Often praised by Christopher Lee as an exceptionally good director with actors, Sharp certainly deserves such commendation judging from the fine performances in *Witchcraft*, particularly in the case of Lon Chaney. The actor was in unfamiliar surroundings among the Britons. Not a terribly stable person at this time, Lon must have been particularly lonely without his wife, Patsy, his Rock of Gibraltar since their marriage in 1937. As a result, his drinking may have been heavier than usual during the film's production.

Sharp confirms this:

> Yes, he did drink heavily. This problem meant that we had to make sure that his dialogue scenes were

completed by lunch time. I found him quite cooperative to work with.

Unfortunately, he was no longer flexible or capable of much variation. In the first scenes we shot with him, I thought I could get what I wanted in his performance by going for more rehearsals or more takes. He would listen carefully to what I had to say and would try to do it. There might be some slight improvement, but then we'd reach a stalemate—he couldn't do any better. He was in a haze. He wasn't in full control, either mentally or in the technical side of his performance. I had to learn when he had reached his maximum and settle for it. Also, the more quickly we got through his scenes, the less time he had in his dressing room with his bottle. Wardrobe staff and one of my assistants said he would drink a bottle of vodka before lunch. I don't know, but certainly he was of very little use in the afternoon. His broad strokes suited the character, but his performance could have been better.

"I didn't spend much time off the set with him. During the day I was very busy, and in the evenings he bordered on the incoherent. In the few times when we did talk, not about the film, the overwhelming impression was of a sad and lonely man. I only encountered the equivalent feeling of loneliness in one other person. That was working with George Sanders [shooting *Psychomania*] not many months before his death.

Ironically, Chaney's unhappiness may have contributed to his performance, because Morgan Whitlock exudes frustration and woe between his bouts of fury.

Script supervisor Renee Glynne's memories of Chaney on this film shed light on Sharp's difficulty in soliciting a good performance from Chaney and also the actor's almost pathetic desire to impress others. "Lon Chaney, Jr., had a briefcase full of booze," she remembers, "and was drunk more or less the whole time. Couldn't remember his lines, couldn't walk from A to B. He looked all right in the finished film, but to get him to do anything was simply awful. We'd be doing 20 takes for just one line. After shooting one day, I was in the bar with Arthur Lavis, the cameraman, and Lon Chaney was sitting in the corner. We were all drinking away and suddenly Chaney went into his soliloquy from *Of Mice and Men* [1939], which he'd done 25 years before. He did it without faltering and it was so beautiful, so wonderful, that we were all in floods of tears. And all this after a whole day in which he can't remember and he can't walk...."[5]

On a short, 20-day shooting schedule that began on January 13, 1964, Sharp was under immense pressure, exacerbated by Chaney's problems. Thankfully, Sharp's understanding, patience, and support for Chaney resulted in a good performance instead of a catastrophe. Evidence does exist in one shot, however, that the director had to settle for a less-than-perfect take. Toward the end of the film, when Todd visits Amy against her uncle's wishes, Chaney walks in on the two of them and angrily says, "I warned you not to come here, Amy [instead of Todd]." The mistake, sandwiched between other rapidly spoken lines, is not easily noticed, but Sharp must have been desperate for a usable take to include it.

In 1964, moviegoers would have expected to see Karloff, Price, Cushing, or Lee playing a character who nurses expensive brandies in an exclusive country club. Each of those actors possessed a charm and dignity as polished as a king's silver chalice. Chaney's characters, however, would have been spotted, sleeves rolled up, pounding down beers at the corner bar, unceremoniously blowing off the head of each foamy mug. Precisely because Morgan Whitlock was a modern blue-collar figure garbed in Victorian threads, Chaney was uniquely qualified to play the role.

Chaney brought something else to his character that the other members of the Professional Horror Actors Society could not offer, because they did not live in the daunting shadow of a more famous father, the Man of a Thousand Faces. Morgan Whitlock is a sweaty, meat-and-potatoes Anglo-Saxon trapped, and eventually destroyed, by a legacy bigger than himself—the Whitlock name. The parallel is unavoidable, and Chaney must have felt it strongly.

Chaney's often loud, enraged, enthusiastic animation contrasts greatly to the quiet, classically trained British cast in this film. This contrast is effective—Morgan Whitlock is of Anglo-Saxon stock, after all—and warranted because of the Laniers' terrible injustices to his family's ancestors. The contrast also works well because Sharp keeps Chaney within the bounds of the rage his character would feel. These emotions are then underlined by the contrast, without allowing Chaney to seem over-the-top.

Although Chaney could slice the ham deliciously thick under good direction to save films like *The Alligator People* (1959, Roy Del Ruth), his hamminess could also contribute to the dreadfulness of other, poorly directed movies like *The Cyclops* (1957, Bert I. Gordon). Sharp, however, nurtured a natural, less affected performance from Chaney. "Unless an actor's performance is based in reality and the circumstances, then it's phony," explains Sharp. "I can't ask an actor to do something phony. There has to be a reality about it. Even if it's a fantasy, it can still work because of something in the character of the person...."[6] Chaney's fine, unobtrusively controlled performance (even while under the influence) probably results from Sharp's meticulous handling and from the strong identification Chaney likely felt with Morgan Whitlock.

Sharp often used Chaney's presence and power as an actor to enhance the themes of the story. For example, during the opening minutes of the film at the Whitlock cemetery, in a formidable, low angle shot, Chaney runs toward the camera, then faces the bulldozer, and screams, "Stop! Stop it! This is blasphemy! Stop it! Go back! Go back I tell you!" Chaney himself looks large and mighty, like a bulldozer, only louder than the real one and bold enough to confront it. As the patriarch of the Whitlock family, he is a perfect match against modern progress at the expense of family honor. Throughout, Sharp uses Chaney's blustery presence to reinforce this central idea.

Yet Chaney could also be subdued when necessary—and Sharp almost seems to pay him homage as a genre star at these moments with terrific, eerily lit close-ups of Lon's mountainous face. For example, in the chapel where the Black Mass is to be performed, Chaney (in a medium shot) quietly says, "Vanessa will be angry.... Yes [smiles cheerfully], she is coming to us. You will see her [zoom-in to close-up of Chaney] tonight, yourself [long, chilling pause, then said in a whisper]—at the Sabbath." This

Whitlock is a blue-collar, grandfatherly devil out for revenge.

wonderfully rendered line captures the nuances of its horrible implications, and Chaney makes a terrifying impression as a grandfatherly devil with his thick, unmatching eyebrows, puffy eyes, and fleshy cheeks.[7] Unlike his contemporaries, Chaney did not look like a horror star, which is why he is so much more realistic and frightening.

The other performers are equally well-cast and effective in their roles. As David Weston points out, most of them "were quite well-established English stage actors, which added to the flavor of it." Jack Hedley is appropriately handsome and sincere, handling his character's gradual move from disbelief to reluctant acceptance of the supernatural in a believable manner. David Weston and Diane Clare display a strong love as Todd and Amy, without becoming maudlin. Clare is not the kind of buxom beauty typical of Hammer films at this time. Instead, she is soft-spoken and possesses an appealing vulnerability. Her sensitive performance implies a deeper problem with her uncle, without giving away the surprise that she has been coerced into his witches' coven. Viewers genuinely like her and, consequently, Amy's sacrifice for Todd has more strength emotionally.

Clare[8] has played in Hammer's *Plague of the Zombies* (1966, John Gilling), Robert Wise's masterful *The Haunting* (1963), and *The Vulture* (1967, Lawrence Huntington). Her best mainstream role is as a nurse in J. Lee Thompson's excellent *Ice Cold in Alex* (1958), with John Mills, Sylvia Syms, Anthony Quayle, and Harry Andrews.

Clare, who appears in most of Chaney's *Witchcraft* scenes, recently recalled her work with the actor: "I was young at the time and, since I was doing a series of films, I tended to be moving (happily) from one set to another. As a consequence, my memories are fragmentary and naive. I had, for example, no idea that Lon Chaney had a drinking problem. I remember him as being completely professional on the set and, as a man, at all times being unassuming, friendly, and unfailingly a gentleman. I liked him. The set was friendly and professional. Most of the English cast had worked together before, which helped, and my impression is that they all felt, for Mr. Chaney, the same as I."

David Weston, who also appeared in Roger Corman's *Masque of the Red Death* (1964) and Jim Clark's *Madhouse* (1974),[9] paints a much grimmer portrait of the actor: "I'd always admired Lon Chaney. *Of Mice and Men* was one of my favorite films, and I remember him being so wonderful in a scene he had in *The Defiant Ones* [1958, Stanley Kramer]. I wanted to talk to him, but I couldn't. He didn't seem to want to make personal contact with anybody. He brought a bottle of vodka around with him all the time and drank from it before he went onto the set. This caused him to sweat a lot. He seemed to do whatever they wanted him to do, but you couldn't actually have any conversation with him. He did his stuff. He got his lines out mostly all right. There weren't lots of takes, but you couldn't make contact with him. We never got to know him. We never got close to him at all. It was sad. I'd love to have spoken to him about his films—and about his father."

Weston believes the movie "does stand up well. Don Sharp made it better than the producers expected it to be, I think. He was good—and a nice man. He didn't get in our way. He made us feel relaxed and gave us our heads. He just let us do it. He banked that we could. For a low-budget picture, *Witchcraft* has great atmosphere, and it was lovely working with Marie Ney, who was a wonderful old actress, and Viola Keats. It was an enjoyable three weeks of my life."

Viola Keats and Marie Ney, as the Lanier matriarchs, came to this film after long, distinguished careers, and they expertly add the initial fear element when the younger Laniers dismiss the supernatural as hokum. Keats' next, and last, film was *The Devil's Own* (1966, Cyril Frankel), for Hammer.

Of his hand-picked British cast, Sharp remembers that he was delighted with their contributions.

> Jack Hedley, our leading man, was quiet, sane, thoughtful, caring, rational—all the facets of Bill Lanier's character. Jill Dixon, a talented actress, possessed a directness and incisiveness in her work, yet she somehow was vulnerable, too. Marie Ney was a grand old lady with a huge theatre background. Diane Clare was new then and full of promise. David Weston, a good actor, was fresh-faced, with an open, honest quality. I chose each based on their abilities and their personal qualities. They were a splendid team of non-starry people whose ordinariness lent a great strength to the situation. If they could believe in, be afraid of, the supernatural threat, then the audience would be

> much easier to convince. Audience identification is so very important in a story where you know you will have to battle to get them to suspend their disbelief. Put a bimbo in the Jill Dixon role and the whole film would have collapsed. They were a lovely cast to work with.

Although most reviews praised *Witchcraft* as an excellent, low-budget, genre film, it did not do especially well at the box office in competition with the slick and colorful Hammer horrors and Roger Corman's Poe films. It was no help that *Witchcraft* was released on a double bill with an unfunny horror farce, *The Horror of It All* (1964, Terence Fisher), another low-budget black and white film produced by Lippert and Parsons.[10]

Criticism continues to be kind to *Witchcraft*. Ivan Butler, in his *Horror in the Cinema* (New York: A.S. Barnes & Co., 1970), credits the film for its "unusually convincing atmosphere of brooding evil... the whole film is pleasantly old-fashioned in appearance." In *A Heritage of Horror* (London: Gordon Fraser, 1973), David Pirie lauds it as "a remarkable little film... with several extremely fine moments which utilise the possibilities of cinema cheaply and persuasively." Phil Hardy's massive *The Encyclopedia of Horror Movies* (New York: Harper & Row, 1985 ed.) calls this "Poverty Row effort... a very well made movie with a particularly good beginning. Sharp's strong point... is the way he can make a set or a location come alive and assume an importance almost equal to that of the actors." John Stanley's *Revenge of the Creature Features Movie Guide* (Pacifica, CA: Creatures at Large Press, 1988) notes that the film "transcends its speedy Robert L. Lippert production values to become a sustaining (albeit minor) chiller...." Don G. Smith, in his chronicle of Chaney's career, *Lon Chaney, Jr., Horror Film Star, 1906-1973* (Jefferson, NC: McFarland, 1996) extols the film's merits: "With the passage of the years... the suspenseful and atmospheric *Witchcraft* has rightfully established a loyal fan following."

Unfortunately, *Witchcraft* has not yet been released to video and rarely turns up on television. Hopefully, one day this skillfully made film will be more widely available, for in it Chaney's misery and alcoholism combine with his talent and the right script and director to create a final tribute to his abilities in the genre that made him famous.

CREDITS: Producers: Robert Lippert and Jack Parsons; Director: Don Sharp; Screenplay: Harry Spalding; Music: Carlo Martelli; Musical Conductor: Philip Martell; Director of Photography: Arthur Lavis; Art Director: George Provis; Editor: Robert Winter; Production Manager: Clifton Brandon; Assistant Director: Frank Nesbitt; Camera Operator: Len Harris; Sound Editor: Spencer Reeve; Continuity: Renee Glynne; Hairdresser: Joyce James; Wardrobe: Jean Fairlie; Make-up: Harold Fletcher; Sound Recordist: Buster Ambler; Assistant Editor: Clive Smith; Production Secretary: Barbara Allen; Filmed in England at Shepperton Studios and nearby locations (including Oakley Court next to Bray Studios); Released 1964 by 20th Century-Fox (U.S.); Black and white; 79 minutes

CAST: Lon Chaney (Morgan Whitlock); Jack Hedley (Bill Lanier); Jill Dixon (Tracy Lanier); Viola Keats (Helen Lanier); Marie Ney (Malvina Lanier); David Weston (Todd

Lanier); Diane Clare (Amy Whitlock); Yvette Rees (Vanessa Whitlock); Barry Linehan (Myles Forrester); Victor Brooks (Inspector Baldwin); Marianne Stone (Forrester's secretary); John Dunbar (Doctor); Hilda Fennemore (Nurse)

Special thanks to Paul M. Jensen, Diane Clare, A. C. Lyles, Don Sharp, and David Weston. Thanks also to David Hanks, David J. Hogan, Brett Miller, Patty Musgrove, Jonathan Rigby, Don G. Smith, and Gahanna-Lincoln High School (Ohio) librarians Dana Johnson, Linda Swarlis, Dr. Duff L. Helvoigt (Ashland University, Ohio) and Huey Walsh.

Chapter Notes

1. Beck, Calvin Thomas. *Heroes of the Horrors*. New York: Macmillan Publishing Co., 1975: 276. Price probably made this comment about Chaney during the making of *The Haunted Palace* (1963, Roger Corman) or shortly thereafter. Chaney was his co-star in that film.
2. Actor David Weston remembers that filming the fiery sequence in which Amy, her uncle, and Vanessa perish "was bloody dangerous." Also, the effective finale of the burning Lanier mansion does not use stock footage. "The art department," explains Sharp, "made inquiries to find if any large, old house was about to be demolished. One such was found. It was on large grounds and was to be pulled down to make way for the erection of a number of smaller, new houses. Normally, the demolition company salvaged doors, windows, interior paneling, etc. We did a deal whereby we destroyed the house by fire and compensated them for the loss of salvageable materials. Obviously, we had to make window details, curtains, etc., to match with our sets and pile inflammable materials into the rooms. We got the okay from the local authorities and warned the local Fire Services of the extent, the time, etc., so they would not interfere and ruin our sequence. They did, of course, have a crew standing by on site in case things got out of hand. It was a huge success, although dozens of neighbors phoned the fire station. Some calls went to a different, neighboring fire station, and there was a panic to head off their engine as it came racing down the road. Luckily, the standby crew persuaded them that it was all under control."
3. In addition to *Witchcraft*, Carlo Martelli composed scores for two Hammer films, *The Curse of the Mummy's Tomb* (1964, Michael Carreras) and *Prehistoric Women* (1967, Michael Carreras), and also *It* (1967, Herbert J. Leder). According to Randall D. Larson's *Music from the House of Hammer* (Lanham, MD: Scarecrow, 1996), "Two minutes of Martelli's music from *Witchcraft* was reused as the end title for *Quatermass and the Pit* (otherwise scored by Tristram Cary)."
4. Don Sharp offers some insights into making effective horror films: "I don't agree with the idea of a horror climax in every reel. This is self-defeating. You get to the stage where each 'shock' has to be more shocking than the previous one or your audience is disappointed. The horror moments become more important than the characters, their relationships, and the story dynamic. If the audience doesn't care about—relate to—the characters, there will be no real involvement with their plight. The audience become mere spectators: 'Let's go watch the lions kill a few Christians.' Cinema is not a spectator sport; it invites the audience in to share what the protagonist is experiencing.

"In certain genres of cinema, expectation equals suspense. You are taken forward fearing, knowing that something is about to happen. Who was it said, 'Suspense is having the courage to go slowly'? Travel slowly, then. Engage the expectations, don't let the audience off the hook, don't give them the relief of action/horror/shock when they expect it. Keep them where Hitchcock had them—on the edge of their seats waiting till almost anything is a relief or release. It is the duration and the quality of the expectation that is important, not necessarily the moment when the shock is delivered."

5. Rigby, Jonathan. "Calling the Shots." *Hammer Horror* 7 (September 1995): 39.
6. Don Sharp interviewed by Colin Cowie in *Little Shoppe of Horrors* 10/11 (July 1990): 53.

7. Chaney's memorable physical appearance in *Witchcraft* was captured by artist Basil Gogos for a colorful cover of *Famous Monsters of Filmland* 67 (July 1970).
8. Diane Clare is married to British author Barry England (*Figures in a Landscape*, *Conduct Unbecoming*, et al.).
9. David Weston offers this anecdote from *Masque of the Red Death*: "Roger Corman was making a big play for Jane Asher. I remember we were sitting at lunch one day—Roger, Jane, Vincent Price, and myself—and he asked her to go out. She said, 'No, I've got a boyfriend.' Roger said, 'What's your boyfriend do?' Jane answered, 'Well, he's a pop star.' Roger replied with words to the effect, 'Listen, darling, pop stars come and go. They're forgotten in six months' time.' And, of course, that was Paul McCartney."

Of Vincent Price, Weston says, "He was lovely, lovely. Almost ten years after *Masque*, I was out of work and ran into him on Sloane Street. He asked me what I was doing, and I told him, nothing. He got me two days on *The Revenge of Dr. Death* [U.K. working title for *Madhouse*]." Weston also worked with Peter Cushing ("a delightful man") in a 1963 BBC-TV production of *Julius Caesar*.
10. Jack Parsons became a producer after selling his chain of cinemas in northern England. For a short time, in the mid-1960s, he kept Shepperton Studios open with his low-budget film productions. David Weston remembers that when he acted in *Becket* (1964, Peter Glenville) at Shepperton, the studio was thriving with stars and busy technical crews, but during the making of *Witchcraft*, it was like a ghost town. They were the only ones there. Script supervisor Renee Glynne reports that, a few years after producing *Witchcraft*, Parsons hanged himself in a Soho Square office (Rigby, Jonathan. "Calling the Shots," *Hammer Horror* 7 [Sept., 1995]: 39).

Don Sharp adds his memories of Jack Parsons and Robert Lippert: "Jack's input was to look constantly worried and to assume that you would take too long and it would cost too much, not a positive or helpful attitude. But, then, Jack was not a creative producer. Away from the studio, he was a friendly, generous man. The change came at the studio gates. Bob Lippert was a totally different personality. He wanted the finished product to be on budget, but he had flair and showmanship. He knew that certain sequences were highlights and needed to be filmed to their full entertainment value. It might put us behind schedule, but if I convinced him that we could shoot other sequences more simply and, thus, regain lost time, he was, well, not happy, but he held his peace until we had shot the 'simple' scenes and were back on schedule. Then he was happy. I liked Bob.

"Part of our problem staying on schedule was due to the peculiar situation throughout the British studios in 1964. As film after film was canceled, the studios began to lay off staff. The rule with dismissing staff was 'Last in, first out.' So, by the time all other productions at Shepperton had been canceled, the studio was staffed by technicians who had been there the longest, i.e., they were the oldest. Quite a few of them had been 'sheltered' by their colleagues for some time. Now they had to do tough jobs they were no longer fit enough to perform, such as elderly 'sparks' [set electricians] climbing the long ladders to the grid. That was no longer a swift operation! It was also an odd feeling to be the only movie—a small, tightly budgeted film—in the enormous spaces of Shepperton Studios."

WORLD'S WEIRDEST MOVIE

FIVE STRANGE TALES OF TERROR FROM BEYOND THE GRAVE!

DR. TERROR'S "GALLERY OF HORROR"

IN PATHÉCOLOR AND TOTALVISION

LON CHANEY · JOHN CARRADINE · ROCHELLE HUDSON

[Courtesy Ronald V. Borst/Hollywood Movie Posters]

DR. TERROR'S GALLERY OF HORRORS (1967)

by John Stell

My mother used to tell me that if I couldn't say anything nice about someone or something, I shouldn't say anything at all. But if I did that when discussing *Dr. Terror's Gallery of Horrors* (1967), this would be a very short piece—and I don't think my editors would like that very much. Sorry Mom. The fact is that this "gallery of horrors" is gallery of ineptitude—acting wise, direction wise, script wise... well, you get the picture. (Get it? Gallery, picture? Badaboom!) In an effort to get somebody to see their movie, American General Pictures did get three "names": Lon Chaney, John Carradine, and Rochelle Hudson. But even talented people can do very little if they receive no support from the cast and crew. *Dr. Terror's Gallery of Horrors* is a low point for all involved.

The film shamelessly tries to cash in on the anthology craze that was kicked off by Amicus' *Dr. Terror's House of Horrors* (1964). (Even the title is a steal!) Even though horror's finest anthology is 1945's *Dead of Night*, that film spawned no imitators. Roger Corman gave us three Poe stories in *Tales of Terror* (1962), and United Artists, three Nathaniel Hawthorne yarns in 1963's *Twice Told Tales*. But with Amicus' five-stories-for-the-price-of-one, a sub-genre was created which includes classics like *Kwaidan* and *Black Sabbath* (both 1964), and *Spirits of the Dead* (1967). Amicus—Hammer's chief rival in 1960s—produced many fine anthologies including *Torture Garden* (1967), *The House That Dripped Blood* (1970), *Asylum* (1972), *Tales From the Crypt* (1972), *From Beyond the Grave* (1973), and *The Vault of Horror* (1973). Although most films contained tales of varying quality, these films were, overall, well produced and well acted—or, in a word, professional.

But professional is the last word one would use to describe the "tales of horror" told to us in *Dr. Terror's Gallery of Horrors*. John Carradine is apparently the doctor of the title, introducing five ventures into the supernatural. But there is nothing terrifying in his comments. He is merely telling us, in a most uninteresting way, events surrounding the stories. At least, that's what he seems to be doing until we actually see the yarns and realize the intros do nothing for the story at hand.

The witch trials of Salem, Massachusetts, for example, provide the set-up for the opening yawner, "The Witch's Clock." A couple (Roger Gentry and Karen Joy) move into a 300-year-old castle and discover an ordinary looking grandfather clock in the basement. (The husband, Bob, says, "I've never seen a clock like that before," which must mean he's never seen any grandfather clock before.) When they get the clock working, a knock is heard at the door and it turns out to be John Carradine as a friend of the former owner. But when it's revealed the last owner was a witch, and that the witch put a spell on a clock, Bob stops the clock from working, causing the visitor and the couple to go up in flames. The conclusion has a new couple move in and find the clock.

This poor opening story sets the tone and mood for the rest of the film: cheap and foul. There is only one set in this part: covered furniture—except for that clock—in a nondescript room. Clearly shot on a sound stage, the actors' voices echo and sound too far away from their boom mikes. The acting is terrible. Gentry and Joy simply read their lines and, when trying to get emotional, they just get louder. Carradine seems to be having fun; at least he grins a couple of times. At one point he starts to hypnotize the missus, but this leads to nothing since the husband happens upon them and quickly starts the fire. The superimposition of the fire over the characters is really... bad. There's not even any smoke.

American International Pictures fans may take delight in the fact that the exterior shots utilized throughout *Dr. Terror's Gallery of Horrors* are from the Corman-Poe-Price series of films. When the castle "burns" in "The Witch's Clock," the destruction is right from *The House of Usher*, as are assorted shots of the castle. It is so obvious that inside and outside are from different sources that the film fails in creating any atmosphere.

Not any better is the second feature, "King Vampire," which has the "modern" London police force looking for a 13-time killer. London? There's nary an accent to be heard from anyone. The police work involved has an inspector visit the streets (we get two sets this time: a police office and a street) calling out, "Who has seen King Vampire's face?" This guy's so upset he's very close to just screaming, "Somebody talk to me!" and then bursting into tears. At one point he gets a description of the murderer: dark hat and clothes, slight figure, and the face of a corpse. Later a comment is made that everyone's been picked up who matches that description!

The twist to the story is that the vampire turns out to be the secretary of the police chief. This might have been interesting if there had been other suspects, or if someone had accidentally thought to give a performance. As it stands now, the reaction to this "surprise" is, "Big deal."

No surprises are even attempted in "The Monster Raid," the third offense. Told in flashback by a rotting corpse (and a rotten looking rotting corpse at that), we find out the cadaver was once a noble scientist (Ron Doyle) trying to... well, it's not exactly clear. It has something to do with knowledge passed down genetically, hypnotism, a truth-telling serum, and, perhaps, mind reading. Anyway, the doctor's wife (Rochelle Hudson) is having an affair with family friend Dr. Savard (Roger Gentry). But Savard is only using her to learn about her husband's formula. The two kill the doctor, but he is rescued by the Ygor-like Desmond (Vic McGee). It seems that the poison actually preserved the doc's vital organs.

So the build-up is in place, and the lovers are about to get their just deserts. And what happens? The corpse shows up, laughs a little, and then strangles them. That's it. What the hell was the purpose of telling us in advance the doctor survives? The story has nowhere to go, no shocks to spring. There's lots of AIP footage in this one (*The Raven*, *The Terror*). There's also a bit of an in-joke here: Dr. Savard was the name of Boris Karloff's character in *The Man They Could Not Hang* (1939), although his name was spelled Savaard.

If you make it through the first three you may as well stick around for number four: "The Spark of Life," perhaps the funniest (unintentionally) of them all. Two medical

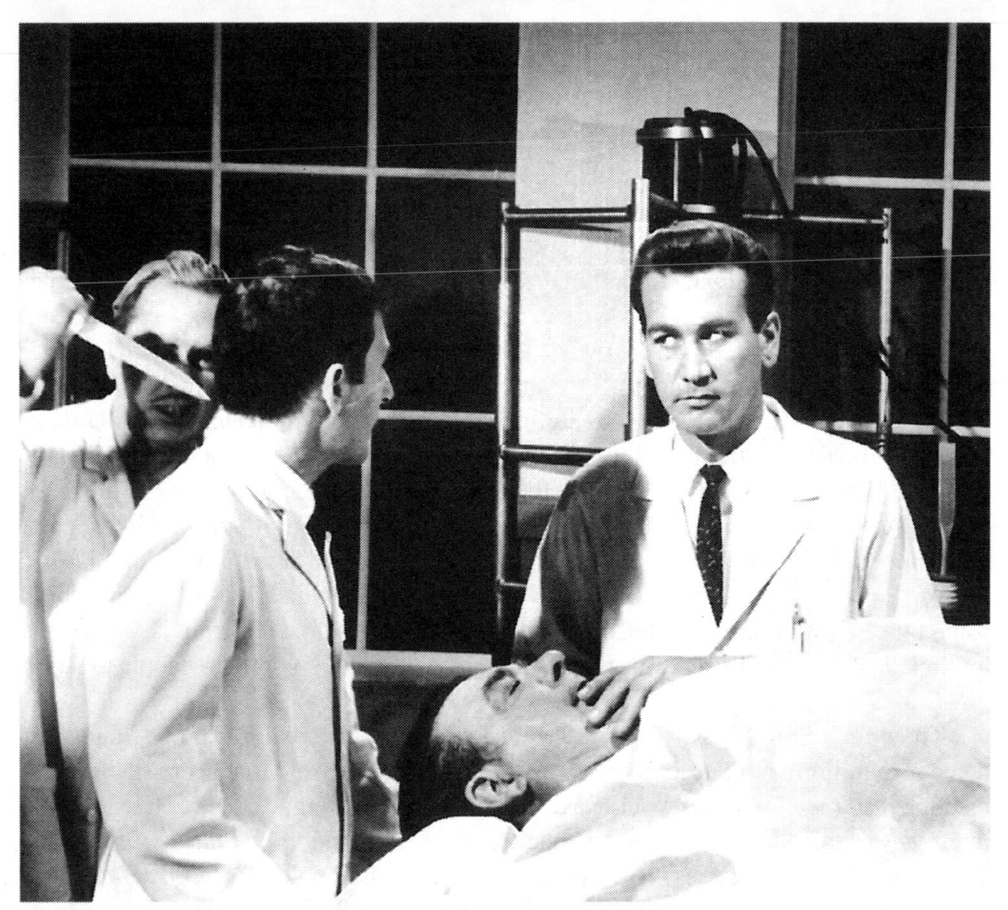

Lon Chaney is the first actor in this film to show any kind of emotion, or, to put it another way, the first person to "act."

students (one of them named Cushing!) learn that their professor Dr. Mendell (Lon Chaney) knew Dr. Frankenstein. (This story supposedly takes place in Scotland but you won't hear any accents or bagpipes.) Mendell too has a theory that electricity may restore life to the dead. "Is electricity life?" he asks them. They decide to test the theory. And in the film's most absurd line, Mendell asks, "How did you think of such a thing?" right after he's explained his theory to them. He decides to help them, and the three revive a recently executed murderer. They quickly decide they must kill the killer. But at the fade out, Dr. Mendell is dead, and the dynamic duo are about to join him.

Lon Chaney is the first actor in this film to show any kind of emotion, or, to put it another way, the first person to "act." But Lon is really overacting—and it's a breath of fresh air. He treats the shopworn material so seriously, so intensely, that his ultimate cry of, "I'm a genius!" is the film's single biggest laugh. Chaney doesn't just walk through the part, he tramples it. In most cases this would be a bad thing. But this time, it actually brings the film its only lively moments.

Last up is the story of "Count Alucard," and you get no points for guessing the subject matter. Mr. Harker (Roger Gentry) visits the Count (Mitch Evans) to sell him the Carfax Abbey property in London. But at night, Harker is visited by Malena (Karen Joy), and you do get points if you can understand one damn word she says to him. Anyway, before she can bite Harker, villagers are heard outside and she flees. Harker joins the party to help them search for a vampire, who turns out to be—surprise (at least Harker acts surprised)—Malena.

Returning to the castle Harker tells Alucard he knows there is another vampire. Just as Alucard is about to "reward" Harker for his cleverness, Harker is revealed to be a werewolf—one who plans on eating the townsfolk himself.

The only possible excuse for this final segment, a not-at-all disguised reworking of *Dracula*, is the werewolf twist at the end. But this is little more than a steal from *Dr. Terror's House of Horrors*. In the final segment of that film, a kindly doctor double-crosses his colleague because the associate's wife is a vampire—as is the kindly doctor. And the town isn't big enough for two doctors or two vampires. So what we're left with is another cheap-jack installment. One might say this is a fitting conclusion.

If anthologies are only as strong as the weakest element, then *Dr. Terror's Gallery of Horrors* boasts no strengths, only weaknesses. The cast just says their lines, director David L. Hewitt just lets the camera roll (notice how the camera rarely even moves!), and the script just churns out the clichés. A film like this probably sounded like a great idea: stories about witches, vampires, werewolves, and mad scientists taking place in spooky castles or on fog-bound streets, with angry villagers nearby. You would think some bit of atmosphere would accidentally sneak in. But no. The truth is, a film this low-budgeted needed the involvement of imaginative and high-spirited people to pull it off.

The three top-billed performers were, sadly, aging stars being paid low sums for name recognition. While Lon Chaney and John Carradine were true genre staples who no doubt had their fans who would pay to see them in anything, Rochelle Hudson had a more "respectable" resume including the classic *Rebel Without A Cause* (1955). The Oklahoma City–born actress made two films with Peter Lorre: *Mr. Moto Takes A Chance* in 1938 and *Island of Doomed Men* in 1940. During the 1960s she appeared in a pair of William Castle films: *Strait-Jacket* (1964) and *The Night Walker* (1965). Clearly her visit to the papier-mâché sets of *Dr. Terror's Gallery of Horrors* was a career low point.

Hudson isn't given a role, really. She's the cliché adulteress, and she's not having a good time with the part. She's given silly lines like when she tells her love she suspects he's using her as a "pawn" to get her husband's formula. Like he was really going to tell her she's right. Later she has a "soliloquy" as she realizes she was correct in her suspicion. If these are supposed to be her "moments," she disappoints. Who could blame her?

John Carradine was appearing in a lot of junk at this point in his career. His late 1960s' efforts include *Billy the Kid vs. Dracula* (1966), *Hillbillys in A Haunted House* (1967), *The Astro Zombies* (1968), and *Blood of Dracula's Castle* (1969). A truly dignified actor, Carradine had done fine work in films such as *The Hound of the Baskervilles* (1939) and *The Man Who Shot Liberty Valance* (1962). He is thought of, by some, as the best Dracula based on his work in Universal's *House of Frankenstein* (1944) and *House of Dracula* (1945). But unlike his horror peers, Carradine never had what one might call a definitive role. Lugosi already had the Dracula crown, and Carradine never attempted Frankenstein's Monster, the Wolf Man, or the Mummy. Frequently he portrayed a "mad scientist" in films such as *Revenge of the Zombies* (1944), *The Face of Marble* (1946), and *The Unearthly* (1957).

But if one had to chose a "classic" performance by Carradine, it may his work in Edgar G. Ulmer's *Bluebeard* (1944). He portrays Gaston Morrell, a crazed artist-puppeteer. He strangles women who model for his paintings, driven insane by the memory of a model he loved who turned out to be a prostitute. Carradine gives a non-hammy, sensitive performance as the title character who is compelled to kill. He cannot seem to help himself, and this tragic self-awareness makes for a touching suspense tale.

Unfortunately, Carradine cannot do anything for *Dr. Terror's Gallery of Horrors*. Serving as our host (Dr. Terror?), he can do little to hide the dull nature of the introductions. Although he stands tall and lectures authoritatively, the lessons coming out of his mouth are unimaginatively conceived, telling horror fans nothing we don't already know: that witches were burned in Salem, Massachusetts; that police techniques have advanced through the years; or that scientists perform sometimes questionable experiments. These segues feel more like time fillers, a way to stretch thin ideas even thinner and get a respectable running time. Carradine is actually better than his role deserves. But, unfortunately, this can hardly be seen as a compliment, even though it is meant as one.

Although John Carradine has the most screen time of the "stars," it's Lon Chaney who gets top billing. He arrives just in time to liven things up too. Although his performance is not exactly good, it certainly isn't bad, and that gets him to the top of the list in terms of acting. He brings energy to his role. He shows more than one emotion. Like Carradine, Chaney gives the part more than it deserves.

In his best performances (Lennie in *Of Mice and Men*, Larry Talbot in *The Wolf Man*), Chaney showed an ability to make his characters instantly likable. He allowed himself to come across as a big teddy bear. Some of that manages to get through in his portrayal of Dr. Mendell. First he's the caring professor who's excited by his seemingly eager students. He seems like a nice enough guy. Then, he's panic stricken at the prospect of trying to bring back the dead. Suddenly, he's excited about the opportunity to test his theory. And there's still more emotion to come! He's horrified when he realizes the revived corpse is a murderer (isn't that always the way it goes?). Lastly, he's sad as he prepares to put the revived fellow back to "sleep." All these emotions are packed into a thinly written part which develops in about fifteen minutes. Chaney's a hurricane compared to his fellow thespians. Actually, if more of the cast had taken Lon's no-holds-barred approach, *Dr. Terror's Gallery of Horrors* might have been a so-bad-it's-good film.

It also wasn't such a good idea to use the same actors in all the stories. Roger Gentry, Ron Doyle, and Vic McGee keep showing up to remind us how bad they were the last time we saw them. Worst acting honors probably go to Karen Joy, whose

[Courtesy Ronald V. Borst/Hollywood Movie Posters]

performance as the vampire Malena is so bad that we're thankful we cannot hear her lines. Vic McGee appears in all but the second tale, so he wins for most roles.

Director David L. Hewitt made several bad genre films during the 1960s: *Horrors of the Red Planet* (1964), *Monsters Crash the Pajama Party* (1965), and *Journey to the Center of Time* (1967). But his anthology is the worst of the lot. The film has absolutely no style or imagination, no suspense or originality. He and his screen writers don't even try to come up with an interesting linking device for the stories. In *Dr. Terror's House of Horrors*, the tarot deck serves to move from "prediction" to "prediction." In *Asylum*, the tales are told by the criminally insane. In *From Beyond the Grave*, the narratives are tied by antiques. And with a title that includes the word "gallery," you would think a light bulb might have gone off and suggested a picture or painting link (which is exactly what Rod Serling did in 1969). But that would have required some thought. And even if there had been a clever linking device, the movie still would have sucked.

I used to believe every "bad" film had its supporters. There are actually people out there who argue artistic merits exist in the film canons of Ed Wood, Jr., Andy Milligan, and Herschell Gordon Lewis. But no one seems to have a kind word for *Dr. Terror's Gallery of Horrors*. Leonard Maltin rates the film a "BOMB" in his annual video guide saying the film is an "utter monstrosity." Bryan Senn and John Johnson rate the film a "1" in their *Fantastic Cinema Subject Guide*. *VideoHound's Movie Retriever* gives the film a "Woof!," its lowest rating: "Goes by many names—stinks in all of them." And in his *Psychotronic Encyclopedia of Film,* Michael Weldon uses such words as "terrible" and "ludicrous" when discussing the film, but ultimately recommends it on that basis! Well, it does have some big laughs.

One of the most telling facts about *Dr. Terror's Gallery of Horrors* is the amount of title changes it has had. You may have seen the film as *Return From the Past*, *The Blood Suckers*, *Gallery of Horror*, or *Alien Massacre*(!). You don't suppose somebody's trying to trick us, do you?

While it's not exactly praise, the fact of the matter is Lon Chaney is perhaps the only thing going for *Dr. Terror's Gallery of Horrors*. The actor had played his last memorable horror role in 1964's *Spider Baby* as chauffeur to a family of wackos. Keeping busy mostly in Westerns, Chaney's last genre credit would be as the mute lab assistant in the late Al Adamson's *Dracula vs. Frankenstein* (1971). Sadly, Chaney's final horror roles could not touch the ones that were made available to him during the 1940s. Anyhow, I hope maybe he and John Carradine shared some pleasant memories while working on *Dr. Terror's Gallery of Horrors*, because there certainly isn't anything memorable about this dreck. The character of Dr. Sedgewick sums it up best: "Well that was all pretty dull." You said it, doc.

CREDITS: Producers: David L. Hewitt and Ray Dorn; Director: David L. Hewitt; Associate Producer: Gary R. Heacock; Screenplay: David Prentiss and Gary R. Heacock; Original stories: Russ Jones; Director of Photography: Austin McKinney; Art Director: Ray Dorn; Editor: Tim Hinkle; Make-up: Jean Lister; Released 1967 by American General Pictures; 82 minutes

CAST: "The Witch's Clock": John Carradine (Tristram Halbin); Roger Gentry (Bob Farrell); Karen Joy (Julie Farrell); Vic McGee (Dr. Finchley); "King Vampire": Ron Doyle (Brenner); Margaret Moore (Mrs. O'Shea); Ron Brogan (Marsh); Roger Gentry (Mob Leader); "Monster Raid": Rochelle Hudson (Helen Spalding); Ron Doyle (Dr. Spalding); Roger Gentry (Dr. Savard); Vic McGee (Desmond); "Spark of Life": Lon Chaney (Dr. Mendell); Ron Doyle (Dr. Cushing); Joey Benson (Dr. Sedgewick); Vic McGee (Amos Duncan); "Count Alucard": Roger Gentry (Harker); Mitch Evans (Count); Karen Joy (Vampire); Vic McGee (Burgermeister); Gray Daniels (The Coachman)

SPIDER BABY, OR THE MADDEST STORY EVER TOLD (1968)

by Bryan Senn

"Fiends and ghouls and bats and bones,
And teenage monsters and haunted homes,
A ghost on the stair, a vampire's bite,
Better beware (heh, heh, heh), there's a full moon tonight.

Sit round the fire with this cup of brew,
A fiend and a werewolf on each side of you,
This cannibal orgy is strange to behold,
And the *maddest story* ever told!"
—Opening and closing stanzas of the *Spider Baby* theme song sung by Lon Chaney, Jr.

"I was pleased to hear people laughing; it's supposed to be funny."
—Writer/director Jack Hill after *Spider Baby*'s "30th Anniversary Showing" at Los Angeles' Nuart Theater.

From the opening theme song, it's obvious that *Spider Baby* is something unusual. What it *is*, exactly, can be hard to define. Is it a horror film, a black comedy, a satire, a cheap exploitation movie? (Given that Lon Chaney, Jr.'s off-key, gravely voice belts out the title tune, it is most assuredly *not* a musical.) Actually, *Spider Baby* is all these things and, more importantly, a film that remains completely unique, one that simply can't be pigeonholed but must be seen to be believed—and enjoyed.

Cannibal Orgy, or The Maddest Story Ever Told (the picture's shooting title) was filmed in twelve days in August 1964 for the paltry sum of $65,000 provided by two real estate developers-cum-movie moguls, Paul Monka and Gil Lasky. "They had been in dramatic school [UCLA]," explained director/screenwriter Jack Hill, "wanted to do a movie, and got a hold of a treatment I had written called *Cannibal Orgy, or The Maddest Story Ever Told.* They'd read scripts before, but never anything like this."* Indeed. (When asked where he received his inspiration for such an offbeat story, Hill was nonplused. "It just came to me in a flash," he said, "and I wrote it down.... It just sounded like a good idea. I can't tell you where those things came from.")

Unfortunately, soon after the film's completion, the bottom dropped out of the California building industry and the two financier/producers wound up in bankruptcy court, resulting in the film being attached by their creditors. "It was locked up in a lab for about four years," related Hill. "[Low-budget promoter] David Hewitt had seen it early on at a screening and tried to get it, and waited and waited, and when it was finally

Lon Chaney clowns with famed comedian Mantan Moreland in this publicity pose on the set of *Spider Baby.*

available, he grabbed it. But by that time (1968) it was pretty difficult to get distribution for a black-and-white movie on the top half of a bill." Consequently, Hewitt (after changing the title to *Spider Baby, or the Maddest Story Ever Told*) initially released it in support of lesser color features. Then, two years later, he retitled it *The Liver Eaters* and sent it around the drive-in circuits, reaping a substantial profit (putting paid the old question of "What's in a name?").

The film begins with Peter Howe (Quinn Redeker) cheerfully reading from a book entitled *Directory of Rare and Peculiar Diseases*: "The Merrye Syndrome, so called because its only known occurrence is among the descendants of one Ebeneezer Merrye, is a progressive age regression beginning about the tenth year and continuing steadily throughout the victim's lifetime. It is believed that eventually the victim of the Merrye Syndrome may even regress beyond the pre-natal level, reverting to a pre-human condition of savagery and cannibalism. Many authorities do not accept the existence of the Merrye Syndrome." At this, Peter looks up (directly at the camera) and says, "Incredible, but true nevertheless. I know—only too well. Of course, there's no Merrye Syndrome any more. It was extinguished, forever, from the human race that fateful day ten years ago—" The image wavers and the flashback that makes up the bulk of the film begins.

A messenger (Mantan Moreland) rides his delivery scooter up to the secluded, dilapidated mansion called the Merrye House. (Exteriors were shot at a house high atop a hill in Highland Park. Though in the film the Merrye Mansion looks removed and forbidding, Jack Hill related that "it was actually surrounded by other structures and telephone poles, etc., so that only one or two angles on the building were possible in order to make it look isolated.") When his knock goes unanswered, the messenger sticks his head through an open window to see if anybody's home—and is promptly hacked to death by a teenaged girl, Virginia (Jill Banner), playing "spider." When Bruno (Lon Chaney), the family chauffeur and caretaker, arrives home, we meet the elder brother Ralph (Sid Haig), who acts like an overgrown toddler, and Virginia's other sibling, Elizabeth (Beverly Washburn). After chastising Virginia for playing spider when it had been forbidden, Bruno reads the letter that the ill-fated delivery man had brought. It's from a lawyer, announcing that he and his clients, distant relations of the Merryes, will be arriving that evening.

Bruno prepares the "children" for the unwanted visitors ("We'll have to keep some secrets," he instructs them), who consist of the officious and abrasive lawyer, Mr. Schlocker (Karl Schanzer, complete with an amusing Hitler mustache and a huge cigar), his perky secretary Ann (Mary Mitchel), their greedy client Emily Howe (Carol Ohmart), and her reluctant brother Peter (Quinn Redeker), who's just along for the ride and wants no part in Schlocker and Emily's plan to bilk their distant relations out of the Merrye fortune.

When Emily and Schlocker insist upon staying the night, Bruno and the children prepare a dinner for them (the main course being a cooked cat(!) which Ralph had caught, and which Peter assumes to be rabbit). Despite Bruno's best intentions and efforts, a night of terror ensues for the intruders as the snooping Schlocker runs afoul of the two sisters: Emily is chased into the woods by Ralph (where he attacks and presumably rapes her), Peter is tied up by Virginia playing her "spider" game (and narrowly escapes the messenger's fate), Ann is kidnapped and taken down to the cellar, and a now-mad Emily wanders back to the house where she mortally wounds Ralph before ending up as a meal for Uncle Ned and company.

With things now completely out of hand, Bruno, having given the dying Ebeneezer Merrye "a solemn oath that I'd never allow their unfortunate malady to become the object of public scrutiny," determines to end the Merrye line once and for all. He steals some dynamite from a nearby construction site, gathers the children around him with the promise of this "new toy," and lights the fuse. As Peter rescues Ann and stumbles out of the house, Bruno gives a final shrug and the Merrye curse ends in a flash of light and a big bang.

The film then returns to the narrating Peter, who finishes, "And so the Merrye Syndrome was extinguished forever with the family that carried it. My own branch of the family, being so distant, we never suffered from the curse." But as his young daughter (the fruit of his subsequent union with Ann) walks out into their suburban garden, she spies a spider in its web and stands, staring and transfixed, while "THE END" comes up on screen—quickly followed by a "?"

By all accounts, the *Spider Baby* shoot was a happy one. "I remember just how much fun we had," recalled Beverly Washburn warmly. "We shot it very fast," added Mary Mitchel, "it was kind of a quick experience, but it *was* fun." Sid Haig concurred: "I *loved* going to work every day." This sense of fun and enthusiasm permeates the production, oozing out through the warped cracks to add an offbeat liveliness to the eccentric characters and bizarre situations.

Spider Baby's opening set-piece (the delivery man's demise) encapsulates the picture's tone and focus, as it's one part grotesque horror and two parts black comedy. When the ill-fated courier sticks his head through the open porch window to see if anybody's home, the sash suddenly slams down on his back, pinning him there like a specimen in a child's bug collection. Immediately, the teen-aged Virginia scuttles out into the room, hunched over, her arms crossed in front, holding two large knives in her hands like the forelegs of some huge insect. "I caught you!" she says gleefully. "I caught a big fat bug right in my spider web." With that she takes a loose makeshift net (her "spider web") and tosses it over the astonished man's head. "And now the spider gets to give the bug a big *sting*." At this, her tongue darts out of her mouth in anticipation and she brings her knives gleefully together—click-click. She then rears up and starts slashing, shouting "Sting!" with each vicious blow.

Director Jack Hill and cinematographer Alfred Taylor's effective staging, combined with precision editing, emphasizes both the horror and the absurdity of the scene. POV shots from the victim's perspective as the bizarre assailant approaches her prey suddenly give way to close-ups of Virginia frenziedly slashing and shouting "sting, sting, sting!" Suddenly an ear falls to the floor and an abrupt zoom briefly hammers the horror home. This gruesome sight is immediately juxtaposed with the humorous one of the man's posterior sticking out of the window on the porch side, his legs kicking comically as the violent assault continues.

The scene then concludes with Virginia brought up short from her continued slashing by a sharp "Virginia!" uttered by her sister, Elizabeth. The camera then shows us Elizabeth: A twenty-something woman garbed in a little girl's pinafore dress with her hair up in pigtails. "Virginia, are you crazy?" she asks scornfully (and the viewer has to chuckle at this obvious question). "You're bad, *bad*," continues Elizabeth, "Bruno's going to *hate* you." Virginia looks down, momentarily cowed, and Elizabeth gives a superior smile and tilt of her head—a five-year-old chastising a misbehaving three-year-old. It's a scene both funny and chilling in its macabre absurdity.

Like another quirky and effective (and better-known) independent, Tobe Hooper's *The Texas Chain Saw Massacre*, the warped "family" in *Spider Baby* provides the film with its most intriguing characters. *Un*like that later terror classic, however, the "normal" people intruding into the bizarre scene in *Spider Baby* remain interesting as well, with scripter Hill taking care to write them as unusual, offbeat characters while *director* Hill makes sure his cast plays them as such. For instance, Emily (played with a wonderful biting arrogance by the sexy Carol Ohmart), while appearing the typical greedy, disdainful relative on the surface, turns into a sensuous hedonist (enjoying twirling about in sheer stockings and black lace) in the privacy of her boudoir.

In contrast, Emily's kindly, oblivious brother Peter hasn't a bad word for anybody. When confronted with the disquieting sight of the bald-headed Ralph acting like an overgrown infant, Peter's face lights up as he says, "Aww, he's just a big kid!" At dinner, Peter enthusiastically helps himself to the grotesque fare offered (unsavory-looking fungus, a wiry mass of weeds, a cooked cat, and some kind of bug stew). When Bruno points out to the others (who prove understandably reluctant to imbibe), "As I told you, our diet is very austere—but it's most healthful," Peter cheerily pipes up,

Bruno (Chaney, Jr.) looks fondly at the children Ralph (Sid Haig) and Virgina (Jill Banner).

"You know, that's great! I think everybody ought to eat like that." One almost expects him to burst into a chorus of Monty Python's "Always Look on the Bright Side of Life."

Quinn Redeker makes Peter an almost farcically likable protagonist, with his open face, wide smiles, and willingness to go along with whatever bizarre events unfold (including playing "Spider" with Virginia—much to his eventual regret).

Still, *Spider Baby*'s focus is on the family. Sid Haig's expressive face and energetic portrayal turn Ralph into a perfectly realized (and effectively exaggerated) toddler. "I tried to do some muscle contraction things," said Haig, "and I just kind of played with it to see if I could make my body work the way I wanted it to. I thought, 'He's on the brink for the animal tendencies to come through,' so I tried to get that."

Jill Banner plays Virginia as a fun-loving, mischievous innocent, whose fascination with (and deadly emulation of) spiders is both amusing and horrific, making her the ultimate "naughty little girl." At one point she comically sticks her tongue out at her sister after Elizabeth tattles on her for killing the messenger, while at another she violently stabs the pieces of a jigsaw puzzle with the tip of her ever-present butcher knife.

As Elizabeth, the blond, pig-tailed Beverly Washburn projects a heady mixture of little-girl coquettishness and ferocious savagery. With her wide, inviting smiles and her goody-goody demeanor, she effortlessly turns from coy flirt to feral killer (her face twisted in fury as she shouts "Kill him! Kill him!" before brutally stabbing Schlocker with a pitchfork).

Then there's Uncle Ned, Aunt Clara, and Aunt Martha kept in a pit in the cellar—the result of the Merrye Syndrome in its advanced state. (Why a pit? "Interiors were shot at a soundstage in Glendale," explained Hill, "which at one time had been an auto garage and therefore had a *pit* built into the concrete floor. This made the stage a very useful place for horror pictures, as building a set with a pit would have otherwise been prohibitively expensive.") Hill wisely keeps these mysterious figures largely out of sight, occasionally showing a filthy, grasping arm while dubbing in disturbing grunts and mewlings. The result is both frightening (for the viewer's imagination conjures up all manner of depraved terrors) and poignant (because we know that this is the inevitable fate of the three Merrye "children").

It's a testament to both writer/director Jack Hill and to the individual actors' efforts that the three Merryes are indeed sympathetic and even likable, each possessing a weird charm that draws the viewer into their world—and their plight.

Caught between the two groups (straddling the normal and the bizarre, as it were) is Lon Chaney as Bruno, the faithful family chauffeur-turned-guardian. His is the only character that can seemingly function in—and relate to—both worlds, and much of the film's humor comes from Chaney's delicate balancing act as he tries to cope with the two disparate groups coming together (with disastrous results).

When Bruno arrives in the car, Elizabeth says, "Bruno, Virginia hurt somebody real bad; you ought to *hate* her," in a little girl nyah-nyah tone (as if tattling on her sister for stealing from the cookie jar). Bruno's response: "Elizabeth, how many times have I told you it's not nice to hate!" Not "Oh my God!" or "What happened!" or even an astonished "What?!!"—just "It's not nice to hate."(!)

Later, Bruno opens the letter from the lawyer, and Elizabeth asks, "It's something bad, isn't it?" At this Bruno replies, exasperated, "How many times do I have to tell you, just because something isn't good doesn't mean it's bad?!" Virginia then chimes in, "It must be very bad." Chaney, struggling mightily to maintain his patience, only answers, "Nothing is *very* bad" (an odd sentiment considering there's a mutilated corpse, still warm, lying not ten feet away).

As Chaney plays him, Bruno is an open, honest, simple man, yet one who is placed in the unenviable position of trying to maintain the charade of normalcy. With his very first scene, Chaney's subtly expressive playing illustrates this dilemma. After properly instructing his ward that "it's not nice to hate," he glances over to see the messenger's body sticking half out of the porch window. Chaney gives a pitying "oh," then looks again and gives a louder, drawn out "ohhh"—this one of disapproval and irritation as he moves toward the corpse. Looking down at the body, Chaney briefly closes his eyes and brings his hands together in front of his chest—as if trying to draw from some inner strength. Opening his eyes again, he says softly, "One time I leave them alone, now this—," and trails off, his hands opening in a gesture of futility and his expression one of troubled resignation.

Then, when Virginia and Ralph first see each other, they both start jumping up and down with joy as Virginia squeals "RalphRalphRalphRalphRalph!" At this Chaney starts to smile at the obvious pleasure of his two charges. But the smile suddenly fades before fully formed, and his eyes drop as he gives a slight shake of his head, realizing the sad absurdity of it all.

With the arrival of the "normals," Chaney makes the most of the opportunities presented for sly comedy. "I'm proud of you, Virginia," Bruno tells his young ward as

Director/screenwriter Jack Hill goes over a scene with Lon Chaney, Jr. on the set of *Spider Baby.*

she tries (vainly) to make a good impression at dinner, "you're doing so well." Chaney beams like a proud parent, and one can't help but feel both affection and anxiety for his character and his doomed task. Then, upon offering a dish of mushrooms to his reluctant guests, Bruno explains, "You see, [Virginia] has an uncanny knack for picking only the—uh—non-poisonous ones." Chaney's honest, smiling face and slight pause adds a welcome touch of humor.

Chaney is not above spoofing his own image (and those of his two most famous monster-characters). At dinner, when Peter asks Ann if she's a horror film fan, she bursts out enthusiastically, "Oh the Mummy, I *love* the Mummy! The way he walks—step-scrape, step-scrape. Oh, and the Wolf Man—grrrr!" At this, Chaney's face falls and he says worriedly, "There's going to be a full moon tonight."

Lon Chaney was Jack Hill's first choice for the role of Bruno. "At first," related Hill, "his agent pretended that, since it was a horror picture, Lon should receive a much higher salary; but we just didn't have the budget for it, and luckily, that same agent also represented John Carradine. So when we asked him to send the script to Carradine, Chaney quickly accepted our offer [a mere $2,500] because he loved the script and really wanted to do the picture—particularly as it gave him a chance to do comedy, which he had rarely been given before—and he didn't want to lose it all to his rival Carradine."

In fact, the actor was so enamored of the project that he remained on his best behavior throughout the filming (perhaps realizing that, though in a low-budget production, he was finally being offered a worthy role—at a time when such opportunities had seemingly dried up). "He was an alcoholic at the time," stated Hill, "but, since he wanted so badly to do a good job on this film, he made a truly heroic effort to stay on the wagon during the shoot, allowing himself only one glass of beer in mid-afternoon in order to get through the day." Chaney remained sober up until the very last day. ("On the last day we ran until four o'clock in the morning—" explained Hill.)

Chaney's determination held fast even under the most adverse conditions, for the shoot proved to be a physically grueling one for him. "He was very uncomfortable most of the time," remembered Hill, "suffering badly from the August heat in a non-air-conditioned building, so that someone had to stand by with a bucket of water and chamois to wipe the sweat off his face between takes."

Hill recalled that Chaney "felt he hadn't gotten the credit in his career that he'd earned. He was justly proud of his performances in *High Noon* and his parts in *Of Mice and Men* and *The Wolf Man*. He was a very underrated actor."

Hill also remembered Chaney expressing some animosity toward another of his horror rivals. "He seemed a bit jealous of Boris Karloff," recalled the director, and was "vocally quite bitter that he was not as highly regarded as Karloff.... Several times he did say, 'That guy isn't one bit better than me.' Lon told me that Karloff's strong suit might have been his ability to do dialogue well. Lon felt he wasn't very good at dialogue, but if you look at *Spider Baby*, he had many lines and he was pretty good. He'd grown up with his grandparents who were deaf, so he felt like he had learned to communicate with his body and wanted more chances to do visual things. But he was good with his lines."

By all accounts, Chaney was both professional and enjoyable to work with. Beverly Washburn recalled that "Lon Chaney was a very gentle and kind man; he was a wonderful man." Jack Hill simply stated, "He was wonderful." Sid Haig concurred: "He was great to work with; he was a lot of fun." Haig told how "on the first day I said, 'Mr. Chaney, they want you on the set.' And he turned on me and said, 'Don't ever call me Mr. Chaney again. We're working together—I'm Lon and you're Sid, okay?'"

Haig recollected that "when [Chaney] was working he was very intense and focused. I think [*Spider Baby*], oddly enough, is one of his better films—particularly in the scene where he decides it's time for the line of Merryes to end. When we shot that, when Jack hollered 'cut,' there was a silence. And I looked around and everyone was crying. An ovation started; they wouldn't let him off the stage for five minutes."

Apart from Lon Chaney, Jr. (and perhaps one-time sex symbol Carol Ohmart, though by this time her brief film career was all but over), the film's most recognizable player was Mantan Moreland. Though, as the doomed delivery man at the film's beginning, Moreland's part is little more than a cameo, the beloved black comic still manages to slip in a few of his trademark quips and pop-eyed glances, setting the stage for the hilarious horrors to come (of which he becomes the picture's first recipient).

Born in 1902 in Monroe, Louisiana, Mantan Moreland ran away from home at age twelve. He subsequently worked in traveling minstrel shows as a barefoot dancer, joined the Hagenbeck Wallace circus, acted in Vaudeville, and worked in various nightclub acts and stage shows before breaking into films in 1937. Moreland appeared in over 125 movies from 1937 (*Sprit of Youth*) to 1973 (*The Young Nurses*). His popularity peaked in the 1940s when he made 103 films in only ten years (including two with his name in the title—*Mantan Messes Up* and *Mantan Runs for Mayor* [both 1946]). Moreland also acted on stage and even worked on Broadway in a 1957 all-black revival of *Waiting for Godot*. Among his film credits are the horror/fantasy entries *King of the*

Zombies (1941), *A-Haunting We Will Go* (1942), and *Revenge of the Zombies* (1943). After suffering a stroke in 1963, Moreland moved (with his wife and daughter) from New York to California. His first film after his recovery was *Spider Baby.*

"Mantan Moreland was a delight to work with," recalled Jack Hill. "He was rather bitter over the fact that the civil rights movement virtually destroyed his career, as it had become no longer fashionable to cast African-Americans in menial or comic roles. Mantan felt that his type of comedy was in no way degrading, that the black audience appreciated it, and that it was most unfair that producers had lumped it together with the Stepin Fetchits, etc."

Upon its brief (and unnoticed) initial release in 1968, *Spider Baby* was ignored by the critics (and even by the trade publications). Only in the last decade has anyone bothered to review or write about it (though not in any great detail)—with generally positive results.

In the Re/Search book *Incredibly Strange Films*, Jim Morton calls the picture "one of the best examples of extreme, idiosyncratic cinema both witty and macabre." Of Chaney he says: "Lon Chaney, Jr.—whose acting was usually somewhat substandard—is brilliant as Bruno, giving the character just the right qualities of compassion and desperation."

In his bio-filmography, *Lon Chaney, Jr.,* author Don G. Smith concurs: "Chaney gives his best performance of the 1960s, and one of the five or six best of his career."

The Phantom of the Movies (in *The Phantom's Ultimate Video Guide*) calls *Spider Baby* "truly unique" and "certainly one of the weirdest stories ever committed to celluloid, sort of like a William Castle vision on psychedelic drugs."

Even mainstream critic Leonard Maltin (in his *Movie and Video Guide*) labels it a "not bad little chiller... at its best it's both scary and funny."

Scary and funny indeed, *Spider Baby* remains one of those illusive rarities in horror cinema (or *any* branch of film for that matter)—a complete original. For Lon Chaney, Jr., it offered the actor one final worthy characterization late in his career (as well as a rare opportunity to play comedy). Chaney rose magnificently to the occasion. The Karloffian has *Targets*, the Lugosiphile has *Abbott and Costello Meet Frankenstein*, and now, thanks to its recent video/laserdisc/big screen resurrection, Lon's Legion has *Spider Baby.*

CREDITS: Alternate Title: *The Liver Eaters* (re-issue title); Director/Screenwriter: Jack Hill; Producers: Paul Monka, Gil Lasky; Director of Photography: Alfred Taylor; Production Supervisor: Bart Patton; Associate Producers: Alan Riseman, Marvin Levine; Art Director: Ray Story; Music: Ronald Stein; Assistant Director: Bart Patton; Assistant Cameraman: Gil Haimson; Script Supervisor: Barbara Bohrer; Gaffer: David Stern; Best Boy: Robert Pickering; Key Grip: Carl Olsen; Wardrobe: Joan Keller; Still Photographer: Frank Zuniga; Sound: Lee Strosnider, John Broadrick; A Lasky-Monka Production; 86 minutes

CAST: Lon Chaney (Bruno); Carol Ohmart (Emily Howe); Quinn Redeker (Peter Howe); Beverly Washburn (Elizabeth Merrye); Jill Banner (Virginia Merrye); Sid Haig (Ralph Merrye); Mary Mitchel (Ann Morris); Karl Schanzer (Mr. Schlocker); and Mantan Moreland (Messenger)

*Quotes attributed to Jack Hill are from interviews by Jeffery Frentzen (*Fangoria* magazine), Michael Copner (*Cult Movies* magazine), the director's appearance at the "30th Anniversary Showing" of *Spider Baby* at the Nuart Theater in West Los Angeles, and correspondence with the author. Quotes from Sid Haig, Beverly Washburn, and Mary Mitchel are from their appearance at the anniversary screening.

WHEN TIME RAN OUT: THE LAST ROLE

by Mark A. Miller

The 1973 advertisement for Ohio's Kenley Players, which appeared in the *Columbus Dispatch*, promised a tantalizing cast for this summer stage revival of *Arsenic and Old Lace*. In addition to Lon Chaney, Jr., Margaret Hamilton, better known as the Wicked Witch of the West in *The Wizard of Oz* (1939, Victor Fleming), was to play Martha Brewster. She bowed out and was replaced by Nan Wilson. Michael Dunn, often remembered for his recurring part as Dr. Loveless on *The Wild, Wild West* TV series, canceled out of his role as Dr. Einstein to make a movie in London, *The Abdication* (1974, Anthony Harvey). The 3-foot-6-inch-tall actor died on August 29, 1973, during the film's production. He was replaced in the play by Art Ostrin.

Finally, the courageous Lon Chaney—plagued by alcoholism, numerous other illnesses, and the loss of part of his vocal cords to cancer—accepted the offer to play Jonathan Brewster, a stage role for which Boris Karloff and later Bela Lugosi had received excellent notices in the 1940s. Chaney planned to use a special throat microphone to be heard and had even made some practice recordings with it. Although he began studying his lines, the performance was not to be. The actor died at his home on July 12, 1973. Chaney's part was given to Peter Lupus, the brawny actor who played Willy Armitage in the long-running TV series, *Mission Impossible*.

LON CHANEY, JR.—ACTOR
by Don G. Smith

In researching my book *Lon Chaney, Jr.* (McFarland and Company, 1996), I continually encountered critical comments disparaging my subject as an actor. According to predominate popular opinion, Chaney was a limited actor who could play a moron with the best of them, but who struggled in roles demanding depth. He was, critics said, the monotonous son of a great actor. Though he was Universal's biggest horror film star of the forties, most critics give him little respect as a good horror film actor either, pointing out that he pales before Chaney, Sr., Karloff, Lugosi, and Lorre. After the forties, Chaney's horror films generally declined in quality, as did the actor's reputation. When one thinks of post-forties horror film actors, Price, Cushing, and Lee come immediately to mind—but not Lon Chaney, Jr. Most of these critics based their conclusions on having seen Chaney's horror films and *Of Mice and Men*—a good sample, I must admit. But Chaney's corpus of work contains much more than horror films and Lennie. I think I can say with confidence that I have probably seen more of Chaney's film and television performances than almost anyone else, and when one considers his work as a whole, a certain respect and appreciation develops.

The purpose of this chapter is to compare and contrast Chaney as an actor with Lon Chaney, Sr., Bela Lugosi, Boris Karloff, Peter Lorre, Vincent Price, and Peter Cushing. I have already compared Chaney and Christopher Lee in my book, so I will not repeat that examination here. I will compare actors knowing that such exercises depend a great deal on personal taste. I think Humphrey Bogart was right in saying that the Academy Award process is flawed. To be fairly judged against one another, Bogart said, the actors in question must all perform the same role and be guided by the same director. Even then, taste will enter the equation. Nevertheless, here we go.

I am not an actor; therefore, I do not have the insights into acting that professional actors have. Like most people, I evaluate actors on the basis of how believable they make the characters they portray. Roles demanding greater depth and versatility require better acting. On that basis, I regard the likes of Laurence Olivier, Michael Redgrave, Spencer Tracy, and Anthony Hopkins as great. There are some others, but Lon Chaney, Jr. is not among them.

Lon Chaney, Jr. vs. Lon Chaney, Sr.

You just know that Chaney, Jr. is bound to lose this evaluation, and he does. For years, most people saw Lon Chaney, Sr. in a handful of classic films such as *The Hunchback of Notre Dame* (1923) and *The Phantom of the Opera* (1925). In the last few decades, other of Senior's films have surfaced, many of them directed by Tod Browning. Interestingly, as these films have depreciated Browning's reputation as a director, they have generally enhanced Senior's reputation as an actor. Chaney, Sr. was an enormous talent who ranks among the greats. He played monsters, soldiers, physically afflicted curiosities, and even a woman, and in every case he holds the audience in thrall. Lon Chaney, Jr. desperately wanted to reprise his father's roles in remakes of *The Hunchback of Notre Dame* and *The Phantom of the Opera*, but in each case he lost the parts to actors with greater name recognition and greater talent. Nevertheless, Junior did get a chance to challenge his father in pantomime in *One Million B. C.* (1940). As Akhoba, leader of a prehistoric tribe, Junior successfully models power and arrogance as he feeds his dogs before he feeds his people, and he successfully elicits pity after being injured by a musk ox. Horror film historian and collector Ronald V. Borst considers Junior's performance here of superior quality, and I stand by what I said in my book—"[in this instance] it is hard to imagine his father giving a superior performance." For years, Junior acted in Senior's shadow, driving himself to equal or surpass his father's legacy. It never happened, and after Universal chose not to renew his contract in 1945, he gave up his dream. With his dream dead and a significant portion of his ego crushed, he referred to himself thereafter as simply "a useful actor." Everything considered, the body of their work leads me to conclude that Senior was a better actor than Junior.

Lon Chaney, Jr. vs. Bela Lugosi

When Lon Chaney, Sr. died, the lead role in *Dracula* (1931) went to Bela Lugosi, who became America's next horror film star. Lugosi and Chaney were completely different types. Though both were tall, Lugosi was aristocratic while Chaney was common, Lugosi was reserved while Chaney was boisterous, and Lugosi exuded European pride while Chaney embodied the American Joe's ideal of hard labor followed by a few beers (or in his case—*quite* a few). Lugosi was trained on the Hungarian stage where he brought the characters of Shakespeare and other great playwrights to life. In America, however, he was hampered as a result of never fully mastering English. As a result, we can only evaluate Lugosi as an actor based on his silent films and on his American sound performances wherein he usually played typecast heavies and red herrings. Still, Lugosi *was* Dracula on both stage and screen, and, in my opinion, he remains today the greatest horror film personality because of a charisma that focuses all eyes on him as long as he occupies the screen. As a result, his presence alone can make an otherwise poor horror film watchable and often enjoyable. Horror films with good screenplays that provide him meaty roles have become classics of the genre.

Chaney, Jr. sometimes brought a certain charm to his roles—e.g., *Sixteen Fathoms Deep* (1934) and *Man Made Monster* (1941)—but never charisma. Chaney's appearance alone could not save a bad film. In this respect, Lugosi towers above everyone else in the genre. But if we compare Lugosi's sound films to Chaney's, we must at least entertain the possibility that Chaney was a more versatile actor. After all, Lugosi's characters were mainly vampires, mad scientists, and servants. Chaney boasts an enormous variety of starring roles: monsters, monster hunters, cowboys, Indians, benevolent college professors, psychologists, artists, etc. He also performed a large variety of character roles on both the big screen and on television. Well, perhaps Lugosi didn't have the chance. That may be, but Chaney did (meaning that studios viewed him as versatile), and he made the most of it. A case can, of course, be made for Lugosi in the versatility category. One need only watch the actor as Ygor in *Son of Frankenstein* (1939), for instance, to see that he could handle the role of a downtrodden villain of lower social status. One might also suggest viewing Lugosi in *Mystery of the Mary Celeste* (1935). Still, Chaney distinguished himself as a versatile (and therefore "useful") actor throughout his career. Lugosi must have wished to be even half as "useful"—which translates as "employable."

Before moving on, however, we must note that both Lugosi and Chaney did play Dracula and the Frankenstein Monster. So how do they compare? With regard to Dracula, Lugosi has an immediate edge since the role of Dracula is that of a European aristocrat—in other words, the Lugosi type. In *Son of Dracula* (1943), Universal passed over Lugosi and cast Chaney against type. For years, conventional opinion dismissed Chaney as an overly corpulent failure as the vampire king. In recent years, however, *Son of Dracula* has grown in critical stature, partly as a result of Chaney's being grudgingly acknowledged as an effective Dracula and because of the film's better-than-average direction and cinematography. One might argue that Lugosi overplays his Dracula as though he were projecting from the stage. Though we all love them, Lugosi's mannerisms are often exaggerated. Chaney, on the other hand, appropriately underplays the role, his voice alternately velvety, commanding, and sinister. Though playing against type, Chaney gives a believable and appropriately eerie performance, certainly not as charismatic as Lugosi's, but damn good nevertheless.

Also, both Chaney and Lugosi played the Frankenstein Monster, Chaney in *The Ghost of Frankenstein* (1942) and Lugosi in *Frankenstein Meets the Wolf Man* (1943). Most readers are by now familiar with the difficult conditions under which Lugosi played the Monster (see my chapter on *Frankenstein Meets the Wolf Man* in *Bela Lugosi*, Midnight Marquee Press, 1995). Add to that the fact that Universal cut all of his dialogue, some of which was necessary to explain his actions, and it becomes clear why Lugosi's performance is generally considered weak. In *The Ghost of Frankenstein*, script limitations require Chaney to play the Monster as a hulking, emotionless brute throughout most of the film. Only at the end is he allowed to infuse the Monster with anger. Given the difficulties under which both men labored, Chaney still gives the superior performance.

Everything considered, Lugosi is the greater horror film personality and the greater screen persona. No one in the horror film genre exceeds his star quality. Though Chaney lacked Lugosi's ability to carry a film, he still must be considered Lugosi's equal (if not superior) in the categories of depth and versatility. Give Chaney a chance and watch the many mainstream films and television shows in which he essays both powerful and poignant character roles, and I think you might agree.

Lon Chaney, Jr. vs. Boris Karloff

Since 1931 to the present, the actor most associated by the public with horror films is probably Boris Karloff—and rightfully so. Along with Lugosi's Dracula, Karloff's Frankenstein Monster is the most identifiable horror monster ever to grace the screen. Both Lugosi and Karloff benefited from acting in the thirties—horror film's golden age. Though Chaney was the number one horror film star of the forties, that decade was silver rather than gold. Most top literary properties had already been produced, and except for the films produced by Val Lewton (often aided greatly by Boris Karloff) for RKO, the forties was largely a derivative era. One exception was Universal's *The Wolf Man* (1941), in which Lon Chaney, Jr. brought to life a new and unique character in

Larry Talbot. Lugosi was Dracula, and Karloff was the Frankenstein Monster, but Chaney was the Wolf Man. The Wolf Man, as he often said, was his baby!

But was Chaney equal or superior to Boris Karloff as an actor? The answer is no, at least not in starring roles. Karloff's performances in such films as *The Bride of Frankenstein* (1935), *The Black Room* (1935), and *The Body Snatcher* (1945) are superior to anything Chaney ever did. In fact they can compete successfully with all other starring roles in the horror genre. For obvious reasons, Karloff could not have played Lennie as well as Chaney did, but Chaney simply lacked the depth and versatility Karloff possessed in creating lead characters. Like Chaney, Karloff played many roles outside the horror genre, usually with great success. Of course, on television he often spoofed his horror film persona, as Chaney rarely did. I would argue, however, that Chaney was often superior to Karloff in performing cameos; in fact, Chaney was a master of the supporting role—truly top-drawer. In fact, there is some merit in Chaney's being advertised as "the screen's master character creator." Take, for instance, his performance as Robert Mitchum's alcoholic father in *Not as a Stranger* (1955). Always underplaying, Lon's watery eyes beg Mitchum for understanding. His slumping body, his imploring hand, and his pathetic entreaties convey the desperate weakness of the alcoholic, yet an alcoholic who knows who and what he is. Consider also Chaney's moving supporting performances in *High Noon* (1952) and *The Defiant Ones* (1958).

Neither Karloff nor Chaney could save a bad film by his presence alone. In that respect they both must bow to Lugosi. The two men, however, did play a number of similar roles, and in that respect we might evaluate them more fairly. Both, for example, played the Frankenstein Monster. As I have already noted, Chaney's Monster was hindered by script limitations. Critics like to point to Chaney's non-expressive Monster as proof that he couldn't act, but a close examination of the script reveals that Lon played the Monster just as the script demanded (see chapter five in my *Lon Chaney, Jr.*). While a more confident actor might have brought more to the part, we cannot criticize Chaney for essentially doing what he was directed to do. Karloff, on the other hand, created the role of the Frankenstein Monster and played it on three occasions. In *Frankenstein* (1931), Karloff plays the Monster as a child (see my chapter on *Frankenstein (1931)* in *Boris Karloff*, Midnight Marquee Press, 1996), bringing to the role emotional qualities missing from Chaney's Monster. Karloff builds on the role in *The Bride of Frankenstein* (1935) turning in one of the most entertaining performances in the horror genre.

Both actors also played versions of the Mummy. Here again, Karloff had an initial advantage in that he plays most of the film without bandages while poor Lon never does. Though Chaney in a few instances emits hatred from his one functioning eye and utilizes his physical stature to elicit menace, Karloff's performance in *The Mummy* (1932) is superior to any of Chaney's appearances as Kharis.

Both actors also played Indians, Chaney on several occasions and Karloff in *Tap Roots* (1948). While Karloff is effective as the medicine man, I prefer Chaney as an Indian. For example, in both *The Battles of Chief Pontiac* and *Daniel Boone—Trail Blazer* (1956), Chaney infuses his characters with great heart and dignity, and in his co-starring role as Chingachgook in the television series *Hawkeye and the Last of the Mohicans*, Lon manages to hit the right notes of kindness and humor. All things considered, Karloff was a better leading actor than Lon Chaney, Jr., though Lon was a better character actor than Karloff.

Peter Lorre, Bob Hope, and Lon Chaney, Jr. in *My Favorite Brunette.*

Lon Chaney, Jr. vs. Peter Lorre

While nobody would cast Peter Lorre as Rhett Butler in *Gone With the Wind*, the diminutive Hungarian-born actor was highly versatile, as proven by the large variety of roles he played over his long career. For example, who could ever forget his harrowing performance as the child killer in *M* (1931), wherein he manages to elicit a degree of sympathy for the most despised of criminals. So versatile was Lorre, in fact, that he probably appears in more mainstream classic films than anyone else associated with the horror genre. Though overweight and ill in later years, he still managed to steal scenes (and sometimes whole films) from his co-stars Vincent Price and Boris Karloff.

Chaney and Lorre were so different as actors that it is difficult to fairly compare and contrast them. I would say, however, that Lorre's case is greatly buttressed by the actor's ability to do comedy. Karloff, Chaney, Price, and some other actors associated with the horror genre could pull off situation comedy, but Lorre was himself funny. In other words, his own comedic ability could generate the laughs regardless of the situation. Though Lon Chaney, Jr. appears effectively in several comedies, he is not himself funny as, let's say, W. C. Fields or Jim Carrey are. That is one reason his *Life of Riley* television pilot failed to generate a series. Lorre *was* funny. He could have made a career as a comedian as well as a horror figure. So, everything considered, I must pronounce Peter Lorre a better actor than Lon Chaney, Jr.

Lon Chaney, Jr. and Vincent Price from *The Haunted Palace.*

Lon Chaney, Jr. vs. Vincent Price

Price and Chaney were different types—Price suave, and Chaney gruff. Price would relish great poetry and art while Chaney would immerse himself in Zane Grey Westerns. In other words, the two actors would rarely have competed for the same parts. I consider Price's best genre performances to be his Verdon Fell in *The Tomb of Ligeia* (1965) and his Matthew Hopkins in *Witchfinder General* (1968, aka *The Conqueror Worm*). In both films, Price gives effective, nuanced performances—but no more so than Chaney gives in *Frankenstein Meets the Wolf Man* or *Strange Confession* (1945). Price could evoke the sinister in a variety of ways, probably in more ways than Chaney could, but Chaney's Talbot in *Frankenstein Meets the Wolf Man* is multi-faceted—sinister and sympathetic, cunning and common. And Chaney's Lennie cannot be overlooked. Not just anyone could play Lennie, as some critics have opined. No one we have discussed so far could have played Lennie as effectively as Lon, unless it had been his father.

Unlike many critics, I have seen little of the hamminess attributed to Price in his serious films. When hamminess is warranted or allowed, Price can deliver it in spades, but generally I just don't see it. Price was a fine actor, a serious actor—and so was Lon Chaney, Jr. Their contrasting types are nowhere more obvious than in Corman's *The Haunted Palace* (1963) in which Price is the sophisticated lead and Chaney the servant.

While Chaney has the smaller part, he makes the most of it as Price effectively engages in a meaty battle against demonic possession.

Both Chaney and Price did a great deal of television work, and on the whole, I think Chaney's work stands up as well or better than Price's. Compare anything Price did on television, for example, with Chaney's *Telephone Time* portrayal as "The Golden Junkman" or his tear-jerking performance in *Wagon Train*'s "The Jose Morales Story." In such an examination, Price comes up a little short. These shows demonstrate that Chaney could elicit pity and sympathy in ways Price never could. On the whole, I think Chaney and Price fight to a draw. They were equally good actors.

Lon Chaney, Jr. vs. Peter Cushing

Here again we are faced with evaluating completely different types of actors. Cushing could not have pulled off much of what Chaney did, and vice-versa. In my estimation, however, Cushing demonstrated in his career more versatility. In private, Cushing was as affable a man as one could imagine—which was not always true of Chaney. Yet Cushing could portray a cold, calculating Baron Frankenstein in ways so effective as to make that character legendary and every bit his own. I consider Cushing's best genre starring roles to be his Sherlock Holmes in *The Hound of the Baskervilles* (1959), his Baron Frankenstein in *The Curse of Frankenstein* (1957), his Captain Clegg in *Captain Clegg* (1959, aka *Night Creatures*), his Professor Hildern in *The Creeping Flesh* (1972), and his John Banning *The Mummy* (1959). Chaney could never have played as effective a Sherlock Holmes as Cushing's arrogant, sophisticated master of disguise, and Cushing brings ranges of emotion to the other roles that I believe Chaney would have found difficult to duplicate. In any case, Chaney was not the type needed for those roles. He was probably at his best in meaty cameos and supporting roles. Interestingly, I think Cushing's most memorable screen moments are in *Tales from the Crypt* (1972) in which he plays the small role of Grimsdyke. As effective as Chaney is in, for instance, *Not as a Stranger*, Cushing's portrayal of the grievously wronged, kind-hearted old Grimsdyke takes top honors. Yes, though the two are hard to compare, Peter Cushing was a better actor than Lon Chaney, Jr.

Though the content of this chapter is anything but scientific, I think certain conclusions are defensible. While Lon Chaney, Jr. was not one of the top actors in the horror genre, I would nevertheless argue that he is a genre legend and a good actor in general. He played the Frankenstein Monster, the Wolf Man, Dracula, and the Mummy—four of the screen's greatest monsters—and his Wolf Man is sympathetic, terrifying, and historically enduring. The fact that he worked continuously as a character actor, that he was constantly in demand by respected producers and directors, is convincing evidence of his fine, though not great, acting talent. He was a type, and he performed certain roles as well as almost anyone could. When cast against type, he often turned in surprisingly good performances. He deserves a prominent place in the hearts of all those who love the horror genre, and he deserves the respect due a hard-working actor who brightened the screen for a solid thirty-nine years.

EPILOGUE
by Mark A. Miller

In 1935, while shooting at Paramount, Lon Chaney, Jr., befriended the 18-year-old A. C. Lyles, Adolph Zukor's office boy. Two years later, Lyles graduated to production at Paramount, where he still works today, but he never forgot Lon. Between 1964 and 1968, Lyles gave him much needed steady employment in eight of his Westerns.

Chaney's alcoholism during that period is, today, often given more attention than his considerable talents. Lyles, however, offers a meaningful alternative view of Lon Chaney, Jr., at that time.

"Lon was just a wonderful, wonderful man," recalls Lyles. "I hired him for a lot of reasons. Number one, he was one of my closest friends. Number two, he was one of the best character actors in town. Number three, he was always prepared and never caused me a minute's worry or trouble.

"I never had that problem [drinking] with him. He was always ready, whether it was 8 o'clock in the morning, when we'd start shooting, or 9 o'clock at night. He knew his lines, and his acting was never compromised a moment in any of those pictures that we made together. I'd send him a script and he'd be ready. He was always one of the first on the set and the last one to leave. Lon would say, 'I'll hang around in case something comes up. You may need me for something.' He helped all the other actors as much as anybody could. He was the ideal co-worker, a professional in every way. I never had a moment's hesitation to use him.

"Offscreen Lon was like a big teddy bear. He had that large frame and that voice—I guess maybe that's why people identified him as a rough, tough man—but he wasn't. He had a wonderful sense of humor. I don't know how many people realized that, because he never did anything particular onscreen that took advantage of it, but he was funny. Sometimes, Lon would pretend to be one of the monsters he had done or something of that sort, just to get a laugh on the set and keep things jolly. He was a pistol.

"In those days I had a little ensemble of actors I used in my Westerns. We used to call it the Lyles Stock Company—Richard Arlen, William Bendix, Yvonne De Carlo, Jane Russell, Dana Andrews, Rory Calhoun, Bruce Cabot, and many others. As long as I made pictures and Lon was able to work, he was one of the first I would call. He loved to work. He really, really did. Lon was just a delightful human being. I adored him and I miss him."

The irony of Lon Chaney's life is twofold. First, the fact that his most famous screen character, Lawrence Talbot, could not free himself from the tragic curse of turning into the Wolf Man becomes the inescapable metaphor for the real man who could not free himself from turning to the bottle. Second, this well-liked actor brought many hours of entertainment to children and adults, yet he was self-tormented and too often existed in a lonely, isolated world of unhappiness.

Let's remember Lon in kindness and with thanks for Lennie, for Lawrence Talbot, and for so many other roles that he made memorable through his unique talents.

Lon Chaney, Jr., Actor, 1906-1973

FILMOGRAPHY

Bird of Paradise (1932)

Joel McCrea is a playboy stranded on a Polynesian island where he meets the lovely Dolores Del Rio. Chaney appears as Thornton.

Girl Crazy (1932)

Wheeler and Woolsey star as tenderfoots who get mixed up in all sorts of troubles. Based on the Gershwin musical *Girl Crazy*. Chaney appears in the chorus.

Last Frontier, The (1933)

Twelve-chapter Western serial starring Dorothy Gulliver and Francis X. Bushman.

Lucky Devils (1933)

A look at the life of Hollywood stuntmen starring Bruce Cabot, William Boyd, and William Gargan. Chaney appears as Frankie.

Scarlet River (1933)

A film star (Tom Keene) turns Western hero as he helps a woman save her ranch from her evil foreman (Chaney). Yakima Canutt would first perform his famous *Stagecoach* stunt with a wagon in this film.

Son of the Border (1933)

Chaney once again appears with Tom Keene in this Western. Keene is forced to kill his friend (Chaney) who has become involved with outlaws.

Three Musketeers, The (1933)

Twelve-chapter serial starring Francis X. Bushman, Jack Mulhall, Raymond Hatton, and John Wayne. Chaney appears as Armand Corday.

Life of Vergie Winters, The (1934)

A tear-jerker starring Ann Harding and John Boles as ill-fated lovers. Chaney portrays Hugo McQueen.

Sixteen Fathoms Deep (1934)

Chaney plays a deep-sea fisherman who needs money for a boat and to marry his girl (Sally O'Neil), but is sabotaged by bad guy Savanis (George Regas).

Accent on Youth (1935)

A secretary (Sylvia Sidney) falls in love with her older boss (Herbert Marshall). Chaney appears as Chuck.

Captain Hurricane (1935)

A tale of sailors and a washed ashore girl (Helen Westley) who falls for a city boy. Chaney appears as Westley's brother.

Girl O' My Dreams (1935)

The lives and loves of a group of college kids. Chaney appears as a track star. Also stars Mary Carlisle, Sterling Holloway, and Arthur Lake.

Hold 'Em Yale (1935)

Another college tale, this time with Buster Crabbe, Cesar Romero, William Frawley, and Andy Devine. Chaney appears as a football player in an unbilled part.

Marriage Bargain, The (1935)

Although unable to find any film listing on this movie, Don Smith lists it in his Lon Chaney, Jr. book as starring Edmund Breese, Audrey Ferris, and Francis McDonald.

Girl O' My Dreams

Shadow of Silk Lennox (1935)

Another obscure film we could find no listing of although Don Smith lists it as starring Chaney, Dean Benton, Marie Burton, and Jack Mulhall.

Ace Drummond (1936)

Thirteen-chapter mystery serial with John King, Jean Rogers, Noah Beery, Jr., and Lon as Ivan.

Killer At Large (1936)

B mystery with Mary Brian, Russell Hardie, Betty Compson, Thurston Hall, and Henry Brandon. Chaney appears as a guard at a wax museum.

Rose Bowl (1936)

College football comedy/romance starring Eleanore Whitney, Tom Brown, Buster Crabbe, and William Frawley. Chaney is a football player.

Singing Cowboy, The (1936)

Gene Autry musical Western where Autry heads for the city to earn money for a little girl's operation. Also stars Smiley Burnette and Lois Wilde. Chaney appears as Martin.

Undersea Kingdom (1936)

Twelve-chapter serial starring Ray "Crash" Corrigan, Lois Wilde, and Monte Blue. Chaney appears as Hakur.

Undersea Kingdom

Angel's Holiday (1937)

Jane Withers appears in this film as a kid who helps save a kidnapped movie star. Also stars Robert Kent, Joan Davis, and Sally Blane. Chaney appears as Louie.

Born Reckless (1937)

Brian Donlevy, Barton MacLane, and Rochelle Hudson appear in this remake of the John Ford 1930 film of the same title. Chaney has an unbilled role as an auto mechanic.

Charlie Chan on Broadway (1937)

Chan solves the mystery of a murdered nightclub singer. Stars Warner Oland, Keye Luke, and Joan Marsh. Chaney appears as a desk clerk.

Checkers (1937)

Jane Withers appears in this racetrack comedy. Also stars Stuart Erwin and Una Merkel. Chaney appears in an unbilled part at the racetrack.

Cheyenne Rides Again (1937)

Cheyenne (Tom Tyler) is hired to infiltrate a gang of outlaws. Chaney appears as Girard. Also stars Lucille Browne, Jimmy Fox, and Roger Williams.

Lady Escapes, The (1937)

Romantic comedy starring Gloria Stuart, Michael Whalen, George Sanders, and Cora Witherspoon. Chaney appears in a bit part as a reporter.

Lon Chaney, Jr. and his bride Patsy Beck at their home at Van Nuys, Califormia, 1937 [Photofest]

Life Begins in College (1937)

Another college football comedy, this one starring The Ritz Brothers. Also stars Joan Davis, Tony Martin, and Gloria Stuart. Chaney appears as Gilks.

Love and Hisses (1937)

Musical starring Walter Winchell and Ben Bernie feuding over the charms of Simone Simon who sings several songs. Chaney appears as an attendant.

Love is News (1937)

Tyrone Power, Loretta Young, and Don Ameche star in this thinly veiled copy of *It Happened One Night*. Chaney appears as an unbilled newspaper reporter.

Midnight Taxi (1937)

Crime film with Brian Donlevy as an undercover FBI agent. Also stars Frances Drake and Gilbert Roland. Chaney appears as Erickson.

Old Corral, The (1937)

Gene Autry saves a Chicago singer from mobsters. Also stars Smiley Burnette, Hope Manning, and the soon to be famous Dick Weston (Roy Rogers). Chaney appears as Garland.

One Mile From Heaven (1937)

A newswoman on the trail of a story discovers a black mother caring for a white child. A court battle ensues over the custody of the child. Stars Claire Trevor, Sally Blane, Douglas Fowley, Fredi Washington, Eddie Anderson, and Bill Robinson. Chaney appears as an unbilled policeman.

Lon Chaney, Jr. and Patsy at the premiere of *Of Mice and Men.* [Photofest]

Second Honeymoon (1937)

Romantic comedy starring Tyrone Power, Loretta Young, Stuart Erwin, Claire Trevor, and Marjorie Weaver. Chaney appears as an unbilled reporter.

Secret Agent X-9 (1937)

Twelve-chapter serial starring Scott Kolk, Jean Rogers, and Henry Brandon. Chaney appears as Maroni.

Slave Ship (1937)

Mutiny on the high seas as a captain wants to give up the slave trade. Stars Warner Baxter, Wallace Beery, George Sanders, and Mickey Rooney. Chaney appears in a bit as a laborer.

That I May Live (1937)

Crime drama starring Robert Kent as a young man forced by criminals to help them in their dirty deeds. Chaney has a small part as an engineer.

Thin Ice (1937)

Chaney has a small part as a reporter in this Sonja Henie musical. Also stars Tyrone Power, Arthur Treacher, and Joan Davis.

This is My Affair (1937)

A man goes under cover to discover a notorious group of bank robbers. Only the president knows his assignment. Unfortunately the president was McKinley who gets himself assassinated. Stars Robert Taylor, Barbara Stanwyck, Victor McLaglen, John Carradine, and Brian Donlevy. Chaney provides an offscreen voice.

Wife, Doctor and Nurse (1937)

Romantic comedy starring Loretta Young and Warner Baxter as husband and wife. Young is jealous of Baxter's nurse, Virginia Bruce. Chaney appears as a chauffeur.

Wild and Woolly (1937)

Jane Withers and Alfalfa Switzer uncover plans for a bank robbery in this comedy. Chaney appears as Dutch.

Alexander's Ragtime Band (1938)

Chaney has a bit as a photographer in this big-budget spectacle. Stars Tyrone Power, Alice Faye, Don Ameche, Ethel Merman, and Jack Haley along with impressive songs by Irving Berlin.

City Girl (1938)

Gangster/romance film starring Phyllis Brooks and Ricardo Cortez. Chaney appears as a gangster.

Happy Landing (1938)

Chaney once again appears as a reporter in this Sonja Henie musical. Also stars Don Ameche, Jean Hersholt, and Ethel Merman.

Josette (1938)

Romantic comedy staring Don Ameche, Robert Young, Simone Simon, and Bert Lahr. Chaney appears as a boatman.

Mr. Moto's Gamble (1938)

Comedy/mystery where Mr. Moto solves the murder of a boxer. Stars Peter Lorre and Keye Luke. Chaney appears as Joey.

Passport Husband (1938)

Gangster comedy where thugs threaten Stuart Erwin. Also stars Pauline Moore and Douglas Fowley. Chaney appears as Bull.

Road Demon (1938)

Gangsters move in on drivers in the racing circle. Stars Henry Arthur and Joan Valerie. Chaney appears as a gangster.

Sally, Irene and Mary (1938)

Musical about girls trying to break into show biz. Stars Alice Faye, Tony Martin, Fred Allen, Jimmy Durante, and Joan Davis. Chaney appears in an unbilled part as a policeman.

Speed to Burn (1938)

Racetrack story where gamblers try to keep a horse out of a race. Stars Michael Whalen, Lynn Bari, and Marvin Stephens. Chaney appears at the racetrack.

Straight, Place, and Show (1938)

The Ritz Brothers and Ethel Merman star in this musical where the brothers inherit a racehorse, but a gang of Russian jockeys are out to sabotage the race. Chaney appears as a chauffeur.

Submarine Patrol (1938)

Directed by John Ford. A crew of misfits shapes up and sinks several enemy subs. Stars Richard Greene, Nancy Kelly, John Carradine, and Preston Foster. Chaney has an unbilled part as a sailor.

Walking Down Broadway (1938)

The film follows a year in the life of showgirls. Stars Claire Trevor, Phyllis Brooks, Leah Ray, and Lynn Bari. Chaney has an unbilled bit.

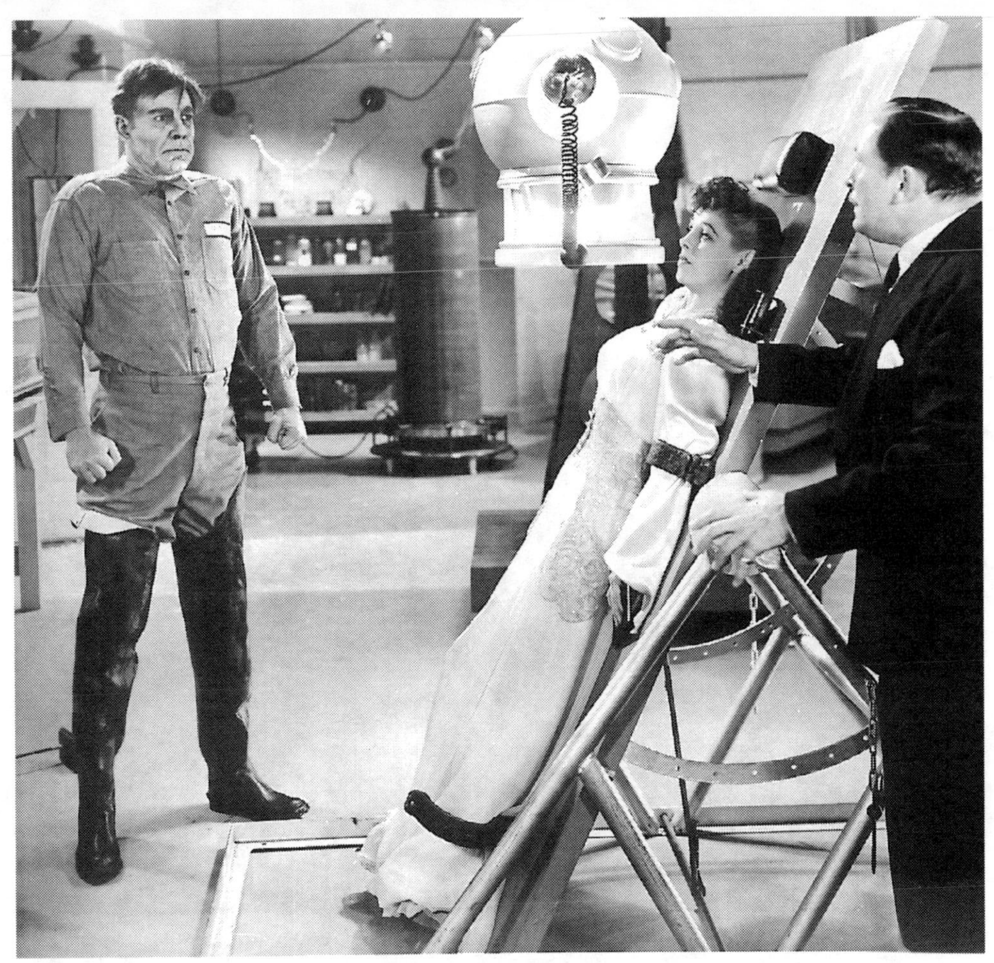

Man Made Monster

Charlie Chan in the City of Darkness (1939)

Charlie Chan investigates the murder of a munitions manufacturer in Paris. Stars Sidney Toler, Lynn Bari, and Richard Clarke. Chaney appears as Pierre, Assistant to Sentinelli.

Frontier Marshal (1939)

Early version of the Wyatt Earp tale with Randolph Scott as Earp. Also stars Nancy Kelly, Cesar Romero, John Carradine, and Eddie Foy, Jr. Chaney appears as Pringle.

Jesse James (1939)

Film version of the story of Frank and Jesse James starring Tyrone Power, Henry Fonda, and Randolph Scott. Chaney appears as a member of the James gang.

Of Mice and Men (1939)

(see chapter)

Union Pacific (1939)

Big-budgeted Western/railroad epic produced and directed by Cecil DeMille starring Barbara Stanwyck, Joel McCrea, Robert Preston, and Akim Tamiroff. Chaney appears as Dollarhide.

North to the Klondike **(Chaney with his Uncle George on the set)**

Northwest Mounted Police (1940)

An Academy Award–winning tale of Mounties, Indians, a Texas Ranger, and the woman he loves. Stars Gary Cooper, Madeline Carroll, Paulette Goddard, Preston Foster, and Robert Preston. Chaney appears as Shorty.

One Million B. C. (1940)

A prehistoric tale of the mountain dwellers and the shell people. Chaney is third billed. Reportedly he created his own make-up for the film but was unable to apply it because of union rules. Stars Victor Mature and Carole Landis.

Badlands of Dakota (1941)

Western about the gold rush in the Black Hills of Dakota and the adventures of Wild Bill Hickok (Richard Dix) and Calamity Jane (Frances Farmer). Chaney appears as Jack McCall.

Billy the Kid (1941)

Another fictionalized tale of Billy the Kid starring Robert Taylor as Billy. Also stars Brian Donlevy, Ian Hunter, and Mary Howard. Chaney appears as Spike Hudson.

Man Made Monster (1941)

(see chapter)

Riders of Death Valley (1941)

Fifteen-chapter Western serial starring Dick Foran, Buck Jones, Glenn Strange, and Noah Beery, Jr. Chaney appears as Butch.

San Antonio Rose (1941)

Universal musical with Jane Franzee, Robert Paige, Eve Arden, and Shemp Howard. Chaney appears as Jigsaw Kennedy.

Too Many Blondes (1941)

Romantic musical involving the bickering of married radio performers. Stars Rudy Vallee and Helen Parrish. Chaney is third billed as Marvin Gimble.

Wolf Man, The (1941)

(see chapter)

Ghost of Frankenstein, The (1942)

(see chapter)

Mummy's Tomb, The (1942)

(see chapter)

North to the Klondike (1942)

Chaney appears as a bad guy trying to drive farmers off their land so he can search for gold. Fistfight between Chaney and Broderick Crawford is the highlight of this film. Also stars Evelyn Ankers and Andy Devine.

Overland Mail (1942)

Fifteen-chapter Western serial starring Chaney as Jim Lane. Also stars Helen Parrish, Noah Beery, Jr., and Don Terry.

Calling Dr. Death (1943)

(see chapter)

Crazy House (1943)

Olsen and Johnson decide to make their own movie. Also stars Patric Knowles and Martha O'Driscoll. Chaney, along with many other stars, appears in a cameo.

Eyes of the Underworld (1943)

Richard Dix is a police chief with a criminal past. Also stars Wendy Barrie. Chaney appears as Benny.

Frankenstein Meets the Wolf Man (1943)

(see chapter)

Frontier Badmen (1943)

Cattlemen come up against unscrupulous dealers in Abilene. Stars Robert Paige, Anne Gwynne, and Noah Beery, Jr. Chaney appears as Chango.

Scream in the Night (1943)

Chaney in a dual role as a detective tracking down a jewel thief and also as the thief's deformed assistant. Also stars Zara Tasil, Sheila Terry, and Manuel Lopez. Originally filmed in 1935.

Son of Dracula (1943)

(see chapter)

What We Are Fighting For (1943)

Patriotic Universal contribution to the war effort. Stars Chaney, Samuel Hinds, and Osa Massen.

Cobra Woman (1944)

Maria Montez as the queen of a cobra-worshipping cult who also appears as her devious sister. Also stars Jon Hall and Sabu. Chaney appears as Hava.

The Mummy's Tomb

Dead Man's Eyes (1944)

Inner Sanctum mystery stars Chaney as Dave Stuart who is blinded by acid. Also stars Jean Parker, Paul Kelly, and Thomas Gomez.

Follow the Boys (1944)

A family of vaudevillians leave New York for California where George Raft marries the star before being shipped overseas. Chaney makes a cameo appearance. Also stars Vera Zorina, Grace McDonald, and Charley Grapewin.

Ghost Catchers (1944)

Bizarre Olson and Johnson film where the boys visit a haunted house. Chaney plays a bear while Andy Devine plays a horse!

House of Frankenstein (1944)

(see chapter)

Mummy's Curse, The (1944)

(see chapter)

Mummy's Ghost, The (1944)

(see chapter)

Weird Woman (1944)

(see chapter)

The Mummy's Curse

Daltons Ride Again, The (1945)

The adventures of the Dalton gang. Stars Alan Curtis, Kent Taylor, Noah Beery, Jr., and Martha O'Driscoll. Chaney appears as Grat Dalton.

Frozen Ghost, The (1945)

Chaney appears as Alex Gregor, a hypnotist who is being driven insane. Also stars Evelyn Ankers, Elena Verdugo, and Milburn Stone.

Here Come the Co-Eds (1945)

Abbott and Costello as custodians of a girls' college. Chaney appears as Johnson aka "The Masked Marvel."

House of Dracula (1945)

(see chapter)

Pillow of Death (1945)

Chaney appears as Wayne Fletcher in this *Inner Sanctum* mystery. Chaney is the suspect in a series of murders. Also stars Brenda Joyce and Clara Blandick.

Strange Confession (1945)

(see chapter)

My Favorite Brunette (1947)

Chaney joins Bob Hope in this classic Hope mystery/comedy. Chaney appears as Willie. Also stars Dorothy Lamour, Peter Lorre, and Reginald Denny.

Abbott and Costello Meet Frankenstein (1948)
(see chapter)

Strange Confession

Albuquerque (1948)

Randolph Scott saves a small stagecoach line. Also stars Barbara Britton, Gabby Hayes, and Russell Hayden. Chaney appears as Steve Murkill.

Counterfeiters, The (1948)

Scotland Yard detective teams up with the Secret Service to stop a counterfeiting ring. Stars John Sutton, Doris Merrick, and Hugh Beaumont. Chaney appears as Louie.

Sixteen Fathoms Deep (1948)

Remake of the 1934 film. Chaney as Dimitri is the bad guy this time around. Also stars Arthur Lake and Lloyd Bridges.

Captain China (1949)

A disgraced sea captain must clear his name. Stars John Payne, Gail Russell, and Jeffrey Lynn. Chaney appears as Red Lynch.

There's a Girl in My Heart (1949)

Musical starring Lee Bowman and Elyse Knox. Bowman tries to swindle Knox out of her property. Chaney appears as John Colton, a music hall owner.

Once a Thief (1950)

June Havoc as the murderer of Cesar Romero. Chaney appears as Gus.

Behave Yourself (1951)

A young married couple find a dog belonging to criminals. Stars Farley Granger and Shelley Winters. Chaney appears as Pinky.

Bride of the Gorilla (1951)
(see chapter)
Flame of Araby (1951)
Chaney plays Borka, one of a pair of evil brothers trying to force Maureen O'Hara into marriage. Also stars Jeff Chandler, Susan Cabot, and Buddy Baer.
Inside Straight (1951)
Western where David Brian engages in a game of cards with Mercedes McCambridge for ownership of her bank. Chaney appears as Shocker.
Only the Valiant (1951)
Gregory Peck as an Army captain who must whip a troop into shape to defend a pass. Also stars Barbara Payton, Ward Bond, and Gig Young. Chaney appears as Trooper Kebussyan.
Battles of Chief Pontiac (1952)
Chaney as Chief Pontiac is called the film's only saving grace by the Motion Picture Guide. Also stars Lex Barker and Helen Westcott.
Black Castle, The (1952)
Stephen McNally is a murderous count out to kill Richard Greene and Paula Corday. Boris Karloff is the hero of the film with Chaney portraying Gargon, McNally's henchman.
Bushwhackers, The (1952)
Chaney appears as Mr. Taylor, the evil boss of a small Western town. John Ireland is the good guy who takes care of the villains. Also stars Wayne Morris, Lawrence Tierney, and Dorothy Malone.
High Noon (1952)
(see chapter)
Springfield Rifle (1952)
Gary Cooper as a Union officer goes undercover to bring a Confederate gang to justice. Also stars Phyllis Thaxter and David Brian. Chaney appears as Elm.
Thief of Damascus (1952)
Paul Henried as Abu Andar joins forces with Aladdin (Robert Clarey), Sinbad (Chaney), and Ali Baba (Philip Van Zandt) to save a city. Also stars Elena Verdugo.
Lion is in the Streets, A (1953)
James Cagney as a sharecropper begins a political campaign to expose corruption. Also stars Barbara Hale and Anne Francis. Chaney appears as Spurge.
Raiders of the Seven Seas (1953)
Swashbuckler with John Payne as a pirate taking on the Spanish fleet. Chaney appears as Peg Leg, his second in command. Also stars Donna Reed and Gerald Mohr.
Big Chase, The (1954)
Glenn Langan is a policeman who chases payroll robber Chaney into Mexico. Also stars Adele Jergens and Jim Davis.
Black Pirates, The (1954)
Pirates search for gold in the West Indies. Stars Anthony Dexter and Robert Clarke. Chaney appears as Felipe.
Boy From Oklahoma, The (1954)
Will Rogers, Jr. cleans up a small town with his rope and faith. Chaney appears as Crazy Charlie.

Casanova's Big Night (1954)

All-star cast supports Bob Hope in the big-budget historical romp. Also stars Joan Fontaine, Audrey Dalton, Basil Rathbone, Vincent Price, John Carradine. Chaney appears as Emo.

Jivaro (1954)

Rhonda Fleming searches for her fiancé in the Amazon jungle. Also stars Fernando Lamas and Brian Keith. Chaney appears as Pedro.

Passion (1954)

Cornel Wilde takes on bandits trying to drive out the ranchers. Also stars Yvonne De Carlo and Raymond Burr. Chaney appears as Castro.

Big House, U.S.A. (1955)

(see chapter)

I Died a Thousand Times (1955)

(see chapter)

Indian Fighter, The (1955)

Tim Holt helps a tribe of Indians stop bad guys. Also stars Noah Beery, Jr. and Richard Martin. Chaney appears as Chivington.

Not as a Stranger (1955)

Olivia de Havilland, Robert Mitchum, and Frank Sinatra star in this soap opera tale of a doctor who thinks he is God. Chaney appears as Job Marsh.

Silver Star, The (1955)

A pacifist sheriff must put aside his beliefs when Chaney, as John W. Harmon, hires killers to do him in. Stars Edgar Buchanan and Marie Windsor.

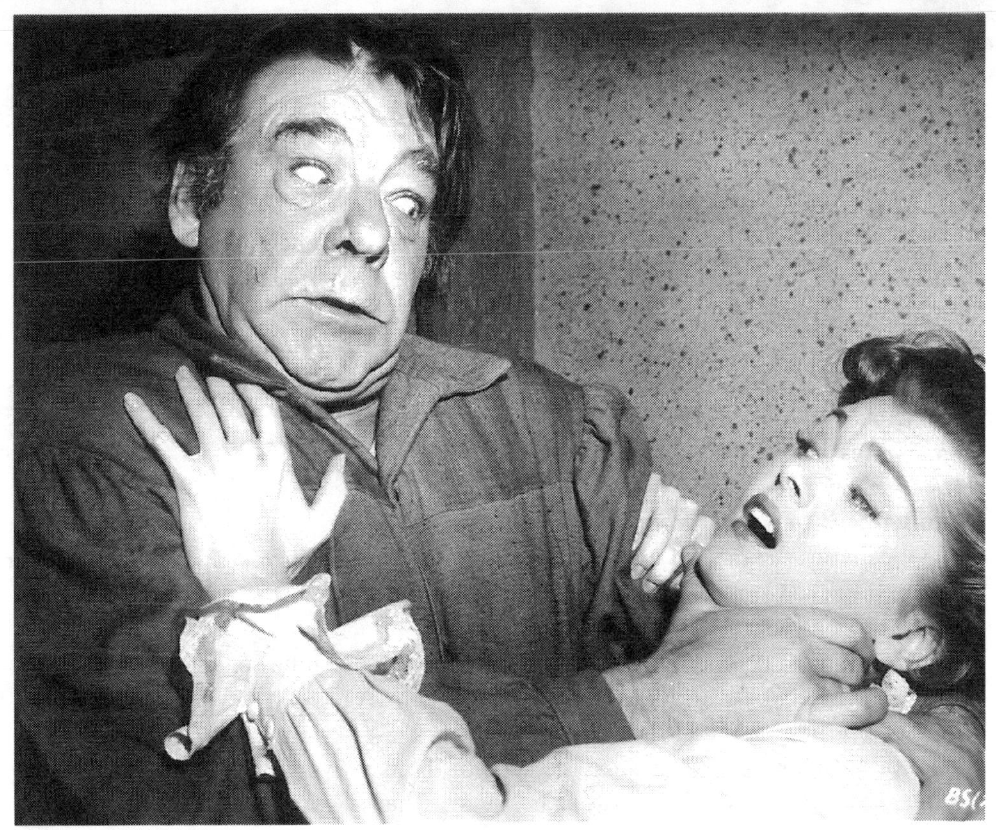

The Black Sleep

Black Sleep, The (1956)

A doctor invents a drug hoping to cure his comatose wife. Stars Basil Rathbone, Akim Tamiroff, John Carradine, and Bela Lugosi. Chaney appears as Mungo.

Indestructible Man (1956)

(see chapter)

Manfish (1956)

Based on two Edgar Allan Poe stories, John Bromfield and Victor Jory seek buried pirate treasure. Chaney appears as Swede.

Pardners (1956)

Martin and Lewis invade the Old West. Along for the ride are Lori Nelson, Jeff Morrow, and Agnes Morehead. Chaney appears as Whitey.

Cyclops, The (1957)

(see chapter)

Daniel Boone—Trail Blazer (1957)

Bruce Bennett as Daniel Boone, who leads a group of settlers against the Shawnee. Chaney is the Shawnee chief, Blackfish. Also stars Faron Young.

Defiant Ones, The (1958)

Tony Curtis and Sidney Poitier star in this Academy Award–winning film of racial tension and a corrupt prison system. Also stars Theodore Bikel and Charles McGraw. Chaney plays Big Sam.

Money, Women and Guns (1958)

Western/mystery with Jock Mahoney searching for the heirs of a murdered prospector. Also stars Kim Hunter and Tom Drake. Chaney appears as Art Birdwell.

Alligator People, The (1959)

(see chapter)

Face of the Screaming Werewolf (1959)

Mexican horror film with Chaney as a mummy/werewolf. Also stars Landa Varle. Actual footage from *La Casa Del Terror*, which Chaney starred in as the werewolf, was used to complete this film along with scenes from *Attack of the Mayan Mummy*.

Chivato (1961)

Americans help some anti-Castro Cubans try to overthrow the government. Stars Bill Fletcher and Jake LaMotta. Chaney appears as Gordo.

Devil's Messenger, The (1962)

(see chapter)

Haunted Palace, The (1963)

Vincent Price stars as a man possessed by his warlock ancestor. Also stars Debra Paget and Elisha Cook, Jr. Chaney stars as Simon Orne.

Law of the Lawless (1964)

A judge must defend himself against a man whose son he sentenced. Stars Dale Robertson, Yvonne De Carlo, Bruce Cabot, and John Agar. Chaney appears as Tiny.

Stage to Thunder Rock (1964)

A sheriff must bring to justice the sons of the man who raised him. Stars Barry Sullivan, Marilyn Maxwell, and Keenan Wynn. Chaney appears as Henry Parker.

Witchcraft (1964)

(see chapter)

Black Spurs (1965)

Chaney tries to divert a railroad so it runs through his land. Stars Rory Calhoun and Linda Darnell.

House of the Black Death (1965)

Chaney and John Carradine portray the De Sade brothers, Carradine the good warlock, Chaney the bad.

Town Tamer (1965)

Dana Andrews as a man searching for the killers of his wife. Also stars Terry Moore and Pat O'Brien. Chaney appears as Mayor Charlie Leach.

Young Fury (1965)

A man returns to town years after abandoning his wife and infant son. Stars Rory Calhoun and Virginia Mayo. Chaney appears as the bartender.

Apache Uprising (1966)

Rory Calhoun and pals stop a gold robbery. Chaney appears as Charlie Russell.

Johnny Reno (1966)

A U.S. marshal gets into trouble with the hysterical townsfolk of Stone Junction. Stars Dana Andrews, Jane Russell, and John Agar. Chaney appears as Sheriff Hodges.

Dr. Terror's Gallery of Horrors (1967)

(see chapter)

Hillbillys in a Haunted House (1967)

Country music stars spend the night in a haunted house. Stars Ferlin Husky and Joi Lansing along with John Carradine, Basil Rathbone, and Chaney as Maximillian.

Dracula vs. Frankenstein

Welcome to Hard Times (1967)

A band of viscious outlaws continually raid a small town. Stars Henry Fonda, Keenan Wynn, and Warren Oates. Chaney appears as Avery.

Buckskin (1968)

A marshal tries to unite the town against a cattle baron who wants to cut off the water supply. Stars Barry Sullivan and Joan Caulfield. Chaney appears as Sheriff Tangely.

Fireball Jungle (1968)

Mobsters invade the stock car circuit. Stars Alan Mixon and John Russell. Chaney stars as Sammy, the owner of a junkyard.

Spider Baby (1968)

(see chapter)

Female Bunch, The (1969)

A group of women live together on a ranch. Russ Tamblyn happens along causing all kinds of trouble. Chaney appears as a hired hand/drug dealer.

Blood of Frankenstein/Dracula vs. Frankenstein (1971)

A sick and tired J. Carrol Naish and Lon Chaney team up for this one last film with Naish as Dr. Frankenstein and Chaney as his slow-witted assistant.

INDEX

AUTHORS' BIOGRAPHIES

Cindy Ruth Collins has contributed to *Midnight Marquee* magazine and books, and is currently at work on a book about Jack the Ripper films. She recently married fellow writer Brian Smith and now lives in Arlington, VA with her wonderful husband and their two adorable cats.

Bruce Dettman is a San Francisco-based writer whose film related articles have appeared in *Filmfax, The Monster Times, Fangoria*, and *Good Old Days*. He also co-authored the book *The Horror Factory* and periodically lectures on horror cinema. He has written for *Military History, True West, Emmy, Alfred Hitchcock's Mystery Magazine*, and *San Francisco* and has authored several stage productions, the most recent being *Hoagy*, the story of composer Hoagy Carmichael.

Dennis Fischer is the author of the book *Horror Film Directors* (McFarland, 1991) and is currently working on a follow-up on science fiction directors. He has contributed to many film magazines including *Filmfax*, *Cinefantastique*, and *Midnight Marquee*.

Kerry Gammill is a storyboard artist and special effects designer in Hollywood, with current projects including the *Species* sequel. Gammill spent the 1980s and much of the '90s as a comic-book artist, illustrating the adventures of *Spider-Man* and *Superman*.

David J. Hogan is the author of *Who's Who of the Horrors and Other Fantasy Films*, *Dark Romance: Sexuality in the Horror Film*, and *Your Movie Guide to Drama Video Tapes and Discs*. He contributes to *Cinefantastique*, *Moviegoer*, *Filmfax*, and *Outré*. Hogan lives with his wife Kim and three children in a rambling house filled with books, music, and movies.

C. Courtney Joyner is a producer/director whose films include *Class of 1999, Desperate Motive, Doctor Mordrid, Lurking Fear*, and *Puppet Master III*. He is a devoted Western fan and is currently working on a book about Western films.

Leonard J. Kohl has contributed to *Filmfax* and is working on a book about the serials of Lon Chaney, Jr., Boris Karloff, and Bela Lugosi.

Mark A. Miller is the author of *Christopher Lee and Peter Cushing* (McFarland) and has contributed to *Midnight Marquee Actors Series: Boris Karloff* and *Bela Lugosi* as well as *Guilty Pleasures of the Horror Film*. He lives in Columbus, Ohio with wife Teresa and teaches English in nearby Gahanna.

John E. Parnum, at the tender age of nine, saw his first horror movie, *House of Frankenstein*, which infused in him a lifelong interest in films of this genre. Fortuitously, he has channeled this obsession into many magazine articles and contributions to Midnight Marquee Press. He resides with his bird-watching wife Edith in a Nightmare Museum in Wayne, PA.

Michael Price is co-author of *Forgotten Horrors* and an internationally syndicated film columnist with the *New York Times News Service*, based at the Fort Worth (Texas) *Star-Telegram*. A lifelong Texan, he is also a professional jazz musician and teaches courses in film appreciation.

Gary Don Rhodes is author of *Bela Lugosi* (McFarland, 1997) and has contributed to *Classic Images, The Big Reel, Filmfax*, and *Cult Movies*. He is also a documentary filmmaker currently working on a film about Bela Lugosi.

Bryan Senn lives in Washington state with his young son Dominic and his wife Gina Beretta, who holds a Ph.D. in *murder* (criminology, actually). When not trying to stay on Gina's good side, he watches old horror movies and writes for magazines like *Filmfax, Movie Club*, and *Midnight Marquee*. Every few years he manages to finish a book: *Fantastic Cinema Subject Guide* (McFarland, 1992; co-authored with John Johnson) and *Golden Horrors: An Illustrated Critical Filmography of Terror Cinema, 1931-1939* (McFarland, 1996). Up next is *Drums of Terror: Voodoo in the Cinema* for Midnight Marquee Press.

David H. Smith is a lifelong aficionado of horror, science fiction, and fantasy cinema. He lives with his wife Lynn and their son in south Florida. Smith has contributed to *Midnight Marquee Actors Series: Boris Karloff* and *Bela Lugosi* as well as *Cinematic Hauntings*.

Don G. Smith is an associate professor in history and philosophy of education at Eastern Illinois University. He has written for *Midnight Marquee, Scarlet Street, Filmfax, Movie Collector's World*, etc. He is also the author of *Lon Chaney, Jr.* (McFarland, 1995). He is currently working on *The Cinema of Edgar Allan Poe*.

John Soister is a teacher of modern and classical languages. He has contributed to *Midnight Marquee Actors Series: Boris Karloff* and *Bela Lugosi* and is currently working on books about Universal's horror/mystery/suspense films of the 1930s, Paramount horror films, and the films of Claude Rains.

John Stell, a CPA residing in Baltimore, contributes to *Movie Club, Monsters From the Vault*, and *Midnight Marquee*. He has contributed to *Midnight Marquee Actors Series: Boris Karloff* and *Bela Lugosi* and is currently working on a book about horror films of the 1980s, *Psychos, Sickos, and Sequels*.

Gary J. Svehla created his first publishing venture at the age of 13, *Gore Creatures*. Thirty-four years later he is still going strong publishing the magazine, now *Midnight Marquee,* as well as overseeing Midnight Marquee Press. He teaches English at North County High School in Glen Burnie, MD.

Susan Svehla is a life-long movie fan and has contributed to *Movie Club* and *Midnight Marquee* as well as *Guilty Pleasures of the Horror Film* and is co-editor of *Midnight Marquee*.

Alan Warren was one of the earliest subscribers to *Midnight Marquee*, back in the days when it was known as *Gore Creatures*. Since then he has written articles and short stories for such publications as *Scarlet Street, Film Comment, The Armchair Detective,* and *Issac Asimov's Science Fiction Magazine*, among others. His first book, *Roald Dahl*, was published in 1988; a second, revised edition followed in 1994. More recently his full-length study, *This Is a Thriller*, was published by McFarland. His mother's cousin, Elizabeth Russell, best known for her roles in Val Lewton's films, appeared with Lon Chaney, Jr., in *Weird Woman* (1944).

If you enjoyed *Lon Chaney, Jr.*, you will enjoy these other fine books from Midnight Marquee Press, Inc.

BELA LUGOSI

"This is what books on specific actors should be...good reads!"—*Monster Scene*

"Informative, colorful, nostalgic, and amusing"—*Video Watchdog*

BORIS KARLOFF

"Like Midnight Marquee's earlier Lugosi volume, this is a treasure trove for horror aficionados and a must for all film fanatics."—*Filmfax*

DWIGHT FRYE'S LAST LAUGH

"A nimbly written, impressively researched biography."—Roger Hurlburt, *Ft. Lauderdale Sun Sentinel*

All books are 6"x9" (unless noted) paperbacks with over 100 photographs, $20.00 each. Midnight Marquee Press, Inc., 9721 Britinay Lane, Baltimore, MD 21234; phone: 410-665-1198; fax: 410-665-9207; Please include $3.00 shipping for the first book and $1.00 for each additional book (US). Canada: $4.50 for first book, $1.50 for each additional book.